# DIGITAL AND OTHER VIRTUALITIES

# NEW ENCOUNTERS
## Arts, Cultures, Concepts

**Published**

*Conceptual Odysseys: Passages to Cultural Analysis*
ed. Griselda Pollock, 2007

*The Sacred and the Feminine: Imagination and Sexual Difference*
ed. Griselda Pollock and Victoria Turvey Sauron, 2007

*Bluebeard's Legacy: Death and Secrets from Bartók to Hitchcock*
ed. Griselda Pollock and Victoria Anderson, 2009

*Digital and Other Virtualities: Renegotiating the Image*
ed. Antony Bryant and Griselda Pollock, 2010

**Forthcoming**

*The Visual Politics of Psychoanalysis: Art in a Post-Traumatic Era*
ed. Griselda Pollock

# New Encounters Monographs

**Published**

*Helen Frankenthaler: Painting History, Writing Painting*
Alison Rowley, 2007

*Eva Hesse: Longing, Belonging and Displacement*
Vanessa Corby, 2010

**Forthcoming**

*Outfoxed: The Secret Life of a Fairy Tale*
Victoria Anderson

*Witnessing Abjection: Auschwitz and Afterimages*
Nicholas Chare

# DIGITAL AND OTHER VIRTUALITIES

## Renegotiating the Image

EDITED BY

ANTONY BRYANT AND GRISELDA POLLOCK

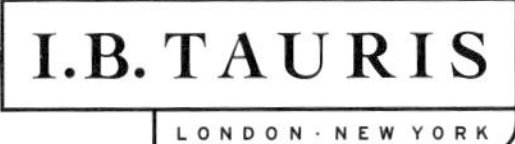

Published in 2010 by I.B.Tauris & Co Ltd
6 Salem Road, London W2 4BU
175 Fifth Avenue, New York NY 10010
www.ibtauris.com

Distributed in the United States and Canada Exclusively by Palgrave Macmillan
175 Fifth Avenue, New York NY 10010



ISBN: 978 1 84511 567 8 (HB)
       978 1 84511 568 5 (PB)

A full CIP record for this book is available from the British Library
A full CIP record is available from the Library of Congress

Library of Congress Catalog Card Number: available

Printed and bound in Great Britain by CPI Antony Rowe, Chippenham
from camera-ready copy edited and supplied by the editors

*For P. B. 1913–92*

# CONTENTS

# ILLUSTRATIONS

**Chapter 10**



**Chapter 11**



**Chapter 12**

# ACKNOWLEDGEMENTS

The research for this book was undertaken with the financial support of the Arts and Humanities Research Council and the University of Leeds. We acknowledge their support with gratitude.

Permission has been granted by the author and the University of Chicago Press to reprint N. Katherine Hayles, 'Traumas of Code', *Critical Inquiry* 33/1 (2006), pp. 136–57, which was originally delivered as a keynote lecture at CongressCATH IV, *The Ethics and Politics of Virtuality and Indexicality*, National Media Museum, Bradford, organized by the Centre for Cultural Analysis, Theory and History, University of Leeds.

Permission has been granted by the author and artist to reprint Juli Carson, 'Legacies of Resistance', which first appeared in the catalogue for the exhibition *Mary Kelly: Circa 1968*, 4 October–17 November 2007, at University Art Gallery, University of California Irvine, curated by Juli Carson.

# SERIES PREFACE

# NEW ENCOUNTERS
## Arts, Cultures, Concepts

*Griselda Pollock*

*How do we think about visual art these days? What is happening to art history? Is visual culture taking its place? What is the status of cultural studies, in itself or in relation to its possible neighbours art, art history, visual studies? What is going on? What are the new directions? To what should we remain loyal?*

*New Encounters: Arts, Cultures, Concepts* proposes some possible ways of thinking through these questions. Firstly, the series introduces and works with the concept of a *transdisciplinary initiative*. This is not a synonym for the interdisciplinary combination that has become de rigueur. It is related to a second concept: research as *encounter*. Together transdisciplinary and encounter mark the interaction between ways of thinking, doing and making in the arts and humanities that retain distinctive features associated with disciplinary practices and objects: art, history, culture, practice, and the new knowledge that is produced when these different ways of doing and thinking encounter one another across, and this is the third intervention, *concepts*, circulating between different intellectual or aesthetic cultures, inflecting them, finding common questions in distinctively articulated practices. The aim is to place these different practices in productive relation to one another mediated by the circulation of concepts.

We stand at several cross-roads at the moment in relation to the visual arts and cultures, historical, and contemporary, and to theories and methods of analysis. *Cultural Analysis, Theory and History* (CATH) is offered as one experiment in thinking about how to maintain the momentum of the momentous intellectual, cultural revolution in the arts and humanities that characterized the last quarter of the twentieth century while adjusting to the different field of analysis created by it.

In the 1970s–1990s, the necessity, or the intrusion, according to your position, was Theory: a mythic concept with a capital T that homogenized vastly different undertakings. Over those decades, research in the arts and humanities was undoubtedly reconfigured by the engagement with structuralist and poststructuralist theories of the sign, sociality, the text, the letter, the image, the subject, the postcolonial, and above all, difference. Old disciplines were deeply challenged and new interdisciplines—called studies—emerged to contest the academic field of knowledge production and include hitherto academically ignored constituencies. These changes were wrought through specific engagements with Marxist, feminist, deconstructionist, psychoanalytical, discourse and minority theory. Texts and authors were branded according to their theoretical engagements. Such mapping produced divisions between the proliferating theoretical models. (Could one be a Marxist, and feminist, and use psychoanalysis?) A deeper split, however, emerged between those who, in general, were theoretically oriented, and those who apparently did without theory: a position easily critiqued by the theoretically minded because being atheoretical is, of course, a theoretical position, just one that did not carry a novel identity associated with the intellectual shifts of the post-1968 university.

The impact of 'the theoretical turn' has been creative; it has radically reshaped work in the arts and humanities in terms of what is studied (content, topics, groups, questions) and also how it is studied (theories and methods). Yet some scholars currently argue that work done under such overt theoretical rubrics now appears tired; theory constrains the creativity of the new generation of scholars familiar, perhaps too familiar, with the legacies of the preceding intellectual revolution that can too easily be reduced to Theory 101 slogans (the author is dead, the gaze is male, the subject is split, there is nothing but text, etc.). The enormity of the initial struggles—the paradigm shifting—to be able to speak of sexual difference, subjectivity, the image, representation, sexuality, power, the gaze, postcoloniality, textuality, difference, fades before a new phase of normalization in which every student seems to bandy around terms that were once, and in fact, still are, challengingly difficult and provocative.

Theory, of course, just means thinking about things, puzzling over what is going on, reflecting on the process of that puzzling and thinking. A reactive turn away from active engagement with theoretical developments in the arts and humanities is increasingly evident in our area of academe. It is, however, dangerous and misleading to talk of a post-theory moment, as if we can relax after so much intellectual gymnastics and once again become academic couch-potatoes. The job of thinking critically is even more urgent as the issues we confront become ever more complex, and we now have extended means of analysis that make us appreciate ever more the complexity of language, subjectivity, symbolic practices, affects and aesthetics. So how to continue the creative and critical enterprise fostered by the theoretical turn of the late twentieth century beyond the initial engagement determined by specific theoretical paradigms? How does it translate into *a practice of analysis that can be consistently productive?*

This series argues that we can go forward, with and beyond, *by transdisciplinary encounters with and through concepts.* Concepts, as Mieke Bal has argued, are formed within specific theoretical projects.[1] But, Bal suggests, concepts can and have moved out of—*travel from*—their own originating site to become tools for thinking in the larger domain of cultural analysis their interplay produces, a domain that seeks to create a space of encounter between the many distinctive and even still disciplinary practices that constitute the arts and humanities: the fields of thought that puzzle over what we are and what it is that we do, think, feel, say, understand and live.

Our series takes up the idea of 'travelling concepts' from the work of Mieke Bal, the leading feminist narratologist and semiotician, who launched an inclusive, interdisciplinary project of cultural analysis in the 1990s with *The Point of Theory: Practices of Cultural Analysis* and *The Practice of Cultural Analysis: Exposing Interdisciplinary Interpretation.*[2] In founding the Amsterdam School of Cultural Analysis (ASCA), Bal turned the focus from our accumulating theoretical resources to the work—the practice of interpretation—we do on cultural practices, informed not only by major bodies of theory (that we still need to study and extend), but by the concepts generated within those theories that now travel across disciplines, creating an extended field of contemporary cultural thinking. Cultural analysis is theoretically informed, critically situated, ethically oriented to 'cultural memory in the present'.[3] Cultural analysis works with 'travelling concepts' to produce new readings of images, texts, objects, buildings, practices, gestures, actions.

In 2001, a Centre for Cultural Analysis, Theory and History was founded at the University of Leeds, with initial funding from the Arts and Humanities Research Council, to undertake what it defines as a *transdisciplinary* initiative to bring together and advance research in and between distinct but interrelating areas of fine art, histories of art and cultural studies: three areas that seem close and yet can be divided from one another through their distinguishing commitments to practice, history and theory respectively. CentreCATH was founded at a moment when emerging visual studies/visual culture was contesting its field of studies with art history, or inventing a new one, a moment of intense questioning about what constitutes the *historical* analysis of art practices, as a greater interest in the contemporary seemed to eclipse historical consciousness, a moment of puzzling over the nature of research through art practice, and a moment of reassessing the status of the now institution-alized, once new kid on the block, cultural studies. CentreCATH responded to Mieke Bal's ASCA with its own exploration of the relations between history, practice and theory through an exploration of transdisciplinary cultural analysis that also took its inspiration from the new appreciations of the unfinished project of *Kulturwissenschaft* proposed by Aby Warburg at the beginning of the twentieth century. Choosing five themes that are at the same time concepts: hospitality and social alienation, musicality/aurality/textuality, architecture of philosophy/philosophy of architecture, indexicality and virtuality, memory/amnesia/history, CentreCATH initiated a series of encounters (salons, seminars, conferences, events) between artists, art historians, musicologists, musicians, architects, writers, performers, psychoanalysts, philosophers, sociologists and cultural theorists. Each encounter was also required to explore a range of differences: feminist, Jewish, postcolonial, politico-geographical, ethnic, sexual, historical. (See <http://www.leeds.ac.uk/cath/ahrc/index.html>)

Each book in this new series is the outcome of that research laboratory, exploring the creative possibilities of such a transdisciplinary forum. This is not proposing a new interdisciplinary entity. The transdisciplinary means that each author or artist enters the forum with and from their own specific sets of practices, resources and objectives whose own rigours provide the necessary basis for a specific practice of making or analysis. While each writer attends to a different archive: photography, literature, exhibitions, manuscripts, images, bodies, trauma, and so forth, they share a set of concerns that defy disciplinary definition: concerns with the production of meaning, with the production of subjectivities in relation to meanings, narratives, situations, with the questions of power and resistance. The form of the books in this series is itself a demonstration of such a transdisciplinary intellectual community at work. The reader becomes the locus of the weaving of these linked but distinctive contributions to the analysis of culture(s). The form is also a response to teaching, taken up and processed by younger scholars, a teaching that itself is a creative translation and explication of a massive and challenging body of later twentieth century thought, which, transformed by the encounter, enables new scholars to produce their own innovatory and powerfully engaged readings of contemporary and historical cultural practices and systems of meaning. The model offered here is a creative covenant that utterly rejects the typically Oedipal, destructive relation between old and young, old and new, while equally resisting academic adulation. An ethics of intellectual respect—Spivak's critical intimacy is one of Bal's useful concepts—is actively performed in engagement between generations of scholars, all concerned with the challenge of reading the complexities of culture.

One of CentreCATH's research strands focused on the concepts of *Indexicality* and *Virtuality*. We aimed to register and bring into dialogue several different debates in contemporary cultural analysis about the impact and potentialities of new media, new technologies and their virtual realities and both their cultural significance and artistic implications. At the same time, we aimed to reflect the renewed interest in the Bergsonian concept of virtuality, paired not with reality or materiality but with actualization, reanimated notably by the philosophy of Gilles Deleuze, in which the term virtuality has radically different connotations, leading us to issues of movement, sensation, time and memory and particularly, theories of art 'beyond representation'.

Indexicality, known to a fairly restricted circle of students of American logician and philosopher C. S. Peirce's semiotic theory, in which Peirce categorizes the sign as icon, index and symbol, re-emerged in cultural theory, notably around photography and cinema, precisely because of the shift from analogue to digital photographic technologies. The index is a sign by virtue of a relation to its object, grounding the signifying relation in existential or indicative relations to real processes or things, in contrast to the icon, which works by resemblance, and the symbol by convention or rule. While earlier theories of photography sought to dissipate the delusion of photography's unmediated reproduction of the real in order to stress the role of rhetorics of the image and ideological overdetermination of the 'truth' effect, faced with the dissolution of the indexical link between photograph and its object in the simple necessity of the two actually confronting one another at some point for the genesis of the image, theorists became interested in the politics of indexicality or its absence in contemporary image-making and theory. This shift invited, therefore, what we might call archaeological reconsiderations of pre-digital technologies but also of theories of cinema and photography that had been deposed by the structuralist/post-structuralist rhetorical and semiotic turns, and which now assumed a renewed interest in relations to both a politics and an ethics of knowledge and its mediations.

What both re-orientations—towards virtuality and indexicality—have in common is the analysis of the relation between new modes, processes, practices and theories of representation and even non-representation on the one hand, and, on the other, both the grounds for knowledge of the world and ourselves and the conditions of thinking embodied human social and sensuous life in the changing conditions of the information era. Bringing together a range of engagements with these concepts across their differences and possible confusions is a gesture towards analysis of contemporary cultural configurations.

This book creates the transdisciplinary encounters necessitated by so complex and varied a theme. It brings together philosophers, literary theorists, cultural theorists, theorists of informatics, film theorists, film makers, artists, and art historians, none of whom merely represent different disciplinary approaches. Rather they have been assembled in order to indicate the manner in which these current, vital, necessary and stimulating concepts are circulating in the expanded field of the image. This field involves critical reflections on both the visible and the invisible, the seen and the overlooked, the unseeable and the over-spectacularized. At the same time, these writers ponder the emotional tone and affective processes of subjectivities generated and mediated by both new and future virtualities. Yet the increasing domain of the virtual in the image-world has generated a renewed interest in the Peircean concept of indexicality, as that which defined analogue photographic imagery, linking representation existentially to the social and material world. New questions arise here. Does indexicality acquire renewed significance and political pertinence in increasingly virtual image-worlds as a political-aesthetic issue? How is it related to our continuing struggle to pierce the illusions of the 'society of the spectacle' and to grasp, through critical representational interventions, our material, social and economic groundedness and embodiment, and our ever-shifting determinations and limitations?

Centre for Cultural Analysis, Theory and History
University of Leeds 2009

# EDITORS' INTRODUCTION

*Antony Bryant and Griselda Pollock*

In 1957, an earth-born object made by man was launched into the universe, where for some weeks it circled the earth according to the same laws of gravitation that swing and keep in motion the celestial bodies—the sun, the moon, the stars […] This event, second in importance to no other, not even to the splitting of the atom, would have been greeted with unmitigated joy if it had not been for the uncomfortable military and political circumstances attending it. But, curiously enough, this joy was not triumphal; it was not pride or awe at the tremendousness of human power and mastery which filled the hearts of men, who now, when they looked up from the earth towards the skies, could behold there a thing of their own making. The immediate reaction, expressed on the spur of the moment, was relief about the 'first step toward escape from men's imprisonment to the earth'.[1]

Seemingly far removed from a contemporary discussion about virtuality and the image in the digital age, Hannah Arendt's opening paragraph to her political reflection on *The Human Condition*, published in 1958, identifies a still pertinent, and paradoxical, relation between the 'human condition' and the technologies humans have created as evidence of their ingenuity. Such technologies have been typically compromised by politically specific, and often military, circumstances of development, while often leading to uses beyond their troubling genesis. The internet was itself propelled, although not initiated, by military research during the 1960s in the search for a resilient, distributed computer network; but this did not prevent its later transformation into a commercialized social technology fundamental to our current communication systems and expanding forms of social networking.

As importantly for our study, Arendt identifies cultural fantasies blossoming around technological advances. In media and military responses to the first satellite's space-circumnavigation of the globe, Arendt overheard fantasies of transcendence of what she would define in her book as the earth-bound conditions for humanity. Such fantasies lead to the misrecognition of the relations between embodied and grounded, yet inventive and masterful, human life and the varied and ever-expanding technologies we produce. In Lacanian-Althusserian terms, Arendt discerned a technological Imaginary, in which the technological products of socially determined human hands and minds are imagined, and then related to, as a means of delivering us precisely from the defining limit(ation)s of 'the human condition'.[2] Reminiscent of Marx's nineteenth-century diagnosis of capitalism's propensity towards the fetishism of the commodity, we repeatedly find the products of social human labour—in this case stored labour in the form of technologies—being endowed, through the inverted mystification of the real relations of their production, with power over the very humans of whose minds and hands they are a product.[3] The dream of a technologically delivered escape from *imprisonment* on earth that Arendt notes after the launch of Sputnik in 1957—the great space fantasy—has not been realized, although it persists imaginatively in science fiction. Is it possible that we are now witnessing another fantasy of technological transcendence that has accompanied the age of cyber-virtuality? What can we make, philosophically and politically, of the later twentieth-century technological events that have generated the current critical debates about information, communication, representation and fabrication—attached to which are fantasies of transcendence through bodiless 'travel', virtual identities and realities, breaching time and space—and of the claims for the radical novelty of a new age that is spawning both utopian and dystopian fantasies?

This book is not another chapter in the proliferating literature on the crisis of representation occasioned by the digital revolution. We will, of course, discuss some aspects of this. Nor is it an apologia for a brave new cyber world, whose implications must, however, be taken seriously. The thinkers, film-makers and artists collected here perform, in many different ways, as makers and theorists, *cultural analysis* in the tradition of Hannah Arendt and Walter Benjamin, whose essay on photo-mechanical reproducibility of the first capitalist eras provides an equally relevant theoretical resource for the current questioning of the digital image in a later phase of globalizing capitalism. That is to say, theoretical reflection, as much through making as writing analytically, investigates the political and cultural effects, significance and long-term impact of socio-historical processes that are extending human uses of image (and sound), technology, and simultaneously affecting their counter-point in aesthetic practices. Aesthetic practices that are being altered in direct and indirect responsiveness to technological innovations, in ways which are both novel and yet continuous with longer histories of art's social interface with earlier technologies. A fantasy of radical novelty can often displace measured appraisal of the more constant interactions over millennia between alterable human attributes and socially produced technologies, one of the most foundational of which is language itself. For example, in their interrogation of the relations between biology and culture, and of the historical and social malleability of human capacities through the technical prostheses from tool use to writing, Paul Hirst and Penny Woolley conclude their exploration of the immense impact of the invention of printing with this caveat directed specifically at an early technicist enthusiast, Marshall McLuhan, whose infamous catch-phrase was 'the medium is the message':

> There are no automatic and general effects of printing or any other technology, no effects independent of social relations and organized systems of beliefs. Print is a medium which *does* have significant effects, but not as a medium in and of itself. This is the primary error of Marshall McLuhan's *The Gutenberg Galaxy* (1962) [...] McLuhan argues that there are standardized typical psychological effects which result from reading the printed page and that these effects are virtually irrespective of context, social relations, and practices, or attributions of significance on the part of the reader. This can be summed up as the dominance of eye over ear, the separation of thought and action, head and heart—the formation of a detached 'typographic man'.[4]

'Typographic man'—the effect of printing and literacy—is now being replaced by notions of virtualized subjects such as cyber-man or the cyborg. Is it possible that the quantitative expansion of technologies of audio-visual image-making that we have witnessed from the 1960s to the 1990s is producing a qualitative shift of significance at the level of human capacities and subjectivities? Or should the measure of change always situate technological advance in relation to the social conditions of emergence or use and to the imaginaries in which such use occurs—conscious and unconscious fantasies inflecting the interface between our machines and ourselves? Donna Haraway's key essay, 'The Cyborg Manifesto' (1985), is a marvellous example of a socialist-feminist dialectical analysis of both the deadly genesis of cyborg technology in the 'Star Wars' of the military-industrial complex and the creative potentiality released by *the political uses of the image* of the cyborg. The cyborg as playfully redefined by Haraway defies both fundamentalist myths of Oedipal origins and salvation histories, and provides instead a cultural mythology for the progressive and politically inclusive transgression of boundaries (gender, race, difference) in the name of a fiction for political affinities and hybrid rather than pure or standardized social identities.[5]

## From reproducibility to producibility

In 1935, Walter Benjamin published the now foundational text 'The Work of

Art in the Age of Mechanical Reproducibility' (*Reproduzierbarkeit* has been mistranslated as reproduction). Benjamin's reflections serve as a model for attempting to 'think' relations between technology and representation with a political reading of both the socio-economic conditions in which they operate and the imaginary effects they may generate. Benjamin's initial purpose in the essay was to confront the transformation of that which had hitherto been imagined as art, surrounded by now-outmoded concepts of mystery, eternal value, originality, creativity, genius and singularity. (This volume also bears that hallmark by asking what new technologies mean for art, and what art tells us about the implications of new technologies.) Art, Benjamin argued, had been transformed, with an inevitable time lag, by the radical economic advent of industrial capitalist production. The impact of its photo-mechanical technologies in the sphere of the image were the reproducibility of representation and new modes of reproducible representations that adjusted to the new constituencies of modernity: the masses, industrial production, urban space, and historical consciousness. Benjamin's complex analysis is not reductive of the image to the economic production. There is no analogy or correspondence, only difficult dialectics. He contemplated the cultural-political significance of the invention of photography and cinema, which he saw not only as lens-based techniques of reproduction but, on the one hand, as regimes of seeing (close-up, aerial survey, montage) and, on the other, as representational screens upon which hitherto undisclosed aspects of social reality and notably the new social entity, the masses, could now be seen, or indeed see/recognize themselves on the historical stage by means of the novel forms of visual representation that could encompass the scale of the masses. Benjamin argued that the technological event of photomechanical reproduction was as much an event for 'thinking'—theory—as it was for perception. Writing with some urgency as a direct witness and later victim of German fascism, Benjamin declares that his analysis will be useless for fascism, which nostalgically reclaims outdated concepts of art for deadly and mystifying purposes; his ideas will serve what he names 'revolutionary demands in the politics of art'.[6] Benjamin's concluding formulation, opposing aestheticization of politics to a politicization of aesthetics, further underlines the challenge thinkers confront now in relation to another phase of 'the work of art (not separate from its technological environment but functioning critically within it) in the age of digital producibility'. In this volume, therefore, critical artistic practices both working on and engaged with photo-mechanical and digital image technologies and their iconic products, by David Haines, Mary Kelly, Martha Rosler and Trinh T. Minh-ha, function as such theoretico-political interventions.

Many have suggested that the later twentieth century transformations of technologies of information associated with computing, the internet, the World Wide Web and digital imaging constitute a rupture or an event of a similar order to that which had begun in 1839 and which Benjamin began to theorize in the mid-1930s. The difference, however, lies in the current rapidity of change and the necessity to produce theoretical reflections on the significance of what is happening almost in parallel with continuous technological innovation, which hardly allows us the lengthy time-frame for reflection exemplified by Benjamin's landmark essay on the period 1839–1935.

The electronic communication of digital messaging between computers was experimentally instituted in the USA in the 1960s in the wake of the launch of Sputnik. By the early 1970s, in the form of ARPANET it offered a potentially global communications service, acquiring a standard format and protocol, later becoming commercially widespread by the 1990s with the invention of the World Wide Web by Tim Berners-Lee and his team at CERN, whose usage became a *sine qua non* commercially by 1996. The combination of internet and World Wide Web now forms what Manuel Castells, sociologist of the information age, names 'the space of flows' that 'links up distant locales around shared functions and meanings on the basis of electronic circuits and fast transportation corridors, while isolating and subduing the logic of experience embodied in the space of places'.[7]

Parodying Benjamin, we have replaced 'reproducibility' with 'producibility'. Digital imaging is not reproduction. Wherein lies the 're'? We are no longer in the realm of reproduction by means of a photographic process, which, however manipulable photographic negatives and printing may be, always practically, as well as theoretically, retained some degree of *indexicality*. Digital photography operates by means of electronic image sensors that record an image as a set of electronic data in binary configurations of 0 and 1. In retrospect, chemical photography, which registers that which is to be recorded through a chemical change to its photosensitive material, is re-specified as 'analogue' imaging. Its logic is formally recognized as indexical in opposition to digital virtuality, whose imitation of existing *forms* of imagery theorist and historian Philip Rosen identifies by the new term, *digital mimicry*.[8] This collection is, therefore, as much about indexicality as it is about virtuality.

## Indexicality

In order to confront this new tension our original, and clumsy title for this book opposed the two terms: *Indexicality* and *Virtuality*. While both are rich with relevant meanings for contemporary culture and cultural analysis, they are hardly part of everyday vocabulary. In recent years, however, the semiotic concept of indexicality has emerged as a site of intense scholarly investigation, as the practice of research responds to the unceasing movement of cultural practice itself. The arrival of new kinds of computer-generated imagery and the possibilities for the fabrication and transformation of images from other technological archives have inspired film theorists to revisit the history and analysis of the cinematic and its relation to the technologies of photography, using in particular the trichotomic formula provided by the pragmatist philosopher and semiotician C. S. Peirce (1839–1914).

Peirce analysed signification under the trio of icon, symbol and index. The index is a type of sign that produces meaning through an existential or phenomenological relation between signifier and referent: for instance smoke and fire, footprints, thunder and so forth. Classic theories of photography initially posited photography as providing a revealing access to the real.[9] In 1960 André Bazin contrasted photography to all previous artistic modes of reproduction: 'For the first time between the originating object and its reproduction there intervenes only the instrumentality of a non-living agent […] Photography affects us like a phenomenon of nature.'[10] Such claims were challenged in structuralist photo-theory by counter-insisting on what Roland Barthes named the coded and the rhetorical character of the photographic image.[11] But for all the justified insistence on the discursive, ideological and social parameters determining the uses and understandings of any photographic image, Barthes, none the less, recognized that in analogue photography and its variants there is always a connection between the photo-image and its event. For a photo-mechanical image to exist, light has had to have bounced off an object to register its trace of an external reality by changing chemically sensitive material within the camera. Roland Barthes argued that 'the Photograph always carries the referent within itself'.[12] This is one aspect of indexicality: an existential or phenomenological connection between image and referent at the level of the trace.

The indexical image, furthermore, as Laura Mulvey has argued, is in a 'privileged relation to time, its moment and the inscription of its duration'.[13] Tracking back through André Bazin's theses on the ontology of cinematic realism—that the value of cinema is that it shows reality as it was in time and space—Mulvey reveals the psychic and metaphysical dimensions that result.

> It is the *indexical* aspect of the photographic sign, located as it is in a preserved moment of time, that allows these movements to take place across the boundaries between the material and the spiritual, reality and magic and between life and death. From this point of view, the most material aspect, the physical link between object and image gives rise to the most elusive and ineffable properties of this particular sign. The photographic index, the most literal, the most banal of signs, inscribes into itself the clouded point at which even Freud allows that the uncanniness of intellectual uncertainty persists into the frame of 'civilisation'.[14]

'The uncertainty of death' and the impossibility of reducing the photograph to language and meaning conjoin in this meeting of photography and the uncanny, strangely bringing the indexical and the virtual into proximity.

In her analysis of the 'emergence of cinematic time', Mary Ann Doane returns to Peirce's theorization of the index as the sign that comes closest to the limit case of the sign, itself evidence of the struggle of thought to master the world. Far from being the most banal (and the least symbolic) of the typology of signs, the index is a kind of limit case.

> Thought and signs, welded together, resist instantaneity or any notion of an immediate present. It would seem, therefore, that there can be no sign that fully or accurately represents or embodies instantaneity. The instant—as an ideal limit—can yield no adequate sign of itself [*because thought takes time, depends upon an interval—GP*].
>
> Nevertheless, within Peirce's own extremely elaborate taxonomy of signs, the index is in fact the form of sign that comes closest to this ideal limit. Just as the present is the effect of the 'pure denotative power of the mind' (that is, attention), the power of the index is a denotative one, forcing the attention to a particular object, here and now.[15]

This links to another aspect of indexicality and photography: the *deictic*. From linguistics, *deixis* is the pointing to or indicative aspect of language which may often accompany the showing of photographs, revealing to us an inherently indicative function: 'Look', 'See', 'Here it is'. Deixis touches on the question of how we can perceive, experience or know the here-and-now, a living historical as well as empirical moment of consciousness of a world, otherness, time, space, and even ourselves as living. Thus the photograph combines the paradox of 'that-has-been' or 'there-ness' (the time/place of a *what* that has been photographed, captured as an image through this combination of light and chemicals) and 'here-and-now-ness' because the photograph brings into its always-open moment of being looked at what it captured in a specific time and space. The photo-image thus simultaneously inhabits its originating past and produces its perpetual present. It is this aspect of encoded, but displaced, history that hits us, out of time, to which Barthes gave the term *punctum*, to signal this piercing trauma of a momentary encounter with time. As trace of time, the *punctum* marks photography's affinity with death, its brush with finitude.[16]

Deixis is, moreover, in some profound way the contemplative foundation of the cinema, itself a technology of modernity and the modernity of technology. Cinema, as Doane argues following both Paul Willemen and Miriam Hansen (herself re-reading Kracauer), becomes a new form of historical experience, namely:

> the historical experience of modernity, of accelerating technological expansion, of the phenomenological and representational dominance of urban space, and of the potential for mass destruction. History here

is not a discourse foreign to theory, not an evocation of a gradual but certain accumulation of knowledge. But the access to contingency, to the imprint of temporality, is made possible by cinema heavily imbued with historicity.[17]

Analogue image-making not only used its specific methods of reproducing an image of something external to it, but has also been theorized in relation to the fundamental element of the temporal trace it cannot but contain through its doubly indexical function of connection and indication.[18] This further binds it to history and our technologically mediated means of becoming conscious of history, not as narratives of events but as a process which, in modernity, is profoundly imbricated with technology. In complex ways the luminous-chemical encounter that the image 'records' and the photographic processing reproduces, materially and notionally anchored the resulting image to a source in time, space and history, however much subsequent chemical processing, cropping, or superimposition may intervene to reshape the final image. Yet, we must counter any risk of simplifying an opposition between analogue and digital imagery in terms of the trace or indexicality of time. It is clearly possible for digital cinema—'the digital film event' as Trinh T. Minh-ha names this moment of possibility—to create a practice within which to inscribe its own, critical self-reflexivity about its specific modes of producing imagery, forms of proposed spectatorship and, crucially, relations to time through the specificity of digital imaging (as well as its other chromatic and acoustic dimensions equally transformed by digital processes).

Classic film-theorizing about cinema—the moving image—as an apparatus reminds us that cinema offers but an illusion of movement. Stills, that is, still photographic images, run through the recording camera or projector's 'gate' at the rate of twenty-four frames per second to reproduce the effect of human movement. In digital cinema, however, there is no such thing as a still image, no punctual moment. There is only a consistent process of *becoming* (and *unbecoming*) based on the binary sequencing of zeros and ones that creates a constant relay of appearing and vanishing, of presence and absence. Writing of her digitally filmed study of modernity and tradition in contemporary Japan, *The Fourth Dimension* (2001) Trinh T. Minh-ha writes of her digital film-making as 'dilating and sculpting time'.[19] She also works with the very oppositions that found the techne of the practice:

Bringing into visibility the invisible would only gain in scope and dimension if, for example, the film takes as part of its subject of inquiry the invisible forces and relations at work in the creative process. The challenge is to find a way to let the film perform the holes, the gaps, and the specific absences by which it takes shape. Sound and silence, movement and stillness are not opposed to one another [...]. Images of the real, produced at the speed of light, are made to play with their own reality as images. There where new technologies and ancient Asian wisdom can meet in all 'artificiality' is where what is viewed as the objective reality underneath the uncertain world of appearances proves to be no more no less than a reality effect—or better, a being time. With digital systems taking part in our everyday thought and work, and with the advent of virtual reality, we are witnessing a profound reality shift, one that radically impacts upon the foundations of our knowledge, and upon our perception of the world.[20]

In a comparable artistic gesture video artist, David Haines, whose video *Three Months* (2004) Adrian Rifkin subjects to a complex, multi-layered reading in this volume, takes one site of virtual communication as simultaneously the space for the circulation of desire which is ever virtual: the internet gay chat-room, and 'translates' its fluid cyber exchanges into performative speech acts and staged scenarios where words and images now collide in disconcerting reformulations. Arguing against the media studies sociologies of users of such 'services', Rifkin elaborates a theoretically rich auto-ethnography about his own investments in and relations to the spaces of his own daily practices on and with the internet, or the practices of these spaces of and for subjectivity that he compares, allegorically, to the devotional rituals of a former sacred age. The 'epiphany' he came to know through Haines' video work was precisely that which constitutes the moment of art as transformation of the coordinates of knowing which he calls 'tracking the old and the new in a complex process of small negotiations'.

## From truth to trust

The shift from analogue indexicality to digital virtuality substantially raises the stakes for our situation in and understanding of these fundamental parameters of bodies, times, and spaces. If older 'truth' or reality claims of photography (and hence cinema) have long since been qualified by emphasis on all the possible modes and codes of manipulation (technical to ideological), the re-emerging recognition of indexicality confers an ethical dimension on analogue imagery, binding a pre-filmic or a pre-photographic event and its process of production both to the image that results and to the experience (of modernity of time and space) it promises to an embodied viewer. What has changed, therefore, in the current technological age of digital producibility is that the indexicality of the analogue photograph has given way to the virtuality of the digital to produce questions that are *forensic* and hence fundamentally political.

The infinitely modifiable electronic image can be processed and altered so that no trace of its layers of processing can be detected.[21] As digitally generated image, it has no original, even while it may have, as part of its electronic interpretation, translation, or in Rosen's term, mimicry, a notional referent that makes its content recognizable. Hence, in digital photography there is no longer a question of truth per se; rather its capacities problematize trust. Apart from self-critical film-making of the kind Trinh T. Minh-ha creates to make us see and work with its gaps, we have now to ask of very image: has what we are seeing a ground in historical time and space at all? Can we trust what we see to be what it shows?

Robert Zemeckis' *Forrest Gump* (1994) was one of the first Hollywood films to use computer-generated imagery seamlessly to insert his star, Tom Hanks, into archive footage. Zemeckis turned to Ken Ralston of *Industrial Light and Magic* to create these visual effects using processes such as chroma key, warping and rotoscoping.[22] Beyond the already-suspended credibility of Hollywood entertainment, however, consider for a moment the blog-led controversy known as Reutersgate over the manipulations of photographs taken after Israeli air attacks on buildings at Qana during the war with Hizbullah in Lebanon in 2006. Adnan Hajj, a Lebanese photographer then working for Reuters—he was subsequently sacked—is now known to have digitally fabricated photographs to make the scene of devastation appear considerably more serious. This manipulation of what was circulated to the world's media was discerned not by reference to an original negative, but only by recognizing in the published image unnaturally repeated 'cloned' configurations of identical smoke clouds.[23] Other staged, wrongly captioned, enhanced or falsified news images have been subsequently exposed through the diligence of bloggers to the point that David D. Perlmutter, an academic at the University of Kansas, writes in a lament for the terminal loss of trust in photojournalism that is the result of exposure of these practices:

> In each case, these bloggers have engaged in the kind of probing, contextual, fact-based (if occasionally speculative) media criticism I have always asked of my students. And the results have been devastating: news photos and video shown to be miscaptioned, radically altered, or staged (and worse, re-staged) for the camera. Surely 'green helmet guy', 'double smoke', 'the missiles that were actually flares', 'the wedding mannequin from nowhere', the 'magical burning Koran', the 'little girl who actually fell off a swing' and 'keep filming!' will now enter the pantheon of shame of photojournalism.[24]

One final example of the effect of digital manipulability comes anecdotally from a radio news item in 2009 about a situation in contemporary Cambodia, where a schoolteacher reported that she was attempting to educate pupils about the history of the Khmer Rouge genocide (1974–9) using analogue photographs from that period. Such was the scepticism born of the students' own easy familiarity with digital image-making that the students simply discounted the veracity of what would otherwise register as documentary evidence of atrocity. Because any image can now be fabricated, these images no longer functioned for the students as exposure to an unquestionable historical truth to any degree. They simply could not access such an experience of the historical through photography.[25]

## Virtuality

The word 'virtual' is a contranym—a word that means its own opposite (examples are dust, transparent, oversight, clip, fast). Virtual means both 'not really existing' and 'almost the same'—for example, virtual reality and 'he is a virtual dictator' respectively. The word gained new resonance in the light of the development of computer technology from the 1960s onwards. Its first usage, in relation to computer software, being something made to appear to exist physically, is recorded in 1959, used in computer science with reference to virtual *memory* and virtual *machine*. Virtual memory is essentially a matter of extending and enhancing the physically real, by 'fooling the machine' into believing its memory is greater than it is, something particularly useful in the early days of computers when physical memory was expensive and, by today's standards (megabytes and gigabytes), very small (measured in kilobytes, or 0.001 of a megabyte). Such an understanding of the virtual was then extended into ideas about 'virtual reality' in the 1990s, whereby users can be 'fooled' into thinking and experiencing things, environments, and interactions that do not have any material existence. This is not the same thing, however, as saying that they are not real; on the contrary, virtually generated experiences can be all too real in their effects.

It is in this sense that we can now talk about virtual space—cyberspace, a term coined by William Gibson in his novelette, *Burning Chrome* (1982), that later became synonymous with the internet through its use in his novel *Neuromancer* (1984). Gibson defined 'cyberspace' as:

> A consensual hallucination experienced daily by billions of legitimate operators, in every nation, by children being taught mathematical concepts ... A graphic representation of data abstracted from banks of every computer in the human system. Unthinkable complexity. Lines of light ranged in the nonspace of the mind, clusters and constellations of data. Like city lights, receding.[26]

In an afterword to the twentieth anniversary edition of the novel in 2004, fellow science-fiction author, Jack Womack suggested the possibility that the imagined worlds of fiction that Gibson named influenced the way in which cybercultures and their technologies were themselves subsequently elaborated.[27]

The technological meaning of 'virtual' then becomes imbricated with pre-existing meanings of the term—but as with many other terms that get taken up and used in the context of information technology, the new meaning eclipses some of the earlier ones; for example terms such as editor, system, and input now almost immediately and exclusively evoke links to computers and information technology. If the virtual is in some fashion a deceit or conceit, so the global financial system can to an extent be seen as a consensual hallucination, or one foisted on everyone by a specific form of exchange and capital accumulation; and the economic meltdown of 2008 can then be understood as virtuality being undermined by materiality—in which context it is important to note the way in which reporting of the meltdown drew a distinction between the 'real economy' and the financial system—although we now recognize the virtual economy as all too real.

## Technology as culture

The work on virtual reality in this collection—see the examples appraised in Katherine Hayles', Samuel Weber's and Antony Bryant's chapters—indicates that often the technology appears to develop in isolation from other considerations—ethical, human, and social. Moreover, the claims for a great deal of this technology turn out to be grossly over-stated—virtual in the sense of not really existing. Transdisciplinary encounters such as the conferences that generated this collection are an important act of resistance to this tendency. It is vital that technologists engage with the idea that technology is not simply the stuff you can kick—or spill coffee over—but is a form of social practice not only shaped in structural relations of contemporary production but also inflected by pre-existing imaginings and projections as well as projected fantasies.

In his remarkably prescient work on computers and technology, dating from the 1960s and 1970s, Jacques Ellul stressed that technology is always a form of mediation, and what has been emerging as the current 'technological system' is a particularly potent form of mediation; leading to a reinterpretation of all problems and all issues as *technical* ones, even though such a distinction between the technical and the social is not sustainable. Existing in this systemic capacity, Ellul argues that technology is never simply a 'means' or an 'instrument', a medium, but always a 'mediation'. Mediation is used here in the dual sense of *passively* forming an adjunct between two elements and *actively* intervening between them. Ellul's concept of mediation relates to and extends the points made concurrently by cultural theorist Raymond Williams about technology being looked for and developed by the societies in which it emerges. Ellul contends, however, that the modern technological system has taken on an ever more active mediation, until it forms a complex and dominating system that 'fragments, simplifies, splinters, divides; everything reduced to manageable objects'.[28] The 'technological environment makes all problems and difficulties technological'.[29] This is what others such as Habermas have termed *technicism*.[30]

In his study of *Television: Technology and Cultural Form*, Raymond Williams tried to balance the analysis of television as a technology with that of television as a cultural form.[31] Williams critiques two typical approaches to their relation: technological-deterministic and symptomatic, which are exemplified in the following statements.

Deterministic:

> Television was invented as a result of scientific and technical research. Its power as a medium of social communication was then so great that it altered many of our institutions and forms of social relationships.

> Television was invented as a result of scientific and technical research, and developed as a medium of entertainment and news. It then had unforeseen consequences, not only on other entertainment and news media [...] but on some of the central processes of family, cultural and social life.

Symptomatic:

> Television discovered as a possibility by scientific and technical research, was selected for investment and promotion as a new and profitable phase of a domestic consumer economy [...].

> Television became available as a result of scientific and technical research, and in its character and uses exploited and emphasised elements of a passivity, a cultural and psychological inadequacy, which had always been latent in people [...].[32]

The two positions, although they appear contrary, share the assumption that technology is an isolated facet of existence, outside society and beyond the realm of *intention*. Anticipating Manuel Castells' argument that technology *is* society, Williams stresses that technology must be seen as being 'looked for and developed with certain purposes and practices already in mind', these purposes and practices being 'central, not marginal', as the symptomatic view would hold.[33] Thus Williams inverts the idea that technology determines culture, to suggest that culture, as the productive and creative dimension of the socio-economic productive relations, shapes the technologies it produces. What we need to read carefully is the actual working through of inventions that while intended, may have unanticipated effects.

Film and media theorist, Warren Sack provides a simplified account of the resulting interactions:

1. When technologies connect or separate people, they become media.
2. Technologies embody social, political, cultural, economic and philosophical ideas and relationships.
3. When a medium is new, it is often used to simulate old media.

4. New media do not replace old media, they displace them.

5. People make media and then media make people.[34]

## Other virtualities

Thus the term virtuality makes obvious reference to current debates about new media, cybernetics, information systems and notions and practices of virtual realities. In this volume, Samuel Weber offers a deconstructive reading precisely into the mirroring of the capitalist economy in virtual realities such as *Second Life* and other massively multiplayer online role-playing games.[35] For its advocates virtual reality is said to promise the realization of a radically new era, pregnant with possibilities and futures hitherto unimagined, with its concomitant transformations of notions of space, the body, time, futurity, subjectivity and global connectivity, the digital, cybernetic, cyborgian virtualities that play in daily life and communication, in film and television, in expanded and thoroughly de-categorized art practices, through the internet, mobile phones and a variety of other instantaneously transmitted textualities and visualities. Yet these claims for the virtual future can be subjected to cultural analysis by literary critics working on science fiction, by philosophers and psychoanalysts as well as Marxist, social and media theorists. Behind the surface of virtual worlds, lie still very concrete processes of material production, labour, capital, and work by grounded beings in space and time. Beyond refusing fetishistic mystifications, however, what does the term virtuality introduce?

From the Latin *virtus* meaning excellence, sharing a root with the word *vir*, meaning 'man', and its adaptation to a Middle English word, *virtuell*, meaning effective, we inherit the still confusing but rich term *virtuality*. 'It is virtually the same', we say; or 'it is virtually impossible'. This everyday usage means 'almost' but not quite. We also say 'it is so by virtue of *x*', meaning having the property of *x*, but not the essence. Virtual suggests something that is effective, operating in parallel to, but at a distance from the concrete, actual, material, or lived reality. There is similarity with the actual thing; but it is not the thing itself. It is not the real; yet it is not false. It displays, none the less, similar enough traits for our interactions with the virtual to function as if they were indeed real. This is not only at an imaginative or fictional level. In this sense we speak of virtual worlds, or the virtualities offered through information technologies and conversations in cyberspace. Virtuality is closely linked with simulation in the technical sense but seems distinct from the imagined or fictive. Yet, in its non-technological sense, virtuality must be understood in relation to the faculty of the imagination and to *phantasy*: the psychic plane of an effective, if not perceptual, reality.[36] In this political sense, the virtual can be manipulated as the site for generating affects that have substantive political consequences. Thus Brian Massumi's chapter in this volume enfolds indexicality and virtuality into the contemporary politics of fear fostered and manipulated post 9/11 and the War on Terror, in which certain indices of events or threats are used pre-emptively to generate affects in anticipation of a virtual event. 'The smoke now precedes the fire', suggests Massumi, in the political manipulation of a semiotics of fear.

Virtuality is thus not merely a new dimension of our worlds shaped by new media technologies. In the quite different register of philosophical thinking, notably in the tradition that runs from Henri Bergson (1859–1941) to Gilles Deleuze (1925–95), virtuality is a gap rich with creative possibility. Virtuality refers to that which could become actual, but is as yet unrealized. Bergson made a distinction between the pairing of the possible and the real, and the virtual and the actual. The possible is only the real in waiting; it must always fundamentally be similar to, and predetermined by, what is real. The virtual, which may be actualized in some precise historical or social forms, is, however, the site of genuinely creative difference.[37] Virtuality is a potential actuality; it is an expandable reality full of promise, that indicates the constant movement of *becoming*, of transformative potentiality in the world. In its creative interruptions as opposed to its semiotic encodings, art can thus be understood as a form of virtuality: a *poiesis* that draws into the realm of the knowable what is new and hence generates genuine difference in contrast to seemingly varied versions of socially limited 'reality'.[38]

### Virtuality, language and the unconscious

The apparent novelty of digital virtuality can, moreover, be contested by an even older concept of virtuality embedded in Western philosophy, language theory and theories of the human psyche. As philosopher Elizabeth Grosz points out:

> The concept of virtuality has been with us a remarkably long time. It is a coherent and functional idea in Plato's writing, where both ideas and simulacra exist in some state of virtuality [...]. [S]ince there has been writing (in the Derridian sense of trace—that is, *as the very precondition of culture itself*), there has been some idea of the virtual.[39]

Thus language, thought, and the psychic apparatus theorized by Sigmund Freud operate with varying kinds and degrees of virtuality. In this collection Anna Johnson's close textual reading of language in artist-theorist Bracha Ettinger's 'writing' and drawing addresses this constellation of aesthetic transformation, theories of subjectivity and the virtualities within alphabets of various languages that facilitate theoretical invention and become the only ground for the articulation of hitherto unsignifiable domains of subjectivity. On the other hand, Katherine Hayles examines the psychoanalytical concept of trauma to analyse the anxieties emerging around the ubiquity of inaccessible machine code as the material infrastructure of the language that we now habitually use in most of our linguistic communications via the computer, texting and mobile/cell phone conversation. Through three case studies of cyber narratives, Hayles interrogates 'the role of code in the cultural Imaginary' and identifies 'the crisis that erupts when code breaks through the representational surface of the fiction to announce its inevitability'. She thus points to the tension between a surface simulacrum of human language (through which we currently communicate with each other) and machinic language (through which machines 'speak' to each other so that we can imagine we are 'speaking' to each other) in which code functions as a contemporary *aconscious*, whose traumatic impacts may be variously negotiated in imaginative works of cyber fiction that explore code as either cure or as virus disintegrating 'real life'.

## Virtuality and materiality

In yet another approach, virtuality might be paired with a different opposite: materiality. Yet what is this materiality? The materiality of the embodied activities of perception, cognition and response continue and are necessary, unaffected by what Grosz specifies as the virtuality of the objects or images created by technologies that offer new degrees of virtual space and imagery. Grosz reminds us, too, that only certain orders of representation can be 'virtualized' while others less so: can there be a substantive difference between a real and a virtual sound at the point of reception? Is this absence of distinction a reminder not of the tension between the virtual and actual (an order of truth) but the virtual and material, which we suggest is indicative of the order of history and politics. Is the virtual an imaginary projection onto technologies of representation that continue much older fantasies of transcendence by means of materially created prostheses for human communication, imagination and interventions in the world and relations between folks?

If, in these older senses of the word, writing and thought are themselves forms of virtuality, we might then need to recover another materiality, denigrated in terms of the dominant linguistic and semiotic turn of later twentieth century cultural theory. In his book *Parables For the Virtual: Movement, Affect, Sensation* (2002) philosopher Brian Massumi has suggested that this materiality is framed by a deeper internal debate in cultural theory. A hegemonic focus on a semiotic concept of culture, stressing mediation and the systemic and the schematic, rendered certain kinds of speculation about the phenomenological and the materially corporeal suspect, marginal or ideologically problematic. The deeply linguistic logic of post-structuralism has had a major impact in shaping feminist discourse on gender and sexuality, so much so that post-structuralist feminist theory has tended anxiously to police every possible suspicion of corporeality in discussions of sexuality or gender for fear of falling out of the social into the miasma of the biologically determined, hence apolitical and unchangeable. But at what price? In what ways has this fear of the corporeal aligned itself with the fantasies of escaping imprisonment in the body that seem to haunt and inspire the embrace of cybernetic virtualities? Culture as text, positionality and coding, or change conceived only as an intervention in linguistic, kinship or other social systems, has precluded analytical theorizations of the virtualities of the body as movement, sensation and affect. Thus Massumi writes that his book:

> was based on the hope that movement, sensation and qualities of experience couched in matter in its most literal sense (and sensing) might be culturally-theoretically thinkable, without falling into the Scylla of naive realism or the Charybdis of subjectivism and without contradicting the very real insights of poststructuralist cultural theory concerning the coextensiveness of culture with the field of experience and of power with culture. The aim was to put matter unmediatedly back into cultural materialism, along with what seemed most directly corporeal back into the body.[40]

To do this, was, of course, a philosophical undertaking, a remodelling of thought based on an engagement with and dissemination of the battle between the dominance of a Lacanian and Derridian Paris and the recharting of a philosophical genealogy in the work of Gilles Deleuze from Henri Bergson and William James. This shift reclaims a space for the aesthetics of affect and sensation in cultural theory and practice while also reframing the discussion of television, film and the internet that demand models of analysis beyond the culturally dominant semiotic or rhetorical modes that are so creatively and politically significant, but which are not sufficient perhaps to account for changes in culture itself that must struggle over situated and simulated affectivity. These changes both register new developments in technologies, social relations and subjectivities while bringing some of their implications and possibilities to the surface and attention of culture itself.

Beyond some 'purely' but never discretely philosophical and theoretical problems, or rather, as their determining foundation (the concrete is always given, even in the head, according to Marx), lie questions about the politics of culture, cultural theory and the social and economic processes that we experience as culture and through cultural practices. Many contemporary artists, film and media theorists, as well as literary critics, practise analysis of the changing landscapes of contemporary societies and cultures neither as uncritical cyber-enthusiasts nor as nostalgic Luddites, but as involved and situated commentators, participants and social historians deeply fascinated by the kinds of subjectivities that are being fostered by new kinds of interface mediated by the virtualities of digital and cyber cultures. The virtual subject, and the virtual gaze are just some themes in recent studies.[41] They suggest that these are important sociological and historical dimensions: there is a need to analyse both the social and economic conditions of the technological and cultural changes produced by digitalization, the internet, simulation and globalization of communication and information systems, not to mention their cultural register and deployment. We are easily and often misled by technological innovation to lose sight of what Marx argued, that machines must be recognized as themselves stored-up human labour, representing the mental and manual work that expedites and transforms the social forces of capitalism beyond the limits that check their unfettered and compulsive drive for profit. Moving from the heavy industrial labour of capitalism's *solid* state into the *liquid* movement—brilliantly identified by Zygmunt Bauman—of its silicon- or crystal-based industries (which are dependent on a globalized and often feminized proletariat manipulated by a new army of technocrats), the question we need to ask is this: are we moving into a radically new era, as cyber-enthusiasts imagine, or are we merely entering into another stage of capitalism?[42] In this apparent 'disappearing'—virtualization—of human labour and its ever present politics and lived worlds, do we not see the familiar tropes and devices that Marx identified in the heavy or solid stages of industrial capitalism: commodity fetishism, spectacle and the so-called phenomenal forms that mystify the real relations? Are real relations *virtual* in their historical materiality, encountered in masked forms that have the immediacy of seductive realities? Was Marx already a theorist of a historically specific mode of virtualization to come? Related as we know to the pressures and needs of the military-industrial complex, generated the better to prosecute new types of warfare, the technologies we now use domestically and for entertainment carry some trace of their dark genesis and certainly remain ciphers of the capitalist conditions of their production and realization. Perry Anderson reminds us of what Marx called 'the character-masks of capital'. Quoting Anderson, Paul Willemen suggests that we need new analytical tools to discern the changing forms of the masks that do not, however, allow us to forget the real relations that may have shifted globally but have not been superseded. In remaining urgently faithful to a historical materialist analysis, we are reminded that Marx already diagnosed capitalism itself as a system in which virtualities and material realities are distinctively configured to transform them into the compelling, seductive surfaces of the former: phenomenal appearance as spectacle. It was the enigmas of these surfaces, images and delusions for which Marx developed his non-realist analytical tools for the specific dialectic of the capitalist mode of production. In this context Willemen's chapter outlines a method for comparative studies in cinema that uses indexicality precisely as a means to pierce the surfaces of diversity represented as global or third or world cinema, in order to identify how we might read the ways in which the specific and local forms of capitalist production of cinema are articulated at the level of cinematic form.

## Post-humanities?

In her book *How We Became Posthuman: Virtual Bodies in Cybernetics, Literature and Informatics* (1999), literary theorist N. Katherine Hayles investigated the formation of a discourse which declares the arrival of a new era: the post-human in which intelligence/information appear to have 'lost their bodies'—become dematerialized and disembodied.[43] In a manner reminiscent of Arendt's questioning of the fantasies of the space age, or Hirst and Woolley's challenge to McLuhan, Hayles investigates how the idea of a mind separated from its bodies emerged and wonders how we came to imagine machines as the final liberation from the human and for the novelty of the post-human. How, she asks, is it possible to dispose of embodied enactment? Working as both historical researcher and textual literary critic, Hayles plots out three interrelating narratives that concern computers, informatics, cyborgs and imaginative constructions based on them. Moving between sociology and informatics, Antony Bryant follows on from Hayles. He analyses the profound misunderstandings of the nature of human beings, thought and cognition underlying many of the claims in the artificial intelligence community about what computers can do in the post-human and the information age. Many commentators on our current, changing conditions of social practice mediated by new technologies and its myths see in the claims and some of the practices a much older dream of futurity that is indexed to social and historical materialities on the one hand, and cultural mystifications on the other.

Where is the practice of art, once the very privilege site of the humanist imaginary, situated? Is the artist to be an enthusiastic and playful user of new technologies or a critical ethnographer of the worlds we are being offered through its ever shinier and facilitated fabrications? Are the new technologies expanded resources to enable affecting as well as cognitive reflections on time, bodies and space? Martha Rosler has a distinguished career producing a range of projects at the intersection of cultural mythologies and the disseminated social imagery from soft porn magazines and advertising to news television and documentary photography. Rosler has tracked the dialectics of artistic engagements with the mediatic and the political while herself performing a series of critical engagements through her own reworking of the spectacles that surround us and through which we travel. Her project in this volume, *Airport*, expands upon a major work, *In the Place of the Public: Observations of a Frequent Flyer* (1999) which links the relentless movement of the artist, travelling within what Appadurai names the globalized 'artscape' with the image-environment of the encapsulated travel-space of the airport, asking us to recalibrate the body's place in the movements of the capitalist economy.[44]

In this move to produce a reconsidered 'archaeology' of the media and technologies of representation of modernity precipitated by a new moment in which they seem at once 'old' media vis-à-vis what is proclaimed as new media, and yet strangely unknown because of that apparent 'historicity', what of television and its medium: photo-emission? Both Martha Rosler, as an artist working with and through the medium of video, and cultural theorist Samuel Weber have reflected on the meanings of television. In his *Mass Medi-auras: Form, Technics, Media*, a confrontation between aesthetics and the rise of new media, Weber draws upon both deconstruction and critical theory to consider what he argues is central to television: the reality of ambivalence.

> For what is ostensibly 'set in place' as the television set is also and above all *a movement of displacement*, of *transmission*. What results strongly resembles what Walter Benjamin, in his work on German Baroque theatre of the 17th century, described as the 'court' that emanates from all allegory […]. Like the allegorical court, television brings the most remote things together only to disperse them again, out of 'indifference to their being-there', or rather, out of the undecidability of their being-there (*Dasein*).[45]

To this mix we can now add psychoanalysis: surely a significant site of reflection on relations of virtuality and indexicality through its own metaphoric language that struggles to think of the somatic/psychic dialectic of subjectivity, the unimaginable yet affecting corporeal materiality of the drives and/as their equally unplaceable psychic representatives, straddling the world of movement, affect, sensation, materialities and those of thought, signification and that most tricky concept, memory, whose aporia is trauma.

Several texts in this volume lean on psychoanalysis for a purchase on current cultural phenomena. Claire Pajaczkowska enters the debate from the left field of textiles, offering a semiotic reading drawing on Peircean categories of the sign to open up the virtuality and signification (affectivity, fantasy, memory) of that most material of materials, cloth. A dossier on a work by American artist, Mary Kelly includes a specially created book-form of an installation work made for the Whitney Biennial in 2004 with the artist's voice in narrative captions. There are two commentaries, one by the artist and the other by art historian Juli Carson on the occasion of the installation of the work at University of California, Irvine. Pondering the role of mediated historical memory, encoded in political photographs or slogans, Kelly identifies the virtual impress of the past, that she suggests functions like a 'political primal scene', linking one generation removed from the historical event to the past it always misses. To explore this Kelly has refabricated, on a monumental scale a chance, but now iconic, news photograph from the Parisian student movement in May 1968. The image is transfigured through material that is not a textile: lint, created by laundering hundreds of pounds of black and white clothing in a domestic tumble dryer whose lint-filter becomes a fragile screen for a vulnerable physicality into which this 'image' is translated, computer calculated block by block, and onto which, when re-assembled, electronically generated light-noise is projected. Undoing the indexicality of the photograph by materializing re-creation, yet animating its surface with light noise that evokes, without reproducing, cinematic flicker as digital pulse, Kelly's reflections on the constitution of political memory is also examined in Griselda Pollock's reading of indexicality and virtual trauma in an earlier Kelly work, which addresses an incident from the Kosovan war. Occasioned by a news photograph and the sound environment of television and radio reportage, Kelly's work an-iconically replays cinematic narrative by linking words (and in performance, voice and music) and a material support. She materializes the virtualized world that comes into our homes through modern communication technologies to focus momentary attention on the 'real' of subjectivity.

## Conclusion

In this collection, the project seeks to allow the play of concepts of virtuality and indexicality within the transdisciplinary realm of cultural analysis, theory and history, and there to shape a range of provisional intellectual examinations of the complexity of our current cultural situation and foundations for knowledge with regard to what is happening to us by replacing reductive opposition with interfacing complexity. If there are many ways to understand virtuality, and many virtualities: cybernetic, linguistic, psychic, socio-material, there are also many modes and conditions of indexicality. All require analysis, as does their interaction. Our sphere in this collection is that virtuality we name culture, a sphere of critical reflection on socio-political and economic conditions and relations as well as on the imaginative-theoretical intervention in their representation at the interface of cognition and the imaginary. This collection emerged out of several gatherings of scholars, filmmakers and artists under a heavy phrasing that seems, so far, to have escaped being pilloried in 'Pseuds' Corner' of *Private Eye*: *The Politics and Ethics of Virtuality and Indexicality*.[46] This cumbersome but necessary conjunction of the two sets of terms locates the theoretical space for the renegotiation of the image. The *ethical* questions the ways in which current regimes of the images and technologies have effects in relation to what, in Arendtian terms, we might consider human interactions, mediated self–other relations, and attendant subjectivities, desire, fantasies and mythologies; the *political* questions power, participation, agency, change, as well as the constant work of critical reflection with historical consciousness that is fundamentally the meaning of any politics.

Leeds 2009

# 1

# TRAUMAS OF CODE

*N. Katherine Hayles*

Language isn't what it used to be. In computer-mediated communication, including cell phone conversations, email, chat room dialogues, blogs, and all documents written on a computer, the language we learned at mother's knee is generated by computer code. Though computer-mediated language may appear to flow as effortlessly as speaking face-to-face or scribbling words on paper, complicated processes of encoding and decoding race up and down the computer's tower of languages as letters are coupled with programming commands, commands are compiled or interpreted, and source code is correlated with the object code of binary symbols, transformed in turn into voltage differences. Most of this code is inaccessible to most people. At the level of binary code, few are equipped to understand it with fluency, and even fewer can reverse engineer object code to arrive at the higher-level languages with which it correlates.[1] As a result, contemporary computer-mediated communication consists of two categories of dynamically interacting languages: so-called natural language, which is addressed to humans (and which I will accordingly call human-only language); and computer codes, which (although readable by some humans) can be executed only by intelligent machines.

The vast majority of the literate public who are not computer programmers become aware of this dynamic interaction through ordinary experiences. The easy flow of writing and reading human-only languages on computers, increasingly routine for the millions who populate cyberspace, is regularly interrupted by indications that unseen forces are interacting with the language flow, shaping, disrupting, redirecting it. I mistype a word, and my word processing program rearranges the letters. I think I am making the keystroke that will start a new paragraph and instead the previous paragraph disappears. I type a URL into the browser and am taken to a destination I do not expect. These familiar experiences make us aware that our conscious intentions do not entirely control how our language operates. Just as the unconscious surfaces through significant puns, slips, and metonymic splices, so the underlying code surfaces at those moments when the program makes decisions we have not consciously initiated. This phenomenon suggests the following analogy: as the unconscious is to the conscious, so computer code is to language. I will risk pushing the analogy even further; in our computationally intensive culture, code is the unconscious of language.

How literally should we take this aphorism, hovering somewhere between an analogy and a proposition? If we take it seriously as a proposition, a sceptic may object that code is easily read and understood, whereas the unconscious is inherently unknowable. Such an objection depends on a naive notion of programming that supposes code is transparently obvious to anyone who knows the coding language. On the contrary, people who have spent serious time programming will testify that nothing is more difficult than to decipher code someone else has written and insufficiently documented; for that matter, code one writes oneself can also become mysterious when enough time has passed. Since large programs—say, Microsoft Word—are written by many programmers and portions of the code are recycled from one version to the next, no living person understands the programs in their totality. Indeed, the number of person-hours necessary to comprehend a large program suite such as Microsoft Office exceeds a working lifetime.[2] In the case of evolutionary algorithms where the code is not directly written by a human but evolves through variation and selection procedures carried out by a machine, the difficulty of understanding the code is so notorious as to be legendary. These examples demonstrate that in practice both code and the unconscious are opaque, although with code it is a matter of degree, whereas the opacity of the unconscious is assumed. Psychoanalysts position themselves as informed theorists and practitioners who can understand, at least partially, the workings of the unconscious; programmers constitute the group who can understand, at least partially, the workings of code.

A more cogent objection is articulated by Adrian Mackenzie in his groundbreaking study *Cutting Code*, where he considers code as the site of social negotiations that structure and organize human agency, behaviour, and intention.[3] His book illustrates the advantages of *not* black-boxing code. This stance is a valuable option, and the rich insights in his work testify to the need for more studies of this kind. Nevertheless, the argument Mackenzie makes for the agency of code—one of his major points—can be appropriated for the case I am making here for code as the unconscious of language. With admirable clarity, he shows that code is not merely a neutral tool but an ordered system of cognitions making things happen in the world, both among humans who can (sometimes) understand the code and those who cannot. The agency of code underscores its similarity to the unconscious in producing effects even when it remains hidden under a linguistic surface.

A framework extending code's effects into the non-linguistic realm is provided by Nigel Thrift's *technological unconscious*.[4] Thrift uses the term to reference the everyday habits initiated, regulated, and disciplined by multiple strata of technological devices and inventions, ranging from an artefact as ordinary as a wristwatch to the extensive and pervasive effects of the World Wide Web. Implicit in his argument is the idea that both the conscious and unconscious are influenced and shaped by the technological environments with which humans have surrounded themselves as far back as the domestication of fire. The argument suggests that the unconscious has a historical dimension, changing in relation to the artefactual environment with which it interacts. Thrift's vision resonates with recent arguments for thinking of cognition as something that, far from being limited to the neocortex, occurs throughout the body and stretches beyond body boundaries into the environment. Andy Clark and Edwin Hutchins, among others, see human thought as taking place within extended cognitive systems in which artefacts carry part of the cognitive load, operating in flexible configurations in which are embedded human thoughts, actions, and memories. For Hutchins, an anthropologist, an extended cognitive system can be as simple as a geometric compass, pencil, and paper.[5] It is not only a metaphor, he asserts, that drawing a line on a navigation chart constitutes remembering, and erasing it is forgetting. Clark carries the argument further to envision humans as natural-born cyborgs who have, since the dawn of the species, excelled in enrolling objects into their extended cognitive systems, from prehistoric cave paintings to the laptops, PDAs, and cell phones pervasive today.[6]

The shift from 'thinking' to 'cognizing' in this model is significant, for it blurs the boundary between conscious self-awareness and nonconscious processes. These include dreams (associated with the Freudian unconscious) as well as cognitions that occur in the limbic system, the central nervous system, and the viscera, which, as Antonio Damasio has argued, are integrally involved in feedback loops with the cortex and thus should legitimately be considered part of the human cognitive system.[7] The idea that the unconscious may be historically specific now appears considerably less contentious. If the dreaming part of cognition is seen in the context of an integrated system that includes, for example, the limbic system and its associated motor functions, it stands to reason that, as motor functions change in relation to a technologically enhanced environment, these changes would resonate through the entire cognitive system. Indeed, from this perspective the Freudian unconscious may appear as a fetishization that privileges the dreaming part of cognition as consciousness' shadowy other, while relegating to mere biological functions the rest of the extended cognitive system.

In view of the long association of the unconscious with dreams, I propose modifying Thrift's terminology to the *technological nonconscious*. The modification highlights a principal difference between humans and intelligent machines: humans have conscious self-awareness, and intelligent machines do not. Along with the capacity to feel emotions, self-awareness remains a distinctively biological characteristic. Nevertheless, contemporary computers perform cognitions of immense power, complexity, and sophistication. The technological nonconscious, impacting human cognition for millennia before the advent of the digital computer, now has a stronger cognitive component than ever before. Human cognition increasingly takes place within environments where human behaviour is entrained by intelligent machines through such everyday activities as cursor movement and scrolling, interacting with computerized voice trees, talking and text messaging on cell phones, and searching the web to find whatever information is needed at the moment. As computation moves out of the desktop into the environment with embedded sensors, smart coatings on walls, fabrics, and appliances, and RFID (radio frequency ID) tags, the cognitive systems entraining human behaviour become even more pervasive, flexible, and powerful in their effects on human conscious and nonconscious cognition. Thomas Whalen references this entrainment when he calls the World Wide Web the *cognisphere*, a term that can be expanded to include many different kinds of human-machine cognitions, including wired, wireless, and electromagnetic communications.[8]

Enmeshed within this flow of data, human behaviour is increasingly integrated with the technological nonconscious through somatic responses, haptic feedback, gestural interactions, and a wide variety of other cognitive activities that are habitual and repetitive and that therefore fall below the threshold of conscious awareness. Mediating between these habits and the intelligent machines that entrain them are layers of code. Code, then, affects both linguistic and non-linguistic human behaviour. Just as code is at once a language system and an agent commanding the computer's performances, so it interacts with and influences human agency expressed somatically, implemented for example through habits and postures. Because of its cognitive power, code is uniquely suited to perform this mediating role across the entire spectrum of the extended human cognitive system. Through this multilayered addressing, code becomes a powerful resource through which new communication channels can be opened between conscious, unconscious, and nonconscious human cognitions.

### Code and trauma

A promising site for the possibility of new communication channels is trauma. In clinical accounts of trauma, such as those presented by Bessel van der Kolk and Onno van der Hart, trauma overwhelms the ability of a human to process it.[9] In this view, traumatic events are experienced and remembered in a qualitatively different way from ordinary experience. The characteristic symptoms of trauma—dissociation, flashbacks, re-enactments, frighteningly vivid nightmares—suggest that traumatic memories are stored as sensorimotor experiences and strong emotions rather than as linguistic memory. Dissociated from language, trauma resists narrative. When traumatic events are brought into the linguistic realm, they are frequently divorced from appropriate affect. As Dominick LaCapra puts it, 'Trauma brings about a dissociation of affect and representation: one disconcertingly feels what one cannot represent; one numbingly represents what one cannot feel.'[10] Moreover, van der Kolk and van der Hart's research indicates that when people experience traumatic re-enactments while sleeping, their brain waves differ significantly from those characteristic of REM dreams. In light of these results, he suggests that traumatic nightmares should not be considered dreams but a different kind of phenomenon; to recognize the distinction, I will call traumatic re-enactments and related experiences that occur outside and apart from conscious awareness the traumatic aconscious.

Experienced consciously but remembered non-linguistically, trauma has structural affinities with code. Like code, it is linked with narrative without itself being narrative. Like code, it is somewhere other than on the linguistic surface, while having power to influence that surface. Like code, it is intimately related to somatic states below the level of consciousness. These similarities suggest that code can become a conduit through which to understand, represent, and intervene in trauma. Code in this view acts as the conduit through which traumatic experience can pass from its repressed position in the traumatic aconscious to conscious expression, without being trapped within the involuntary re-enactments and obsessive repetitions that typically constitute the acting out of traumatic experience.

This possibility was explored in the early days of virtual reality, through simulations designed to help people overcome such phobias as fear of heights, agoraphobia, and arachnophobia. The idea was to present a simulated experience through which the affected person could encounter the phobia at a distance, as it were, where fear remained at a tolerable level. As the person grew habituated and less fearful, the simulated experience was gradually intensified, with habituation occurring at each step. When the stimulus reached real-life levels and the person could tolerate it, the therapy was considered successful.[11]

Useful as these therapies may have been for particular phobias, they focused on a narrow range of traumatic experiences and used code in a purely practical way without deeper theoretical resonances. More interesting from a theoretical perspective are recent cultural productions that explore through fictional narratives the ways in which code can be appropriated as a resource to deal with trauma. Precisely because these are works of the imagination, they can shape their narratives to probe the deeper implications of what it means for code to entrain human behaviour. They consequently have much to say about the ways in which the technological nonconscious operates with unprecedented cognitive power in conjunction with the performances of intelligent machines; they explore the implications of these enactments for the computational present and the even more computationally intensive future; and they meditate upon the ethical significance of enmeshing human agency within the optic fibres, data flows, and smart environments of the cognisphere.

To explore these interrogations of the role of code in the cultural Imaginary, I will focus on three works, each setting up a different relationship between trauma and code and each produced within a different medium. First, William Gibson's print novel *Pattern Recognition* represents a complex transmission pathway for trauma in which code plays a central role, by breaking the cycle of obsessive repetition and allowing the trauma to reach powerful artistic expression that can touch others and even initiate a process of healing.[12] *Pattern Recognition* makes extensive use of ekphrasis, the verbal representation of a visual representation, creating through its verbal art the representation of video segments released on the internet (and therefore mediated through code).[13] The footage, as the 135 segments are called by those who avidly seek them out, becomes a topic of intense interest and speculation for the online discussion site F:F:F (Fetish:Footage:Forum), leading to a confrontation with trauma staged on multiple levels. Second, Mamoru Oshii's film *Avalon* explores a different problematic, how code controls and delimits the space of representation.[14] Compared to the sensory richness and infinite diversity of reality, computer simulations are necessarily much more limited, typically evolving only within the parameters specified by the code. The film sets up a structural dichotomy between real life and the eponymous virtual reality war game Avalon. Death is the ultimate signifier separating the real world from the simulacrum, for in the game 'reset' can be called and the game replayed. Code lacks the seriousness of real life because it provides only a simulacrum of death, not the thing itself. Paradoxically, the inability to experience the ultimate trauma becomes itself the presenting trauma of *Avalon*, a condition generated by and mediated through code. Finally, Jason Nelson's online fiction *Dreamaphage* takes this implication to its logical conclusion, presenting code as an infectious agent that inevitably leads to death.[15] The three works thus present a spectrum of possibilities, from code opening the way to overcoming trauma, to code becoming so ubiquitous it threatens the very idea of real life, and finally to code as a virus eating away at life from the inside. Their differences notwithstanding, all three works entwine code with trauma and explore code's ability to influence and entrain human conscious, unconscious, and nonconscious cognition.

The different thematic significations of code in these works correlate with how deeply code entered into the work's production, storage, and transmission. As a print novel, *Pattern Recognition* was produced by manipulating electronic files. Indeed, digital encoding has now become so essential to the commercial printing process that print should properly be considered as a specific output form of digital text. Code thus generated the text but was not necessarily involved in its transmission or storage. Code was also used in the production of *Avalon*, created through a combination of filming live actors, generating special effects through computer graphics, and using non-digital effects such as hand mattes. In contrast to the print novel, code was also involved in transmission and storage processes, especially in marketing the film as a DVD. For the online work *Dreamaphage*, code is obviously crucial in all phases of creation, storage, and transmission. As code enters more deeply into the production and dissemination of these works, they become more concerned about the adverse effects of code on the fabric of reality. Thematic anxiety about code within the text thus appears to be reflexively entwined with how deeply code was involved in the production of the work as an artistic object. The more the work depends on code, the more it tends to represent code as not merely involved with traumatic pathways but itself the cause of trauma.

At crucial points in the narratives, each work highlights a doubled articulation, as if acknowledging the double address of code to humans and intelligent machines. The specific configuration of the doubling serves as a metaphor for the work's exploration of the ethical significance of coupling code with trauma. In *Pattern Recognition*, the doubled articulation connects a physical wound with the representational space of the footage, suggesting that the transmission pathways opened by code can overcome dissociation by forging new associations between life and fiction. In *Avalon*, doubling blurs the boundary between life and simulation; rather than promoting healing, the interpenetration of life and code troubles the quotidian assumption that there can be life apart from code. In *Dreamaphage*, doubling takes the form of imagining a physical virus that is indistinguishable from viral computer code. Here the transmission pathway opened by code is figured as an epidemiological vector along which disease travels, with fatal results for human agency, consciousness, and life. The implication is that code is a virulent agent violently transforming the context for human life in a metamorphosis that is both dangerous and artistically liberating. Notwithstanding the different ways in which the encounter with code is imagined, the works concur in seeing code as a central component of a complex system in which intelligent machines interact with and influence conscious, unconscious, and nonconscious human behaviour.

### *Pattern Recognition:* interpolating code

'Only the wound, speaking wordlessly in the dark.'[16] This is Cayce Pollard's thought when she finally succeeds in tracking down the maker, the artist responsible for the compelling segments of the footage. Cayce's search for the maker leads her to Nora and Stella Volkova, whose parents were killed by a bomb planted by the political enemies of their powerful and very wealthy uncle, Andrei Volkova. Nora was severely injured in the explosion when the triggering device of the claymore mine was driven deep into her brain. As a result, Nora is unable to speak or focus on anything around her, but Stella notices that Nora seems to attend to a nearby screen. She has a computer and monitor installed by Nora's bedside, and Nora, a student film-maker before her injury, begins creating the images that become the footage. The only times she is intellectually and spiritually present is when she works on the footage; otherwise she lapses into an unresponsive state that Stella describes by saying Nora is simply not 'there'. The footage, then, is both antidote and witness to the trauma Nora has suffered.

The breakthrough in Cayce's search comes when a group of Japanese footage heads discover that the images are watermarked. (Watermarking is a computational version of steganography, defined as hiding a message within another message.)[17] When decrypted, the hidden message depicts a T-shaped city map, presumably the city where the footage's action takes place. A pattern-matching program discovers, however, that the shape corresponds to no known urban geography; instead it is a perfect match with the claymore mine trigger. In this complex entanglement of signifiers, the hidden message points in two directions at once: inward to the physical object that is the immediate cause of Nora's injury and outward to a representation that promises to link the footage with the world. This doubleness is mirrored by the footage's effects on trauma. It helps to give Nora's life focus if not meaning. It also has a profound effect on others, particularly Cayce, for whom it initiates a chain of events that helps her partially overcome her own traumatic symptoms.[18] The transmission pathways associated with the footage depend for their construction and dissemination on computer code. Without the mediating code, Nora could not create, others could not be affected by her creation, and the footage could not become the glue binding together the globally dispersed community participating in the F:F:F discussion site. Like the doubleness of the T-shaped map, this insistence on the mediating role of code is articulated twice over: once in the computer code that, when executed, creates the footage by making visual images and again in the steganographic message hidden within the executable code.

Although the footage segments are not numbered, many who follow their release believe they should be assembled to create a narrative, although in what order remains a matter of intense debate, as does whether they should constitute a narrative at all. The *articulated* narrative, of course, is the plot built around the ekphrasis that creates the footage through verbal representation. On this level too code plays a crucial mediating role. Cayce is able to make contact with Stella Volkova after she obtains her email address through a backdoor connection to the National Security Agency, the branch of the US government charged with overseeing the encryption and decryption of code. Sitting in a London park at the foot of a statue of Peter Pan, Cayce enters a trance-like state in which she writes an email to an unknown addressee, whom she presumes to be the footage's maker:

> We don't know what you're doing, or why. Parkaboy thinks you're dreaming. Dreaming for us. Sometimes he sounds as though he thinks you're dreaming us […] We become part of it. Hack into the system. Merge with it, deep enough that it, not you, begins to talk with us […] We may all seem to just be sitting there, staring at the screen, but really […] [we are] out there, seeking, taking risks.[19]

The passage hints at a connection between Cayce, her fellow footage heads, the wound-marked Nora, and the code that mediates their connection to 'the system' with which they merge on conscious, unconscious, and nonconscious levels. The connection remains latent until Cayce, still in a trance-like state, hits the send button. The gesture, taking place as a somatic action below awareness, initiates the events that create a transmission pathway between Cayce's individual traumatic symptoms, those of the community whose presence she evokes, and the healing possibilities of the footage.

Although we never learn the precise nature of the originating trauma, Cayce's symptoms bear witness to its existence. The triggering stimuli are commercial logos, especially Bibendum, known in the US as the Michelin Man. The symptoms, including panic attacks, flashbacks, nausea, inappropriate affect, and uncontrollable repetitions of the talismanic phrase 'He took a duck in the face', exist before the death of Cayce's father, Win, in the 9/11 Twin Towers disaster, but become worse afterwards. The symptoms seem to be connected with Cayce's inability to follow her father's advice to 'secure the perimeter'—a phrase that summed up his strategy as a security expert, the profession he adopted after retiring as a CIA operative. After his death, the phrase connotes for Cayce a haunting sense of vulnerability. One of its manifestations is pervasive paranoia; another is a deep sense of a rift between body and spirit that makes Cayce feel her soul is trailing after her as she jets around the world, tethered to her body by an invisible thread she feels she must reel in to achieve a wholeness that nevertheless eludes her.

These intuitions are embedded in a narrative in which, for nearly 300 pages, nothing much happens. The effect of delaying all the decisive action until the end is to envelop the reader in an atmosphere of murky apprehension, searching for the pattern amidst a welter of precisely drawn details that do not quite cohere into plot.[20] The murkiness finds explicit articulation in the belief of Cayce's mother, Cynthia, that her dead husband is trying to communicate with Cayce through EVP, Electronic Voice Phenomena. Cayce has been named, we learn, for Edgar Cayce, the 'sleeping prophet' famous for falling into a self-induced trance in which his mind could seemingly transcend the limitations of time and space.[21] Cayce follows her father in refusing to believe in EVP and other paranormal phenomena, debunking the mindset that Win called 'apophenia [...] the spontaneous perception of connections and meaningfulness in unrelated things'.[22] Yet the narrative seems finally to validate EVP, for, as the action accelerates, Cayce perceives (receives?) messages from her dead father that intervene by rescuing her from harm. In all but one instance, the messages come to her amidst electronic noise, mediated through electronic circuitry. Indeed, they can be seen as a special kind of steganography, for they are messages hidden within the noise of other texts.

The connections thus created between Nora's wound and her creation of the footage, on the one hand, and Cayce's traumatic symptoms and her EVP experiences, on the other, extend the scope of code's mediating function to transnational proportions. As the action jumps from New York City to London, Tokyo to Moscow, computer-mediated communication is pervasive, from the F:F:F website to email and electronic music to the creation and rendering of the footage. Representing the cognisphere in which, as a mass-market print novel, it is also enmeshed, *Pattern Recognition* brings to conscious articulation the pattern we are thereby enabled to recognize: the crucial role of code in allowing trauma to be released from the grip of obsessive repetition, emotional disconnection, and aconscious re-enactment so that it can achieve narrative expression. In this sense *Pattern Recognition* is a self-referential fiction, for its ability to create a narrative about creating a narrative through code reflexively points back to the role of code in its own production as a material artefact. At the same time, the possibility that the footage, compelling as it is, may not finally be a narrative at all hints at the vulnerability of narrative at a time when Lev Manovich, among others, asserts that the database has displaced narrative as the dominant cultural form.[23] The apprehension that permeates the novel thus operates on two levels at once: as the visible trace of trauma that bodies experience in the text and as the text's latent fear that the penetration by code of its own textual body could turn out to be traumatic for the print novel as a cultural form.[24]

### *Avalon:* traumatizing code

In *Pattern Recognition*, there is never any doubt that the world of flesh and blood exists in its own right as something other than code. This is precisely the premise that Mamoru Oshii's *Avalon* draws into question. Filmed in Poland by a Japanese director and crew, featuring Polish dialogue and actors, and Japanese and English subtitles, the film was released in Japan, the US, and Europe. It thus shares with *Pattern Recognition* an international milieu and the computer technology necessary to coordinate a transnational enterprise. Even before the titles play, the film presents action in which code does not merely mediate but actually creates the world of the illegal virtual reality game Avalon. The opening scenes depict the terrifying events of a war zone—bombs dropping, tanks rumbling down city streets, civilians screaming and running. The signs of potential trauma are everywhere. But when the film's protagonist Ash (Malgorzata Foremniak) turns and shoots a young soldier drawing a bead on her, his body explodes into pixellated fragments as she calmly remarks, 'You are not ready for Class A yet. You might want to spend a little bit more time in Class B'. In the Avalon war game, death is evacuated of the finality that makes it the ultimate signifier, for it means merely that a player is ejected from one level of the game and must start again at a lower level. Moreover, even that simulated death becomes a matter of choice, for when the pressure becomes too intense and threatens to overwhelm a player, he can always call 'reset', whereupon the game is aborted.

No sooner are these ontological boundaries established, however, than the film renders them ambiguous. The game's dangers are not exclusively simulated; players who push too far too fast can experience brain death and become Unreturned, condemned to live as institutionalized vegetables. When Ash meets Stunner (Bartek Swiderski), one of her former teammates from Wizard Party (as one of the VR teams is called), she learns that their leader Murphy (Jerzy Gudejko) suffered this fate. Stunner suggests that Murphy was searching for the gate that would lead to Special A, a secret, ultra-high level where one cannot call 'reset' and must play the game to the end. The sign that signals proximity to the gate is the Ghost, a mysterious apparition manifested as a luminous, floating young girl. 'Killing' her opens the gate, but her appearance is also accompanied by grave danger. Murphy's mistake, Stunner suggests, was to go after the Ghost, and as a result he became Unreturned.

Although Wizard Party was so good that its exploits were legendary, it broke up when one of its members disobeyed orders, panicked, and called 'reset', thereby bringing ignominy upon the team. Unaccustomed to defeat, the members thereafter loathed one another, and the team was dissolved. The guilty player, so rumour goes, was none other than Ash. Ironically, the 'reset' call, designed to abort the game when it threatens to become traumatic, itself becomes for Ash the source of her traumatic symptoms, associated with a potent brew of intense fear, shame, and repulsion at her inability to control her emotions. She exhibits classic indications of trauma, including dissociation, flashbacks, and isolation. Her sole companion is her dog, a lugubrious basset hound. The film's representation of her condition is heightened by the landscape of urban blight she inhabits, the dreary communal kitchens where she watches Stunner wolf down disgusting gruel, and the sepia-coloured cinematography. Given this grim world, it is no wonder that disillusioned young people prefer the excitement of the virtual reality game or that the authorities have declared it illegal. Entering the game world is a relief not least because it offers an objective correlative for trauma in a context where one has at least a theoretical possibility of winning the game. The game's addictive appeal is clearly evident in Ash's lifestyle. Surrounded by code, immersed in code, she experiences simulation as if it were life, investing in it all her emotional energy, and lives life as if it were a pale imitation of the virtual reality war game. The ironic motto of the US Army's Program for Simulation Training and Instrumentation, *All But War Is Simulation*, has come true for her.[25]

After Ash's encounter with Stunner, she experiences in her next game a wrenching flashback, involuntarily returning to the traumatic experience in which Wizard Party fights its last battle together. The violent experience is so upsetting that she rips off the VR helmet and vomits, in a symmetrical inversion of the scene where the camera gives us a long close-up of Stunner's repulsive gorging on the food she bought for him as a bribe for information about Murphy. The entanglement of food with trauma continues as she compensates for her involuntary re-enactment by splurging on real meat, real vegetables, and real rice so she can lovingly prepare a magnificent feast—for her dog. But when she turns around to find him in her small one-room apartment, the animal has inexplicably disappeared. Since he was her only friend and companion, his disappearance precipitates her realization that she can no longer put off confronting the source of her symptoms. She accordingly decides to go in search of Murphy, which in a sense means going in search of death.

This decision prepares for her entry into the game's next level, a transition signified by the image of her body surrounded by concentric rings of flashing code, emphasizing the massive computations necessary to propel her into this realm. When she emerges, she finds herself not in the war-torn game world but, significantly, back in her own apartment. Previous shots had shown her reclining with her head encased in a VR helmet when she was in the game world, establishing a clear boundary between simulated action and the real world. Moreover, to access the VR equipment she went to a cavernous game hall, the locale's specificity emphasized with long shots of her walking down the hallway, riding a grungy trolley home, and trudging up a flight of steps to her apartment. Now that geography collapses, along with the distinction it created between the game world and her drab everyday existence.

Glancing at the computer screen, she is informed she is now in 'Class Real'. A screen interlocutor tells her that a rogue player has illicitly entered this level, and her task is to find and kill him, which corresponds, her interlocutor says, to acting as a debugger and eliminating a virus from the system. She and the intruder will be the only players; everyone else is a 'neutral'. If she kills or injures one of them, she loses the game. If she succeeds in terminating the intruder, she will be allowed to join the privileged group whose members are successors to the game's original programmers. Warned that 'Class Real' is a much more complex game level than any she has previously seen, she finds beside her computer an evening dress and a gun.

Now comes another rupture in the fabric of reality, for when she goes out, she discovers not the dark and sombre world where she has lived but a bright, bustling, European metropolis, filled with light, colour, and people. All this suggests that her supposedly 'real' world was merely another level of the game, and she has now graduated from being a creature within the game world and been allowed to enter the real world, the one we ourselves inhabit. In this 'Class Real' world, she sees a poster advertising a musical concert of Avalon; decorating it is a picture of her beloved basset hound, underscoring his function as a signifier of the real.[26] Following the breadcrumb trail of posters, she is led to the concert hall, where she discovers, mingling among the concertgoers, her old teammate Murphy.

This discovery reinforces the suspicion that she is now in the real world, in which case the instruction telling her that killing Murphy amounts to eliminating a virus appears as a lie designed to overcome any scruples she might have about murdering her comrade. The discrepancy between what she has been told and the audience's understanding of her task hinges on the meaning of the death Murphy would suffer. Is he a person or a bit of troublesome code? Would his death represent an irrevocable finality or merely another move in a simulated world where the game can always be played again? The ambiguity is heightened by the Avalon concert, sung by a magnificent soprano backed by a full chorus and orchestra. In the Arthurian myth, Avalon is of course the island where, as the words of the song remind us, 'departed heroes go'—departed from one world but somehow still living in another.

Ash confronts Murphy as he perches on a World War I cannon, a reminder of the war game in which they were comrades. As the camera pans around her and Murphy, the music rises toward a climax, with jump cuts between their confrontation on the lawn and the ongoing concert in the hall. She charges Murphy with deliberately arranging the disaster that tore apart Wizard so he could continue on alone and reach this level of the game, deserting his teammates after they had ceased to be useful and becoming, as she says, a hollow shell. 'Do I look like a hollow shell?' he asks incredulously. He ripostes with what the audience has already surmised, that he has escaped from the game and now chooses to inhabit this world. 'Reality is only what we tell ourselves it is,' he asserts.

As the tension mounts and the action moves toward the inevitable moment in which one will kill the other, Murphy tells Ash that when the body actually bleeds instead of disintegrating into pixels she will know they are no longer in the game. Anticipating that moment, he asks her to 'imagine what it's like to actually be shot [...] to experience that pain'. When Murphy draws his weapon, Ash shoots him repeatedly in the chest, whereupon he opens his hand and drops the bullets that, unknown to Ash, he has refused to use. As he predicted, his body bleeds and he writhes in pain. Trauma returns, it appears, as the signifier of the real. At the next moment, however, this normalizing interpretation is subverted, for at his death his body does not simply become inert but rather dissolves into the concentric rings used to signify the game death of advanced players. The double signifiers of his bleeding body and its disintegration into code create an unresolvable ambiguity about whether this world is a simulation or reality. Somehow it is both at once, and death functions simultaneously as the ultimate trauma and as a disjunction separating one round of game play from another.

With Murphy dead and erased from the scene, the antagonist that Ash must face shifts to those who control the game. The shift has been anticipated in Murphy's final words. He tells Ash, 'Don't listen to what they tell you. Never go back. This world right here is where you belong.' That the game is continuing into another round (perhaps at another level) is further indicated by what Ash does when Murphy's body disintegrates. As a result of his sacrifice, she has something the programmers of the game could not have predicted—the unused bullets he left behind, which she loads into her gun. The implication is that she intends to make those who control the game pay for their deception. But what does a loaded gun mean when the status of death is ambiguous? How can Ash kill the makers of the game when she may still be inside the game, as Murphy's pixellated body suggested? These questions are not so much answered as intensified by the action that follows. She slowly walks into the now-deserted concert hall, at the front of which appears the Ghost. As the girl lifts her head and smiles with an expression that is somehow menacing, the camera cuts to a game screen with the message, 'Welcome to Avalon'.

What are we to make of these mysterious final moments? Does Ash make it to Avalon because she has a loaded gun and the will to use it or because she refrains from shooting? How can the Ghost, an unearthly apparition possible only within the simulation, appear in the concert hall previously understood as located in the real world? In an interview, Oshii commented that

> Hollywood films about virtual reality always end with a return to the real world. However, because those real worlds exist within film they themselves are lies. Reality is a questionable thing. I didn't want to do a movie where the characters return to reality.[29]

As his remarks suggest, the conundrums of the final moments are unresolvable as long as we cling to the belief that the world of simulation, the world generated and maintained by code, is separate from the real world in which we live. The appearance of the Ghost indicates that 'Class Real' is yet another level of the game. Since this new world is indistinguishable from our own, we are left with the conclusion that there is no escape from the simulation; we too are creatures of code. If the realm of code has expanded so that all death is simulated, this does not mean that trauma is absent. Although death has (perhaps) been divested of its pre-eminent position as the ultimate trauma, it is revealed as covering over the actual traumatic experience, which is nothing other than the discovery that reality itself is generated by code. Hence the double signifiers of Murphy's bleeding body and its pixellated disintegration, respectively identified with reality and code; their juxtaposition indicates that reality and simulation no longer constitute mutually exclusive realms but now interpenetrate one another. Derrida's famous aphorism, 'Il n'y a pas de hors-texte' has been replaced by its computational equivalent *Il n'y a pas de hors-code* (there is no outside to code).[28]

### *Dreamaphage:* infecting code

In Jason Nelson's online digital fiction *Dreamaphage*, code penetrates reality by first colonizing the unconscious. The backstory is narrated by Dr Bomar Felt, investigating doctor for the Dreamaphage virus. People infected with the virus start dreaming the same dream every night; the dream differs from person to person, but for any one person it remains the same. Becoming increasingly obsessed with the dream, the infected person finds that it starts looping, a term significantly associated with the programming commands of machine cognition rather than the putative free will of humans. Soon the dream occupies waking thoughts as well as sleeping visions. Within three to four months after initial onset, the infected person slips into a coma and dies. Dr Felt has encouraged patients to keep dream journals, and he suggests that they may hold the key to understanding the virus.

The next screen, an interactive animation programmed in Flash, shows rectangles whirling within a frame, suggesting that the work proceeds as an exploration of this digital space rather than as a linear account. Represented in diminishing perspective, the space seems to recede from the screen, intimating that it is larger than the screen can accommodate, perhaps larger than anyone can imagine. The navigation requires the user to catch one of the rectangles and, with considerable effort, drag it into the foreground so it can be read. The task is difficult enough so that the user may feel relieved when she finally succeeds and finds the rectangle imaged as a small handmade book. If so, the relief is short-lived, for she discovers that the book's contents can be accessed only by laboriously catching onto the lower page corner and carefully dragging it to the other side, as if the work was punishing her for her desire to return to the simplicity and robustness of a print interface.

The dream journal narratives are wildly incongruous, telling of chairs impossible to move, grocery coupons exploding under the shopper's hat, and skin cells inhabited by couch potatoes. They are accompanied by clever interactive animations that do not so much act as illustrations as performances accentuating the surrealistic mood. The following illustrates the logical disjunctions that the verbal narratives enact:

And by sunlight I mean those sparkling particles the super-intelligent viruses manipulating the fiery burst we call the sun use [*sic*] to control our, deceivingly harmless, aquarium fish. But then that's another story now isn't it. Moving on, this substance holds our world and all other worlds together. It makes us sad and happy and hungry for humping.

Sometimes this goo collects between two people [...] [b]ut love has nothing to do with goo. Instead love is governed by a complex system of ropes and wires haphazardly connected to cattle in the Texas panhandle.

Lucky for us it seems the cattle haven't yet discovered their power over love.[29]

Although the text presents itself as narrating a linear causal chain, the connections it posits are preposterous, from sunbursts to aquarium fish to love controlled by wires and ropes running through Texas cattle. Recall the interactive animation from which this text was pulled; with its swirl of many different shapes receding into the distance, it suggests a large matrix of reading trajectories, which I have elsewhere called a possibility space.[30] The narratives make no sense qua narratives because they function as if they were constructed by making random cuts through the possibility space and jamming together the diverse elements, resulting in texts that present themselves as sequential stories but are socially illegible as such. This does not mean that the narratives (or, better, pseudonarratives) fail to signify. They do so, powerfully, testifying to a cognisphere too dense, too multiply interconnected, too packed with data flows to be adequately represented in narrative form.

This intricately coded work, with its interactive animations, accompanying sound files, and complex screen designs, testifies through its very existence to the extent to which code has become indispensable for linguistic expression. If, as noted earlier in the discussion of *Pattern Recognition*, database is displacing narrative as the dominant cultural form of our computationally intensive culture, here we see that process represented as an *infection* of narrative by data. Generating the linguistic surface, the code infects that surface with its own viral aesthetics. The symptomatic monologic dreams indicate that the unconscious has been colonized by the Dreamaphage virus, a screenic word generated by the underlying code (as are all the screen images). Readers of Neal Stephenson's *Snow Crash* will recognize in the Dreamaphage virus a remediation of the idea that computer viruses can be transmitted to humans and make them behave as if they were computers, here specifically by making them execute an endless programming loop consisting of the dream.[31] Since it is not clear in Nelson's text how the virus is transmitted, we may suspect that viewing the screens of computers infected with the virus is a disease vector for human transmission (as in *Snow Crash*). In this case, the word that appears on the screen, *Dreamaphage*, at once names the phenomenon and spreads the infection, an implosion of signifier into signified that is possible because code is the underlying causative agent for both the screenic word and the disease it signifies. In a certain sense, then, the disease consists of nothing other (or less) than collapsing the distinction between artificial and human cognitions and a consequent conflation of computer code and human infectious virus. The code-virus pre-empts the normal processes that produce dreams and installs itself in their place, creating visions of the cognisphere, its native habitat, that appear nonsensical when forced into the linear sequences of human-only language. It is not the virus that is diseased, however, but the human agents who cannot grasp the workings of the cognisphere except through stories no longer adequate to articulate its immense complexity. The individual patients may die, but the cognisphere continues to expand, occupying more and more of the terrain that the unconscious used to claim. That at least is the story *Dreamaphage* enacts, a bittersweet narrative that exults in the power of code to create digital art even as it also wonders if that power has exceeded the capacity of humans to understand—and by implication, control—the parasitical ability of machine cognition not merely to penetrate but to usurp human cognition.

## Code/coda

Although previous arguments have established that code is available as a resource to connect with trauma, they do not fully explain why, as our culture races over the millennium mark, this resource should be taken up by contemporary cultural productions. To explore that question, I want to reference a moment in Joseph Weizenbaum's *Computer Power and Human Reason: From Judgment to Calculation*, when his secretary becomes so engaged with the ELIZA computer program mimicking a psychoanalyst's routine that she asks him to leave the room so she can converse with the machine in private.[32] The moment is all the more extraordinary because, as he notes, she's fully aware how the program works and so is not deceived by the illusion that the machine in any way understands her problem.[33] Shocked by the intensity of her engagement, Weizenbaum feels compelled to issue a stern warning about the limits of computer intelligence. Humans must not, he argues, think that computers can make ethical, moral, or political judgements—or indeed engage in any judgement at all. Judgement, in his view, requires understanding, and that is a faculty only humans possess.

I propose to revisit the scene with the secretary and ask again why she was so intensely engaged with what she knew was a dumb program. Let us suppose she was suffering from a traumatic experience and was using the computer to explore the significance of that experience for her life. What qualities does the computer have that would make it the ideal interlocutor in this situation? It does not feel emotion and so cannot be shocked or repulsed by anything she might reveal; it does not betray anyone (unless programmed to do so) and so can be assumed to function in a perfectly logical and trustworthy manner; and—precisely the point that so bothered Weizenbaum—it does not judge because it lacks the rich context of the human life-world that would make it capable of judgement. In brief, it possesses the kind of cognitive state that psychoanalysts train for years to achieve.

After four decades of research, development, and innovation in information technology, computers are becoming more human-like in their behaviours. Research programmes are underway to give computers 'emotions' (although as software programs they remain very different from human emotions mediated by the endocrine system and complex cortical feedback loops). Object-oriented languages such as C++ are designed to mimic in their structure and syntax human-only languages, making possible more intuitive communication between humans and computers. Neural nets, within the parameters of their feedback information, can learn to make a wide variety of distinctions. Genetic programs use diversity and selection to create new emergent properties, demonstrating that computers can achieve *human-competitive results* in such creative endeavours as electronic circuit design.[34] In addition, more and more code is written by software programs rather than humans, from commercial software like Dreamweaver that does HTML coding to more sophisticated programs designed to bootstrap computer-written software through successive generations of code, with each program more complex than its predecessor.

The present moment is characterized, then, by a deep ambivalence in the roles that computers are perceived to play. In certain ways they remain like the relatively primitive machine on which Weizenbaum created the ELIZA program—unendingly patient, emotionless, and non-judgemental. In this guise they are seen as interacting positively with humans to provide transmission pathways for the articulation of trauma. In other ways, however, they are taking over from humans more of the cognitive load, a manoeuvre widely perceived as an implicit threat to human autonomy and agency. The double speaking that characterizes my three tutor texts—in *Pattern Recognition* the map/trigger, in *Avalon* the bleeding/pixellated body, and in *Dreamaphage* the code-virus—signifies more than the double addressing of code to humans and intelligent machines. Rather, it interrogates the ambivalence inherent in the double role that the computer plays, as the perfect interlocutor and as the powerful machine that can not only penetrate but actually generate our reality.

Increasingly computers are seen as evolutionary successors to humans that are competing for the same ecological niche humans have occupied so successfully for the past three million or so years. The evolutionary progression that gave humans the decisive advantage over other species—the development of language, the coordination of larger social groups and networks that language made possible, and the rapid development of technologies to make the environment more friendly to the species—is now happening with intelligent machines, as computers have ever more memory storage and processing speed, as they are networked across the globe, and as they move out of the box and into the environment through interfaces with embedded sensors and actuators dispersed across the world.

The issues at stake, then, go well beyond linguistic address (although this is, I would argue, the fundamental characteristic from which other behaviours evolve, just as language was the fundamental development that initiated the rapid development of the human species). As the technological nonconscious expands, the sedimented routines and habits joining human behaviour to the technological infrastructure continue to operate mostly outside the realm of human awareness, coming into focus as objects of conscious attention only at moments of rupture, breakdown, and modifications and extensions of the system. Trauma, the site in these fictions through which the ambivalent relations of humans to intelligent machines are explored with special intensity, serves as the archetypal moment of breakdown that brings into view the extent to which our present and future are entwined with intelligent machines. No longer natural, human-only language increasingly finds itself in a position analogous to the conscious mind that, faced with disturbing dreams, is forced to acknowledge it is not the whole of mind. Code, performing as the interface between humans and programmable media, functions in the contemporary cultural Imaginary as the shadowy double of the human-only language inflected and infected by its hidden presence.

# 2

# OF MICE AND MIEN
## Or Perhaps of Mouses and Mien? (anyway with apologies to John Steinbeck)

*Antony Bryant*

In April 2005 I attended a workshop at the London School of Economics (LSE), which centred on the topic of *Mobile Interaction*,[1] one of those increasingly common phrases where each of the individual terms has a relatively clear meaning, but taken together there is more than a little ambiguity. No doubt there are countless examples of this, but I can offer the following: a book entitled *The Leadership of Civilization Building*, and the frequently used term *Re-usable Learning Objects*—which I assume is meant to encompass things such as books, articles and notes.

One of the presenters at the workshop was Kevin Warwick.[2] The name may not be immediately familiar or recognizable; but you may recall reading or hearing about someone who frequently subjects himself to various forms of *cyborg experimentation*. Warwick excels at courting publicity—whether this is matched by his actual achievements is another matter. He has been nicknamed *Captain Cyborg*; and that is meant to be ironic rather than reverential.[3]

In 2004 Warwick was in the news announcing his discovery that watching *Richard and Judy* on television for half an hour was the best thing to improve IQ test performance, and that reading a book was bad for you. He has also surgically implanted a trivial chip in his arm, which allowed sensors to detect his presence and do things like turn on lights and open doors.[4] He then broadcast this in the media, explaining gravely that he was now a cyborg: 'Being a human was OK,' he said, 'But being a cyborg has a lot more to offer.'[5] It should be noted that he could have achieved the same results by carrying the chip in his pocket. Amongst his wilder predictions is that before the end of the twenty-first century machines will take over the planet.

After the Soham murders in 2002, Warwick announced that he was going to implant a locating transmitter in an 11-year-old girl, in case she was abducted. It does not take any great insight, however, to note that any kidnapper would simply have to remove the device—probably painfully and messily—to render it worse than useless. As usual Warwick garnered a flurry of media coverage, but with no actual result.

There are many other examples of Warwick's well publicized feats. A volleyball competition between teams of intelligent robots slipped into farce when all entrants apart from Warwick's own Reading University team were given the wrong dimensions of the court. Despite this, Reading University came last. ROGERR the robot was designed by Warwick to run a half marathon, following two metres behind Warwick himself. Warwick wore a transmitter on his back which beamed out a signal for ROGERR to follow. After about twenty paces ROGERR veered violently to one side and smashed into a kerb, causing irreparable damage. The robot had tried to follow the sun's infra-red rays rather than those in the transmitter.[6]

At the workshop at LSE Professor Warwick was at his most bullish. One of his most recent experiments involved setting up a mechanical hand that was then connected to his own hand via the internet. He could make the mechanical hand mimic his own hand movements, and claimed that movements of the mechanical hand would create similar movements in his own hand. In fact it quickly became apparent from his description of the set-up that this was not the case. The movements of the mechanical hand produced signals which, when transmitted to the receiver implanted in Warwick, caused him to feel a series of sensations. Warwick then described how he had then to learn to interpret these sensations as equating to particular movements made by the robot arm—which he then could mimic.

He did not seem to grasp the significant difference between his claim that the mechanical hand made his hand move in a particular way, and the reality that he had to learn to interpret the signal from the mechanism. On the contrary, he saw his experiment as yet another stage in the inexorable move towards a cyborg future. He asked: 'If you could network your brain into the internet, would you do this?' But he then conveniently evaded the issue of who the 'you' refers to in this question,[7] and in what sense can that 'you'— that conscious, choosing subject—be considered distinct from and the owner of an object called the brain. He went on to argue that this sort of work would eventually lead to the obsolescence of speech—since there would be direct signalling from one brain to another. My immediate response was that if it became true then at least it might mean being able to *dis*connect, and so not have to listen to any more of his presentations![8]

So far so bad. Yet the reason for dwelling on Warwick's ideas and pronouncements is that whenever he talks about communication and cognition, he exemplifies—albeit in a grotesque parody and absurd-beyond-logical-extreme fashion—a far more pernicious, because often disregarded, set of assumptions; and we all perpetuate these, albeit in smaller and quieter ways.

Katherine Hayles has pointed to the nature of this misconception in her book *How we became Posthuman* which she begins by noting that it

> began with a roboticist's dream that struck me as a nightmare. I was reading Hans Moravec's *Mind's Children* […] where he argues it will soon be possible to download human consciousness into a computer. […] How, I asked myself, was it possible for someone of Moravec's obvious intelligence to believe that mind could be separated from body?[9]

Part of her answer is that we are all too ready to go along with this separation, in terms of our philosophical beliefs, our understanding of the relationship between humans and machines, and our everyday use of language.

A more recent example can be seen in *The Observer* newspaper, in an article titled 'Britain's leading thinker on the future offers an extraordinary vision of life in the next 45 years'. The article profiled Ian Pearson, head of something called 'the futurology unit' at BT.

> 'If you draw the timelines, realistically by 2050 we would expect to be able to download your mind into a machine, so when you die it's not a major career problem,' Pearson told The Observer. 'If you're rich enough then by 2050 it's feasible. If you're poor you'll probably have to wait until 2075 or 2080 when it's routine. We [*Pearson does not clarify whom he means by 'we'—AB*] are very serious about it. That's how fast this technology is moving: 45 years is a hell of a long time in IT.'[…] He believes that today's youngsters may never have to die, and points to the rapid advances in computing power demonstrated last week, when Sony released the first details of its PlayStation 3. It is 35 times more powerful than previous games consoles. 'The new PlayStation is 1 per cent as powerful as a human brain,' he said. 'It is into supercomputer status compared to 10 years ago. PlayStation 5 will probably be as powerful as the human brain.'[10]

Note the leap from the speed and capacity of games consoles to brains; a leap based on the assumption that the brain is no more than a superfast computer, so that once computer speeds have increased sufficiently they will be operationally equivalent to the brain. Some form of caveat is required here, perhaps an appropriate one might be the one used on the London Underground warning passengers of the space between the train and the platform: '*Mind the Gap*'.

Moreover predictions such as Pearson's—and Warwick's—need to be placed alongside others, such as those from the 1950s which predicted that by

1970 we would all have robot butlers, maids, chauffeurs et cetera; that cars would fly; that energy supplied would be clean and inexhaustible; and that everyone would have sufficient food and water, and be holidaying on Mars.[11]

There is a Talmudic saying: 'If you want to amuse God, talk about your plans for the future.' To which should be added: and if you want to give God a really good laugh, talk about your ideas regarding the future of technology. The prognostications of people such as Moravec, Pearson, and Warwick are, however, more portentous than amusing. Their ideas are part of a general trend of associated work with a trajectory aimed at a cyborg future—to rephrase Hayles' title—*How we are becoming Posthuman*.

## Data-out, data-in

Warwick sought to give some support for and grounding to his ideas and zany experiments by pointing to some examples of this associated work; and I offer a brief account of some of these efforts in order to indicate what is going on, and to explain and exemplify the claims being made about its nature and objective.

The first example is the *lamprey cyborg experiments* in Chicago where researchers have built a cyborg: a half-living, half-robot creature which connects the brain of an eel-like fish to a computer. The device consists of the brain stem from the larva of a lamprey, a bloodsucking fish, attached by electrodes to an off-the-shelf Swiss robot.

> In an arrangement reminiscent of the genesis of the Daleks, the living brain floats in a container of cool, oxygenated salt fluid. Placed in the middle of a ring of lights, the robot's sensors detect when a light is switched on. It sends signals to the lamprey brain, which returns impulses instructing the robot to move on its wheels towards the light. When all the lights are off, the robot stays still. When one of the robot's eyes is masked, the disembodied brain is temporarily confused, but learns to compensate. [...] [A] marriage of baby bloodsucker and Swiss engineering [...].[12]

The researchers state that their objective is to create advanced, brain-controlled prostheses for people whose normal ability to control their limbs has been disrupted by a stroke or Parkinson's disease. As we shall see this sort of claim-cum-justification is a common trope among researchers. Meek also quotes one of the leaders of the project, Dr Mussa-Ivaldi, as follows: 'The focus of our work is not so much to create a cyborg as to create a tool for investigating the organisation of the brain.'

The common term for this work is Brain–Machine Interface (BMI) research and it involves creating outputs from or inputs to the brain that are additional to those that occur naturally; and then investigating the flow across these interfaces. There are two possible directions of data flow: data *from* the brain *to* outside machinery, and data *to* the brain *from* outside machinery. As we will see there is one indisputable conclusion to this research: the brain is a much more adaptable organ than it was previously thought to be. The more cyborg-oriented 'findings' are more equivocal and ambiguous.

One major objective of BMI research is to create a system that will allow patients who have damage between their motor cortex and muscular system to bypass the damaged route and activate outside mechanisms by using neuronal signals. This would potentially allow an otherwise paralysed person to control a motorized wheelchair, computer pointer, or robotic arm by thought alone. This is a significant step beyond the sort of mechanisms used, for instance, by Stephen Hawking and Christopher Reeve. As is often the case the early experiments have involved mice and rats.[13]

Chapin and his co-workers have taught rats to obtain water via a bar-pressing task. The task was designed to get the rats to think about the action that the bar was having on the arm, not on the immediate task of pressing the bar. If the rats simply held the bar down then the cup would rotate past the water dropper; and if they never released the bar then the arm would never come back to its resting position near the cage, so that the rat could drink the water. Four out of the six rats (not coincidentally, those with the highest number of active task-related neurons) were routinely able to use the brain activity-derived signal to accomplish the task. 'The rats were theoretically able to control the arm with brain activity alone (e.g. ignoring the bar), and this dissociation between the bar movement and robot arm movement did occur, *but only after extended practice*.'[14]

A similar device has also been tried with humans. Though there are no systems that move arms, researchers Philip Kennedy of Georgia Tech and Roy Bakay of Emory University have implanted electrodes in humans with amyotrophic lateral sclerosis (more commonly known in America as 'Lou Gehrig's disease') or strokes in their brain stems.[15] These patients cannot move a muscle but are cognitively alert. According to reports, the 'implants allow them to move an icon over a virtual keyboard and slowly tap out messages, simply by thinking'.[16] This has been hailed as the first example of a human brain communicating directly with a computer.

> Kennedy and Bakay implanted two glass cones, each about the size of a tip of a ballpoint pen, into the brain of Johnny Ray, a 53-year old brainstem stroke victim who is completely paralyzed. His brain functions perfectly but the signals don't get anywhere. With special chemicals, Kennedy and Bakay induced neurons in the motor cortex—which controls movement—to grow into the glass cones, ensuring that the electrodes would stay in place. Ray was told to think about moving his finger. A circuit routed this signal to an icon on the screen instead of into his

arm. After practicing, Ray eventually learned to will the cursor to move right or left and up or down. The brain signals act as a computer mouse. They move the cursor across the screen and select pre-scripted phrases, such as 'See you later. Nice talking with you,' or 'I'm thirsty.' […] Beyond these initial human tests, the emerging field of neural prosthetics is embroiled in many controversies. One major quandary is where to place electrodes within the still-mysterious brain.[17]

This work on *data-out* BMIs is slowly blurring the line between human and machine; and researchers are keen to learn about the way that the human brain adapts to the new interface. But it is important to attend to the ways in which these sorts of developments are described—both by the researchers themselves and by others reporting their work. A recent report in *Forbes Magazine*—under the heading Health described another neural prosthetics experiment where five quadriplegics will each have a tiny microchip implanted under their skull, with a wire running to a nearby computer.

> Neuroscientists will ask them to think about moving a cursor on a computer screen, and if the chips record their thoughts correctly, the cursor will move by itself. The goal of the firm running the trial, […] is to help the severely paralyzed regain some function—dialing a phone, switching on lights—through thought power.[18]

The report went on to note that

> Neural prosthetics have long been the stuff of science fiction. Morpheus and his crew from the *Matrix* series, and Case, the hero of William Gibson's *Neuromancer*, all jack their brains directly into computers. But the science is catching up with the fiction […].

After noting that many of the experiments were complex and expensive, and that existing achievements were only scratching the surface, the writer stated that 'the human brain is a difficult computer to harness'.

The report also noted that current developments are based on earlier work 'eavesdropping on the brains of rats and monkeys'. Some of the researchers on similar recent work with monkeys—reported in *New Scientist*—noted that eventually 'you could apply this cognitive approach to language areas of the brain'; and that it will then 'be possible to decode the words someone was thinking'. The researcher interviewed commented that "'[i]n the future you could apply this cognitive approach to language areas of the brain" […] By doing so it may be possible to decode the words someone was thinking'.[19]

I could give several more examples. All of them involve similar types of work, and all use the same imagery of sending thoughts, or information, or messages from the brain to a receiving device of some kind. Many researchers, as well as those reporting the work, apply simple cerebral localization to the brain, referring to 'the planning area of the brain', or 'the place in the brain where thoughts are born'. Many invoke the image of the brain as a super-powerful computer, and as something distinct from the person with that brain. Warwick is not alone.

One should also note that such devices and inventions—real or imagined—are almost always justified and rationalized in the name of helping the disadvantaged, the disabled, the injured, the elderly, and so on. Yet in reality it is best to recall Ian Pearson's point about the rich benefitting before the poor—perhaps a very long time before the poor.[20]

It is inevitable, I hope, that as these projects are described they evoke in the reader suggestions of several highly unethical or problematic, state-controlled or corporate-controlled applications of this technology: such projects may well be those that are far more likely to receive funding. If you recall the film *Enemy of the State* (1998), starring Will Smith as a hapless victim of state surveillance, he only finally manages to rid himself of all the tracking devices planted on him by taking off all his clothes.[21] But what if he also had a chip inserted under his skin! He would then have had to consider more drastic strategies such as those employed in *The Terminator* and *Total Recall*.

Work on the brain–machine interface has thus far developed a long way, perhaps well beyond what most of us would think currently feasible, although nowhere near the more common flights-of-fancy of sci-fi writers. In most cases such work has focused around *data-out* systems, where the subject controls external machinery. But to return to Warwick, let me remind you that he was claiming to have established a *data-in* system, where his movements were controlled by external machinery. Moreover he then extended this claim by talking about linking people together via similar devices so obviating the need to use language.

Now as we shall see, and as perceptive readers may already have grasped, these researchers, and those reporting on the research, have completely misunderstood the nature of communication and the role of language. Furthermore they have even misunderstood the brain, or at the very least used only a very simplistic and one-sided view. This leads to profound misconceptions regarding ideas of control, guidance, and agency, with the ramifications of their misconceptions becoming apparent in the ways in which the imagery used to describe and explain these technical advances, and the technology itself, are then applied to concepts concerning the brain, the mind, thought, thinking, cognition and communication.

This is nothing new, since innovative and pervasive technology often becomes the dominant metaphor for what is hard to conceptualize. In the 1950s the brain was likened to a telephone exchange, before that it may well have been likened to a network of telegraph machines with Morse code signals being sent from one part or node to another. I am old enough to remember reading the children's comic *The Beezer*, which had a wonderful comic strip set of characters called The Numskulls. These guys each had a particular task within someone's brain; depicted in terms of what we might call a cerebral division of labour, or a cartoon phrenology. As one website notes, 'The Numskulls stood out from the other comic strips in that it addressed the metaphysical questions that fascinate only children and philosophers such as—Where do thoughts come from and why do people do as they do?'[22]

Clearly the brain is involved in cognition, but what exactly is the brain? According to Susan Greenfield it is 'a sludgy bumpy thing'; so she asks:

> Where do we start if we're trying to examine what kind of brains we're going to have in the future and how, conversely, the technologies of the future are going to impact on what kind of brains we have? It's a two-way street because for the first time ever possibly, we have access to technologies that have the power to pervade and invade our brains as never before.[23]

She terms this the carbon–silicon interface, and then describes various examples of pathological brain conditions where the sufferer managed to overcome the effects of the pathology; leading to the conclusion that the brain is constantly adapting and changing to a greater extent, and for a far longer period of our lives, than was thought only a few years ago. Moreover in the light of current and potential technological interventions, she argues that the two-way street between brain and technology will build on and enhance this *plasticity*; in many cases leading to the amelioration or reversal of trauma, or deterioration connected with aging or illness. In this regard she concurs with the researchers mentioned earlier; but she differs from people like Warwick and others in stressing that your brain is not something distinct from you. On the contrary

> [T]he brain is the personalised you, and as you live your life it becomes ever more you. […] You are born, in the words of the great William James, into 'a booming buzzing confusion' which you evaluate in terms of how sweet? how cold? how fast? how bright? how loud? Gradually these sensations will coalesce into people or objects, and those people or objects will start to acquire labels and will feature in certain events in your life. They all acquire a meaning, and the way the brain registers this is by forging connections relating to that coalescence of abstractions to a person, a place, an object, and then into the wider context of a memory. So connections are all-important.

Meaning will develop, and the way the brain registers this is by forging connections relating to that coalescence of abstractions to a person, a place, an object, then into the wider context of a memory. So connections are all-important. As we grow and learn we develop more and more connections, and as we grow old some of these connections are lost. Those suffering from Alzheimer's disease lose many of the connections. 'Gradually the world means less and less and you revert to your childhood.'

> A primary area of loss is in the hippocampus, which is related to memory. The hippocampus featured in a very elegant and simple study that captured the imagination of the press a few years ago and is an extreme example of plasticity in everyday life. This was the London taxi driver study. London taxi drivers have to master 'the knowledge'. They have to remember all the street names of London, all the one-way systems and so on, so they're using their memories all the time. In this study their brains were scanned and compared with those of non-taxi drivers of the same age, and behold, their hippocampus was bigger than other people's. […] And it's not that having a big hippocampus predisposes you to being a London taxi-driver because the difference was more marked the longer that people had been taxi drivers.

Greenfield notes that this sort of research shoots down 'that old and silly dichotomy of mind versus brain, of mental versus physical. Everything you're feeling has some kind of physical substrate although we don't yet know what it is'. Whether or not she has thereby resolved the paradox of Cartesian dualism, what she goes on to say is critical to our current concerns. She stresses that it is not possible to explain brain function in terms of a gene or a single brain region. Nor is it meaningful to talk about 'downloading yourself on to a chip', and thereby to hope to achieve immortality.

> Think about downloading a memory. If it's an episode it needs to be given a certain space and time, it needs to have a history to it, it needs to have expectations or thoughts or feelings. So if you wanted to download my memory, not your interpretation, you would have to download my thoughts, my feelings, a whole raft of prejudices and hopes and fears. You cannot isolate memory. That's a nonstarter.

So much for Moravec's vision: as far as a leading expert in brain physiology is concerned, Hayles' nightmare is exactly that; a phantasm, devoid of any substance.[24]

## Beyond the conduit metaphor

Such projects should draw our attention to processes and concepts concerned with thinking, communicating, and so on. It should not be only children and philosophers who are fascinated by metaphysical questions such as—Where do thoughts come from? How do people think? Why do people do as they do?

Unfortunately most of us, as we grow and develop neural connections, lose this fascination and questioning behind a barrier of everyday language which speaks and thinks for us, doing this to a large extent through metaphor.

You may have noticed that many if not all of the examples and explanations used so far for cognitive processes such as thinking, thought, communication and so on, used metaphorical language. Most of these metaphors derive from a view of communication that sees it as a process in terms of flows of bits of information through a channel, to some form of storage, with the brain seen in terms of a computer, and learning as a process of filling the computer's memory.

Metaphor must not be thought of as a restricted linguistic device, employed purely for literary and dramatic effect. Our vocabulary is largely built on metaphors. We use them, though perhaps not consciously, whenever we speak or write. Moreover metaphors play an active role in thought and cognition. In particular, metaphors are seen as a crucial aspect in the spread and understanding of new ideas and concepts.[25] Metaphors do not interfere with and interpose in our cognitive processes. On the contrary, they create and establish the ways in which we gain access to reality and develop our understanding. They are actually indispensable in *constituting* that reality. Metaphors serve in a powerful, creative fashion, producing genuine insight. Yet on the other hand they also can and do constrain our ideas. In so doing they may help enlighten us in some ways, but simultaneously conceal other key aspects.

Donald Schön sees metaphors operating as symptoms of a process of '*carrying over* of frames or perspectives from one domain of experience to another'. To substantiate this he has investigated areas where there are conflicting frames, demanding 'frame restructuring'—i.e. which emanate from conflict and contradiction between different ways of constructing reality, and where the only recourse is to 'restructuring, coordination, reconciliation, or integration of conflicting frames'.[26] He illustrates his argument with reference to a group of researchers seeking to develop a new paintbrush. This new product used artificial bristles instead of natural ones. The brush failed to give the same smooth finish as its bristle counterpart, leaving a surface that was marked by discontinuous application of the paint. The group had observed that bristles produced 'split ends', whereas synthetic ones did not. So they split the ends of the synthetic brush, but with no marked improvement. Real progress was made, however, when one of the team remarked that 'a paintbrush is a kind of pump'; and that applying paint is actually achieved by using the *spaces* between the bristles as channels through which the paint can flow. This directed the team's attention to a range of new factors, such as the curve formed by the bristles of the non-synthetic brush. What in strict terms might be thought of as a mistake—a paintbrush is a pump—resulted in the generation of new perspectives, explanations and inventions. Schön's concern is to point out that this cognitive process of using metaphors is not simply one of 'mapping' from one domain (pumps) to the other (painting). The initial response is one of 'unarticulated perception'—a gut-feeling—only followed later by efforts to clarify the relationship by interpreting ostensibly different 'tools' as examples of a single category.

If the paintbrush example seems trivial, Schön's more extensive illustration concerns housing policy. He exemplifies this with reference to the conflict between those who see the issue of urban housing in terms of 'slum clearance and removal of urban blight', and those who see it in terms of 'natural communities that must be protected or restored'. 'It is precisely because neighborhoods are not literally diseased that one can *see* them *as* diseased. It is because urban communities are not literally natural that one can see them *as* natural.'[27]

Schön's solution to frame conflict is what he terms 'frame restructuring [...] constructing a new problem-setting story, one in which we attempt to integrate conflicting frames by including features and relations drawn from earlier stories, yet without sacrificing internal coherence or the degree of simplicity required for action'. He argues that frame-restructuring and the making of generative metaphor are closely related. 'In both processes, participants bring to the situation different and conflicting ways of seeing [...] there is an impetus to map the descriptions [...] but [they] resist mapping [...] the participants work at the restructuring of their initial descriptions—regrouping, reordering, and renaming elements and relations [...]'.[28]

With regard to communication we tend to be far too unaware of the dominant metaphor. We fail to see that the language used by Warwick, Pearson, Moravec and many others is peculiar and specific, and needs to be brought to the fore and challenged. We need to introduce some frame conflict, challenging the dominant—and mostly unspecified—metaphor: the conduit metaphor.

This term is taken from an important paper by Michael Reddy, in which he specifically raises the issue of the dominant metaphor that English speakers use when talking about communication—*the conduit metaphor*—i.e. one that evokes images of waterways, channels, ducts, pipes, streams, and so on. Reddy poses the question: 'What do speakers of English say when communication fails or goes astray?' He answers his question with examples commonly found in everyday English; these include:

- 'Try to get your thoughts across better'

- 'None of Mary's feelings came through to me with any clarity'

- 'You still haven't given me any idea of what you mean'[29]

At first sight, all these examples seem unremarkable, perhaps devoid of metaphors. Yet Reddy argues that all of them—and many more of their ilk—

involve the idea that information is transferred from one point or person to another. Good communication then appears to resemble friction-free, blockage-free flow. Good reception involves extraction and unwrapping.

Reddy lists over 100 variations on these general themes, divided into seven categories, of which the major four are:

- *Transfer:* 'Implying that human language functions as a conduit enabling transfer [...] from one individual to another'—e.g. *put, get, give, send*

- *Embed within external signals:* 'Implying that, in speaking or writing, humans place something within the external signals, or else fail to do so in unsuccessful communication'—e.g. *capture, fill, include, overload, force*

- *Signals convey or contain:* 'Implying that signals convey or contain something, or else fail to do this in unsuccessful communication'—e.g. *carry, convey, contain, be empty of*

- *Listening or reading as unloading or extracting:* 'Implying that, in listening or reading, humans find something within the signals and take them into their heads, or else fail to do this in unsuccessful communication'—e.g. *find, uncover, overlook, be buried in, expose*[30]

There is a strong resemblance here between the conduit metaphor and the classic engineering model of communication developed by Claude Shannon and his colleagues at Bell Labs in the US in the 1940s. Shannon's model comprises a source, a transmitter, a receiver, and a destination. The source provides a message that the transmitter sends as a signal, and which is received as a signal by the receiver. The receiver then passes this signal on as a message to the destination or target. Source and destination may be 'a person or thing'. The transmitter and receiver are connected via a channel. This might be a telephone line or some other communications link. For an ideal process the message transmitted is the same as that received, but this might not always be the case. Shannon's model specifically incorporates the possibility of *noise* altering the signal. The noise may occur in the channel, or be introduced either by the transmitter or receiver. With telephone lines in the 1940s, noise was often actually heard by source and destination in the form of crackling or bursts of static. Noise will distort or change the message so that the received message is not the same as that sent. Whether or not the discrepancy between the two can be remedied will depend on the signal-to-noise ratio and also the level of *redundancy* in the message. If I send you a series of sentences in English, perhaps the words of a well known speech, you will probably be able to reconstruct them even if they are received in an altered or distorted form. For instance if you receive the following—*Governmend of th5 pe-ple, by t6e 5eople, fjr the peopl6*—then you will probably be able to understand the original message and strip out the effects of *noise*. On the other hand if I send you a series of numbers for opening a safe, then it may be almost impossible to reconstruct what was sent initially. So if you receive the message *45 %5 g6 778 870-43* you will have no way of being able to retrieve the original message. Even if the message received consisted entirely of numbers there would be no way of knowing if the message sent was the same as that received—unless of course the safe could be opened, and even then that is no guarantee, since the combination received might have been correct, but the message sent may not have been.

Shannon's work was critical in enabling people to develop ways in which the received message could be checked to see if it had been the subject of any distortion or alteration. In some cases remedial action could be taken to reconstitute the initial message, but in others all that could be done was to request a retransmission.

For Shannon, and other communications engineers, this model provided a basis for a mathematical understanding of the processes necessary to verify that the received signal is identical to the transmitted one—and if not, then to offer ways in which the latter can be altered. Thus Shannon's model had a crucial impact on the development of many of the communications technologies which we now take for granted, and from which most of us derive some benefit—for example in the form of digital technologies, CDs, and so on. But it is the general extension of Shannon's model, as metaphor, into the realm of cognition which is more problematic, and where the effects have to be exposed, confronted and challenged. This is where Reddy sees the necessity to highlight the limitations and impairments caused by the conduit metaphor.

Reddy characterizes what he terms the four categories that constitute the critical features of the conduit metaphor:

> (1) language functions like a conduit, *transferring* thoughts bodily from one person to another; (2) in writing and speaking, people *insert* their thoughts or feelings in the words; (3) words accomplish the transfer *by containing* the thoughts or feelings and conveying them to others; and (4) in listening or reading, people *extract* the thoughts and feelings once again from the words.[31]

Reddy further points out that one sub-component of this *conduit metaphor* characterizes thoughts and feelings as being 'ejected [...] into an external *ideal space*', where they are reified, and take on an independent existence; and from where they may or may not 'find their way back into the heads of living humans'.

Having demonstrated the impact and ramifications of the conduit metaphor, Reddy offers an alternative metaphor to assist in what he terms—following Schön—'frame restructuring'. 'In order to engage in frame restruc-

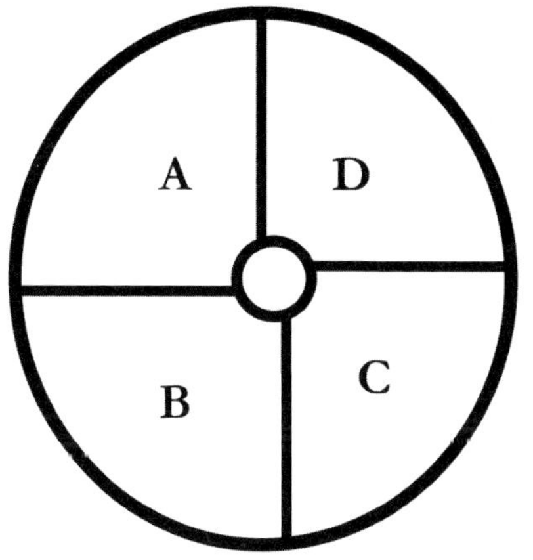

2.1   The Toolmakers Paradigm, after Michael Reddy, 'The Conduit Metaphor', p. 172.

turing about human communication, we need first an opposing frame.' Reddy terms his alternative *the toolmakers paradigm*.[32]

This paradigm is best understood through Reddy's own example, which needs to be described at some length. He supposes that there exists a community of people living in a compound—see 2.1. Each person has their own sector, and no two sectors are alike. The hub of the wheel contains a mechanism for delivering paper messages from one person to another, and this is crucial in people passing on their ideas about how best to survive in terms of building shelters, developing tools, and so on. People cannot visit each other's sectors, nor can they exchange products. At best they can circulate crude blueprints. Any individual only knows about the existence of others as an inference from the exchange of pieces of paper, plus other supporting deductions. Reddy calls this the 'postulate of radical subjectivity'.

Now suppose that the person living in sector A develops a tool, a rake for clearing away leaves and other debris. She goes to the hub and draws three identical sets of instructions for fashioning this tool, leaving copies for B, C, and D. A's environment has a lot of wood and trees in it, but B's sector is mostly rocky. So B tries to copy the design for A's rake, using a wooden handle and a stone head. Person A did not specify the material for the handle or the head—both were wooden—since there seemed no alternative. B completes the 'rake', but finds it unwieldy and heavy, and wonders at the strength of A. He is also somewhat bemused at the tool itself, and guesses that A uses it to clear away small rocks in her sector. He adapts the tool for his own environment, and eventually decides that a better form of the tool will be one that has two prongs to unearth large rocks. This is far more useful for B's sector. B then sketches out his tool design and makes three copies for the others to study.

Persons C and D then develop their own tools on the basis of the plans from A and B. Person A makes a tool along the lines suggested by B, but can see no use for it in her own rock-free sector. She also wonders if B has misunderstood her original design, and so produces a more detailed one for circulation. The interchange between A and B goes on for some time, until A comes across two small pebbles in her sector, and she begins to understand that her assumptions about wooden materials and organic debris may not be universally applicable. The result is that A and B raise 'themselves to a new plateau of inference about each other and each other's environments'.

The fundamental difference between the toolmakers paradigm and the conduit metaphor is that for the latter successful communication appears to be gained without effort, whereas for the former human communication 'will almost always go astray unless real energy is expended'. Moreover the conduit metaphor assumes that communication is perfect unless there is some failure in encoding, decoding, transmission or reception. The norm for the conduit model of communication is fault-free, noise-free communication. Conversely the toolmakers approach does not see communication failure or divergent understanding as aberrant; on the contrary it assumes such outcomes are the norm, and that further and continuous efforts are required to sustain communication.

In order for any communication to occur, all parties to the communication must have access to both the *code* and the *set of alternatives*. Reddy calls this an 'a priori shared context'; what might be thought of as a shared set of values and understandings. In the example of the toolmakers paradigm, this is a very limited and simple set of assumptions regarding interchange via pieces of paper at the hub of the wheel. It might be argued that even this set of shared assumptions has been learned, and so requires some effort and some still more fundamental set of assumptions. There is no way of avoiding this conceptual infinite regress, but it must be stressed that this does not invalidate Reddy's argument. The issue of infinite regress can in part be evaded by treating these assumptions as an independent variable along the lines proposed by Alexander and Smith in their outline for a cultural sociology where they

> subscribe to the idea that every action, no matter how instrumental, reflexive, or coerced vis-à-vis its external environments is embedded to some extent in a horizon of affect and meaning. This internal environment [...] [is] an ideal source that partially enables and partially constrains action.[33]

There are strong parallels between this view of communication and the encoding/decoding model associated with Stuart Hall.[34] Both Hall and Reddy stress that communication is a fundamental social process, requiring effort from all parties involved. Reddy, using the work of Shannon, focuses on the effort itself, contrasting it with the seemingly effortless communication enjoyed by those with access to contemporary information and communications technology (ICT). Hall's work stresses the political aspects which provide the context within which what he terms the 'moments' of encoding and decoding take place. Hall's model of encoding/decoding is often contrasted with Shannon's mode, the latter seen as ignoring all social and political aspects. But it is also important to note that both incorporate the concept of *selection*, in the sense that the encoder chooses what to encode. In Shannon's model this is stated in terms of entropy and probability; in Hall's it is bound up with power, dominance and hegemony.[35]

This characterization of communication applies not only to linguistic communication, but also to non-linguistic and non-verbal forms. Aspects such as gestures, tone of voice and body-language can all be considered to be drawn from a repertoire—selected and somehow relayed as signals. Indeed the balance of activity and effort may well lie far more markedly with the 'receiver' than with the 'sender' than it does for linguistic communication. In some cases the 'shared context' may not be as mutual as the participants assume—gestures being notoriously context- and culture-specific, similarly tropes such as irony and sarcasm when conveyed by extra-linguistic facets such as facial expression or cadence. (The postulate of a shared context, whatever its origins and however it is developed and sustained, is inherently associated with cultural values and beliefs.)

The toolmakers paradigm is also important in highlighting that it is not the *message* but the *signals* that are transmitted. Only signals are mobile. They are transmitted, received and decoded. Moreover, if the process works correctly, or adequately, the received signal will be identical to the transmitted signal, and this can then be used in the process of decoding from received signal to received message. This should then result in an identical message at the destination to that at the source.

The signal does not *contain* anything; it *does* something that leads to an activity. Communication is that activity—and perhaps the gerund form, *communicating*, would be a more apposite and accurate term, less prone to be misunderstood in the form of conduits, message-passing and passive reception. Communicating can involve some or all of the following—words, gestures (conscious and unconscious), body-language, written texts, pictures, grunts and so on.

Reddy concludes his paper with a revealing story that amplifies the example of the segmented circular compound introduced earlier. He supposes that individuals A–D begin to develop and enhance their interchanges; making slow progress, but always aware of the effort needed to secure adequate communication. Indeed they retain 'a distinct sense of awe and wonder that they could make the system work at all'. But this is all undermined by an evil magician who hypnotizes them, so that, once they have accomplished some technical feat through arduous communication, they will forget that this happened. Instead they will have the false memory 'that the object had been sent to them directly from the other person'. The result is that the communication system falls into disuse, and the participants assume that any technical construct has been presented complete, ready and working by its originator. This leads to each individual blaming the others both for faults in any artefact that has been collectively developed, and for feeling that they themselves are inadequate.

As far as Reddy is concerned, the wicked wizard is the English language, and the hypnotic spell is the 'bias imparted to our thought processes by the conduit metaphor'. It results in our acting as if communication is something that can be accomplished without effort, or certainly without effort on the part of the receiver—reader, listener or whatever.

Far too many of those writing about communication, particularly in the context of the wonders of ICT, and ways in which human activities can be entirely replaced by silicon-based ones continue to labour under the magician's spell. If communication is seen as effortless, then the advances in communications technology simply present technical issues related to access, speed, retrieval and so on. Hence the ideas and claims of people like Warwick, Pearson, *et al.* are used to support projects based around increasing technological involvement in the process of communication.

Writing in the 1960s, Raymond Williams was acutely aware of the primacy of communication, and pointed out the error of relegating communication to a secondary role. It is erroneous to think that 'there is, first, reality, and then second, communication'. On the contrary we have to understand that 'society is a form of communication, through which experience is described, shared, modified, and preserved'. 'What we call society is not only a network of political and economic arrangements, but also a process of learning and communication.'[36] Williams stressed the key role played by language in communication, and argued that linguistic forms had to change to encompass this view of society as a form of communication.

Reddy takes this further with his introduction of the toolmakers paradigm, and specifically addresses the point at issue—communication.

> We have the greatest, most sophisticated system for mass communication of any society that we know about, yet somehow mass communication becomes more and more synonymous with less communication. Why is this? […] We have the mistaken, conduit-metaphor influenced view that the more signals we can preserve, the more ideas we 'transfer' and 'store'. We neglect the crucial human ability to reconstruct thought patterns on the basis of signals.[37]

Reddy makes his points within the context of his description of the toolmakers paradigm. In more general terms there seems to be an overwhelming tendency for people to resort to conceptual categories that are inherently concrete and technological. The conduit metaphor is just one, highly significant and influential example of this.

So what can we learn from this? Well, we can use our understanding of the limitations and effects of the conduit metaphor to do some deconstruction of standard reports of conduit-type research. As an example we can use Cobb's article 'Mind Meld' referred to earlier, describing the work being done by Krishna Shenoy. The title 'Mind Meld' is taken from the ability of *Star Trek*'s Mr Spock to read the thoughts of another being.[38] The article is replete with phrases rooted in the conduit metaphor (CM) or in the idea that brain function can be explained in terms of a gene or a single brain region (SBR).

- 'Shenoy [...] is devising ways to tap into a monkey's brain and read where the animal plans to reach its arm' (CM; SBR)

- 'Electrodes set in the brain will talk to robots or stimulate distant muscles' (CM; SBR)

- 'the scientists snooped into the monkey's brain' (CM)

- 'Messages zip along as electric pulses' (CM)

- 'And that's exactly what Shenoy is trying to do—hear the monkey's thoughts' (CM)

- 'But even for a computer, reading these buzzing thoughts is tricky' (CM)

- 'Shenoy's group placed electrodes deep in the brain, in an area called the "parietal reach region." This area of the brain first specifies where to you want to go, and precedes any formal plan for how to get there. It's the place where thoughts are born' (SBR)

- 'Most other researchers place electrodes in the motor cortex of the brain, which is the last place thoughts visit before they exit the brain for the spinal cord' (CM; SBR)[39]

Cobb is on stronger ground in certain other parts of the article: 'Three steps are involved in building such a device: plucking neural signals from the brain, making sense of them, and carrying out the intention encoded in the signals' (shades of Shannon, and hinting at Reddy); but on weaker ground in others: 'Information is contained in the speed and intervals at which neuron cells fire their electric pulses' (CM—signals are transmitted, not information).

Examples such as this abound in both the specialist literature and more popular and accessible sources. The conduit metaphor is alive and well; based on a misconceived premise, it continues to exert significant influence on our daily lives, on the R & D agenda, funding and resources. Some of these ramifications are political and ethical in nature. Reddy concludes that 'the conduit metaphor is leading us down a technological blind alley. That blind alley is mass communications systems coupled with mass neglect of the internal, human systems responsible for nine-tenths of the work in communicating'.[40] Twenty years on we can see that this mass neglect has tangible effects, leading people to pursue technological advances based on the conduit metaphor that will lead to ever more monitoring of our lives at all levels: at the level of genes, molecular events, more screening, and potential for engineering for good and ill—probably ill rather than good. Two examples from recent events indicate some of the aspects of this technological blind alley; and what results from ignoring *the mien* and focusing on *the mice*.

The first example concerns the analyses and responses to the devastation of the Asian Tsunami in December 2004. The devastation led to an unremitting demand for more technology, particularly in the form of some intricate early-warning communications system—what amounts essentially to an embodiment of a super-fast conduit. Yet in the reporting of the events the tale of one ten-year-old schoolgirl stands out. Tilly Smith was on the beach in Phuket with her family when she noticed that 'the water started to go funny'.[41] She had been taught about tsunamis a few weeks previously in a geography lesson, and so understood what it meant when the sea receded, and boats on the horizon started to bob violently up and down. She told her mother that there was going to be a tsunami. Her parents alerted those around them, and by evacuating the beach and the hotel many people survived who otherwise would probably have perished. Those now advocating expensive and elaborate technology to provide an early warning system need to heed this example. Two aspects are particularly important, and neither is dependent on technology. The first is that people have to know how to interpret the signs of an impending devastation. Many others saw what Tilly saw, but failed to act appropriately. Second, there must be a relationship of trust and mutual understanding between the person raising the alert and those responding to it: not everyone would take a ten-year-old's warning seriously. These are prerequisites for effective communication, and so for effective use of ICT; they can only flourish if there is better understanding of the true nature of communication—i.e. some regard for the toolmakers paradigm, not sole and exclusive reliance on the conduit metaphor. Given the title of Congress CATH 2005, *The Ethics and Politics of Virtuality and Indexicality*, it must be noted that the tsunami offers a powerful example of the workings of indexicality, with the intensity of certain stimuli indicating the impending deluge, at least for some of those involved. But it must be noted that it was animals and birds who acted on the index appropriately; most humans did not or could not.

The second example is even more apposite to the subject of the ethics of indexicality. The details are taken from a report in *The Washington Post*, an article headlined 'As Ukraine Watched the Party Line, She Took the Truth Into Her Hands':

Natalia Dmytruk did not have to learn sign language at school. Her first words had to be mimed. Both her parents are deaf. […]

Dmytruk, 48, made sign language her vocation and today interprets for Ukraine's state-run television. Her face and hands appear in a little box at the bottom of the screen as she sends out the news on the mid-morning and early afternoon telecasts to the hearing-impaired.

During the tense days of Ukraine's presidential elections last year, Dmytruk staged a silent but bold protest, informing deaf Ukrainians that official results from the Nov. 21 runoff were fraudulent. Her act of courage further emboldened protests that grew until a new election was held and the opposition candidate, *Viktor Yushchenko*, was declared the winner. […]

Election monitors had reported widespread vote-rigging immediately after the runoff between Yushchenko and the Russian-backed prime minister, *Viktor Yanukovych*. With Yanukovych leading by a slim margin, the opposition urged Ukrainians to gather in Independence Square in front of the parliament building to protest the results.

Each time Dmytruk went to Independence Square with her 20-year-old son and teenage daughter and saw the thousands of protesters, she felt herself transformed.

'I was impressed by the expression on my children's faces. I was so fired up by other people I observed passionately voicing their discontent,' she said in an interview this week. 'It was that special spirit and energy of people coming together, uneasily at first, but looking in the same direction.'

Dmytruk would then return to work and broadcast the state's version of events.

'I was observing it from both sides, and I had a very negative feeling,' she said. 'After every broadcast I had to render in sign language, I felt dirty. I wanted to wash my hands.'

The opposition had no access to the state-run media, but Dmytruk was in a special position as a television interpreter to get their message out.

On Nov. 25, she walked into her studio for the 11 a.m. broadcast. 'I was sure I would tell people the truth that day,' she said. 'I just felt this was the moment to do it.'

Under her long silk sleeve, she had tied an orange ribbon to her wrist, the color of the opposition and a powerful symbol in what would become known as the Orange Revolution. She knew that when she raised her arm, the ribbon would show.

The newscaster was reading the officially scripted text about the results of the election, and Dmytruk was signing along. But then, 'I was not listening anymore,' she said.

In her own daring protest, she signed: 'I am addressing everybody who is deaf in the Ukraine. Our president is Victor Yushchenko. Do not trust the results of the central election committee. They are all lies… And I am very ashamed to translate such lies to you. Maybe you will see me again—' she concluded, hinting at what fate might await her. She then continued signing the rest of officially scripted news.

Dmytruk's live silent signal helped spread the news, and more people began spilling into the streets to contest the vote.[…][42]

So here are two clear examples of the indexicality of communication; a social accomplishment that is very much more concerned with *mien* rather than *mice*—mechanical or animate. Schön has argued for frame restructuring, defining it as a process where participants bring to the situation different and conflicting ways of seeing. Where the participants then work at the restructuring of their initial descriptions; regrouping, reordering, and renaming elements and relations, and where the only recourse is to 'restructuring, coordination, reconciliation, or integration of conflicting frames'. As I think I have shown, there is an urgent need for this work to be continued and intensified, with extensive efforts aimed at bringing conflicting frames to the attention of those such as Kevin Warwick, Hans Moravec, *et al.*

# 3

# A VIRTUAL INDICATION

*Samuel Weber*

The title of an article in the *New York Times* in 2005 speaks directly to the subjects of indexicality and virtuality. The article reported on the spread of video games as a source of income not just for its developers or owners, but for its players; its title announces: 'The Game is Virtual. The Profit is Real'. This headline precisely describes two aspects of current game-playing that concern us here. First, the interdependence and overlapping of virtual and real; and second, the financial medium of that interdependence: not just money, but *profit*. To provide some of the context for this particular aspect of computer games today, especially for those not familiar with the games themselves, here is an excerpt from the article:

> For many people, what are known as massively multiplayer online games have become significant sources of income.
>
> Web sites have sprung up that allow players to use real currency to *buy items—like weapons or real estate*—that they may want or need for the games.
>
> Games like *Second Life*, *World of Warcraft*, *Ultima Online* and dozens of others offer the opportunity to interact with thousands of players worldwide in *virtual environments* that *continue to exist* whether or not *any particular person is playing at the moment*. The virtual broadsword you found in the dragon's cave (or that dream house you built) before logging off on Tuesday will be right there on Wednesday.[1]

Let me interrupt this citation to underscore a few points. *First*, the games require the acquisition of certain 'items' that can or must be purchased with 'real money'. Thus, it is not just the games themselves that are commodities, but the wherewithal with which they must be played. This aspect distinguishes this kind of computer game from its more classic predecessors, such as card games, chess or checkers (but not entirely from games of sport, which also require purchase of equipment and of training to be played successfully, or at least at a certain 'level'). Second, the necessity to purchase items in order to play the computer game successfully introduces an element of 'reality' into the very heart of the game or, as the story describes it, of the 'virtual environment'. Such purchases both presuppose financial resources of a non-virtual kind (although as a medium of exchange, even what the journalist calls 'real currency' or 'real world cash' is hardly devoid of a virtual dimension). Nevertheless, there is clearly a difference between 'real currency' operating outside the game, and 'game currency' subject entirely to it. It is precisely the way this difference is bridged, however, through the interaction of 'game' and 'real' currencies, that fascinates the journalist:

> A thriving market has sprung up in which players spend real-world cash to buy game currency *or desirable items* from other players. Transactions take place on eBay or on sites like gamingopenmarket.com or www.ige.com. Payments are made through PayPal and other online services. Players then log into the game and transfer the virtual goods or currency.

And what do these players then do with the 'virtual goods or currency' they have purchased? Some play, others speculate, and still others both play and speculate, in what then seems to resemble a kind of meta-game attached to and yet distinct from the 'real' virtual game.

This brings us to the title hero and main focus of the article, with whom it begins and ends: Jason Ainsworth of Las Vegas (where else?), a real-life developer and contractor who initially had absolutely no interest in gaming until one day, while watching his ten-year-old daughter play *The Sims*, he noticed that 'certain players' would leave the game after 'selling their assets. So I figured, buy low, sell high'. After shopping around a bit, Jason decided that it was not *The Sims* which offered him the best prospects for accomplishing his program, but rather another game, called appropriately enough, *Second Life*. This game, the journalist notes,

> is less a game than a three-dimensional environment in which players can do whatever they choose. There he [Jason] […] leveraged his real-life experience—he is a developer and contractor—into an online business. In 14 locations in Second Life's virtual world, he owns enough 'land' to rent space to nearly 50 retailers, who in turn earn virtual money selling everything from jewelry to clothing to art (all nonexistent, of course). Mr. Ainsworth converts his game profits into real money on sites like eBay, IGE and gamingopenmarket, which charge a small fee, and he includes that income on his tax returns. […] 'I have good months and bad months, but the work is fun.' […]
>
> Who buys this stuff? One Second Life *resident* [*note that the game-participants here are described as 'residents' rather than as 'players'*—*SW*], who asked

to be identified only by her screen name, Diamond Hope, said she spent $10 to $15 a month on clothing and other accessories in Second Life, but would spend more if she could afford it. 'With all the things you can buy in Second Life,' she said, 'it's hard not to want them, just like real-life stuff.'

Of course, already Marx, and long before him Nicholas Barbon, had asserted that 'desire implies need' and even more significantly, that need implies desire, which, according to Barbon, had to be considered as 'the appetite of the mind, [...] as natural [to it] as hunger [is] to the body. ... The greatest number (of things) have their value from supplying the wants of the mind.'[2] Marx himself, unequivocally adopts this point of view at the very beginning of *Capital*, when he defines commodities as 'first of all, an external object, a thing which through its qualities satisfies human needs of whatever kind. The nature of these needs, whether they arise, for example, in the stomach, or in a yearning [*Verlangen*] makes no difference'.[3] If the difference between physical or physiological 'need' on the one hand, and a spiritual or emotional 'desire' or 'yearning' on the other was already recognized as essentially irrelevant from an economic point of view before 1700—Barbon's *Discourse of Trade* dates from 1690—the fact still remains that the desire-driven consumption of goods that are *essentially* 'virtual'—i.e. that have no material or localizable existence outside the computerized game-world—has today acquired a quantitative scope that clearly brings with it qualitative changes—and opportunities:

> With about 10 million people worldwide playing at least one of the 350 or so massively multiplayer online games, there is no shortage of income-producing possibilities for the imaginative. Steve Salyer, a former game developer, [...] now president of Internet Gaming Entertainment [...] estimates that players spend a real-world total of $880 million a year for virtual goods and services produced in online games—not counting sales of the games themselves, and monthly subscription fees, often around $10.[4]

Now, apart from the general interest of this already substantial and rapidly growing market for 'virtual' goods and services,[5] what this phenomenon demonstrates is how misleading it is today—but not just today—to try simply to 'oppose' something like 'virtuality' to something ostensibly more material, more real, such as 'indexicality'.[6] The emergence of a thriving and expanding market for virtual goods and services with respect to computer games—role-playing games as well as competitive games—suggests rather that the relationship of these two terms can hardly be reduced to the relatively simple form of a mutually exclusive opposition. In this sense, already the title of the article—'The Game is Virtual. the Profit is Real', is far too oppositional. As the story itself demonstrates, 'the game' itself is not simply 'virtual', particularly if by virtual is meant something that *excludes* reality or is independent of it. The critique of such a notion of the virtual was, of course, precisely the point of departure for what even today remains the most influential and elaborate attempt to define this concept in contemporary thought: that of Gilles Deleuze in his 1968 book, *Difference and Repetition*. Deleuze begins his discussion by insisting that the virtual should not be opposed to the 'real', since it itself has its own reality, something that we have just seen at work in 'massively multiplayer games', which has seen the emergence of a very real market for virtual game-goods and services. However, in his effort to define the virtual, Deleuze by no means entirely abandons what can be called a 'logic of opposition': rather, he attempts to shift its focus. Instead of opposing the virtual to the *real*, he opposes it to the 'actual', a word which, it should be noted, in English does not quite mean the same thing as it does in French or German, namely: the 'here and now'. For Deleuze, then, the virtual defines itself as that which is *not* 'here and now', whereas conversely, what is 'here and now' is to be understood as not being 'virtual'. Although the *New York Times* article notes that the world of game-playing consists in 'virtual environments that continue to exist whether or not any particular person is playing *at the moment*'—i.e. independently of any particular here-and-now—it also frames, and is framed by, a picture of 'Jason Ainsworth at his home in Las Vegas'. The caption under the picture goes on to state that 'He owns virtual real estate in a multiplayer online game that earns him enough real money to cover his monthly mortgage'. Thus, by means of this caption, which sums up the trajectory of the story itself, the virtual world of computer games is framed and delimited by the very real monetary benefits that game-playing can bring to those who never lose track of the 'real' world outside. The immediate message thus seems to be that the virtual is framed and instrumentalized by the real, which has as its manifestation the profit that pays Jason's monthly mortgage.

To many this would be a very reassuring message in an age of increasing uncertainty. But upon closer inspection the clear-cut opposition, and subordination, of virtual to real begins to break down. First of all, just to take the information conveyed by the picture, it is difficult to overlook the fact that the so-called real world 'outside' the game-world is itself depicted as being an enclosed and somewhat cramped interior. Jason is seated in front of a curved workbench, itself placed against a windowless wall, upon which hangs a few pictures and photographs. The workbench surrounds him in a half-circle. Directly in front of him is a monitor and between it and him a keyboard; off to his right on the workbench sits a laptop, a desktop computer and a printer, while to his left there is another monitor and keyboard. Jason is leaning back in his chair as though to keep a certain distance, overview and control over this circle of equipment and the windowless wall behind it. If this site is the condition of a certain virtuality, the site itself is anything but virtual: it suggests a very particular kind of 'here and now'. The cramped space suggests a 'cell' in the double sense given that word today in the era of mobile phones: absolute independence of locality, and utter imprisonment in mobility itself.

But the cell is also a home, and more particularly, a *home office*. In the past, remunerative work was generally done outside of the home, at least in non-rural areas. Now, work has migrated to the home, together—and this is not just a fortuitous convergence—with what is called 'theatre': *home-theatre*. The electronic equipment necessary to do many types of computer related jobs has become smaller, more portable, less expensive. With this shift, the distinction between work place and domestic space established over the past four centuries has lost much of its relevance. Not however the distinction between 'virtual' and 'real'. Without simply being identical, these terms tend to interact and proliferate. As we have already noted, the picture is framed by its caption, which tells us that Jason's 'virtual real estate' business earns him enough money 'to cover his monthly mortgage'. His home is assured, it implies, by his ability to play games with the virtual. But the very fact that Jason, like the vast majority of American home-owners, has a monthly mortgage to pay for an extended period of time, reminds us that the virtual is by no means restricted to the world of computer games. For his mortgage testifies to the fact that Jason is by no means the sole proprietor, and probably not even the primary owner of his 'home'; as a result, his home is not actually *his* home at all, not at least *here and now*; it is his only virtually, as a promise to the future which will be realized only when the promissory note is paid in full. If the notion of 'home' implies accessibility, reliability, security, then Jason's home, like that of most Americans, is not 'actual' but 'virtual'—not in the sense of lacking material existence or physical location—its virtuality does not exclude its reality—but in the sense of its not *belonging to* or at least being *under the control of* the person who *resides* in it. It is perhaps not always necessary to be an owner in order to consider one's residence one's home. But insofar as a home is defined not just as a 'dwelling place' but as a place where one can 'abide'— an 'abode'—it implies the kind of control and accessibility usually reserved to ownership: that is, to full ownership and not 'co-ownership' with a bank.

Perhaps this begins to explain why some of the most sought-after objects in this virtual commerce have to do with real estate, including some of its more legendary forms: i.e. castles. If 'my home is my castle', presumably the converse works equally well: 'My castle is my home'. The *New York Times* article notes that 'Hard to find items like castles could fetch up to $500 at the top of the market'. It also mentions 'Weapons or real estate' as two exemplary objects of virtual commerce. The linkage is probably not fortuitous: under condition of virtualization, including economic and financial, a 'home' is not just a 'castle' but as such also a very conspicuous and inviting *target*. To acquire it, and then to keep it, is facilitated by the use of weapons. If this is what goes on in the 'virtual environment' of *Second Life*, then it would seem that this Second Life is not all that different from the First.

In this respect, it is therefore probably not sufficient to assert, as Deleuze does in *Difference and Repetition*, that the 'virtual' has a structure marked by the qualities of 'singularity' and 'difference', or that it defines itself through the tendency to become something else or to take place somewhere else. While it seems probable that this possibility constitutes part of the attraction of developing a fictional character and assuming a pseudonym such as 'Diamond Hope', the very insistence on 'character' in the development and playing of such games, whether 'competitive' or 'role playing', single- or multiplayer, suggests that the goal of many such games, both on the side of 'residents' and of developers, has become that of placing the 'virtual' in the service of the Self. And the notion of Self usually is defined by its ability to *stay the same over time and space*; in other words, *stay the same while changing location*. This is why the 'automobile' has served so well as the symbol and paradigm of such a Self: its claim is to embody and safeguard autonomy in movement—or perhaps more precisely, autonomy through locomotion (change of place). The game-player accomplishes the same task without necessarily having to actually move from one place to another. Residence in such a world complements the picture of Jason Ainsworth surveying his computer equipment in the half-arc of his windowless (monadic?) home office. Through expense and speculation, 'Diamond Hope' on the one hand, and Jason on the other, seek to accomplish in and through their Second Life what they have not been able to achieve in their first one.

But they do this in very different ways. 'Diamond Hope' does in *Second Life* what is rarely done in the First: she gives herself her name, just as she presumably hopes to give herself a new life. This self-given name signifies the goal of its bearer, and creator, in a way that presumably her given name could never accomplish: a hope that is as hard and bright and cutting as a diamond— and that like a diamond, refers to the body that in the virtual environment of the game will never as such be tangible. Diamond Hope is an *imaginary* name in the sense that Lacan gave to the term: it seeks to render representable, imaginable, that which it names. As self-given and self-fulfilling, such a name also seeks to deny or expunge the indebtedness to others that is inseparable from so-called 'proper' and 'familial' names outside the game-world. In naming itself, the pseudonymic self seeks to assert its autonomy and independence. But this autonomy still remains subject to the rules of the game. Despite or because of the virtuality of the game environment—it goes on everywhere and yet in no one particular place, all the time and yet at no one particular time—the 'resident' player requires a safe place of its 'own' from which to organize its activity. And since there are a multitude of other player-residents, the place or places—the (virtual) real estate—of individual players must be secured and defended. Hence the desirability and value of 'weapons and real estate'.

So much for the pseudonym, 'Diamond Hope'. Not by accident it is only mentioned after the story is well underway. The article itself, however, begins with an ostensibly proper name: '*Jason Ainsworth* plays the online game *Second Life* at least four hours a day'. The virtuality of the game-environment and the exchange of goods and services it makes possible are framed, as it were, by the real-life person and name of Jason Ainsworth. To see how this journalistic account stages the relation of virtuality to indexicality, it is helpful to recall how the index is defined by Charles Sanders Peirce: 'I define an Index as a sign determined by its Dynamic object by virtue of being in a real relation to it. Such is a Proper Name [...] such is the occurrence of a symptom of a disease [...].'[7] Note the surprising and suggestive juxtaposition of 'proper name' and 'symptom of a disease': in both cases, as Peirce will make clear elsewhere, 'being in a real relation' with what the index signifies entails, negatively, that there is no internal, intrinsic relation of 'similarity' or 'resemblance'. Now given the tendency to oppose the indexical to the virtual, it is worth recalling that Deleuze employs the same kind of negative definition to distinguish the 'virtual' from the 'possible': the possible, he argues, *anticipates* the real to which it relates through the category of 'similarity', whereas the virtual is its own 'reality', to which it is related not by similitude but rather by difference.[8] In this respect, Deleuze's notion of the virtual, defined through difference and singularity, overlaps with Peirce's concept of the index, equally determined through dissimilitude and singularity. But as the following passage from Peirce makes clear, his notion of the virtual entails a third aspect through which it is distinguished from Deleuze's account of the virtual:

> Indices may be distinguished from other signs, or representations, by three characteristic marks: first, that they have no significant resemblance to their objects; second, that they refer to individuals, single units, single collections of units, or single continua; third, that they direct the attention to their objects by blind compulsion.[9]

The notable exception comes at the end: whereas for Deleuze it is 'structure' that above all constitutes 'the reality of the virtual',[10] for Peirce it is not the structure but the effect that constitutes the third essential constituent of the index, namely, its power of *directing attention to the objects signified 'by blind compulsion'*. The index, thus construed, is defined by its *power to compel*: its ability to seize 'attention' and then direct or redirect it toward the *singularity* it signifies.

Now how does all this apply, not simply to 'the virtual environment' and its commerce, but to the way it is framed by a journalistic discourse that itself is thoroughly indexical, striving to seize and direct the attention of its readers toward its subject—not simply the virtuality of game-playing but more specifically to the fact that certain persons are capable of extracting real-world profit from that virtuality? These persons may play the games 'four hours a day', as does Jason Ainsworth, but there are still 20 hours left over for other, presumably less virtual activities. In beginning by naming one of these putatively real-life persons, and naming him properly, the story implicitly foregrounds the distinction between real-life proper names and virtual, improper pseudonyms; the latter, totally immersed in virtuality, *spend* (Diamond Hope, for instance), while the former (Jason Ainsworth) *speculate* and reap sufficient awards 'to cover the monthly mortgage'. In one case, then, what the story calls 'the overlap between actual and virtual finance' is controlled and exploited, and in the other it is abandoned to desire and consumption. And even if at times the journalist points to certain unresolved questions that result from the 'overlap', such as the question of 'who owns virtual goods—the players or the game company', such questions do not in the slightest alter the perspective that informs the article, which from beginning to end remains focused upon the individuals that turn the virtual speculation into 'real money', and even more, into real-world profit. Again and again, the real world that appears as dominating the virtual environment. Thus, if Jason Ainsworth seems to be financially successful in the various games he plays, it can only be because he has 'leveraged his real-life experience—he is a developer and contractor—into an online business'. Note the use of the financial term, 'leveraged' here: Jason has leveraged, i.e. *borrowed* from or on the capital of his real-world professional experience, in order to invest that capital in the virtual world of game-playing, not in order to play the game but in order to turn a profit: Jason acknowledges that he was wholly uninterested in computer games until he realized that there too it might be possible to 'buy low' and 'sell high'. The game-medium may be somewhat different from what he was previously used to, but the goal and bottom-line remains the same: to make a profit, pay off his mortgage and accumulate wealth in the 'real' world. At the same time, the story that began by naming him, also gives him the last word: 'As soon as it quits being fun [...] I quit.'

The article thus begins with a proper name and ends with a quote suggesting that the bearer of that name remains in total control—of himself, of the game and above all, of the relation of the virtual to the real. In constructing its story around this attitude, the journalistic account itself also remains in full control: it knows what it's talking about and encourages its readers to also think that they know. It is a discourse that, in Peircean terms, is both indexical and *symbolic*. It is indexical in compelling attention and directing it toward its object. But it is symbolic insofar as that object, despite its proper name, does not so much 'indicate any particular thing; it denotes a kind of a thing'.[11] In pointing to an individual, it nevertheless seeks to impart a general lesson: the virtual game-world can be, and is being exploited to personal advantage. Ultimately, the newspaper article, like the entrepreneurs it is describing, is there to turn a profit. And for this it mobilizes the indexical and the virtual but always in the service of a certain kind of reality: that of the private appropriation of wealth. In order to be fully appropriated privately, however, such wealth can never be definitively identified with any of its manifestations, any of its 'here and nows'. It has to retain a certain virtuality, although ultimately this virtuality is placed in the service of that which transcends it: which is not 'singular and differential' as Deleuze puts it, but *individual* and *selfsame*. This is why its trajectory moves from a proper name, through pseudonyms, toward its conclusion with a direct quote in the first person singular. And this direct quote, in which the individual speaks for itself, has to have an essentially negative character. To be a self, to stay the same over time, transcend all changes of place, the self has to be able to disassociate itself from whatever it has been doing. It has to be able to say, without complex, just what Jason says at the end of the story: 'I quit.'

To grasp just what is at stake in this first-person assertion with which the *New York Times* article concludes—and more generally, how the journalistic discourse on the virtual and the real *takes part* in what it seems simply to *describe*, we need only recall the very different ending of another, far more elaborate staging of the virtual environment of game-worlds: David Kronenberg's film, *eXistenZ* (1999). The game-world portrayed in this film is also one of commerce and speculation, but they take place in the background, barely visible, displaced by other, more overtly violent forms of conflict, conspiracies and constraint. *eXistenZ* tells the story of a game-developer, Allegra Geller, whose new game getting its first try-out also gets increasingly out of hand and is caught up in struggles between shadowy groups that are impossible to identify univocally. Scenes of flight, betrayal and battle are not so much concluded as interrupted by the anguished question of a Chinese waiter, who has already been 'killed' once in the film-game. Finding himself once again, for perhaps the last time, facing a revolver and the possibility of certain or uncertain death, he reacts as one does in the midst of a nightmare, by asking: 'Are we still in the game?' In response, the screen goes blank, or rather black, thus suspending the answer by placing it outside the frame of the narrative and leaving it up to the audience to decide, or at least to ponder: Where does the game begin and end? What does it mean to survive the end of the story?

Between Jason's concluding words, 'I quit'—which for an American audience, at least, can be read as an effort to trump the celebrated 'You're fired!' of American's most recent culture and media hero, Donald Trump—and the waiter's 'Are we still in the game?' it is possible to discern what is perhaps the most interesting question the story I have been discussing allows us to address: Can the virtualization of environments made not just possible but *palpable* by digitalization and electronic media be *appropriated* by the capitalist subject—which is to say, by an 'I' understood as autonomous individual, as an ultimately indivisible Self capable of staying the same over time and providing the necessary anchor for the accumulation of property that is both profitable and private?

If I prefer to describe the 'virtualization of environment' encountered in the current game-world as something 'made palpable' rather than just 'possible' by electronic media, it is because in a certain sense such virtualization has a history much older than the introduction of the digital technologies with which it is generally associated. The struggle of the Ego to appropriate itself (as Self) through virtualization has, I believe, been on the agenda of Western modernity ever since the Reformation, at least, and it finds its first systematic philosophical articulation in Descartes' effort to transform the pangs of doubt into the construction of absolute *self-certainty*. To do this, Descartes, as is well known, withdrew from the public world into the safety of a domestic interior that he describes in considerable detail in his *Meditations*. Seated before the hearth and reflecting upon the transformation of a piece of wax over time— its being melted and altered by the warmth of the fire, Descartes sought to construct a space and time that would be both singular and self-contained, contained by the self that he deemed alone would be able to provide the certainty he demanded. Those aspects of Descartes' operation that concern us directly here are first, his attempt to withdraw from the external world, both historical and sensory, of space and of time, into a quasi-domestic, limited and protected private space organized around a hearth (if not a home); and second, his attempt to construct a secure self-contained space and time of reflection, not of a *cogito*, as is commonly assumed, but far more problematically, one a *res cogitans*—of a thinking thing thinking nothing but itself thinking. Not *Cogito ergo sum*, then, but *cogitans ergo sum* was his attempted solution, and the difference between the two involves nothing less than the effort to come to grips with the virtuality of the actual, of the here and now of a singular living being. In this perspective, Descartes' move from the first person present indicative (*cogito*) to the gerund (*res cogitans*) is significant. Here is Descartes' version, or anticipation, of a scenario which has become the implicit video-game of Western modernity; note the play of tenses and the implicit significance of timing in the following passage:

> But what am I then *now*: when I suppose that some very powerful and, if it is permitted to say so, malign deceiver has [...] deluded me as much he could have? Can I affirm that I have even some minimum of all the things that I have just said to pertain to the nature of the body? I pay attention to them, cogitate, return to them—nothing occurs to me, *I get tired of repeating*. But what about those things I attributed to the soul? [...] To think? Here I find it: it is thinking; this alone cannot be torn from me (*me divelli nequit*). I am, I exist, that is certain. But for how long? (*Quandiu autem?*) *Only while I am thinking, of course* (*Nempe quandiu cogito*); for it could also happen that if I ceased entirely to think, that I should

likewise cease altogether to exist. I now admit nothing except what is necessarily true: I am therefore precisely only a *cogitating thing* (*res cogitans*), that is, a mind, or animus, or intellect, or reason: words with significations previously unknown to me. But I am a true thing and truly existing (*et vere existens*). Yet what kind of thing? *A thinking thing*, as I've said.[12]

Thus, Descartes, who begins by bracketing the *here and now* of actuality, since the sensuous experience it affords can provide no reliable or certain knowledge, and yet who also excludes the *there and then* of tradition and history—Descartes finds as sole temporal medium capable of providing the cer tainty he seeks that of the *present participle* and its nominal form, the *gerund*. For the medium of time, like that of space, is a medium of potential alteration and of empty meaningless repetition—'I get tired of repeating'—and it can only become one of possible certitude insofar as it is framed by the activity of a subject which is also its own object: a 'thing' *thinking itself thinking*. This alone can be said with certainty to be, and *only during the uncertain and limited duration of the present participle*. The present participle, in its reflexive form—thinking thinking itself—is the attempt to domesticate the alterity of a repetitive movement that allows for no purely internal principle of closure, but can only be determined, defined and framed by being interrupted, as it were from the outside. 'Nothing occurs to me; I get tired of repeating,' complains Descartes, until and unless he discovers a principle capable of transforming that repetition by bringing it full-circle as a movement of self-reflection. But this transformation remains subjected to the temporality it seeks to transcend. And so, the gnawing question, 'For how long?' receives as its equivocal response the impatient admission: 'Only while I am thinking, of course.'

It is this question and its response that both *motivates* and also *limits* all attempts at virtualizing the worlds of singular living beings. It *motivates* virtualization through the realization that the actuality of the here-and-now is ultimately incompatible with the demands of the self and of self-identity to endure, i.e. to stay the same over time and through space. The uncertainty and precariousness of the actual, of the here-and-now, of a certain indexicality, was precisely what Descartes started out to overcome:

> The fact that I am *now here* (*ut iam me hic esse*), sitting by the fire, clothed in a winter robe, holding this paper with the hands, and similar things. Truly, by means of what reason could it be denied that these hands themselves and this whole body are mine? Unless I were perhaps to compare myself with […] insane people.[13]

In short, the indexical actuality of the here-and-now is so unreliable precisely because its singularity is irreducible to self-identity, self-cognition, self-consciousness. Like the present participle, and unlike the present indicative, it does not contain its principle of closure, of determination, within itself. The 'here and now' can be that of an insane person, or of someone sleeping, or hallucinating: of someone who *in fact* is *actually* elsewhere, in another here and now of which he or she knows nothing. The reliability of knowledge is defined by its ability to transcend such singular here and now's and still retain its validity: which is to say, still remain identically reproducible, independent of its singular actuality. Nothing less than the constitution of the Self depends on precisely such knowledge: the Self *is* in this sense necessarily *self-conscious* and self-consciousness in turn presupposes the ability to *stay the same over time*, which is to say, to reproduce itself identically above and beyond the singularity of its here-and-now. Such identity thus tends to subject the actual to a certain virtuality—a virtuality that is certain of itself. But at the same time, if the example of Descartes teaches us anything, it is that the transcendence aspired to by the virtualization of self-consciousness remains subject to the very temporal dimension, and ultimately to the very corporeal here and now it seeks to overcome. For by its own admission, the certitude it provides is valid only as long as a certain repetition can be said to come full-circle, i.e. only as long as *thinking can think itself without imploding into pure tautology and redundancy*.

This is where the notion of a '*proper* name' and 'proper noun' come in. For they, and perhaps they alone, seem capable of appropriating the singular by virtualizing it, while at the same time retaining its indexical link to a certain actuality, without which the singular would no longer be distinguishable as such. At the same time, no name is entirely proper, in the sense of being the inalienable property of the person or thing named. And yet, it is only this fiction of an essential *properness* of the *proper name*—defined and supported by an entire legal code and tradition, as well as by the social and political system that enforces it—that makes it possible for property that is inevitably virtual—whether in games or outside them—to be converted into the real profits that can be appropriated by private individuals.

But this is also why the 'proper name' cannot, as Peirce argued, be associated exclusively with the 'index': like any name, its functioning requires a recognition, both individual and social, which, in its iterable[14] structure, exceeds the scope of any purely individual being or thing, (assuming that such exists or is conceivable, which strictly speaking it is not: the *singular* is precisely not reducible to the *individual*). Thus, when Peirce tries to define an index as a sign that would be 'physically connected with its object' with which it would form 'an organic pair', and with which it would be linked entirely independently of an 'interpreting mind', he overlooks the fact that a *proper* name requires precisely the kind of conventional, 'triadic' legitimation or sanction that he otherwise associates with the *symbol*. The same holds for the other example he gives of the index—the 'symptom of disease'—with the additional dimension of making explicit the relation between the singularity of the index and the function of the body in *situating* that singularity. At the same time, the mention of 'disease' foregrounds the exposed finitude of all bodily existence—precisely what worried Descartes and what drove him to seek an alternative in the virtuality of self-consciousness as what I would call *gerundive self-enactment*—thinking thinking itself.

The paradoxical fragility of this project is what informs the attempt, discursive and economic, to reduce virtualization to yet another means of generating surplus-value. Jason Ainsworth dips into the virtual world of computer gaming in order to continue and increase his net worth and pay for his mortgage—while insisting that he has the freedom to 'quit' any time his gaming ceases to be fun. 'Diamond Hope', by contrast, is not a speculator but a model consumer, wishing she could consume more than she can afford. Through the virtuality of her consumption she can hope to develop that 'second life' that is the name of the game in which she has taken up residence—but that also perhaps names the game in which Western modernity has taken up residence ever since the advent of the Christian era. Descartes' anguished question—'How long?—now receives the answer, 'as long as you can spend and consume'. Spend and you shall save—save, and you shall be saved.[15] In the project of *spending to survive*, *Second Life* names not just itself, but what Benjamin once called 'the cult of capitalism'.

*          *          *

I had originally intended to relate some of these issues to a problem I have been working on for some time—that of the *Uncanny*. I will, therefore close by indicating a few (virtual) links between my originally intended essay and the foregoing discussion.

The oppositional logic that governs the Deleuzian discussion of virtual as the negation of the actual—but that is also undercut by the interdependence and overlapping of both with the Peircean notion of index—this oppositional logic is suspended in and as the Uncanny. The Uncanny is not the opposite of the 'canny'—the dependable, the clever, the knowable—it marks their convergence. 'A word is canny, secretive and yet familiar [*heimlich*],' Freud writes in an infinitely equivocal and ambiguous sentence, 'whose meaning develops in the direction of an ambivalence, until it finally falls together with its opposite uncann(il)y [*Unheimlich*].'[16] A similar suspension of the oppositional either-or by one of ambivalence also marks Heidegger's different discussions of the Uncanny, but nowhere perhaps more radically than in the text I had originally intended to discuss: Heidegger's 1942 lecture course dedicated to Hölderlin's poem, 'Der Ister' (the ancient Greek name for the Eastern portion of the Danube River). In these lectures, Heidegger elaborates a connection between what he calls, developing a term used by Hölderlin, the '*Stromgeist*'—the stream-spirit—of the river. The movement of the river, as Hölderlin articulates it, at least according to Heidegger, involves not a unidirectional *flow* but a *streaming* that, like much digital streaming today, goes in two opposite directions at once, not just spatially however, but also temporally. The Ister (Danube) is the sole major European river that flows from West to East, but to the poet it 'almost seems' to flow backwards, and Heidegger suggests that this 'counterturning' involves a temporal movement as well—one that streams not just from the present into the past, but also from the past (premonitorily) into the future. The term he coins for such a virtually unimaginable movement—or perhaps, more precisely for a movement that is only imaginable or figurable 'virtually', is 'counter-turning' (*Gegenwendig*).[17] Heidegger's entire discussion of Hölderlin's poem is informed by the need to rethink the challenge of the Uncanny, whether as that which situates the 'unhomely' at the heart of what is familiar and domestic—the 'hearth' for instance—or whether understood as the uncanny in the sense of a *knowledge* and *ability* that is reliable. Heidegger's discussion of the Uncanny in this lecture course held in the summer of 1942, is itself uncanny in many respects. In focusing upon a reading of the second chorus of Sophocles' *Antigone*, it repeats, expands, but also considerably transforms an earlier reading he had undertaken of the same chorus in 1935, but which had not been published at the time. After the war, it was this first reading alone that was published during Heidegger's lifetime, as part of the book entitled *Introduction into Metaphysics*.[18]

Unfortunately, to discuss Heidegger's reading of this chorus in any detail would require a further chapter. I will therefore close by simply quoting what is perhaps the key passage in the entire chorus for this reading, since it can, I hope, suggest how Heidegger's reading of Sophocles can complement and enrich some of the thoughts on the relation of the virtual, the indexical and the media I have been trying to develop here. In Sophocles' play, the chorus that Heidegger reads, spoken or sung by Theban elders, comes right after the startling discovery that someone, as yet unidentified, has ignored Creon's decree that the corpse of Polyneices not be buried, but instead be left to rot and be picked apart by vultures and dogs. It is upon hearing the news of this disobedience that the Chorus begins its ode by proclaiming 'much and many-sided is the uncanny' but nothing more so than man.[19] It then goes on to describe how man sets forth to conquer the earth and subdue its powers, on the earth, in the water, in the mountains—but that however great his power and cunning, there remains one obstacle that even he can never overcome:

> Everywhere making his way, but with no way out,
> He comes to naught.
> Against one assault only unable, against death,
> Through any flight ever to defend himself,
> Even if debilitation through illness
> He has successfully avoided.

> Possessed of his wits, machinating,
> Skillfully mastering beyond all expectation,
> He succumbs at times to misfortune
> Still, at times accomplishes great things.
> Between the laws of the Earth and the
> Conjured order of the Gods he wends his way.
> Rising far above the sites [*hypsipolis*], deprived of sites [*apolis*]
> Is he, to whom always *unbeing being*
> For the sake of the venture.
> Let not such a one become familiar at my hearth,
> Nor share with me his madness my knowledge,
> Who brings this to be in a work.[20]

The destiny of human beings as singular living beings drives men to develop all sorts of machinations and devices—Heidegger will translate them as *techniques*; it requires these beings to be situated, but at the same time goads them on, driving them up and out of their sites, leaving them not so much *apolitical* as without a home or a homeland (*apolis*). The result of all this is then described in what is probably the most enigmatic line of the chorus, since it suspends the most basic, axiomatic oppositional value of them all, that which opposes being to unbeing. The two are no longer said to be mutually exclusive but instead are simply juxtaposed, without even the benefit of a copula to regulate their relationship as one of subject and predicate:

> Rising far above the sites, deprived of sites
> Is he, to whom always unbeing being
> For the sake of the venture.[21]

In this phrase, which, in Heidegger's rendition at least, does not even form a coherent proposition or sentence, humans are described as always ready to treat unbeing as being—which means not so much virtualizing the real as *realizing the virtual*—trying to make the virtual into the home they lack, a place where this time they might be able to abide, as *virtual reality*. It is this 'madness' that the Chorus seeks to keep out of its home and far from its hearth, but again its own words belie the effort to separate what is inseparable:

> Let not such a one become familiar at my hearth,
> Nor share with me his madness my knowledge,
> Who brings this to be in a work.

Like Descartes, who also sought to purge his 'hearth' from all possible contaminants, impurities and above all, to protect it against the deceptions of that *malin génie* he supposed to be *virtually* everywhere, the Chorus of *Antigone* seeks to exclude from its hearth the one who it itself has just described as the epitome of human being and destiny—and hence to which it must also count itself. The Chorus, in its effort to oppose the Uncanny to the Canny, the Unhomely to the Hearth, nevertheless formulates its conjuration in a way that confirms the futility of its attempt: 'Nor share with me *his madness my knowledge*'. What the Chorus claims as its 'knowledge'—as its property: '*my* knowledge'—rubs shoulders in the sequence of its own phrase with its other: '*his* madness', leaving nothing but a breath to keep them apart.

Today, more than ever before, perhaps, with the world's single superpower sworn to defend its 'homeland security' by going after the 'axis of evil' wherever it may be—and of course it is everywhere—we would do well to dwell for more than a moment on the significance of that *silent breath, virtually* inaudible, which, in seeking to safeguard the 'knowledge' of the *self* from the 'madness' of the *other, virtually indicates* their inseparable disunity.

4

# THE FUTURE BIRTH
# OF THE AFFECTIVE FACT
## The Political Ontology of Threat

Brian Massumi

**Future superlative**

'The next pandemic', screams a 2005 headline in Quebec's reputedly most sober newspaper, 'does not exist yet'. Beneath, in a supersize, full-colour portrait, deceptively innocent-looking, peers a chicken. 'The threat, however, could not be more real.'[1]

*Observation:* We live in times when what has not happened qualifies as front-page news.

Human-adapted avian flu is just one of many nonexistent entities that has come from the future to fill our present with menace. We live in times when what is yet to occur not only climbs to the top of the news but periodically takes blaring precedence over what has actually happened. Yesterday was once the mainstay of the journalist's stock in trade. Today it may pale in the glare of tomorrow's news. 'I think we agree,' prophesied a future president on the cusp of a millennium whose arrival was overshadowed by a nonexistent bug of another colour, 'the past is over.'[2]

*Question:* How could the nonexistence of what has not happened be *more* real than what is now observably over and done with?

Threat is from the future. It is what might come next. Its eventual location and ultimate extent are undefined. Its nature is open-ended. It is not just that it is not: it is not in a way that is never over. We can never be done with it. Even if a clear and present danger materializes in the present, it is still not over. There is always the nagging potential of the next after being even worse, and of a still worse next again after that. The uncertainty of the potential next is never consumed in any given event. There is always a remainder of uncertainty, an unconsummated surplus of danger. The present is shadowed by a remaindered surplus of indeterminate potential for a next event running forward back to the future, self-renewing.

Self-renewing menace potential is the future reality of threat. It could not be more real. Its run of futurity contains so much more, potentially, than anything that has already actually happened. Threat is not real in spite of its nonexistence. It is superlatively real, because of it.

*Observation:* The future of threat is forever.

## Futures past

*Rewind:* It is the summer of 2004. George W. Bush is campaigning for a second term as president. He is on the defensive about the War in Iraq, as pressure mounts for him to admit that the reasons his administration set forth to justify the invasion, in particular the allegation that Saddam Hussein possessed an arsenal of weapons of mass destruction, had no basis in fact. For the first time he admits what had been known all along to those who cared to examine the evidence. He goes on to argue that the lack of factual basis for the invasion does not mean that he made the wrong decision.

> Although we have not found stockpiles of weapons, I believe we were right to go into Iraq. America is safer today because we did. We removed a declared enemy of America, who had the capacity of producing weapons of mass destruction, and could have passed that capability to terrorists bent on acquiring them.[3]

The invasion was right because *in the past there was a future threat*. You cannot erase a 'fact' like that. Just because the menace potential never became a clear and present danger doesn't mean that it wasn't there, all the more real for being nonexistent. The superlative futurity of unactualized threat feeds forward from the past, in a chicken-run to the future past every intervening present. The threat *will have* been real for all eternity.

It will have been real because it was *felt* to be real. Whether the danger was existent or no, the menace was felt in the form of fear. What is not actually real can be felt into being. Threat does have an actual mode of existence: fear, as foreshadowing. Threat has an impending reality in the present. This actual reality is affective.

Fear is the anticipatory reality in the present of a threatening future. It is the felt reality of the nonexistent, loomingly present as the *affective fact* of the matter.

Once a nonexistent reality, always a nonexistent reality. A past anticipation is still an anticipation, and will remain having been an anticipation for all of time. A threat that does not materialize is not false. It has all the affective reality of a past future, truly felt. The future of the threat is not falsified. It is deferred. The case remains forever open. The futurity doesn't stay in the past where its feeling emerged. It feeds forward through time. It runs an endless loop forward from its point of emergence in the past present, whose future it remains. Threat passes through linear time, but does not belong to it. It belongs to the nonlinear circuit of the always will have been.

*Proposition:* If we feel a threat, there was a threat. Threat is affectively self-causing.

*Corollary:* If we feel a threat, such that there was a threat, then there always will have been a threat. Threat is once and for all, in the nonlinear time of its own causing.

## Double conditional

The felt reality of threat legitimates pre-emptive action, once and for all. Any action taken to pre-empt a threat from emerging into a clear and present danger is legitimated by the affective fact of fear, actual facts aside.[4] Pre-emptive action will always have been right. This circularity is not a failure of logic. It is a different logic, operating on the same affective register as threat's self-causing.

The logic of affectively legitimated fact is in the conditional: Bush did what he did because Saddam could have done what he didn't do. Bush's argument doesn't really do justice to the logic of pre-emption. Saddam didn't actually even have the 'capacity', and that poses no problem for pre-emptive logic which is based on a *double conditional*. 'The Pentagon neocons argued that the CIA overemphasized what Saddam *could do* instead of stressing *what he would do if he could*.'[5]

Bush was being modest in a CIA kind of way. From the prevailing neo-conservative perspective, he was understating why he was right. He was right even though Saddam did *not* have the capacity, because Saddam 'would have if he could have'. The case remains open. At any moment in the future, he could have acquired the means, and as soon as could, he would. Would-have, could-have: double conditional.

Present threat is logically recessive, in a step-by-step regress from the certainty of actual fact. The actual fact would have been: Saddam Hussein has WMD. The first step back from that is: he had the capacity to have WMD. The next step is: he didn't have the capacity, but he still would have if he could have. The recessive assertion that he 'would have' is based on an assumption about character and intent that cannot be empirically grounded with any certainty. But it is proffered with certainty. It carries a certainty, underivable from actual fact, which it owes to the affective fact of the matter. The felt reality of the threat is so superlatively real that it translates into a felt certainty about the world, even in the absence of other grounding for it in the observable world. The assertion has the felt certainty of a 'gut feeling'. Gut feeling was proudly and publicly embraced by Bush as his peak decision-making process in the lead-up to the war in Iraq and beyond.[6]

Pre-emption's logical regress from actual fact makes for a disjointedness between its legitimating discourse and the objective content of the present context which its affirmations ostensibly reference. Its receding from actual fact produces a logical disjunction between the threat and the observable present. A logical gap opens in the present through which the reality of threat slips to rejoin its deferral to the future. Through the logical hatch of the double conditional, threat makes a runaround through the present back toward its self-causing futurity.

The affect-driven logic of the would-have/could-have is what discursively ensures that the actual facts will always remain an open case, for all pre-emptive intents and purposes. It is what saves threat from having to materialize as a clear and present danger—or even an emergent danger—in order to command action. The object of pre-emptive power, according the explicit doctrine, is 'not yet fully emergent *threat*'. The doctrine doesn't say emergent danger—let alone clear and present danger.[7] And again (and again), when threat strikes it is once and for all.

*Problem:* How can pre-emptive politics maintain its political legitimacy given that it grounds itself in the actual ungroundedness of affective fact? Would not pointing out the actual facts be enough to make it crumble?

*Observation:* Bush won his re-election.


## Right again

*Fast forward:* One year later, summer 2005. For the first time in the polls, more than two years after the invasion, a majority of Americans oppose the War in Iraq. The legitimation of pre-emptive action—or that particular action at any rate—is faltering. The downturn had begun long after the lack of actual facts behind the decision to invade had become common knowledge. It began with the counter-affective strike that came with the release and widespread circulation of shocking images of torture at Abu Ghraib.[8] It was only then that the lack of actual-factual basis for the invasion began to resonate with a voting public rendered less receptive, for the moment, to the logic of pre-emption by the affective counter-coup of torture graphically revealed. Bush makes a valiant attempt to kick-start the logic of pre-emption again. He delivers a major radio address to the nation explaining his refusal to withdraw. He deploys an argument that he will continue to use for at least the next two years.[9]

'Some may agree,' he says, 'with my decision to remove Saddam Hussein from power, but all of us can agree that the world's terrorists have now made Iraq a central front in the war on terror.'[10] The presence of terrorist links between al-Qaeda and Saddam Hussein had been the second major argument, behind WMD, originally used to justify the invasion. The Bush administration had already been obliged to withdraw the assertion long before this speech. The fact that al-Qaeda had *not* been in Iraq at the time of the invasion now becomes the reason it was right to invade. The fact that they are there now just goes to prove that if they could have been there then, they would have.

The could-have/would-have logic works both ways. If the threat does not materialize, it still always would have if it could have. If on the other hand the threat does materialize, then it just goes to show that the future potential for what happened had really been there in the past. In this case, the pre-emptive action is retroactively legitimated by future actual facts.

Bush does not point out that the reason al-Qaeda is now in Iraq is *because of* the invasion that was mounted to keep it out of Iraq. That the pre-emptive action actually *brought about* the result it was meant to fight.

*Observation:* Pre-emptive action can produce the object toward which its power is applied, and it can do so without contradicting its own logic, and without necessarily undermining its legitimation.

*Proposition:* Because it operates on an affective register and inhabits a non-linear time operating recursively between the present and the future, pre-emptive logic is not subject to the same rules of non-contradiction as normative logic, which privileges a linear causality from the past to the present and is reluctant to attribute an effective reality to futurity.

### Flour attack

*Pause:* Around the same time, a state of emergency is called at the Montreal airport. There has been a 'toxic substance alert'. White powder has been seen leaking from a suitcase. The actual facts of the case are still two weeks in the future after the necessary lab work will have been done. Action, however, cannot wait. It *could be* anthrax. That potential threat must be acted upon. The airport is closed. Highways to the airport are closed. Men in white decontamination suits descend. SWAT teams and police pour in. Terrified passengers are sequestered in the terminal. News helicopters hover overhead. Live coverage takes over the local airwaves. All of the actions that *would be* taken if the powder were anthrax are taken pre-emptively. The dramatic rapid-response of the public security apparatus causes a major disruption of commerce and circulation. The site is quickly decontaminated, and life returns to normal.

*Observations:* Pre-emptive power washes back from the battlefield onto the domestic front (even in countries not militarily involved). On the domestic front, its would-have/could-have logic takes a specific form associated with public security procedures involving the signalling of alert. The alert, set off at the slightest *sign* of potential threat, triggers immediate action. The actions set in motion in response to the threat are of the same kind and bring on many of the same effects as would have accompanied an actual danger. The pre-emptive measures cause the disruption to the economy and everyday life that terrorist attacks are designed to produce beyond their immediate impact.

*Proposition:* Defensive pre-emptive action in its own way is as capable as offensive pre-emptive action of producing what it fights. Together with the increasing speed and vigour of defensive action, this blurs the boundaries between defence and offence, between domestic security and military action.

Two weeks later, the powder is identified. It is flour. News articles following up on the story after the discovery of no toxic substance continue to refer to the incident as a 'toxic substance alert'.[11] No one refers to the incident as a 'flour alert'. The incident is left carrying an affective dusting of white-powdered terror. Flour has been implicated. It is tainted with the fear of anthrax, guilty by association for displaying the threatening qualities of whiteness and powderiness.

In pre-emptively logical terms, the incident *was* a toxic substance alert—not because the substance was toxic, but because the *alert* was for a potential toxic substance.

*Observations:* An alarm may determine the generic identity of a potential threat, without specifically determining the actual identity of the objects involved. This declares what will later prove actually to have been innocent objects (or in other circumstances, persons) as officially threatening for the duration of the alert, based on their displaying material qualities answering to the generic description. Afterwards, they remain tainted by their affective involvement in the incident, for they really always will have been associated with the fear produced by the alert, and fear feeds threat forward.

*Proposition:* The affective reality of threat is contagious.

*Proposition:* Threat is capable of overlaying its own conditional determination upon an objective situation through the mechanism of alarm. The two determinations, threatening and objective, coexist. However, the threat-determined would-be and could-be takes public precedence due to its operating in the more compelling, future-oriented and affective, register. This gives it superior political presence and potential.[12]

The incident comes to a close with follow-up articles about improvements in government safety procedure as a result of the toxic substance alert. The false alert is presented in the news media as having palpably increased the security of airplane passengers.[13]

*Proposition:* The security that pre-emption is explicitly meant to produce is predicated on its tacitly producing what it is meant to avoid: pre-emptive security is predicated on a production of insecurity to which it itself contributes. Pre-emption thus positively contributes to producing the conditions for its own exercise. It does this by capturing for its own operation the self-causative power native to the threat-potential that it takes as its object.

## Specifically imprecise

*Rewind:* New York City, October 2005. Mayor Michael Bloomberg puts the city on alert, citing a chillingly specific threat to bomb the metropolitan subway and bus system simultaneously at 'as many as nineteen' different locations. 'This is the first time we have had a threat with this level of specificity,' he says at a televised news conference.[14] The FBI announces that arrests related to the plot have already been made in Iraq, based on 'reliable' information. 'Classified operations have already partially disrupted this threat.' Although offensive pre-emptive action has already been taken, there is still felt to be a menacing remainder of threat. Pre-emptive action is retaken, this time defensively. Transit passengers on the home front are briefed on security procedures and asked to contribute to the city's surveillance by keeping an eye out for suspicious persons and objects. A suspicious bottle, which could have been filled with hazardous material, is sighted at Penn Station. It is isolated and destroyed (if it could have, it would have…).

The next day, the Homeland Security Department weighs in to say that 'the intelligence community has been able to determine that there are very serious doubts about the credibility of this specific threat'. The threat had been 'very, very specific. It had specific time, specific object and modality', the city police commissioner assured. 'So, you know, we had to do what we did. […] I believe in the short term we'll have a much better sense of whether or not this has, you know, real substance to it.'[15]

A threat can have specificity, and lead to decisive pre-emptive actions with a corresponding level of specificity, without having 'real substance' or objective 'credibility'. The pre-emptive actions taken in response to the threat are still logically and politically correct if they were commensurate with the urgency of the threat, if not with the urgency of the actual situation. They will still have been justified even if the information proves objectively imprecise and there was no actual danger.[16]

*Proposition:* An alert is not a referential statement under obligation to correspond with precision to an objective state of affairs. The measure of its correctness is the immediacy and specificity of the pre-emptive actions it automatically triggers. The value of the alert is measured by its *performance*. Rather than referential truth-value, it has performative *threat-value*. More than any correspondence between its semantic content and an objective referent, it is the performed commensurability of the threat and the triggered actions which qualifies the alert as correct. Its correctness, felt as a question of collective security, is directly political. The threat alert, as *sign of* danger, is subject to different criteria of reliability and effectiveness than referential language *about* danger.

*Proposition:* Threat has no actual referent.

*Corollary:* Pre-emption is a mode of power that takes threat, which has no actual referent, as its object. When the politics of pre-emption captures threat's potential for its own operation, it forgoes having an actual object of power.

## 'The 9/11 generation'

*Fast forward on rewind:* It is now the lead-up to the 2008 US presidential elections. Ex-mayor Rudolph Giuliani of New York is revving up his campaign by looping back to 9/11, toward future pre-emptive action. He writes an article in *Foreign Affairs* taking a hard-line neoconservative position in continuity with Defense Secretary Donald Rumsfeld's first-term Bush administration policies. The article argues that the 9/11 attacks inaugurated a new world-historical era. The fall of the Twin Towers was an originating moment of what he calls, following Rumsfeld, the 'Long War' against terrorism, in much the same way that the building of the Berlin Wall inaugurated the Cold War, according to Giuliani. 'We are all members of the 9/11 generation,' he declares.[17]

9/11 was an actual event that put thousands of lives in immediate danger. People were agape in shock at the enormity of it. The immediate shock gave way to lingering fear, relaying the danger into a remainder of surplus threat. 9/11 was an excess-threat generating actual event which has perhaps done more than any other threat-o-genic source to legitimate pre-emptive politics. It has been continually cited by the Bush administration to reinvoke potential threat for use in legitimating policy. Candidates of both parties in the 2008 race to succeed Bush also invoked it regularly in order to establish their own national security credentials.[18] And yet…

*Question:* Can the threat-potential fuelling pre-emptive politics have an identifiable origin?

There were precursors to 9/11. The 'war on terror' was declared by President Richard Nixon in the early 1970s. Between that time and September 2001, there have been any number of attacks characterized as terrorist, including the earlier, less successful, 1993 bombing of the World Trade Centre. Since 9/11 there have been further attacks. If the historical and geographical parameters are enlarged, attacks that could be qualified as 'terrorist' stretch indefinitely.

*Observation:* 9/11 belongs to an *iterative series* of allied events whose boundaries are indefinite.

An event where threat materializes as a clear and present danger extrudes a surplus-remainder of threat-potential which can contaminate new objects, persons, and contexts through the joint mechanisms of the double conditional and the objective imprecision of the specificity of threat. Threat's self-causing proliferates. Threat-alerts, performatively signed threat-events, are quick to form their own iterative series. These series tend to proliferate robustly, thanks to the suppleness and compellingness of the affective logic generating them. As an indication, according to the Homeland Security Department in the US, in 2003 alone there were 118 airport evacuations. In 2004, there were 276. None was linked to a terrorist attempt, let alone an actual bombing.[19]

As the series proliferate, the distinction between the series of actual attacks and the series of threat-events blurs. At the same time, the range of generic identities under which the threat and its corresponding performance may fall also expands. The terrorist series includes torpedoing buildings with airplanes, air missile attacks, subway bombs, suicide car attacks, roadside bombings, liquid explosives disguised as toiletries, tennis-shoe bombs, 'dirty' bombs (never actually observed), anthrax in the mail, other unnamed bioterrorist weapons, booby-trapped mailboxes, coke cans rigged to explode, bottles in public places… The list is long, and ever-extending. The mass affective production of felt threat-potential engulfs the (f)actuality of the comparatively small number of incidents where danger materialized. They blend together in a shared atmosphere of fear.

In that atmosphere, the terrorist threat series blends into series featuring other generic identities. There is the generic viral series including threats, real and nonexistent, as heterogeneous as human-adapted avian flu, SARS, West Nile virus, and the Millennium Bug, just to mention a few from the first years of this century. There is no apparent limit to the generic diversification of threat, which can cross normative logical boundaries with impunity, like that between biological and computer viruses. Or food and pathogens: 'Comparing junk food to a possible avian flu epidemic, provincial Health Minister Philippe Couillard said yesterday that the province is preparing a crackdown to get sugar-laden soft drinks and junk food out of schools.'[20] The series combine and intertwine, and together tend to the infinite, pre-emptive action in tow.

The atmosphere of fear includes this tendential infinity of threat series on the same performative basis as actually occurring terrorist attack. The generic identity of threat overall stretches to the limit to accommodate the endless proliferation of specific variations. The object of threat tends toward an ultimate limit at which it becomes purely indeterminate, while retaining a certain quality—menace—and the capacity to make that quality felt. The portrait of a chicken can embody this quality and make it felt as reliably as a terrorist's mug shot.

At the limit, threat is a *felt quality*, independent of any particular instance of itself, in much the way the colour red is a quality independent of any particular tint of red, as well as of any actually occurring patch of any particular tint of red. It becomes an abstract quality. When threat self-causes, its abstract quality is affectively presented, in startle, shock, and fear. As presented affectively, its quality suffuses the atmosphere. Threat is ultimately *ambient*. Its logic purely *qualitative*.

*Proposition:* Threat's ultimately ambient nature makes pre-emptive power an *environmental* power.[21] Rather than empirically manipulate an object (of which it actually has none), it *modulates* felt qualities infusing a life-environment.

*Question:* If 9/11 is not an origin, what is it? How does it figure in the tendentially infinite series to which it belongs? Is it possible to periodize pre-emptive power?

Rather than assigning it as an origin, 9/11 may be thought of as marking a threshold. It can be considered a turning point at which the threat-environment took on an ambient thickness, achieved a consistency, which gave the pre-emptive power mechanisms dedicated to its modulation an advantage over other regimes of power.

*Proposition:* To understand the political power of threat and the pre-emptive politics availing itself of threat-potential, it is necessary to situate pre-emptive power in a field of interaction with other regimes of power, and to analyse their modes of coexistence as well as their evolutionary divergences and convergences.[22] In a word, it is necessary to adopt an *ecological* approach to threat's environmental power.

*Corollary:* Each regime of power in the ecology of powers will have its own *operative logic* implicating unique modes of causality and having a singular time-signature. The causal and temporal processes involved will endow the objects of each regime of power with an ontological status different from those of any other regime. Correlative to its ontology, each regime will have a dedicated epistemology guiding the constitution of its political 'facts' and guaranteeing their legitimation. The political analysis of regimes of power must extend to these metaphysical dimensions.

## Stop

*Question:* What is an operative logic?

Call an operative logic one that combines an ontology with an epistemology in such a way as to endow itself with powers of self-causation. An operative logic is a productive *process* that inhabits a shared environment, or field of exteriority, with other processes and logics. It figures in that field as a formative movement: a *tendency* toward the iterative production of its own variety of constituted fact. The forms of determination it brings into being as fact have an inborn tendency toward proliferation, by virtue of the self-causative powers of their formative process. An operative logic is a process of becoming formative of its own species of being.

*Question:* What does an operative logic want?

Itself. Its own continuance. It is autopoietic. An operative logic's self-causative powers drive it automatically to extend itself. Its autopoietic mode of operation is one with a drive to universalize itself. Depending on the logic, that drive will take fundamentally heterogeneous forms (from the ecumenical to the imperialist, from the pastoral to the warlike).

*Proposition:* An operative logic is a will-to-power.

This will-to-power is impersonal because it necessarily operates in a field of exteriority in perpetual interaction with other operative logics, with which it is always in a dynamic state of reciprocal presupposition. It is a field phenomenon. The interaction actualizes in a diversity of regimes of power cohabiting the same field in reciprocal exteriority and potential interlinkage. An operative logic's actualization may be to varying degrees, in more than one regime. An operative logic not fully actualized in any regime of power interacts with the others virtually (anticipatorily, as a present force of futurity; or, as 'negatively prehended').[23]

*Question:* In the case of threat as an operative logic, how can an effective analysis of it be carried out, given that the kind of fact it constitutes is affective and largely independent of actual fact, not to mention that its object is superlatively, futurely nonexistent?

There is a common category of entities, known to all, which specializes in making what is not actually present really present nonetheless, in and as its own effect: *signs.* The sign is the vehicle for making presently felt the *potential force* of the objectively absent.

*Proposition:* To understand pre-emptive power as an operative logic it is necessary to be able to express its productive process of becoming as a *semiosis.* Since pre-emption's production of being in becoming pivots on affect as felt quality, the pertinent theory of signs would have to be grounded first and foremost in a metaphysics of *feeling.*

## Smoke of future fires

Imagine a dreamer who suddenly hears a loud and prolonged fire alarm.

> At the instant it begins he is startled. He instinctively tries to get away; his hands go to his ears. It is not so much that it is unpleasing, but it forces itself so upon him. The instinctive resistance is a necessary part of it […] This sense of acting and being acted upon, which is the sense of the reality of things—both of outward things and ourselves—may be called the sense of Reaction. It does not reside in any one Feeling; it comes upon the breaking of one feeling by another feeling.[24]

A fire alarm is the kind of sign C. S. Peirce calls *indications* or indexes. Indexes 'act on the nerves of the person and force his attention'. They are nervously compelling because they 'show something about things, on account of their being physically connected to them' in the way smoke is connected to fire.[25] Yet they *assert nothing*. Rather, they are in the mood of the 'imperative, or exclamatory, as "See there!" or "Look out!"'.[26] The instant they 'show' we are startled: they are immediately performative.

A performative always strikes as a self-executing command. The indexical sign effecting the command may assert nothing, but it still conveys a form. 'The form conveyed is always a determination of a dynamical object of the *command.* The dynamical object [...] means something forced upon the mind in perception, but including more than perception reveals. It is an object of actual *Experience.*'[27]

Now what happens when there is no fire and the alarm sounds nonetheless?

The sign of alarm has asserted more nothing. It is still just as imperative, still as automatically executing of a command. It still startles us awake to a sense of a reality of things, outwardly and selfward at once. It still forces attention, breaking into the feeling before with a transition to a next. Something still happens. A sign-event has transpired. This is an actual *Experience*, including, all the more more-than-perception reveals.

It is not just that the putative object of experience, the fire, is nonexistent. It is that it is absent from perception essentially, not just circumstantially. There is no fire. The alarm was in error. How can a falsity have a superlatively real hold on experience?

How could it not? For Peirce, the 'dynamical object' is not the fire. The dynamical object is the innervated flesh to which the sign performatively correlates 'fire', existent or nonexistent. The nervous body astartle that is 'the object of the command' to alertness. That performance takes place wholly between the sign and the 'instinctively' activated body whose feeling is 'broken' by the sign's command to transition to a new feeling. At that instant, nothing but this transitional break exists. *Its* feeling, the sudden bustle, fills the still dreamily reawakening world of experience.

The form 'conveyed', the dynamical object exclaimed by the sign of alarm, is nothing other than the dynamic form of the body at this instant of reawakening to its world on alert, imperatively altering. It is nothing else than the activation event launching the body into a transition to a next experience in which its waking world will have undergone a change. Everything takes place between the activated body and the sign of its *becoming.* Fire or no fire, transition to and through alert is made.

What happens when the fire is not falsely nonexistent, but nonexistent in a future tense? What happens if the smoke is that of fires yet to come? What happens if the sign-event is triggered by a future cause?

That is the semiotic question of threat.

Semiosis is sign-induced becoming. It is the question of how a sign as such *dynamically* determines a body to become, in actual experience. It is the question of how an *abstract force* can be *materially* determining. The question is the same for a nonexistent present fire signed in error, and for the futurity of a fire yet to come. There is one difference, however. For the future-causal fire, there can be no error. It will always have been pre-emptively right.

That one difference makes all the difference. The question becomes, what are the experiential political implications of the a priori rightness of smokes of future fires? What are the existential effects of the body having to assume, at the level of its activated flesh, one with its becoming, the rightness of alert never having to be in error? Of the body in a perpetual innervated reawakening to a world where signs of danger forever loom? Of a world where once a threat, always a threat? A world of infinitely seriating menace-potential made actual experience, with a surplus of becoming, all in the instant?

Imagine a waker hearing a sudden and loud alarm and therewith falling forward back into a world where the present is a foreshadow cast retrospectively by the future. Where the present's becoming is the back-cast dream of a future's will have been.

### A bustle of it all

Peirce insists that the sign's forcing itself upon the body, and the 'resistance' the body instinctively feels 'in reaction', cannot be 'distinguished as agent and patient'.[28] The bodily activation event occurs at a threshold of reawakening where there is as yet no distinction between activity and passivity. This means that the body cannot distinguish its own 'instincts' from the reawakening force conveyed by the sign's formative performance.

The zone of indistinction between the body reactivating and the action of the sign extends to the shared environment that encompasses and ensures their correlation. Is not the waking distinction between the body and its environment one of activity in a surrounding passivity, or of activity coming from the surrounding to passively impress itself on the body? Prior to the distinction between agent and patient, in the bustle of the reawakening, there is no boundary yet between the body and its environment, or between the two of them and the correlated sign. Or between the dream and the event. These distinctions will re-emerge from the bustle, after a transition, in the settle into a next determinate feeling. The form conveyed is a felt dynamic form of unbounded activation germinal of determinate feeling. Pure affect. In a re-dawning universe. This is what the sign 'shows'.

To understand the political ontology of threat requires returning thought to this affective twilight zone of indexical experience. In that bustling zone of indistinction, the world becomingly includes so much more than perception reveals. For that reason, thought's approach cannot be phenomenological. It must be unabashedly metaphysical. It must extend to that which conditions what is appearing *next*, itself never appearing: what Whitehead terms the reality *of* appearance.

The reality of appearance is the ontogenetic effectiveness of the nonexistent. It is the surplus of reality of what has not happened, paradoxically as an event, and in the event happens to be productive of a startling transition toward more determinate being.

Look out!

'The occasion has gathered the creativity of the Universe into its own completeness, abstracted from the real objective content which is the source of its own derivation.'[29]

This 'results from the fusion of the ideal with the actual', in a mutual immanence of contemporary occasions 'allied to the immanence of the future in the present'.[30]

See there!

'The light that was never was, on sea or land.'[31]

*Last question:* Does it shine beyond pre-emption?

5

# FOR A COMPARATIVE FILM STUDIES

*Paul Willemen*

### Preliminaries

The turn to cultural relativism that accompanied the questioning of the established, mainly modernist, Euro-American theorizations of cultural dynamics, was in many respects both inevitable and salutary.[1] Especially if cultural relativism is seen for what it is: an initial move preparing the ground for a better theorization of cultural dynamics, capable of taking into account the different layers of determination and functioning which the previous theorizations could not or did not discern sufficiently clearly, being trapped within the confines of their own socio-cultural horizons. In that respect, the problem with Western cultural theories is not, or should not be, that they are Western, but that they fail adequately to take into account that they are shaped and bounded by the very social-economic factors that make the West into a pertinent geo-political, or better, geo-historical field. In other words, what is wrong with Western theory is not that it is Western, but that so much of it fails to realize that it is Western. Alternative modalities of cultural theory, marked and bounded as they are by other geo-historical formations, are not necessarily better or less limited. The real challenge is to find a way of overcoming the limits that any intellectual paradigm suffers from by virtue of, necessarily, being elaborated within a specific geo-historical field. In other words, the challenge is to find ways of overcoming the limits of any cultural relativism, any fetishization of geo-political boundaries, and to elaborate a cultural theory worthy of the name. At present, cultural theory, wherever practised, must be regarded as still mired in its prehistoric phase, precisely for being incapable of coming to terms with its own historicity. A breakthrough in cultural theory analogous to the achievement in physics of a Mendeleev table of elements or, in biology, of DNA profiling (metaphorically speaking, the construction of the DNA sequencing of cultural formations) is, unfortunately, unlikely as long as the financial resources required for such a project are withheld. Those resources will continue to be withheld for as long as religious modes of thinking about social and personal relations benefit the current power elites. As Peter Uwe Hohendahl concluded after a detailed investigation of the ways in which literature became a national literature in Germany between 1830 and 1870, neither the emergence nor the erosion of the bourgeois concept of culture can be correlated linearly with the development of organized capitalism:

> It was the interplay of capitalist organization and state intervention, with its rich potential for conflict, which gave rise to the formation that Adorno and Horkheimer were to characterize in the twentieth century as the culture industry. [And only] a new concept of industrial culture can offer a starting point for investigating the cultural change that occurred after 1870. Such a concept would have to begin by avoiding all culture-critical prejudices and debate anew the problematic correlation between the conditions of production (organized capitalism), social formation, and political struggle (state intervention).[2]

That is the context within which I want to pose the question of a possible comparative film studies, a project that must necessarily proceed by way of a collaboration between intellectuals from different geo-historical formations.

The precondition for such a collaboration is that the participants should be prepared to consider their own intellectual formations and thought-habits as symptomatic constellations shaped by the very same dynamics that animate historicity itself. To date, such a programme of work has been thought of, in my view correctly, in terms of the possibility of a historical materialist theory of culture. But in the same way that no theory has as yet been elaborated capable of reconciling Einsteinian physics and quantum theory, so there is no single theory available to us that is capable of articulating cultural dynamics with the socio-economic field. Reflection theory has been discredited for nearly a century, and its opposite, assuming a non-correspondence between the economic and the cultural, has, of course, merely muddied the waters. The long march to the theorization of cultural dynamics has barely begun, mainly because to date we have been able to identify only some of the directions in which we should *not* go.

The working hypothesis underpinning this call for a possible comparative practice of film studies assumes that cinema, a cultural form on the cusp of the economic and the cultural, is particularly well suited to provide a way into the question of how socio-economic dynamics and pressures are translated into discursive constellations. The second, perhaps even more contentious assumption, is that cinema dramatizes the very processes of modernization understood as the differential encounters with capitalism underpinning what in Marxist theory is called combined and uneven development. The third, yet more risky hypothesis informing my own approach to these issues, is that there are two crucial questions to be addressed if we are to outline, however roughly, a map to orient ourselves on the long march. The first one is the further elaboration of a theory of subjectivity-in-history (with associated questions of individuation, modes of address, regimes of looking and so on). The second one is the as yet still unasked question of how the transformation of physical energy into labour power, which is the founding dynamic of capitalism, happens to present itself in cinematic discourse. The problem underpinning a comparative film studies would then be: how do cinemas emerging from within different socio-historical formations negotiate the encounter between capitalist modernization and whatever mode of social-economic regulation and (re)production preceded that encounter?

### From world literature to world cinema

At the turn of the millennium, Franco Moretti published a stimulating essay in the first issue of the *New Left Review*'s newly designed and numbered series: 'Conjectures on World Literature'.[3] In 2004, the *NLR*'s publisher, Verso, followed this up with a collection of essays edited by Christopher Prendergast called *Debating World Literature*. Although in publishing terms the book is triggered by Moretti's essay, which features centrally in Prendergast's collection, the editor claims that his book's point of departure is in fact Pascale Casanova's *La république mondiale des lettres*, published in Paris in 1999. However, Casanova's book is about the ways nation states competitively market their cultural productions. On the other hand, Moretti's essay, and Prendergast follows his lead in his introduction, regards the concept of world literature not as referring to national collections of marketable products or objects, but as a problem requiring a new conceptualization of the way literature is to be studied. That is to say, the notion of world literature is a theoretical question pointing to a series of problems in the way literature is studied and read. Prendergast's collection of essays provides a useful way into that theoretical problem.

The first thing to note about this problem for cultural theory (of which the theory of literature is one region) is the timing of its arrival on our agenda. Intellectuals have been concerned with the problem for many decades, even centuries (from Goethe and Marx to Auerbach, Spitzer and others) and the concern has even been institutionally enshrined in university departments of Comp Lit and associated journals, books and so on. Since the 1920s, that concern has been translated into adjacent academic fields such as comparative social history (Marc Bloch) and aspects of social anthropology. While Moretti acknowledges the importance of the work done in Turkey (by German émigrés in conjunction with Turkish intellectuals), Japan (Kojin Karatani and Masao Miyoshi) and the impact of Fredric Jameson's work, Prendergast notes that the concern with world literature as a theoretical problem takes the form of a swelling wave of interest in the areas of Comp Lit and Postcolonial Studies in the US, following in the wake of the El Niño effect known as globalization. The wave focused attention on the re-examination of national and diasporic public spheres in books such as Arjun Appadurai's *Modernity at Large*[4] and in numerous journals, including *Positions, Traces, Public Culture, Inter-Asia Cultural Studies, Boundary 2, Critical Inquiry, Social Text* and many others.

Much of the wave is taken up by the froth of ruminations about the spread and impact of electronic media, which makes the Comp Lit people feel neglected and unhappy. I share their unhappiness, but for different reasons. I have no wish to join the nostalgics for the Republic of Letters. The destructive impact of attributing too much cultural power to *littérateurs* of various types, usually a barely displaced way of installing a new priesthood, is all too evident in the role played by Lit and its Crit in Britain throughout the twentieth century, and still today. The inhibiting and blocking effects of literature's domination in a nation's ideological state apparatus are also plainly evident in the history of French, British, German and American film theories: the centrality of debates around the triad of authorship, narrative and genre, together with an emphasis on literary and theatre-derived notions of performance and character, testify to that. This domination is now further extended, as Moretti correctly notes, by the apparent obligation imposed on (film) theorists to conduct their work in the form of close readings of individual texts. As Moretti writes, close reading as a strongly favoured type of engagement with texts, the heartland of which is currently in the US literary and publishing establishments, makes sense only if you think that very few texts really matter: 'If you want to look beyond the canon […] close reading will not do it. It's designed not to do it; it's designed to do the opposite. At bottom it's a theological exercise—very solemn treatment of very few texts taken very seriously.'[5] That is the context in which the current plethora of film books dedicated to single-text analyses has to be seen: a covertly anti-theoretical, theological exercise enforced by the power of an Anglo–US coalition for whom canons are an appropriate way of marrying religious modes of thinking to cost-saving marketing imperatives. It does not really matter which works are included or excluded from the canon. What matters is the maintenance and propagation of Canonic Law, regardless of whether this comes in the form of bestseller lists or other listings or codifications (the 100 best of this; 50 milestones of that, etc.).

In the current, early twenty-first-century context, canons are no longer— or only incidentally—part of campaigns to exemplify aesthetic frameworks: classicism, realism, modernism, critical vanguardism and so on. Their use-value has become transmuted into marketing value and it is no longer even relevant to examine which items appear on the listings, as Peter Wollen does in a challenging discussion of canons, arguing that in cinema canonic listings performed a function in the spread of a modernizing (not quite modernist) critical paradigm.[6] Instead, they perform their authoritarian task, enjoining us to consent to a theological mindset for which the commandments are promulgated by a journalistic-administrative priesthood in the service of the culture business.

However, the shift of focus from the literary to electronic media also has other nefarious effects for the case for the time being and probably for the foreseeable future. The specialists in matters of iconic discursiveness, such as the historians and theorists of painting and other art historians, have as yet barely begun to think about electronic media as discursive practices. Instead, the field has been left wide open for the assorted peddlers of globalizing techno-hype. That computers can do other things besides combining telephony with calculators is still an unending source of quasi-mystical wonderment for most teachers and artistic practitioners of 'new media'. The vast majority of writing and exhibiting under the banner of new or digital media reminds me mainly of cargo cults and of the first Parisian spectators in 1895 who are said to have ducked in panic when they saw a film of a train arriving at the La Ciotat train station. I have no wish to contribute to the globalization soap opera which never seems to want to talk about exactly what is being globalized. An answer to that question has already been given some years ago by, among others, Jameson, when he pointed out that the issue is the ability of Wall Street, by way of the US Government, to project its power across the world in ever more varied ways.

This is also why discussions of globalization tend to be so frustrating and misleading: it is an ideology which teaches us to forget history while equating capitalism as a mode of production with its contemporary US version. The globalization soap opera encourages us to confuse the centuries-long dynamic of modernization, which describes the changes resulting from a social formation's encounter with capitalism, with the five decades-long process of Americanization. In this way, by substituting the taken-for-granted medium-term dominance of US capitalism for capitalism as a mode of production with its own long-term history, it is the latter that is made to vanish from our horizon. The late founder and director of the Rotterdam Film Festival, Hubert Bals, once remarked that he attached special importance to films that made mistakes in interesting ways. Moretti's essay stands as a theoretical equivalent of such films. It proposes extraordinarily suggestive mistakes, especially if we take it as an initial formulation of an intuition and systematically read 'cinema' where he writes 'literature'.

Moretti begins with the formulation of something that he calls a Law of literary evolution: 'the modern novel first arises not as an autonomous development, but as a compromise between a Western formal influence [...] and local materials.' The materials that he has in mind—and he cites Jameson's introduction to Karatani's work on the novel in Japan for the purpose—are those that make up the fabric of social experience and which, in turn, are shaped by the socio-economic conditions put into place and managed by the institutional network that underpins and defines a nation state. Moretti then goes on to give examples drawn from the many studies that have charted the development of prose and particularly of the novel form in various regional and national cultures. In a footnote referring to the last chapter in his own *Atlas of the European Novel 1800–1900*, he gives three more such laws: 'the formal compromise itself is usually prepared by a massive wave of West European translations', 'the compromise itself is generally unstable' and finally, that 'genuine formal revolutions' result from the successful matching of a foreign form to local social experience.[7]

In terms of the cinema, a wave of translations is better envisaged as the international distribution and exhibition of (mostly American) films, dubbed or subtitled. Like translations, this circulation of films in altered forms of expression adapted to 'local' conditions is often supported and subsidized by national governments seeking to derive prestige and profits from the export of the products of their cultural industries (or their industrialized cultures). In that respect, film distribution and exhibition confirm Pascale Casanova's view that nation states transform a selected range of cultural materials and transform them into nationally branded product lines which are then competitively marketed abroad.

That such an approach has long underpinned the US film industry is particularly evident in the massive state subsidies allocated to the Hollywood companies (in the form of tax incentives, market research, protectionism, legalized accounting scams, publicly funded public relations and marketing campaigns, and so on), subsidies amounting to billions of dollars over the last two or three decades.[8] In fact, Hollywood is by far the most lavishly subsidized film industry in the world. An early, amusing example of the US government's thinking behind this massive transfer of tax revenues into the pockets of corporate Hollywood, can be found in a publication by the US Department of Commerce and the Office of International Trade, *World Trade in Commodities*. In the late 1940s (volumes 6 and 7) they issued a series of reports on the trade in motion pictures and equipment compiled by the US Government's embassies and consulates all over the world. The reports gave a brief history of motion pictures in their territories, especially from the industrial point of view, listed trade restrictions and opportunities, censorship issues and made a special point of noting the influence that Hollywood films could be said to have on the sales figures of US merchandise in the countries concerned. The films were deemed to be excellent advertising for the marketing of refrigerators, cars, foodstuffs, toys, fashion products and so on. The report on the Philippines, dated January 1948, states confidently that 'as in the United States, the appearance of merchandise in the movies stimulates a desire to possess it'.[9] However, most of the reports admitted that there was no reliable way of quantifying the impact of Hollywood's films on the sales of other commodities in the countries concerned. The point of this example, though, is that it draws attention to the fact that the US Government was not simply looking at ways of selling films and film equipment: the export of films is seen as having a multiplier effect on the sales of other US merchandise, even if there was no easy way of calculating it, and the sale of film equipment was seen as a way of preparing a local market, through the stimulation of local film production and exhibition, for all manner of US exports as well as for its films. This opens up a whole range of possible research projects into the 'real' profits accruing to US companies from the film industry as well as into the value of government subsidies to Hollywood. Instead of simply concentrating on tax credits and other financial measures or trade barriers within the US which channel public funds into the Hollywood companies, the public relations and market research functions performed by government agencies also need to be taken into account, not to mention the enormous sums devoted by cultural and educational institutions of all kinds to format the kinds of viewers and consumers required for Hollywood's products.

Moretti's third Law states that the compromise between locally produced cinematic narratives and the formal aspects of the Hollywood models is unstable. In fact, the compromise between local material and foreign form is, as far as cinema is concerned, not particularly unstable. It yields many films, some very lucrative in their domestic markets. The films may perhaps best be described as products of an industrial cinema from which the most obvious American socio-cultural dimensions have been stripped away. In the most depressing cases, these films try to emulate and compete with Hollywood's productions or at least try to gain access to the US market by seeking to conform to (often naive) ideas about how Hollywood films function. In the more interesting cases, the cinematic narrativization of local social experience bears the stamp of its encounter with the forces that shape and energize the industrialization of culture locally. How the difference between those alternatives can be read or assessed constitutes one of the challenges that a comparative theory of cinema will have to meet. Of all national cinemas, Hollywood displays the forms of industrialized culture most nakedly, perhaps because much of American culture has been shaped by the industrialization of US culture since the 1880s, with a second major 'formatting' wave in the 1920s and again in the mid-1970s and early 1980s (from the adoption of saturation release practices massively promoted on television to the synergistic growth of the video and music industries). In Hollywood, the fit between social experience and cultural forms is tightest, which also makes that cinema more difficult to decipher than films that adopt forms that fit less easily with the social experience they try to convey in industrialized forms.[10] And cinema, because of the capital-intensive aspects of its production, distribution and exhibition, is by necessity an industrialized cultural form. How types of industrial organization and development are expressed in cultural forms must thus also become one of comparative cinema's main concerns. What *is* unstable is then not the compromise between local material and foreign form, but between local material and the transformative power and impact of industrialization itself, which is never simply 'foreign'.

Moretti's fourth Law thus also needs to be reformulated if we are to avoid falling into the trap of equating American (Western) cultural forms with the forms generated by the industrialization of culture itself, that is to say, the forms generated by the encounter with capitalism. Hollywood's forms are generated by that encounter just as much as any other national cinemas. The formal aspects of, say, Thai or Indian or Chinese cinematic narratives are not (simply) to be measured against the way Hollywood does things. They are to be seen, just like the American cinema, as locally specific encounters with capitalism, rather than as simulations of the way that encounter turned out in the US. The problem is to sort out which of those local industrialized forms relate to the encounter with capitalism *by* and *within* the local formation, and which relate to an address or an imitation of the American models of industrial cinema. The currently hegemonic position of US capitalism, and thus of its cultural forms, should not blind us to the fact that, in the pre-World War II period, the cinemas of reference for the modernizers in many Asian and Latin American countries were the French, Soviet or German cinemas, not the American one. Indeed, French and to some extent Italian cinemas offered the templates of modernity for the US cinema itself prior to the First World War, as Richard Abel has shown in his analysis of Pathé's role in the US before 1914.[11]

The formal revolution Moretti has in mind does not come from the realization of any 'impossible programme' (Miyoshi's phrase) allegedly matching Western form to local experience, but from the elaboration of a form of expression appropriate to the local forms of content generated under the pressure of capitalism's drive towards the industrialization of culture. This is what is occulted in Moretti's first Law stating that 'when a culture starts moving towards the modern novel, it's *always* as a compromise between foreign (Western) form and local materials'.[12] No, it isn't. It is *always* as a compromise between local materials and capitalist modernization, and that is just as true in the West as it is elsewhere. Each culture moves towards modernity in its own way and at its own pace. Merely because the West has a longer history of doing so than many non-Western countries does not mean that that which non-Western narrative forms move towards is the particular compromise achieved in one particular Western country, however dominant it seems to be.[13] Of course, it is also possible that in some cases the Hollywood forms have been taken as the norm to be emulated, but this mainly applies to films made for export, that is to say, films expressly produced to try and reap profits in the US market. For the most part, when film makers extol the normative value of Hollywood films, they are merely using a convenient shorthand to refer to obscurely sensed aspects of those modern narrative forms generated by the industrialization of culture, a process that has formatted the West's cinemas for just over a century. In fact, what drives both Western and non-Western narrative forms equally is one and the same dynamic: capitalism's re-formatting of social relations, that is to say, modernization. But as the social relations being re-formatted differ from state to state and region to region, so must the cultural forms generated by the industrialization of culture differ among themselves. The differences are programmed by local histories, the similarities are produced by the encounter with the same socio-economic dynamic as much, if not more so, than by conscious imitation.

This conceptualization of the ways cultural production has of negotiating modernization thus opens the way towards tackling cinematic narration in a comparative framework: how does the encounter with capitalism generate specific cultural forms in particular geographical areas? That question can then be reformulated as: how and by which social sectors are factors operating in a local history[14] formulated to render the specifics of the fabric of social experience in that locality. The answer to that question requires a multi-layered analytical investigation animated by two foundational theories: a still-to-be-elaborated theory of semiosis capable of accounting for the connections between history and textuality, and one (at least one) theory of history as a process (for instance, historical materialism or, for short, Marxism, especially as revised in David Harvey's brilliant book, *The Limits to Capital*, first published in 1982).[15]

## The comparative question for cinema

When asking the comparative question in relation to cinema, a number of conceptual magnetic fields suggest themselves as areas for research, profiling the gateways to areas of investigation likely to produce an understanding of how and why particular cinematic forms (both of expression and of content) obtain at particular times in specified, more or less state-regulated zones of film production. The theoretical intuitions required as starting points for a comparative project are fairly easy to identify. Much of the work has been done already and the main initial work is to elaborate new sets of connections between aspects of familiar theoretical paradigms.

For the required theory of history, I have already pointed to the Marx–Harvey nexus as a good starting point, probably to be complemented by the economic histories of Giovanni Arrighi and Robert Brenner as well as that of the Regulation School of economic analysts and the historians who, following the likes of Fernand Braudel, D. D. Kosambi and Romila Thapar, take such analyses seriously into consideration when producing histories of specific social formations.

As for the required theory or, more likely, theories of signification, the issue is perhaps a little more contentious. Firstly, there is no need to embark on a critique of reflection theory as the assumed direct mirroring of text and context has been discredited decades ago by the Russian and Czech formalists. What does need to be addressed is a fairly basic critique of the notion that representation involves a substitutive relationship in which one thing stands for another.[16] A return to aspects of C. S. Peirce's work, first put on the agenda by Peter Wollen in the late 1960s, provides a useful way forward. We have to begin by abandoning the prevailing misreading of Peirce's work which alleges that he identified three different types of sign: the index, the icon and the symbol. Instead, we have to understand Peirce as talking about the three dimensions present in any given sign (but present in differing hierarchies of prominence). Then the door opens towards a type of textual analysis that can treat signs as partly representational (through their iconic and symbolic dimensions) and partly non-representational (in their indexical dimension). The latter does not involve a substitutive relation, but one of expressive contingency, profiling an ontological connection between sign and referent. A first theoretical exercise then suggests itself: identify the three dimensions of any given film image by specifying the indexical, iconic and symbolic relations at work in the image.

The second theoretical domain to be mined in the Comp Cinema Project is Louis Hjelmslev's set of distinctions as reformulated by Christian Metz: the distinctions between matter, substance and form of both expression and content, constituting six further dimensions.[17] Particularly the distinctions between the substance and the form of expression and of content appear to hold great promise for the comparative project at this stage, especially in the light of Roland Barthes' identification of the cultural codes (substances of content) as one of the five codes structuring narration.[18] The combination of Peirce and Hjelmslev, spiced up with Barthes, then allows us to explore the iconic, indexical and symbolic dimensions of the substances and forms of expression and content of a given film text. Of course, such a bricolaged combination of elements from different theoretical configurations is open to all manner of objections connected with the particular selection of theoretical tools from each framework. For example, to ignore Peirce's notion of the interpretant as a defining element of the sign while retaining his identification of three dimensions of signs may be seen as an unwarranted truncation of Peirce's semiotic theory. On the other hand, I see no particular need for fidelity at this stage since my aim is not to argue for a Peircean way into the problems posed by a comparative approach to film studies. I do not need to accommodate Peirce's notion of the interpretant because this would lead me to the verbal, dictionary definitions of semantic units that are a defining aspects of signs. The need to take Peirce's interpretant into account may come back when the question of inner speech is raised as a dimension of signification, that is to say, when the thought processes that accompany the orchestration of discursive functions as described by Jakobson have to be considered in relation to primarily non-verbal signs.[19] The relevance of particular interpretants will then depend on the modulations of the process of address according to the activation of what Jakobson identifies as the metalinguistic function. Peirce's interpretant operates as an element of a (linguistic) code interacting with what Barthes called the cultural codes and which, together, constitute the metalinguistic dimension of a text or a textual fragment (such as a sequence in a film).

There are also other difficulties which need to be addressed in greater detail if the route advocated here is to become practicable. One of the main issues in this respect is the fact that a film's form of expression is itself an exceedingly complex composite amalgam of different forms: the film's commodity form—which changes, along with a number of its expressive codifications, when a film made in 35mm is circulated on 16mm or on video—the musical, spoken and written linguistic forms, the recorded noise patterns, and so forth.

In this context a rough example, illustrating what my proposed bricolage might mean, will have to suffice. The *indexical dimension of a cinematic narrative's form of expression* would be determined by the available technology deployed in the making of the film (indexing a particular kind of industrial organization, division of labour and investment flows). In this respect, an identification of the lenses used, the type of camera used, the film stock, lighting equipment, studio facilities, printing techniques, colour process, special effects and so on, would all combine to index a particular kind of industrial organization of production in terms of the value tied up in the machinery deployed. The indexical dimension of technologies also points to the need to distinguish between, for instance, the role and possible structuring impact of different kinds of capital: constant (equipment and raw materials) or variable (labour power), circulating (raw materials and labour power) or fixed (plant), not forgetting the importance of fictional capital (land, of course, but also the potential values constituted by dime novels, newspaper items, old novels and plays, songs and so on, which often acquire value only after having been transformed into the raw material of a script or story outline, at which time these items are transformed and fenced into private property domains liable to yield monopoly rents).

On the other hand, the use of sound in Ridley Scott's *Gladiator* (2000) and in numerous other Hollywood productions may, as *the iconic dimension of the form of expression*, alert us to the analogy with the use of music in the retail trade, as in boutiques and fashion shops, whereas the older convention of discreet background music would iconically evoke muzak in elevators and waiting rooms. This iconic dimension of the form of expression could further signal, at *the indexical level of the substance of content*, the industrial psychology work that led to the widespread adoption of such silence-killing devices and to the manipulative public relations ideology underpinning such research. An example, for instance, would be to research the approach to music manifested in the cue-sheets and scores for silent films and to examine whether this changed (as I think it probably did) with the development of industrial psychology and the spread of public relations strategies as manifested in initiatives such as the BBC's music-while-you-work programmes in World War II.

*The iconic dimension of a film's form of content* may alert us to the analogy between, say, the narrative structure of Robert Altman's *Short Cuts* (1993) and a television programme such as *Hill Street Blues* (1981–7) as well as the design of shopping malls catering for a range of niche audiences or shoppers. In other words, we not only need to learn to identify the iconic, indexical and symbolic dimensions of substances and forms of content and expression, we also need to consider the probable connections between these various dimensions as they interact within the same text.

The combination of Peirce and Hjelmslev thus offers a way of envisaging a film's relation to economic structures, the range and type of technologies available, the circulation of different types of capital involved, the ideological configurations that must be in place for these particular forms and substances to be able to structure the filmic narrative, and so on. In short, different aspects of the text acquire, through their expressive-indexical dimension, value for something that could be called a forensic or an archaeological reading. In addition, such a reading would be able to identify the longer-term social dynamics which overdetermine the kinds of shifts and mutations chronicled, for instance, as formal renewals in the writings of Roman Jakobson and Yuri Tynianov on the evolution of literary—or cinematic—styles. In this context, the detailed research conducted by David Bordwell and his colleagues on the so-called classic American cinema could also provide useful clues.

A third theoretical domain to be taken into account is Roman Jakobson's identification of six functions of discourse, especially if enhanced by Emile Benveniste's distinction between *histoire* and discourse. This conjunction offers a most useful way into the analysis of modes of address. Jakobson's work appears to be capable of suggesting how the conjunction between Hjelmslev's and Peirce's dimensions of discourse can be orchestrated into a textual fabric organized around intricate shifts of emphases among six overlapping axes of address. Moreover, in the analysis of shifts and reverberations between functions of discourse, Peirce's three and Hjelmslev's six additional dimensions of textuality is likely to yield an insight into the way meanings can migrate from, say, an indexical dimension at the level of the form of expression to an iconic dimension at the level of the substance of content or an iconic dimension at the level of the form of content. In other words, the analysis may begin to show how the representational aspects of a text may be conditioned by their non-representational aspects, and how regimes of address orchestrate (energize and regulate) the dynamics at work in the textual fabrics. This is why I would like to suggest that, at this initial stage of the project, the most productive way into the problems of comparative cinema studies is by way of an analysis of a text's mode of address. The subject positions thus identified would then, in the light of a forensic reading, be mapped (analogically, indexically or symbolically) on to the actual social subject positions (interest groups) in contention in the social formation that presided over the formulation of the text in question, a procedure that would be able to place the text as a 'field' dramatizing the tensions between historically attestable positions occupied by different interest groups and to ascertain the vectorial impetus underpinning the text. In other words, such a reading would be capable of identifying from which historical position the text is primarily (never exclusively) enounced and in which direction, towards what kind of society, the text seeks to pull or push the addressee.

This brings me to the fourth theoretical constellation that has to be mapped into the field of comparative film studies: Freud's identification of four processes of distortion in the dream work, seen through the prism of Walter Benjamin's notion of fantasy. It may be useful to quote from Benjamin at some length at this stage. Noting that Marx had already dismissed the idea that conditions of life were reflected in ideologies, Benjamin wrote in his notes for the unfinished *Arcades Project* that:

> The economic conditions under which society exists are expressed in the superstructure—precisely as, with the sleeper, an overfull stomach finds not its reflection but its expression in the contents of dreams, which, from a causal point of view, it may be said to 'condition.' The collective, from the first, expresses the conditions of its life. These find their expression in the dream and their interpretation in the awakening.[20]

This is also the context within which Benjamin developed his theory of dialectical images:

> It is said that the dialectical method consists in doing justice each time to the concrete historical situation of its object. But that is not enough. For it is just as much a matter of doing justice to the concrete historical situation of the *interest* taken in the object. And *this* situation is always so constituted that the interest is itself performed in that object and, above all, feels this object concretized in itself and upraised from its former being into the higher concretion of now-being [*Jetztsein*] (waking being!).[21]

A little later, after quoting a passage from Marx on the way individual machines merge in the production process into a collective machine capable of continuous production, Benjamin wrote: 'Film: unfolding […] of all the forms of perception, the tempos and rhythms, which lie preformed in today's machines, such that all problems of contemporary art find their definitive formulation only in the context of film.'[22]

That film texts relate in some way to the historical dynamics which preside over their production has been commonly intuited for many decades. That they do so primarily by virtue of the indexical aspect of the formation of their substance of expression is a hypothesis worth pursuing, as is the certainty that the translation from the real to the text, whether expressively or representationally, must be subject to the four distortion processes identified by Freud as being responsible for structuring fantasy and dream texts.

One of the consequences of adopting that hypothesis is that it becomes possible to differentiate between two distinct, though related, levels in texts where fantasy processes are at work. At the level of *the substance of content*, a menu of culturally determined fantasy scenarios—ideological paradigms of a sort—exert pressure on the way networks of ideas are knitted together into secondarily elaborated ideological or philosophical frameworks or semantic fields underpinning the orchestration of a particular 'form': the particular version of the fantasy performed by/in the text. At the level of a text's *substance of expression*, it is the way the physico-sensoral aspects of cinematic signification are transformed into menus of expressive procedures (such as the recourse to special effects emphasizing iconicity over indexicality or expanding the range of possible actorial gestuality by means of stunt doubles or suspending actors on wires, using digital editing and amplified soundtracks) which constitute a substance of expression that, by virtue of its very selective aspect, vehiculates another kind of fantasy scenario. For instance, a techno-fetishistic fantasy relating to a desirable corporate-industrial organization of film production may thus come to 'double' the oedipal scenarios at work in the narrative of a film such as the Wachowski brothers' *The Matrix* (1999). Going one step further, it is probable that it is the relation between these two distinct levels of fantasy embedded in, respectively, the substances of expression and content, which accounts for whether a film 'clicks' with a contemporary audience or not. On the other hand, historical changes (cultural shifts or changes in personal maturation) might highlight alignments or discrepancies between these two levels which remained unnoticed by contemporary audiences targeted by a given film's marketing strategies. In this respect, reviews, if read symptomatically, often contain a kind of *plumpes Denken* (Brecht's phrase for rough-and-ready thinking) commentary on whether the two fantasy orchestrations are deemed to be in the proper alignment for a given economically significant consumer group.

Peter Wollen, who was the first to draw film theory's attention to Peirce and Hjelmslev in his pioneering *Signs and Meaning in the Cinema*, first published in 1969, identified a telling example of this kind of *plumpes Denken* in an essay on 'Architecture and Film' reprinted in his book *Paris Hollywood*. He notes how studies of film architecture seem to gravitate unreflectively towards the small group of films which feature architecture as 'star'. Focussing particularly on Dietrich Neumann's book *Film Architecture* (1996), Wollen quizzically comments that

> what comes across from Neumann's selection of great 'film architecture' is that it is clustered in the genres of dystopian science fiction, horror and crazy comedy. Architecture as star represents criminal lunacy, pathetic farce or untrammelled despotism. With this in mind, it seems strange that architects themselves should be attracted by this vision of their art, even if it makes them the centre of attention![24]

The apparent contradiction relates to the discrepancies between two layers of fantasy at work in the films concerned. The fantasy generated at the level of the substance of expression stimulates the positive appreciation of the architectural designs; the fantasy underpinning the formatting of the substance of content does indeed suggest criminal lunacy, pathetic farce or untrammelled despotism. The former fantasy layer, because it is anchored in the substance of expression, makes a 'positive appreciation' possible through its implication in the economic aspects of film production. The bulk of the films singled out where architecture features as a star (*Metropolis* (1927), *L'Inhumaine* (1924), *Aelita* (1924), *Just Imagine* (1930), *Things To Come* (1936), *Lost Horizon* (1937), *The Fountainhead* (1949), *Blade Runner* (1982), *Batman* (1989), *Dick Tracy* (1990) and so on) are all very expensive productions mobilizing the industry's resources to showcase 'what cinema can do' when it embarks on prestige projects designed to make loads of profit (even if this intention is not always realized on the films' release). These films constitute a celebration of the film industry's corporate financial as well as cultural power, even if, at another level in the text, such power is presented as problematic.

At the level of the substance of expression, it is what might be described as the film industry's own criminal lunacy (its spectacular displays of corporate power deploying massive resources, mostly acquired by fraud, sharp practice and unfettered greed), pathetic farce (evident from just about any account of the production of 'big' films) or untrammelled despotism (by factory bosses, financiers, bureaucrats and their representatives on the studio floor and, in aspirational forms, by the way film-makers address viewers) that are being celebrated by way of the spectacle starring architecture. From the industry's point of view, all these things are positive features of the great achievements of the culture industries and operate to the greater glory of the hegemons controlling the industry's resources. Hence the prominence given to the quantity of resources used in the marketing of such films. Architects such as Neumann simply disregard the substance of content fantasies (which betray a populist ideological strategy) and appreciate, perhaps intuitively, the role allocated to architectural design in the 'real' display of corporate power underpinning the populist rhetoric decrying corporate rule. In that respect, Neumann's celebration of films starring architectural design is similar to the corporate support extended to, for instance, Reaganite rhetoric against 'big government': Reagan's backers and those hoping to profit from his election realized that the populist rhetoric merely masked a drive to increase corporate power and even bigger government. They were not shooting themselves in the foot by backing him. Quite the contrary. Similarly, Neumann was right, in a *plumpes Denken* kind of way, to intuit that regardless of the populist rhetoric deployed against corporate power by the 'star architecture' films, these were, in fact, celebrations of corporate power at the level of the 'indexing' and display of the expressive resources so spectacularly on show. In these films, the two levels of fantasy operate simultaneously but are, from one point of view (Wollen's), somewhat out of ideological alignment. However, from another point of view (Neumann's), the fantasies conveyed through the way the industry's self-celebratory image is indexically encrusted into its substance of expression, easily outweigh any importance one might attach to the 'surface rhetoric' bad-mouthing the totalitarian aspects of the very untrammelled, despotic corporate power shamelessly spectacularized by the industry itself. These films celebrate the power, both cultural and financial, of the industries that produced them, in the same way that Vicente Minnelli's *An American in Paris* (1951) or Cecil B. De Mille's *Cleopatra* (1934) celebrate the resources at Hollywood's disposal, or as Ridley Scott's *Blade Runner* (1982) and Verhoeven's *Robocop* (1987) celebrate the triumph of corporate America simply by signalling, at the level of the expressive means deployed to make the film, that if you like *that* kind of cinema which so ostentatiously relies on the central control of masses of labour power and gigantic quantities of dead labour, you cannot object to the kind of social relations that must be in place to make it.

Similarly, most disaster movies and post-apocalypse movies celebrate, in the very display of productive resources that constitutes the 'spectacle', the kind of organization of social relations that is on course to create the joyous spectacle of global mayhem. 'Blockbusters' and the mainstreaming of exploitation cinema as a business strategy (as opposed to the occasional 'epic' celebrating the joys of monopoly production) not only signify the rule of finance capital over the film industry: they also demand that we, the viewers, take delight in finance capital's utopias. The films acknowledge that there may be some rotten apples in the barrel of finance capital, but the decent chaps have our interests at heart. The kind of social organization of labour that can bring us Cameron's *Titanic* (1997) or Michael Bay's *Armageddon* (1998) and even sell us wars (as in Spielberg's *Saving Private Ryan*, 1998) may have its flaws, but isn't it hugely beneficent and worthy of support? Films do indeed speak with a forked tongue, and, as Peter Wollen is probably the first to realize—remembering his arguments in appreciation of the formal(ist) qualities of Orson

Welles' *Citizen Kane* (1941)—fantasies inscribed at the level of substance and form of expression often speak louder than apparent story contents, the latter so often given false prominence in plot synopses and film journalism.

It now falls to the new discipline of comparative film studies to begin to explore, more systematically, how social-historical dynamics impact upon and can be read from films. Such a reading has to proceed with forensic care, paying attention to the ways in which, in different geo-cultural regions, films orchestrate their modes of address, the relations between the indexical, iconic and symbolic dimensions of substances and forms of content and expression, paying due attention to the co-presence of a dual fantasy structure vehiculated by that network of signifying relations. The programme of work is vast and must be done, and discussed, transnationally if it is to make any significant headway.

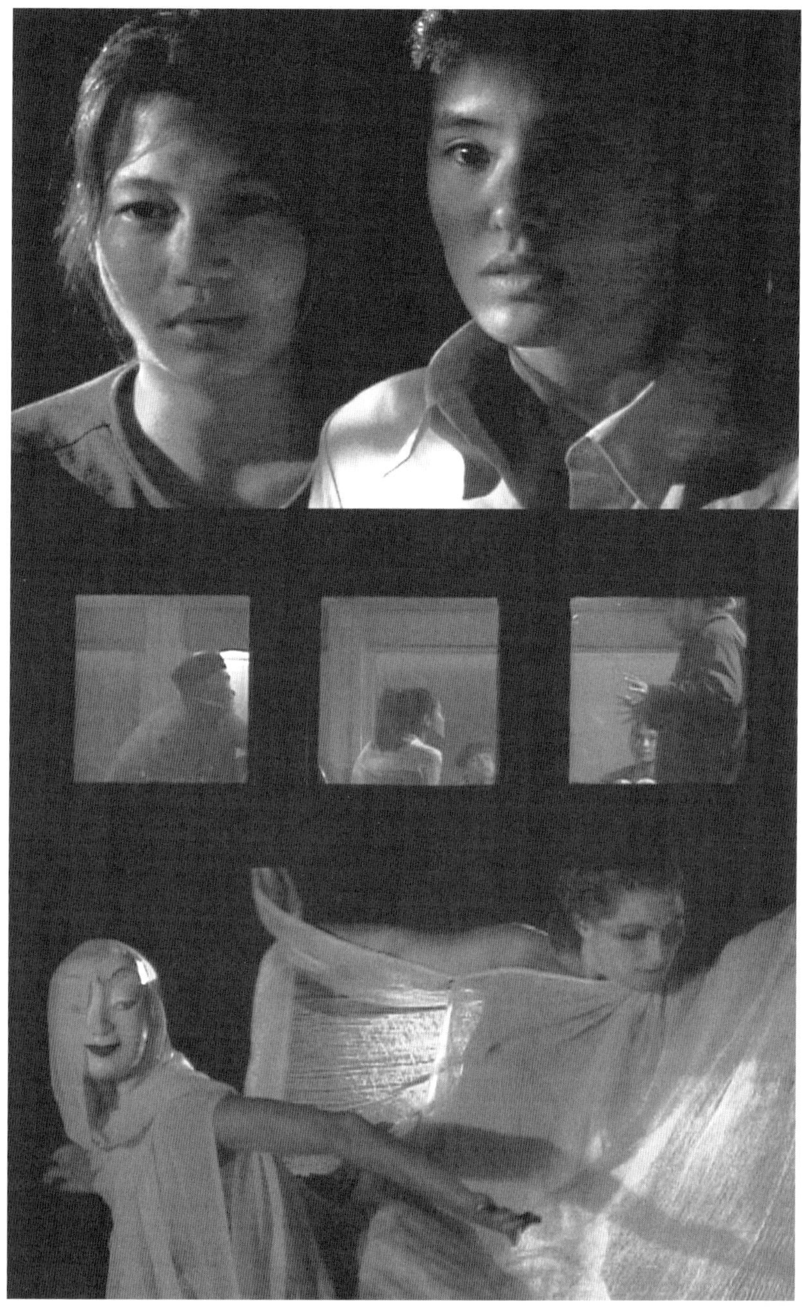

6.1–6.7   Trin T. Minh-ha and Jean-Paul Bourdier, *Night Passage* (2005), ©
Moongift Films.

6

# *NIGHT PASSAGE*
## The Depth of Time

*Trinh T. Minh-ha interviewed by Alison Rowley*

### Somewhere from the middle

*Alison Rowley:*   I have been reading *Milky Way Railroad* by Kenji Miyazawa, which was written in 1927, because I was curious about why you chose this novel as a starting point for your digital film *Night Passage*. In the introduction to the English translation of the book I read that Miyazawa was Japan's best-loved children's writer, as well as one of its three great modern poets. He was a chemist and government agricultural agent, and also worked as a school-teacher. Although he was well known in Tokyo's literary circles, he lived hundreds of miles away from the capital in the isolated province of Iwate in the North of the country, and that while he was knowledgeable about most branches of modern science he also searched for a belief system that would accommodate the religious teachings of both Buddhism and Christianity. Miyazawa was born in 1896 and died in 1933 so his life and work coincide with the high point of Western modernity. They also, it seems to me, correspond with the observations you made about contemporary Japan in *The Fourth Dimension*. The film attends to the encounter between the rituals of traditional culture as they persist today in the everyday life of the country, and sophisticated new technologies of communication and representation, which are structured by their own ritual forms. In *The Fourth Dimension* and in *Night Passage* the train is, quite literally, the narrative vehicle of the films. In *The Fourth Dimension* it travels between past and present, in *Night Passage* the journey takes place between life and death. There is a moment in *The Fourth Dimension* when we see a young woman asleep on a modern Japanese train. Does she dream the story of *Night Passage?* This is a way of asking: are the two films companion pieces? How do you understand the relationship between them?

*Trinh T. Minh-ha:*    Great questions that need no answer after all. You have somehow situated this entire film within an image sequence of another film and linked it to the sleep state of a woman in the train. What a wonderful way to connect *Night Passage* with a previous film of mine and to see them in relation as a dream within another dream. As viewers, one often forgets that each film, each image has its own history and trajectory.

We have to begin somewhere, so it's normal that you start with Miyazawa. The information you gave could be helpful to the reader unfamiliar with the name, which is often the case when the latter is from the non-Western world. But although I am not indifferent to biographical details of his life, they are of limited use here. I would rather begin somewhere in the middle: with the spirit of his work, which was how I met him on the page, and with what I retained from the book, *Milky Way Railroad* or *Night Train to the Stars*. The relation that *Night Passage* maintains toward this book is that of inspiration—and not of illustration, imitation, description or realist rendition.

In other words, viewers need not read Miyazawa to enter the film. The question of 'source' or 'influence' is of little relevance, for what compels me to make the film after having read his book is not its mere content—the story, the message or the information—although these have a role and are quite wonderful in his case. It is rather the sparks generated by our encounter, the freedom, and the insight for new possibilities that the book opens up to. As one of the vehicles of the life-and-death passage—the others being for example, the bicycle, the boat and the ship—the train runs at the core of his voyage, not as one that begins and ends the story, but as one that gives access to the Milky Way and allows its passengers to rediscover, at each stop, the queerness of human desire and yearning.

Life is not explicable when it is lived intensely, with magical freshness. What I kept of Miyazawa in *Night Passage* were: spirit, structural forces, and field of action. His story has no development, so to speak. Broadly speaking, it is composed of an opening and a closure, and in between the two, a space of free-flow happenings and encounters. It was the freedom provided by such a framework that appealed to me initially. In coming up with a night train of my own, the only traces of his that I retain in the film can be found in its beginning and ending, and in some incidences on the train. The rest, the middle, is where the ride to an elsewhere happens and where everything comes alive in the journey. The train appears in the middle of Miyazawa's story and it is from this middle that possibilities abound.

As in ancient Asian praxes, practising the Middle Way does not mean being halfway. No compromise, indecision or non-commitment is implied here. On the contrary, middle is where there's no duality, no leaning on one side or the other, hence no foreclosures due to barriers. The form that emerges is like the moon of realization: empty in its fullness, with neither beginning nor end. Deleuze and Guattari picked up a grain of Zen and became very attuned to this particle of the East when they recalled how Eastern arts always grew

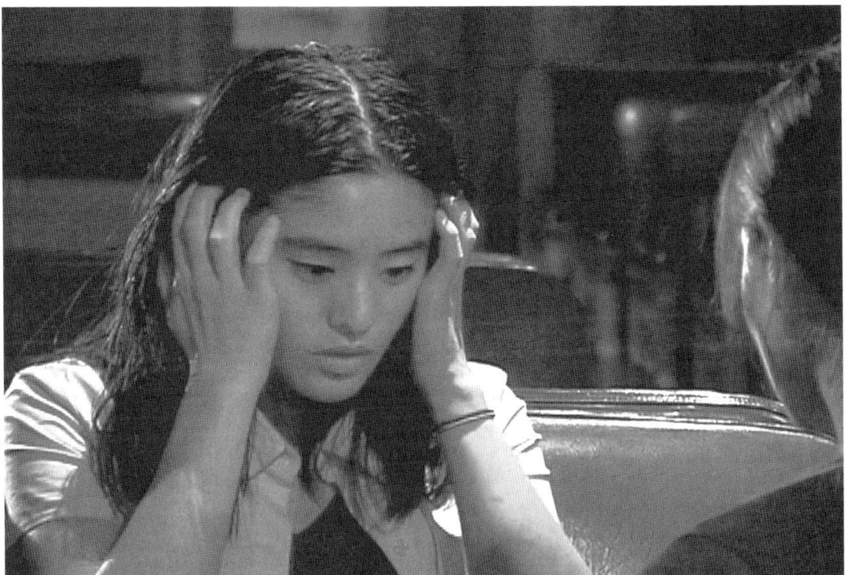

from the middle and urged us to start again from the middle—so as to work with new relations of speed and slowness, thereby enabling new possibilities of assemblages.

Inter, between, midway: what comes to our senses is always on the go, already in motion. Each scene, each sequence could be an autonomous gesture with a centre of its own. Story and plot are minimally retained only to set free the field of affects. We may use them as a way to 'humanize' a larger-than-life event, reducing it to the size of our mouth so that we can digest and regurgitate in putting it to words.

For me, the term 'dream' in its normative sense is not quite adequate when applied to the different passages at work in *Night Passage*. Night travellers and film face infinity with the multiplicity of comings and goings offered in the middle. Rather than leading from one point to another, passages are middles: intervals within intervals, since life itself is an interval between birth and death, and each life is an interval within numerous other lives.

This is all in response to your situating *Night Passage* somewhere in the middle of my film body's trajectory—already in motion in *The Fourth Dimension*. We can even travel further in time, in and out of the digital realm, if we return, let's say, to the sonic plane of the train in yet another fiction film of mine, *A Tale of Love*.

## Cinematic, industrial, digital

*Rowley:*    Trains, and the idea of the magical journey, figure at the very beginning of cinema's existence. The famous sequence of a train pulling into a station made by the Lumière brothers, shown in 1895, and George Méliès' fantasy *Le voyage à travers l'Impossible* (1902), initiate the two dominant strands in cinema history, the documentary and the fiction film. For me a sense of the nineteenth-century industrial technological revolution pervades *Night Passage*. To take just one instance of many: at the 'Word and Sound Station' the three travellers enter a corridor that reminds me of the organization of cabins on an ocean liner. A door leads them down a metal staircase into the bowels of what could be a ship's engine room. A sound, the subtle transmutation of the train's horn into a ship's Klaxon, strengthens the association. Or again at another point in the film the travellers push a trolley through what looks like a gallery in an underground mine into what turns out to be a sculptor's work-shop. And the sculptor, working in welded metal, acknowledges a debt to constructivism. Thus are linked the ideas of industrial technology, revolution and art. At the same time *Night Passage* is a profound engagement with the possibilities of twenty-first-century digital technology. There is a poetic synchrony between these two historical moments of great change in our experience and understanding of relations between time and space as they have been, and continue to be, inscribed in cinematic practice. This is a compelling aspect of the film for me, and I am reminded of Philip Rosen's project in his book *Change Mummified* to examine relations between cinema and the category of history as it crystallized in the West in the nineteenth century along with fully developed industrial capitalism.[1] Is this an idea you set out to explore in the film?

*Trinh:* The time factor, the shifts in perception, as well as the simultaneous engagement with both phases of technology are very adequately captured in the examples you gave. I spoke at some length, in *The Digital Film Event*, about this relation between the mechanical and the digital as two major historical moments of change that inform and are determined by our imaging practices. I was invoking the former not only through Lumière and Méliès, but also through Eisenstein and Vertov. The link between technology, art and revolution became more manifest in time. As a Russian painter (Kasimir Malevich) remarked almost a century ago, the revolution in the arts via movements such as cubism and futurism foreshadowed the revolution in politics and economics.

In the scene with the sculptor, Joe Slusky who performs himself and improvises while addressing his own work, speaks of colour and form in terms of touch and 'automotive paint'; a fluid 'beyond flesh and bones'; or else, an 'urban undersea with all this kind of blue'. He talks about the *unknown* being 'the whole trip', about 'finding these structures going upriver, excavating' whatever drives them, and then going back again and again to see what else can be 'unloosed'. He summarizes his welding work in two words: breath and oxidation. Breath cutting through metal.

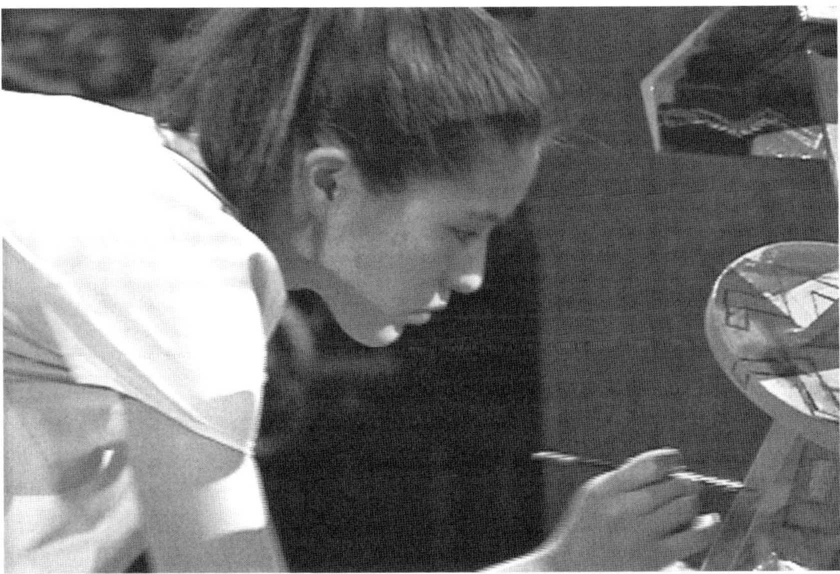

Technics and spirit brought alive. Tactility, motility and liquidity in the field of light and matter. Viewed in the context of *Night Passage*, such an improvisation is quite perfect—a qualification that couldn't be farther from Joe's mind, for he had then no idea how it could affect the film. It was not easy to go on rambling in front of a camera, but with him, every take was unique, and we only did two takes of that scene because we realized Joe couldn't repeat himself. These are the kind of quirky monologues that effortlessly unfurl while he's at work. Having often listened and laughed with them, we decided—Jean-Paul (Bourdier, the co-director) and I—to ask Joe to do just that on camera. This was how we worked with a number of artists in the film. The scene with the two Black scientists and experts in technology was initially conceived with a similar spirit. These largely unscripted or at times self-scripted interventions constitute the documentary parts of *Night Passage*.

Joe's spiel on his art trips gives us a glimpse of how the unknown lies at the core of revolution. Far from being preset, reality and events manifest themselves in a state of constant adaptation and growth. While showing the industrial and the mechanical via digital performativity, the film features technology's mediation in a spiritual passage of life–death transmutation. Your putting to question the category of history as it crystallized in the West—and I would add the category of visibility to it—is here very relevant. This regime of imposed linear time and chronology has not only given rise to unremitting divisions between official and non-official historicist narratives; it also invites us to indulge in the delusion that *knowing all* there is to know— where we're going and what, how or even when the end will be—is all there is to life.

Depending on how we live it, our relation to speed or time-space and knowledge, as well as to memory and anti-memory could free or deeply enslave us.

### Cinema screen, strip of celluloid and electronic train windows

*Rowley:* The opening sequence of *Night Passage*, before the title appears on the screen, is a stunningly economic condensation—which makes it incredibly beautiful—of the idea of cinema as a form of what Rosen calls modern historicity. The reduction of the three dimensionality of the railway carriage to the dense black two-dimensional matting of a row of illuminated windows recalls a flat strip of celluloid, the traditional base material of cinema itself. The camera's track along the length of the carriage demonstrates in slow motion the old linear animating mechanism, the persistence of vision at twenty-four frames a second. When the camera stops tracking for a moment it zooms in to the brightly lit squares of window to focus on the illusion produced by the mechanical operations of camera shutter and projector gate, namely the illusion of life in depth, which at the same time is merely a projection and the windows a cinema screen in the darkness of the auditorium. In addition we know that the moving images we are watching are not mechanical at all but electronically produced with digital technology. Visually there is a lot going on in a very short sequence.

*Trinh:* Yes. The responses I got from a number of viewers on this very opening sequence was, further, that somehow the row of windows reminded them more of those of a ship than those of a train. I was quite astounded when I first heard that comment, because I did try at one stage while editing the film to give the feeling of a train running on water.

An after-effect of that intention may still linger on, perhaps in the way motion and movements come through to the viewer in this one-minute sequence. At work is a net of fluid, spatial movements that can be quite difficult to rationalize: these are the horizontal move of the series of windows across the screen surface, followed by the vertical move into or slow close-up on these windows, or the gradual closing-in of the camera lens (with reversely, the small details growing larger)—what one can call the visible time courses of a virtual depth.

Aside from introducing the viewer to the visual core of both the story in the film and digital imaging itself, as you have so accurately described, what this short sequence potentially invites the viewer to do, right from the start of the film, is to come into the world of sonic imaging otherwise than through the binary of form and content, or of physical and virtual reality. Disappearance is made tangible with appearance, and the unseen, see-able in what is shown. ('What are they looking at?' is a question inscribed in the images of that sequence as well as along the entire film.) There are many ways to enter cinema and our responses here are only two examples. Experiencing the forces that drive the film—its undercurrents, movements, frequencies, dynamisms, modulations, tonalities and rhythms, for example—certainly leads us to a wealth of possibilities in reception that make conventional interpretation of meaning, theme, character and storyline quite stale and reductive.

## Going into darkness

*Rowley:*   The sound in the opening sequence has a particular resonance for me. There is the echoing blast of the train horn, some bars of saxophone music. When the title of the film appears and the text divides to give depth to the screen, there is a sound like a birdcall, followed by the distinct hoot of an owl. I was reminded at this point of Tracey Moffatt's treatment of the title of her film *Night Cries*, in which the text is accompanied by an ambiguous sound. Is it a cry of distress, human or animal, or the wheels of an abruptly breaking train on its rails? It is impossible to tell which. Moffatt plays on the B-movie, gothic horror tradition of sound and graphics for her effect. Her sound evokes nightmare, yours dream, so really they are very different in tone and meaning. I think, however, there are important links to be made between the two films around the figure of the train. In both it is associated with escape from the hardships and unhappiness of daily life, with the suddenness of death, and crucially the vehicle is a signifier of nineteenth-century expansion. The final act of colonizing, imperial capitalism in the Australian outback is played out in all its complexity between two women, the indigenous Australian and the white settler in Moffatt's 'Rural Tragedy'—the film's subtitle. In *Night Passage* 'The Men of the Night', the two storytellers, the African American and the Irish American are reminders of earlier phases of violent colonial, economic expansion. The young travellers from the West Coast of America embody its contemporary realities.

*Trinh:*   I like the association with Moffatt's work, and your suggestion of a sonic fabric that connotes an earlier phase of colonization is fascinating. The example of the storytellers on the train is certainly indicative of such a context of power relations, although I was working here more explicitly with the question of Voice—which is what I also see as crucial in Moffatt's *Night Cries*. A couple of viewers also said that the film's journey brings to mind Conrad's *Heart of Darkness*, especially as it led them to the scene with the young women paddling along the river and being lit up by the spectacle of fire dancers. But frankly, Conrad has never come to my mind—neither in my writings nor in my films—and neither does Moffatt's work in *Night Passage*, although it is much closer to my heart.

Perhaps in relation to these associations, I can discuss the element of darkness. One of the passages of the film repeatedly invoked and quoted by several crew members as well as by some film reviewers is when one of the men of the night, the Irish storyteller, calls to the two main characters as they head out of the train: 'Remember the rules of night passage. Don't stop in the dark or you'll be lost. Move to the rhythm of your senses. Go where the road is alive.'

I am reminded here of a famous Zen *koan* that tells about an event between a master, Ryukan, and a freedom searcher, Tokusan. The searcher had travelled from afar to study with the master. One night, as he was working with the master far into the night, the latter noted that it was getting late and told him to retire. As Tokusan lifted up the door curtain to leave, he turned back to Ryukan, saying, 'It's dark outside.' The master lit a candle and handed it to him, but as the searcher was about to take it, the master blew it out. At this, Tokusan suddenly had a deep realization and made a bow. There's much more to this simple and rich story, but I'll stop here to dwell on what leads me to it: travel and darkness.

We each have our darkness. Where's *yours*? What would you encounter and who would appear on your night train? In my 'vision researches', I have time and again tried to function without my heavily corrective glasses, and for me, if myopia proves to be initially an acute form of darkness, it also turns out at times to be an unexpected form of light. Not only did I realize the capacities with which I could still function, but also I was able to see certain things I couldn't with my glasses on. For many of us, our everyday is our darkness. What our peers do to us (making of us a laughing stock for example, as with Kyra in the film) and what we do to them in revenge; our moments of cruelty and inhumanity; our colonial quest, our warring instincts or blind pursuit for what ends up sapping our vitality as well as our sense of freedom; these are the facets of daily life we can't escape and are bound to walk into as darkness meets us.

In other words, how do we travel? How does the world come to us? Through which window (hearing, touch, taste, sight or smell, for example)? And by what light in the night? These are structural questions in *Night Passage* that also fare as some of the undercurrents in my other films. Going into the dark anew with each film, stepping into the world, entering the known unknowingly have allowed me to actualize capacities of mine I was not aware of. Even though I didn't recognize them at first, they were always there, awaiting the ripe moment to manifest or disappear. These 'flashes' from 'the river under the river' are so many light bulbs that switch on by themselves to sustain our creative practices. Darkness has no beginning nor ending. But there, where the night seems darkest is also where we are most likely to light up and where the road becomes alive as we trust the rhythm of our senses. 'I am the light!' says a laughing traveller of the dark, with the fire literally burning on top of his head in the film.

Miyazawa's darkness is very different in tonality from the one explored by the young women in the film. His train flight leads his male protagonists to the starry sky or to the Silver River (the Japanese term for the Milky Way) above, whereas the ride in *Night Passage* leads rather to the River of golden light below, further into the depths of earthen water. This is where the drama of dying and drowning unfolds in the twin and multiple dances of bodies coupling, struggling and irresistibly being lured into dark waters. Ultimately, everything is bound in the journey to *dissolve* (as digital technology makes it all too easy for our belief-images to fade in and out of sight). It is by riding, walking and paddling into loss, betrayal and mortality that Kyra, the main character, merges into light—her own—at the close of the film.

The deeper the shadow, the brighter the light. One cannot fully rise unless one goes far down into the substance of the dark. The downward–upward movements of consciousness meet in freedom. In an interview with Woody Allen, which Jean-Luc Godard captured in his film *Meetin' W. A.*, there's a very insightful moment when they discuss darkness. The differences between these two men of fame became most telling when upon hearing Godard mention the freedom to go into the dark and to come out from it, or to go into the dark to find light, Allen asked if Godard meant 'to go to the cinema', to which Godard answered, 'no, to make film'. For Allen, going to the cinema is going to the movie theatre, which is most enjoyable because 'light is always disappointing' and darkness offers him 'a place to escape to'. Similarly, when asked about the editing of his films, his response was that the editing room 'is not cold'.

Although his answers are quite genuine, it seems to me that Allen is primarily an actor, and that he enjoys tremendously internalizing the role of the everyday man—even and especially when he is not supposed 'to act' with the interview format. He speaks of film from the consumer's rather than from the maker's point of view, and for him, darkness connotes physical comfort as in a sleep that promises only refuge and rosy dream. Escape, rather than freedom. This could account for the fact that, despite his vehement swearing to normality, his fans attribute his very effective portrayal of daytime neuroticism to his personality rather than to his acted character. Night-time is stabilized and reductively conceived as being opposite to daytime, and the cinema that results from such a binary has been the endearing staple of mainstream productions.

## The body and technology

*Rowley:* In 'Time Paths', the lecture you presented for CentreCATH at the University of Leeds in 2005, as part of its research theme *The Ethics and Politics of Virtuality and Indexicality*, you spoke of the implications of the move from analogical to digital technology for your work of imaging and sound

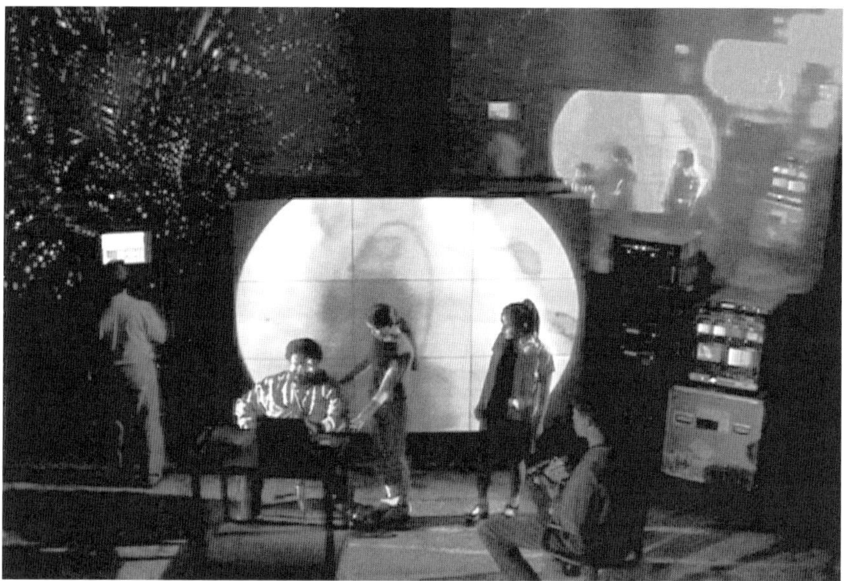

recording the complex locations of transcultural encounters in time. In addition it seems to me that in *Night Passage* you are using the technology to explore as well the complex *spaces* of *transhistorical* encounters.

This point leads me to ask you about an aspect of *Night Passage* I find quite difficult to articulate accurately. It has to do with a particular quality of the *mise en scène* of the station stops on the train journey. The manipulation of digital image and sound material with computer software has been a major resource in the production of science fiction film for special effects. As one writer puts it, 'A creative imagination roams through digital domains unencumbered by the constraints of corporeal existence that are a way of life for analogue artists.'[2] Because Miyazawa's story is a kind of science fiction narrative, generically it lends itself to this kind of treatment. *Night Passage*, however, is full of sounds and images of embodied knowledge and skill: flute and drum playing for example, various traditions of dance, rhythm, movement, the simplest production of light with fire, the sensual appreciation of food. A commitment to the 'analogical' limits of the pro-filmic event at the level of the image is an obvious way in which *Night Passage* does not square with the out-of-body utopian rhetoric of some digital imaging, and theorizing around virtual reality.

*Trinh:* Yes, that rhetoric is widespread and quite misleading. Largely based on the deep-seated duality between mind and body, spirit and matter, it's easily recognizable in certain reactions from viewers, programmers and critics who seem to know what digital is all about. Although it's a commonplace, linking exclusively the corporeal to the analogue seems rather illusory and needlessly reductive. For me, the more cutting-edge studies of digital media focus precisely on the vital role of embodiment in our experience of reality—manifested in its manifold forms, both phenomenal and virtual, to use a dysfunctional binary. These include all the researches aimed at extending the body, giving rise to distinctions between the body image or the body as object, and the body schema whose field of operation is preconscious and subpersonal.

Yet, as in a spiral, the move forward in novelty is also a leap back in time, for this is where new technology potentially meets the ancient Asian science of living, whose spiritual praxes refer not to one but seven bodies in a human—the physical, emotional, mental, astral, etheric, celestial and ketheric. Here, the physical body is only one among others, whose centre channels the earth's energy, grounds us in the material world, and is located at the base of the spine. It can be viewed as being at the end or beginning of the human body, but what about the rest? Seven and yet one. The term 'body' itself is used very differently in this context. We have a lot to learn of ourselves, for we do not live in eternity; eternity lives though us. When spirit and soul are indivisible, there's no separation between higher and lower. As the part of us that takes in the obtrusive and the dark of matter, soul is what makes the world 'real' and is made real by the world. Interestingly enough, rather than achieving immersion through the illusionism of virtual reality spaces that characterizes mainstream VR researches, artists' media projects today often privilege the unfolding behaviour and bodily movements of the participant.

Some of the ideas developed at the initial stages of installations which I've made in collaboration, like *L'Autre marche* (2006–now, at the musée du Quai Branly in Paris) and *Nothing But Ways* (1999, at the Yerba Buena Center for the Arts, San Francisco), call for full interaction between human body and technology to determine letters' mobility in their projections on the one hand, and to produce sound through motion sensors and contact microphones on the other. For financial reasons, the mutual interaffect called for in the former project was not realized as conceived (partly because of the costs raised by the very large scale of the installation). But these are two examples among many in media arts. As you have acutely noted, far from removing experience from materiality and embodiment, technical and cinematic mediation in *Night Passage* makes use of the flexibility of digital technology to feature the (spiritually) interpenetrable relation between human and machine, intermittently inscribing the human computer interface in the transient formation of its images.

In the journey on the River, it is this interaffective exploration of the human and the machinic that manifests itself through embodied vision, knowledge and skills. The human body, a mortal vessel of immortality, stands out in the film as one of the vehicles of light and darkness mentioned earlier. The means to move on one plane are the means of artistic inscription and communication on another plane. The use of the bicycle and the small boat are examples of technics and body singing in tune: to ride, to move, one has to pedal or paddle. Too much control and the body-mind stiffens; too much leaning on one side or the other and one falls; balance is then lost unless one learns to loosen up and let go. 'Remember the rules of night passage. Don't stop in the dark or you'll be lost.' It is in rowing along the shore of the River that the young women catch sight of the body-fire dances turning into light writing on night sky and water. And as you may remember, Kyra returns to life by bicycle.

The train she takes to travel in time 'is weird' for it neither runs on steam nor on electricity—an imaged train caught somewhere between appearances: the material look of metal vividly brought about via immaterial light. Her descent with Nabi and Shin into what you have so accurately identified as 'cabins on an ocean liner' and further as 'the bowels of what could be a ship's engine room' is the descent into the womb of 'the ship of death'—an image immediately recognized and named as such by many viewers at screenings of the film in Japan. Bicycle and boat of life, train of transit, ship of death; ultimately life, transit, death are here interchangeable.

What immediately comes to my mind is the image of embodiment and self that Roland Barthes offers with his *Argo* ship: each piece of this white luminous ship is gradually replaced by the Argonauts such that they end up with an entirely new ship—without having to alter the name or the form, but leaving nothing of its original identity. A vessel whose parts keep on changing and whose totality is in constant motion: this is also a way of digital imaging, and this is how *Night Passage* works for me as digital film event.

**Not so cool: the eye hears, the ear sees**

*Rowley:*   There is, however, another such aspect of the film, no less obvious but that some viewers find uncomfortable. This is what I call the DIY, the 'do-it-yourself' look of the magical *mise en scène* of the station stops. For me this is bound up with your sensitivity as a cinematic translator of Miyazawa's novel, which is, at one level, a children's story with children as its main characters. I'm thinking, for example, of the very simple way of spatializing the mysterious sound terrain at the 'Sound and Word Station' by drawing with coloured pigment, first on the beach, and then on asphalt mapped out in patterned sections as if for a game in the street or playground. While the image is simply made, the sound engineering in that sequence is, by comparison, very sophisticated, and in fact you reveal the sound engineers at work recording the sound of the travellers eating at a dinner gathering in the otherwise ordinary environment of a friend's apartment. In this way the digital manipulation of recorded sound that produces the mysterious effect of moving around the coloured drawing in the earlier sequence is de-mystified. You show how the sound is made, and once we see the process reattached to human causality, it is no more mysterious a process than is making a drawing with coloured pig-

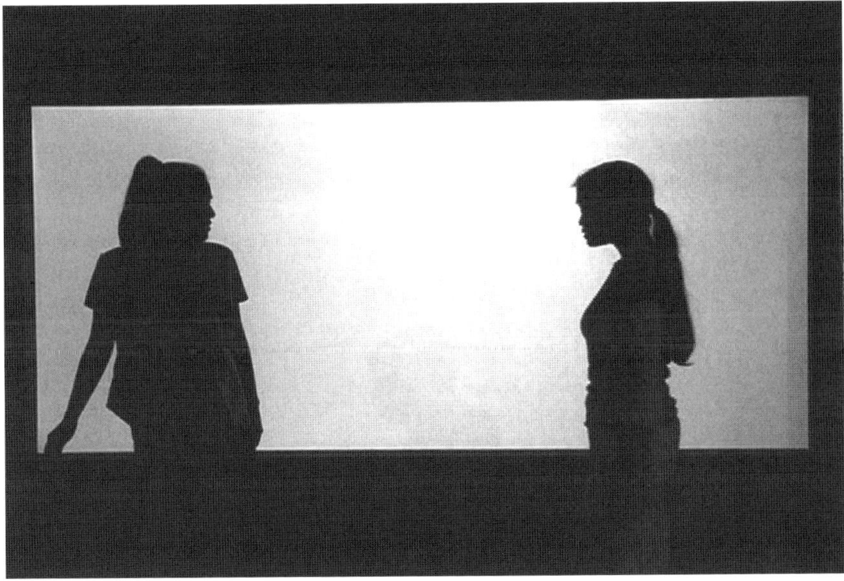

ment. There is a complex play going on here between a politics of translation (of the novel), which involves fidelity to the particularity of Miyazawa's work with the science fiction genre, using the appropriately flexible resources of digital media that is associated with infinite, rapid, disembodied 'special effects' in mainstream, commercial science fiction films. Some of which you proceed to demystify in your film by showing the material conditions of their production.

The whole magical *mise en scène* of *Night Passage* has the quality of the imaginary places and events children create with the bits and pieces of everyday material and objects they have to hand; paint, cardboard, shards of broken mirror, string and clothes pegs. The Immortals, for instance, are just like the projectors I used to construct as child with batteries, bits of wire and torch bulbs under cardboard boxes with holes cut in their side. So imagine my delight when it is revealed that it is by their light that the figures of the two young women are thrown in silhouette on a screen in an image of the very beginnings of cinema itself. For me it is an image that also recalls the beginnings of feminist political analysis of cinema spectatorship in Laura Mulvey's demonstration of how the unconscious of patriarchal society structured narrative cinema, with the silent image of woman as bearer, not maker of meaning. The robot prototype whose mark of humanity is cigar smoking, is that a reference to Freud?

*Trinh:*   Yes, for many feminist viewers, it certainly is. Some saw this scene as being fully reflexive, both in relation to the film and digital imaging, and to language and discourse. Worth noting here again is the collaboration that went into the scene with Uncle Borges and his House of Immortality. It is co-scripted with Tom Zummer, an artist and philosopher, whose impressive erudition is characterized, among other singularities, by a gargantuan appetite for learning and passion for books—one that incorporates their materiality (quality of paper, print, fonts, texture, size, design etc.). I wrote the part on the immortals as inspired by the work of Jorge Luis Borges, and the rest is his: both the creation of the robots and their presentation. As with the sculptor, Jean-Paul and I have heard Tom speak while showing us his robots. We love his drawings and the attention he brings to infinitesimal details, his incredible humour and his mind 'excesses', so we asked him to share them on film. It is often in the small, the trivial and the daily that we realize the extent of our social conditioning. Although I enjoy it, I have little to do with the unique index of humanity being also a mark of gender and sexuality in the world of robots.

You have a wonderful eye for subtle details in the examples you gave of the film. Concerning the work on the transcultural and the transhistorical, which you noted earlier, in this scene with the Immortals, there's the example of silhouette and shadow work that recalls the beginnings of cinema—and rather than returning to Plato's cave, which often serves as a reference for Westerners, I am thinking here of the inter-Asian origins and histories of puppetry and shadow performance (Chinese, Indian, Javanese, to mention the more known ones). But with these diverse beginnings of cinema, there are also the questions of screen histories and of digital postphotographic imaging. (Yes, all these convoluted inter-, trans-, and post- prefixes that define our times!) Presented in that scene are three screen surfaces and spaces: those of cinema, video and still photography (here, transparencies), and in addition, running across the surface of the images of that entire sequence are light squares (or what one can see as spirit-and-soul projections of the light boxes or the Immortals)—with no photorealist content. This is an example of the transhistorical scope of the film, one that I can only bring to discussion once it has spoken to viewers like yourself.

The other scenes you mentioned are those featuring bodily responses to the sound of colour and of food in the instance of their consumption—what my films have always invited the viewers to do in the instance of watching them. Already with my first 16mm film, *Reassemblage*, viewers have expressed, through controversial, baffled, angry or elated comments their visceral responses to a form of primary, radical discomfort. And as one of them excitedly shared in a public debate, what the film offers him is an experience of film in which, literally, 'I hear with my eyes and see with my ears'.

Sound is neither merely temporal nor merely spatial. As you have noted, spacing and spatialization play an important role in sound work. The sound in the scene focused on colours is actually quite simple in conception: to each colour corresponds a sound emitted upon *touch*. The surface of the touch screen—sand, asphalt—matters. And since the three characters each have their own particular rhythm in simultaneous bodily responses, what you hear ends up sounding quite complex: almost as if organized from a score written for an electronic musical ensemble.

*Rowley:*   I have had conversations with some viewers of *Night Passage* who have difficulty with these childlike, homemade aspects of the film. There is a tendency to mistake your pol(e)itical, reflexive work with new technology for an embarrassing *faux naïveté*, or something like that—it's hard to name the reaction precisely—but it is particularly noticeable in academic environments, as if *Night Passage* represents a falling away from the level of sophistication of your previous work.[3] There is an inherent judgement of quality in such responses. Is this a reaction to the film you have encountered?

*Trinh:*   No, this is the first time I've heard of this, although I can understand where it may come from. Interestingly enough, it just so happens that the scenes mentioned concerning colour and food are the most commented upon. Many listeners, musicians, sound technicians and educators from grade schools as well as high schools pick these out as their favourite scenes. The child mind, the beginner's mind comes in as many forms as there are individuals. The discomfort with the not-quite-child and the so-called lack of sophistication has a role here. You have already expanded on this earlier and provided a substantial, on-the-mark answer by focusing on the politics of translation, exposures and incorporation of the 'how', and especially by sharing the joys and magic of imaginary creatures and events you create, or make do as a child with the bits and pieces of everyday material available. There's not much more for me to add to this.

Perhaps, to reopen the space of reception, I would take a slightly different direction and relate this negative discomfort precisely to the impact of technology in commercial productions of the film industry. When it comes to new technology, people tend to recognize it only in products with a *high-tech look*. This is the look that sells, with its dazzling artifices and pithy gadgets. Anything other in appearance tends to be 'not cool'. Money also produces believability and credibility; the money image is what many continue to value as promoted through the media's untiring pursuit of artificial naturalism. In other words, all is in the look and the sophistication of the make-believe apparatus. This ever-more-hip-cool-coarse-or-slick image effect has become quite a cliché, and ironically, the look of discontinuity or the inclusion of processes, which were so dear to experimental filmmakers, are now 'in' for popular mainstream cinema. This being said, shallow imitations and appropriations on the level of the look have little to do with the vision researches of radical experimenters.

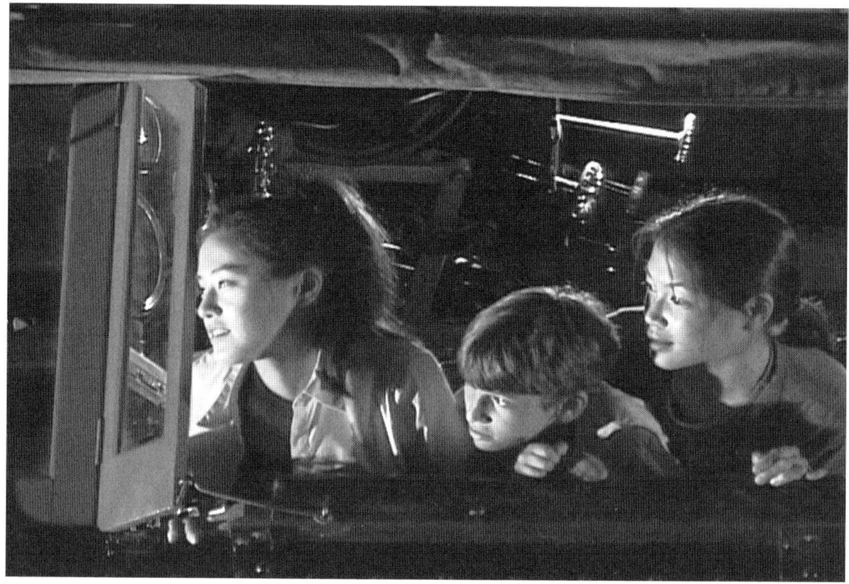

In these times of postcolonial struggles, postmodern recovery and 'green sustainability', to use a trendy term, I would say that we need to be at once very primitive and very cultured. Awkwardly, efficiently 'low' and competently, unfittingly 'high'; shuttling effortlessly between the avant- and *arrière*-garde and surfing in and out from the middle. In other words, marginalized groups could be all at once sophisticated, provocatively high-tech, and defiantly vernacular. Rather than entering the film with judgements on whether the film's portrayal of the child's 'naïveté' looks 'real' or 'faux' (I'm working here with these words that are not mine and not really appropriate to my undertaking in *Night Passage*), it may be more timely to shed these old standards and especially judgements of quality, so as to come to terms with the transhuman mind of new technology. To return again to my film *Reassemblage*, which has had a very difficult and controversial start but has since then enjoyed very wide exposure across cultures—here is a film with a bare-bones budget that *anyone can make*, whether in artistic, social or technical terms.

In previously published conversations, I have also expanded at length, for example, on the primordial work of rhythm in cinema; or on slowness and rituals (including the rituals of new technology) being fully assumed as a form of resistance and a mode of experiencing. The play on the senses in the sound scenes mentioned earlier can be experienced as an individuated but non-representational encounter between sight, sound and human touch; or else, as embodied forces, rhythms and sensations. Deleuze, who also gives a primary role to rhythm (and not metre) in his analyses, speaks of it as a base commonly shared between words, lines, colours, and sounds, and I would add, body. To quote him, 'Rhythm appears as music when it invests the auditory level and as painting when it invests the visual level.' And I would add, as dance when it invests the bodily level. Cézanne calls it a 'logic of the senses'—'neither rational nor cerebral'.[4] Again, what is thought to be modernist often turns out to be ancient practice: Asian artists of old did not separate the visual from the verbal and the musical, for being a painter and a poet was one and the same. Through calligraphy what is manifested is not 'art' so to speak, but *ch'i* or *ki*—breath-spirit—and song from matter.

After all, isn't 'cool' a term that one would also apply to people who have a pace and a rhythm of their own, and who either do not let themselves be distracted by pressure from their peers and external events, or they simply tune in fully with any current that crosses their path? Working at the junction of the analogical and the digital in film, one is bound not only to challenge tendencies to determine what the quality new tech look should be like, but also to question this all too dominant exclusive investment in the look (of quality via believability)—often expressed through a sightless vision.

## Continuity in the digital passage

*Rowley:*   You observe the conventions of analogical film-making for much of the time in *Night Passage*. Instances in the film when you do manipulate the digital image are, therefore, quite striking because they are relatively rare, and most telling when they are barely visible. This brings me back to your choice of the Miyazawa story as a starting point for the film. In your 'Time Paths' lecture at Leeds you spoke about the potential of digital technology for 'sculpting and dilating time in new ways', and your interest in the 'infra-ordinary' use of post-production special effects. In the scene in which the unhappy Kyra sits down with the flute player and homespun philosopher an astonishing example of the 'infra-ordinary' occurs. As the man speaks the words 'confront the night until you see the light in there' a square expands starting at the centre of the frame. I don't know what the technical term for the effect is, however that non-diegetic movement within the image produces, for a split second, the illusion of sculptural relief. This is, if I am not mistaken, the first instance of a post-production visual special effect in the film, and, as an 'impossible' manifestation of the (analogical) cinematic image, it functions to open the passage of the film's title—the passage between life and death—where the narrative of Miyazawa's novel takes place. This is a brilliant example of using a post-production technique unique to digital imaging as a formal tool for translating the 'magic realism' of the narrative from literary to cinematic form.

*Trinh:*   You specifically grasp these visual details in their functions. I wouldn't be surprised that a number of viewers see them as technical errors, but still, errors that they readily attribute to digital duplication or projection. The digital makes its reappearance in quite surreptitious and unexpected ways! I prefer that the touch of new technology be light in the film. Unlike escape, freedom is dangerous in its creativity, and prone to misappropriations and misunderstandings. I assume that by 'conventions of analogical filmmaking' you are pointing to photographic realism, or the use of photographic image in its reference to and visual likeness with lived reality. If so, then yes, I was not doing away with photographic realism but using it otherwise. I was working in between, with both the film look and the video look, and within these two, with instances of non- and post-photographic digitization whose data space does away with external reference. The series of light squares related to the Immortals, whose motion across the screen recalls the train windows of the opening sequence, is another example I discussed earlier.

In realizing a film event, I work less with digital per se than with the way of the digital. It's not a question of producing a non-human, automated vision, nor that of turning every live action image into data for manipulation and special effect purposes. Understanding what is radical to digital imaging allows one to work differently with the experience of film and imaging, while soliciting from the viewer *a new seeing*, one in which the human, although all too visible, remains an other among others, no longer superior to the machine in terms of sight and speed, for example. In other words, we would have to learn to see wide into the depths of time, and hence, to see not with our ordinary eye.

In *Night Passage*, the image's surface of visual realism is punctuated with imperceptible (not invisible) disturbances. As with my other films, form is arrived at only to address the formless, for rather than being set in opposition, they constitute the two facets of every reality. Constantly in dissolution on the canvas of time are the many forms of life that appear while others disappear. Liquidity and dissolution run through the film. Since the focus is on passages, it is mostly in the transitions, in the in-between of shots and sequences that digital undoing and dissolving of the image—disintegration, decomposition, vanishing and passing from image to non-image—is perceived in its time course.

The touch of time travel in the film is also light. The journey between the third and the fourth dimensions, between the departed, the living and the dying, or between what we call past, present and future is realized with little and barely perceptible effects. The same may be said of the way time is stretched in the relation between the bicycle ride, the journey on and off the train, and the death of one of the main characters. Despite the seemingly realistic look, very little of what may be viewed as the conventions of feature narratives is actually kept.

To mention yet another example, one of the aesthetic choices that came in the process of working on the blueprint of the film was to have each main scene actualized in a long take and a camera gesture of its own. In other words, Jean-Paul and I have mostly discarded the standard procedures of breaking a scene into master shots, medium shots and close-ups. (Unlike in my previous 'documentary' films, there are very few close-ups in this one.) In this cells-and-rhizomes structure where each scene has a temporality, a space and a place, a beginning and an ending of its own, we have also done away with the cutting back and forth between over-the-shoulder shots and reverse shots that is standard in scenes with conversation between two or more people. Instead, the camera's movement is choreographed so that it constantly moves—in the dark to the rhythm of our body-in-reception—until it achieves its full gesture in its time sequence. As with Borges' city, this could be said to be a film event in which centres are everywhere and peripheries are nowhere.

The substantial, reflexive, and transformative role that transit and transition play in the film is relevant to both its story and its use of digital technology. For me, one of the very significant shifts that digital technology has introduced in film-making and especially in cinematic storytelling concerns our very *perception of continuity*. With the immense flexibility that digital technology gives us in post-production, what we keep or discard from the golden rules of film continuity is widely up to us and to our creativity. In other words, if experimentation in film has allowed us to challenge them, digital technology has freed us from the conventions around matching in action, location, camera position and screen direction (that is, the spatial dynamics within the film frame or how a subject travels across the screen). Today there are so many possibilities in making transitions that we no longer need to follow the rules to achieve continuity, and those of us who have little need for a 'continuity supervisor' on the crew, can now relax.

It is interesting in these times of rapid globalization to note, for example, the widespread use of certain facile transitional devices that require no knowledge of film conventions, no visual nor mental investment—and no creativity. To achieve the trendy 'cool' look and effect of high-tech action and high-speed mobility, and to tell viewers, for example, that the protagonist (who is now mostly a lone fighter on the run and an unbound world traveller) has changed his whereabouts on the globe, it suffices to show, through a rapid cut, a postcard shot of a city with its name in caption. Recklessly, we scan the unending violence and leapfrog through a dozen capitals, from Washington to Berlin to Casablanca, during the unfolding of the narrative, with no need for any visual link between the shot or the cities, nor any rational connection in the flight across first world and third world nations (the *Bourne* series is one example). Amazing; spectators don't call these amateurish, because the high tech money image is there. Despite the semblance of freedom in creativity, their spread is symptomatic of the complexities of our time-bound conditioning. How mainstream feature narratives quickly appropriate and dilute the demanding work of fragments, discontinuity and exteriority inherent to experimental arts is intriguing.

## Man the passenger and women's time

*Rowley:*   In 'Still Speed', your conversation with Elizabeth Dungan about *The Fourth Dimension* in *The Digital Film Event*, you speak about what Paul Virilio calls 'the third interval, the interval of speed-light that is neither temporal nor spatial', and you name such an interval '"Women's Time," as possibly defining Japan's Time'.[5] In *Milky Way Railroad* Miyazawa's travellers are two young male friends; in *Night Passage* the companions on the journey are two young women. Generally, I am not surprised by the change given your history of engagement with feminist politics, but it also suggests a specific structural link between *Night Passage* and *The Fourth Dimension*. *Night Passage* concerns another kind of 'third interval', an interval that is neither life nor death traversed in the bond of friendship between two women. Miyazawa's story, and the gender transposition its translation from literary to cinematic form allows you to make, provides, it seems to me, the perfect vehicle for a more poetically resolved figuration of 'Women's Time' than could be achieved in *The Fourth Dimension.*

*Trinh:*   Great way to end and reopen our conversation. *Night Passage* showed to a number of audiences in Japan, and for me, the most memorable ones so far were those populated with 'experts' on Miyazawa. I was expecting blows of all kinds, partly because Miyazawa has become a cultural monument after his death (for it is always difficult to touch a national icon), and partly because of the choices I've made in remaining loyal to him—not by illustrating the story, but by keeping its spirit. This entails, as you know, a certain freedom in sketching my own night passage, and in the realm of form, the question of gender is not accidental; it is rather foundational. But for once, my attempt to brace up in getting ready for adversary, fault-finding comments proved to be useless.

The receptions I have had there from artists, poets, writers, scholars of the 'Kenji circle' (as a friend of mine calls it) and people of other professions who love or are related to Miyazawa were very intense, insightful and moving. Viewers were struck by the scenes around the ship of death, the land and water border voyages, the nocturnal dimension of the journey, and the importance given to the work of light. Comments on the forms and trajectories of light in lighting abound. ('I' in Miyazawa's poetry is a 'blue illumination'.) Since these audiences know the story well (which is not necessarily the case with teen audiences), they were very attentive to details and to the how in what the performances came to actualize.

After *Night Passage* showed in Tokyo and in a few other cities of Japan, I was invited to present the film at Miyazawa's birthplace, in the prefecture of Iwate, as part of the Hanamaki City cultural activities and on the occasion of the 110th anniversary of Kenji's birth, when an International Conference on his legacies was also held. At the screening of *Night Passage* at the Iihatobu Center, whose audience knew little about my background and feminist work, I did get provocative questions related to the shift of gender. But as far as I could tell, they came largely from a place of curiosity, and the questioners seemed appeased when I linked the necessity of that shift to the role of inspiration; the difference in imagery and desire between boys and girls, or between Miyazawa and myself; and the foundational role of the experiential body in the descent into dark waters (as compared to Miyazawa's ascent to heaven— a yearning seemingly closer in its image repertoire to Christianity than to Buddhism).

A male viewer further told me, somewhat reluctantly, after this same screening that actually, he thought 'the switch of gender made the film much stronger—stronger than the original story'. He said he was a bit annoyed at first, because he was pretty sure that such a bold change wouldn't work and came into the film with a lot of scepticism as to what I could do. But he was ultimately surprised by the whole journey.

Another unexpected response was, for example, the one given to me by the scholar Nishi Masahiko, whose refined contribution to the Miyazawa event reminded the audience, among other things, of Tokyo imperialism and the shame of the colonized through the plight of peoples of the North and North East like the Tohoku (Kenji's birth region), and through the work on mythical epics by an Ainu woman, Chiri Yukie, who also died young, while in her bloom, in the same year as when Kenji's sister died (1922). Nishi noted how *Night Passage* seemed 'to have moved the disciples of Kenji, [who] discovered a new type of force, which had been latent in Kenji's work'. He thought that my translation had given a different direction to previous understanding of Kenji, and further said that he was particularly moved by the 'homosexual friendship' and by 'the absolute youth of the two girls/boys'.

This comment, which, for me, is very rich in what it does for the film, provides me with a link to your remark on 'the third interval' and 'Women's Time'. Nishi recalls Chiri in reading Miyazawa, just as I saw the death of Kenji's sister through every line of his poetry, and got intensely involved in the D-passage (the dissolving digital passage and the three D's invoked in the film) via his *Night Train to The Stars* or *Milky Way Railroad*. This is where the term transfer and shift of gender seems more adequate than 'change' or 'switch'. These crossings in gender time, culture, geography and technology bring to the fore the question of formed, barely formed and unformed relations. Viewers in the US involved in queer cultural politics have, for example, given insightful feedback on the multiplicity of forms of coupling, pairing, doubling, and team-

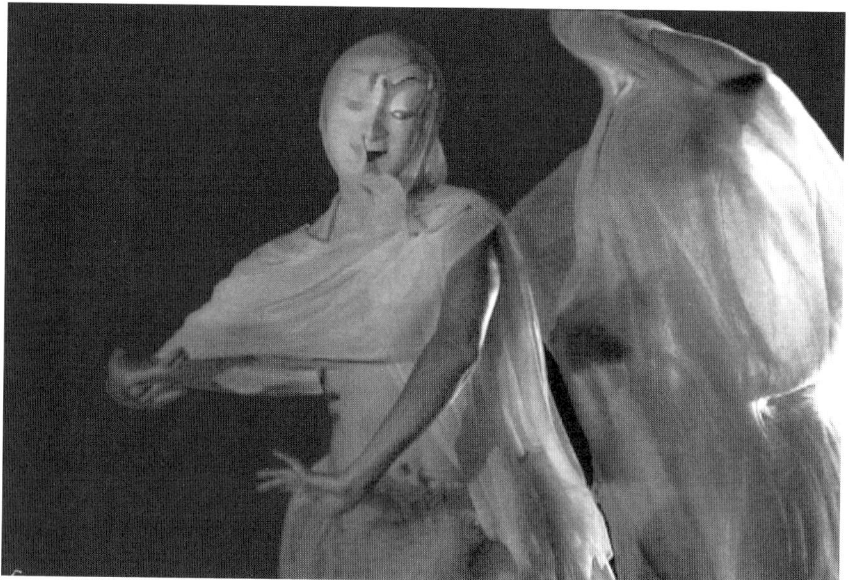

ing that are highlighted not only in the scene of the fire dancers, but throughout *Night Passage*. Elated, as some of them told me, they were very attentive to the way the film focuses on the many possibilities of liaisons and alliances in relationships.

Time lived in its course; space experienced in its indefinite multiplicity; bodies, metabolic and metallic, interpenetrating in their mutual affects on the surface of densely layered time. In a daring analysis of patriarchy, war, sexuality and the economy of violence based on movement and vectors in *Negative Horizon*, Virilio wrote about man being the passenger of woman, not only in the way he came to the world through birth, but also in their sexual relations. In other words, woman is the first transportation vehicle for the species and, in terms of both economics and politics, 'the first transportation revolution'. In offering him free time, she 'became "the future of man," his destiny and destination'. I will not go into this, but of interest to us here is women's time in relation to what he critically sees as the emergence of the locomotive body of the passenger and the acceleration of movement assimilated to a progression and to progress—'a curious blind alley in the history of movement', as he puts it.

The passage-interval that characterizes women's time is what Julia Kristeva called intra- and extra-subjective time; cosmic time; the time of 'unnameable *jouissance*'. In feminist struggles, one recognizes the double political gesture, which consists of inserting women into history, all the while refusing the limiting linearity imposed by history's time—time as departure, progression and arrival. Linking the interval of speed-light to this double gesture of women's time, one can also put to use Deleuze's musical notions of pulse time as related to optical vision in striated space and non-pulse time as related to haptic vision in smooth space. Between the double structure of internal tempo and external measure that characterizes the evolvement of Western music, and the free-flowing, non-measured rhythm of extra-European music, there is a third interval that is neither temporal nor spatial. And in the context of a transnational feminist temporality, I would simply say that between you and me, there are so many travellers—among both the living and the dead.

7

# TENSION, TIME AND TENDERNESS
## Indexical Traces of Touch in Textiles

Claire Pajaczkowska

The emergence of the new mass cultures of digital and virtual representation have enabled new enquiry into the significance of the role of the body in culture, and more particularly the significance of the hand in making culture. This essay suggests that semiotics is helpful to such enquiry, explaining why the trace of the hand within representation is capable of signifying memories of profoundly affective states. The semiotics of 'the textile' is needed in order to show how the specifically material meaning in textiles is founded on embodied knowledge and affect, and that these exist as indexical traces of the touch, handling and holding that are the presence of an absence of the body. This level of meaning is found in all concepts containing the linguistic root 'tain', or 'ten' (Latin, *tenere*, to hold), such as tension, tend, tendency, tenderness, and attain, maintain, pertain, entertain, and these refer meaning to the pre-symbolic material substrate of bodily emotional experience. The ideational content of this indexicality is discussed here in relation to the 'haptic', and to psychoanalytic theories of 'holding' and 'containment', and it is argued that textiles, through this indexical relationship to unconscious memory, convey meanings of complex pre-symbolic relationality. Semiotics facilitates the emergence of textiles as cultural 'object', which will enable a more sophisticated knowledge of its specificity as a cultural practice to emerge.

Textiles has developed a discourse in which consideration is given to the relationship between materiality and meaning, comparing the tension between matter and meaning in similar design practices in order to find the processes common to all practices that work with materials and to find the practice specific to textiles.[1] Similar discourses have already developed in art, literature, cinema, fashion, architecture, music and theatre, as these are cultural practices in which it is easier to differentiate 'form' from ideational 'content', whereas in textiles form and content are either very close, or indistinguishable.

The meanings of textiles have referred to their function, use, means of man-ufacture or technological history, so that whilst the semiotics of art, litera-ture, cinema, fashion, architecture, music and theatre are now well established, the semiotics of textiles has yet to find articulation, both internally, with the other components of textile discourse, and in its relation to the semiotics of other systems of signification. Here the semiology of Ferdinand de Saussure and the semiotics of Charles Sanders Peirce are both developed in relation to the specificity of materiality and meaning in textiles.

One reason for the relative absence of textiles from the semiotic field is the paradoxical status of cloth as simultaneously ubiquitous and invisible. It takes a specific kind of consciousness to enable textiles to achieve the status of a cultural object. Elsewhere, I have suggested that cloth and its component ele-ment, thread, have a cultural position that has endowed them with both an excessive materiality and an almost irrational immateriality.[2] Textiles have a privileged relationship to the senses and society, a relationship that is inscribed within the ritual, magical, superstitious and religious uses that articulate the meaning of cloth in culture.

A relationship of intimate proximity is created by the fact that bodies are universally adorned in fibre, and that the individual body is usually covered in cloth, which is for most of the time in contact with most of the surface of the skin, the body's largest and most sensitive organ. Related to this is the way in which human culture extends the pre-natal amniotic 'containment' of the body through the parental care that 'holds' the emerging self until culture itself takes on the role of providing the environment that facilitates subjec-tivity. This evolutionary strategy for survival results in the tendency of humans to 'ignore' their immediate environment, perceiving it as ambience rather than system. Much of the human ambient environment is textile, from domestic interiors to medical materials. These cultural facts overdetermine the rela-tionship that textiles have to the haptic sense, and give rise to the curious phe-nomenon of cloth being experienced as simultaneously physically ubiquitous and conceptually absent. There are analogies in this logic of ubiquity causing a kind of 'invisibility', however. To explore the ways in which textiles have both matter and meaning it is useful to investigate a method that will enable us to determine the extent to which textiles can be considered as a 'language-like' structure, given that language is the predominant articulation of culture. It is through language that the differences between nature and culture are identified, and it is, according to structural anthropology, the founding state of culture itself. So we can start by considering textiles within the conventional 'science of meaning': semiotics. Should we take Saussure's semiology, or Peirce's semiotics, as our method? Let's try both, and observe the differences between these methods in order to see which yields more relevant meaning.

Saussure suggests that signifying systems depend on patterns of the com-bination of signs, as well as the internal structure of those signs. The sign is a relationship between the signifier, which is the material substrate, and the signified, which is the ideational content. When material and ideational are connected, there is meaning. When signifier and signified are articulated, there is a sign. Few signs have autonomous meaning, and most depend on their relation to other signs within two axes of difference, the paradigmatic and the syntagmatic—or, in other words, the axis of selection and the axis of combination. This collection of differences between things, like the intervals in the resonances that make up musical notes, is the pattern that Saussure identified as the structure of meaning.

One of the most interesting uses of Saussure's work to analyse the meaning of material was made by Roland Barthes in his essay on plastic, published in his *Mythologies*.[3] In the book's introductory essay, 'Myth today',[4] Barthes argues that Saussure's method of analysing language-like systems within a general theory has relevance for a range of contemporary popular cultures such as television, advertising, cinema, toys, garments, vehicle design, architecture, photography and so on, showing how the structure of meaning in representation contains within it the structure of ideology, as the 'first order'; signification of denoting carries a 'second order' signification of connoting. Barthes' essay on plastic materials explores the introduction of these, the new materials, into daily life in France, and he finds a mythology of the new scientifically derived substances located in a history that dislocates plastic from its industrial manufacture, and where the connotations, or 'second order' signification of the feel, look and names of plastics are discussed as generating meanings of both modernity and timelessness. Although a literary scholar by training, Barthes' passion for the mythologies of contemporary culture enabled him to make some sense of design practices. Later, Barthes' analysis of dress in *The Fashion System* explored the semiology of sartorial style.[5] But the culture and practice of textiles remains uncharted territory for semiology.

Fifty years after Saussure's lectures were collected and published they generated a conceptual revolution in European thought, a movement of 'structuralism' that reached every area of science, theory and philosophy. For example, uses of Saussure's work include Claude Levi-Strauss' structural anthropology of myth, Jacques Lacan's concept of the psyche as signifying system, and a whole movement within literary theory, from semantics (Emile Benveniste) and poetics (Roman Jakobson) to narratology (Vladimir Propp) and genre studies (Todorov on fantasy). Emerging in Western Europe after the expulsion of Russian Formalists during the Stalinist reaction against the movement, the structuralism inherent in European theories of culture soon spread throughout the Anglophone world. Although semiology offered no specific method for investigating the structure of the image, cinema was one of the first cultural forms to attract a serious, sustained semiological approach, because of its status as part of a twentieth-century popular culture of urban modernity, and its proximity to the narrative structures of myth.[6]

Whatever the limitations of studying design as a signifying system, rather than as a process or practice, the structuralist method of analysis offers an important perspective that augments the largely descriptive, empirical, historical approaches that have constituted the theory of textiles to date. Textiles have been studied extensively, from the anthropological perspective of material culture, from the social historical perspective of both the history of technology and the history of labour, and from the perspective of design history as aspects of fashion or costume history, or furnishings of interiors. There is, however, a need for sustained inquiry into the meaning of textiles as ambient environment and signifying object, and as a cultural language, and it is to this inquiry that semiology can contribute.

How, in Saussurean terms, might we understand the 'language of textiles'? It may be useful to use Saussure's distinction between *langue* and *parole* to differentiate between textile as a generic noun, as in 'textile thinking', and the specific uses of textiles in the plural which, like the infinite variety of language use in *paroles*, are always multiple. The meaning of fabrics will always include reference to the means and methods of their manufacture, because textiles display the evidence of their tactility in the structure or surface of the material. This transparent evidence of the signs of the method of their making, ranging from the earliest hand-made felts and non-woven cloth to elaborate, computer-aided Jacquard weaves, digitally printed surfaces, and polymeric electro-conductive fibres integrated within cloth, has resulted in the discourse of textiles being primarily technical or historical, and in both cases essentially descriptive rather than analytical.

## Tension

Flat-weave fabrics include a range of different ratio arrangements between warp and weft yarns, and a range of different looms and technologies of production. The difference between various cloths with pile, from velvet, brocade and corduroy to flocking, generates meanings that relate to texture and touch. The flat-weave satins produce meanings that relate to smooth surfaces, sheen and sight. The meaning of each fabric depends on its relative place within a system of paradigmatic choices, say between flat-weave denim or velvet, and choices within a system of combination, such as denim in combination with PVC, or silk, lace, fur or knit, for instance. Many of these aspects of particular fabrics have been discussed by Barthes in *The Fashion System*, and although fashion clothing is the largest single manifestation of fabric in the world today, the semiology of textiles needs to extend beyond garments into other uses of cloth, and into other levels of meaning and abstraction.

What about the meaning of 'stitch' for example? The stitch, as sign, would depend on the relationship between its functional quality and the ideas that it connotes. This meaning will depend on the type of stitch used, considered as one of an innumerable series of different kinds of stitch. And the meaning will also depend on the relationship that the stitch has to other elements in the sequence of combined features. For example, a garment—say a jacket—may have a number of different types of stitching. Buttons are stitched; buttonholes edged, visibly, by machine; seams, lining and hems are stitched invisibly, by machine; and there may be a hand-sewn saddle stitch running along the outer edge of the lapels and collar.[7] Each type of stitch derives its meaning in part from its function, such as securing the button to the fabric, sealing the edges of the buttonhole neatly, making a strong but invisible seam or hem, or providing a neat line of hand-stitching. In addition to its functionality, however, the stitch derives its meaning from its selection within a range of types, such as the difference between the ways in which buttons are attached (a toggle of wood secured with cotton cord twist; a horn toggle secured with leather thong; a mother-of-pearl two-hole button secured with parallel stitch; a moulded plastic four-hole button secured with con-trasting cross-stitch; or a leather weave knot button with rivet fastener signi-fying the absence of stitch and the presence of machine-tooled fastener). The decorative use of stitch will comprise a selection from a range of types of embroidery stitch, such as running stitch, petit point, satin stitch, chain stitch, machine or hand stitch, so that the choice of cross stitch rather than saddle stitch, or blanket stitch across the edges of lapels, will produce different mean-ings, and again will accrue meaning from its combination with different fab-rics, colours, tailoring, draping and silhouette—that is, elements chosen from the 'axis of combination'. The stitching of the garment entails a number of choices taken from the 'axis of selection', such as hemming or fused interface lining, single seam or flat 'French' seam, heat-welded seam, or knitted seam. Likewise, the meaning of the stitching will also depend on the relationship it has to the other components of joining, securing and surface decoration that exist on the garment. Buttons secured with rivets or studs, the stitching of a motif or logo, contrast stitching, or self-coloured, invisible stitching—these all form patterns of significant differences within the two axes of selection and combination, sometimes conceived diagrammatically as vertical and hor-izontal axes, that Saussure identifies as the structuring axes of signification. But how can this systematic ordering of differences tell us anything mean-ingful about 'the language of stitch'?

An identifying characteristic of a language is the fact that its patterns of combination and selection have an 'unmotivated' or 'arbitrary' relationship between their form and meaning, analogous to the arbitrary relationship between the sounds of words and their meaning. Can this be said of the ele-ments of textiles—for example, the stitch as a means of securing two or more surfaces? This could manifest itself as the securing of patterns of pleats in curtains, in an interior design context, or the suture in surgery, or the stapler in the office, or a chain link fence around a sports field or car park, or a means of securing sails to a mast, walls to a roof structure, or sections of a vehicle shell structure. The stitch then has meaning as one selection from a range of possible ways of joining edges, materially, imaginatively or symbolically. This characteristic of the stitch as paradigmatic of a set of devices for 'linking' disparate elements gives it the status of a 'verb' within a syntax of materials.

The advantages of conceiving textiles as a 'language-like' structure are many, but the first is that the textile is no longer conceived as inert matter but as an active material system in which matter is inextricably imbued with meaning.

Is the stitch a verb, or a form of punctuation? Does sewing have the function of an ampersand in grammar, simply connecting terms without differentiating between the quality or type of connection? Or is sewing more like a verb, with an infinite range of differences?

Where the stitch exists as a structural element of the fabric, as in knit or jersey, and as the structuring element of a culture ('*couture*' means sewing, in its literal translation), in the arts and crafts of embroidery, patchwork, quilting, crochet, lace-making, petit point, or the textile art of the avant-garde, the stitch can accrue a very wide range of meanings, which multiply in inverse relation to its status as a functional means of conjuncture. This is a point at which stitch acquires, most visibly, its dual meaning as a point of articulation. It conjoins both matter and ideational content. The craft of stitching may also function to join together the disparate elements of a self that needs time 'to oneself', or may serve to bring together a number of people for a specified time and place as part of a ritual of sociability, such as the quilting circles, sewing bees and knitting groups that have functioned in a range of social, historical and cultural contexts, from pioneer homemakers of nineteenth-century America and the post-war suburban cultures of domesticity to the activity of avant-garde artists working with textiles today. In these cultures it is possible to find an episteme that derives from the specificity of the *techne*, which shares some of the features described by Richard Sennett as the 'ethics of the craftsman',[8] but extends beyond this to provide what Anton Ehrenzweig calls 'pre-articulate knowledge'.[9] The structuralist method can be used to further develop these ideas for textiles.

Peirce's theory of semiotics, developed in his 33 volumes of writings on philosophy and theories of knowledge, offers an alternative method. For Peirce, the relationship between signifier and signified takes place across a spectrum of relational qualities that can be identified at three points of qualitative difference. Peirce called these firstness, secondness and thirdness, or icon, index and symbol. Each has a different level of proximity between the signifier and its signified, with the firstness of the icon having the most direct, proximate relationship of resemblance. For example, an iconic image of the sun might be a diagrammatic circle with rays spreading outwards from the periphery. There is a relationship of visible resemblance between the icon and its meaning. The indexical relation to sunlight might be a photograph, where traces of sun exist in the form of chemical changes in the photographic process. A symbolic representation of sun exists in the word 'sun', which bears no resemblance to the signified except through convention and encoded patterns of difference.

The level of secondness, or indexicality, corresponds to a relationship of contiguity between signifier and meaning, so that the sign bears the trace of the presence of the signified. For example, the mercury expanding in a thermometer gives a trace of the heat that it measures through the pointer on a calibrated scale, and the weather vane gives a visible trace of the direction and movement of the wind. A photograph, taken with a SLR camera that exposes light onto plastic film coated with silver nitrate and developed into a negative, then printed onto light-sensitive paper and fixed, is a sign that has an indexical relationship to its object: the light reflected by the object is a trace of its existence.

Thirdness, or symbol, relates to those signs that have a relationship of 'unmotivated', 'arbitrary' or entirely abstract connection between signifier and meaning. Spoken or written language, for example, uses words that have no relation or resemblance to their ideational content. Onomatopoeia is an interesting exception that proves the rule, as are jokes like puns and 'double entendres'.

Although all three levels of semiosis are, according to Peirce, rarely found in isolation, and are approximate points along a scale of difference rather than absolute and mutually exclusive categories of difference, there is something to be gained from considering these as guidelines for thinking about meaning. This is especially useful with a form such as textiles, where the materiality of fabric plays such an important part in its significance, and where the symbolic levels of 'thirdness' are often found as one aspect of more iconic and indexical qualities. The very concept of proximity and distance as a means of differentiation has real purchase on a language of materials that are experienced as so liminal and ambient that they are often not perceived as having an 'objective' status at all. The complexity of the meaning of textiles as 'subjective objects' and as 'objective objects' is interesting, and is a complexity that confounds many analytic methods of classification, description and analysis.

We might use Peirce's semiotics to bring textile into clearer focus as a cultural object. As an artefact that always bears the traces of the process of its making, it tends to draw on the indexical level of 'secondness'—but textile culture makes full use of both 'firstness', iconicity, and 'thirdness', symbol. The iconic use of cloth is very much present in the logic of 'the fold', as the drape has been present in rituals of shrouding and mourning in all cultures. Textiles have themselves been subjected to ritual burial and entombment, as well as playing an important role in the burial rites of humans and their treasures. The drape is iconic in that it literally denotes the invisibility of things that are 'gone', 'lost' or 'dead'. The hiddenness that the textile can create, and therefore signify, is the relationship between perception and memory, which is the element common to both forms of signification (we can make visible, or present in representation, referents which are no longer present to our senses, and we can, through representation, sustain a memory of what once was but no longer is). Thus the twin aspects of mourning and representation are combined in the icon of the drape (the French language retains the traditional association between death and sleep: bed sheets are known as *draps*).

The absorbent quality of cloth is also part of its capacity to signify as iconic, seen in the way that stains which indicate the capillary action of fibres retain the meaning of mark-making. The body as topos of conflict between nature and culture is, traditionally, prevented from staining fabric. There are many examples of the capacity of textile to signify through its use as symbol. Because textile absorbs liquid, it can be dyed to hold colour. Imperial purple (from the shells of Mediterranean shellfish), eighteenth-century military scarlet (from South American beetles), the gold embroidery of ecclesiastical garments, and the black clothes of European mourners (produced by expensive repetitive immersion in dye baths), are all examples of textile as symbol, although the association of the value of specific colours with the financial cost or rarity value of the dyestuffs adds a level of 'motivation' to the otherwise entirely symbolic association between colour and meaning. Deleuze suggests that the fold also contains symbolic Baroque meaning within the iconic, and certainly this is evident in the architectural conventions in which stone and marble and other hard materials are made to imitate or signify the pliability of the textile drape and fold.[10] The vestigial remains of the ceremonial curtains we find at the cinema and the theatre and in other display contexts have symbolic meaning, with their indication of codes of spectatorship.

It is the Peircean concept of indexicality that is especially interesting to textile research. This is because of the way that textiles have indices of both tacit and tactile meaning contained within whatever other levels of semiosis they may denote. For example, how else to account for the meaning of the Yoruba tradition of producing elaborate stitching on fabric which is then dyed, so that the stitched cloth resists the dye, leaving an elaborate tracery of absent stitches when the stitching is unpicked? This is not the same as an applied form of surface decoration, such as print, nor is it a means of creating pattern through materials within the weave, but is rather a signifier of the action of laborious hand-stitching that once was present, but is now no longer, except as trace of resistance to immersion in dye.

Other ceremonial and ritual uses of textile are evident in the British Museum textile archives, which include examples of sub-Saharan/central African woven back-strap bands, in which the weave is augmented with elaborate stitching, which is cut with a sharpened stone tool to create a 'pile' fabric. This labour-intensive form of signifying tactility has meaning that is different from the meanings of the geometrical patterns that can be produced by variations in the weaving technique itself. Even in societies where metals have not been discovered, needles are made from bone and are used for stitching in a way that is both functional and symbolic.

## Time

Time is present in a number of ways within the meaning of textile as cultural object. The temporality of the tactile, haptic quality of the textile as sign depends on a paradox of presence and absence. The sign denotes meaningfully when it pertains to a referent that is absent. The sign then performs a memory-like function of retaining, in consciousness, what has been lost to the senses. The iconic serves to retain visual similarity, whereas the indexical serves to commemorate haptic presence, and it is the interplay between the absence of the contact and the presence of the sign which sets in motion the memory of a time in which tactile contact was present. This play of memory serves to form a connection in consciousness, to the unconscious bodily memory of the past body. The fact that the ego is a world of representations does not alter the fact that the ego is, as Freud asserted, 'first and foremost a body-ego'.[11] It is the textile sign that most powerfully sets into play the symbolic equivalence between different sensory modalities. The modalities of tactile and optical refer us to a developmental process in which the bodily is gradually replaced by the virtual, symbolic and cerebral. If mapped as an imaginary line of 'ascent', the cultural narrative of human, sensory and moral growth should lead us from an existence of instincts and drives, transmitted through the smell, taste and touch of corporeal proximity, through the optical and acoustic sense of relative distance, towards the goal of complete abstraction of verbal and written language. This imaginary lineage has served as the moral narrative of the Western episteme, embodied in the Cartesian *cogito* and in the monotheist fantasy of the divine, especially as a pedagogy and as the ideology of imperialism. The time connoted in the meaning of the textile sign is the presence of the absence of touch. This gives textiles their power to convey, and elicit, memories of lost affect and relation. This may be why Winnicott's 'transitional object'[12] is usually a textile object.

The meaning of stitch contains within it the index of the time it takes for the hand to complete the gestures required for its production. The traces of this temporality, which is always a time prescribed by the body and the temporalities of embodiment, convey meaning which is somewhat specific to textiles. As the cultures of industrial manufacture and electronic reproduction generate a temporality of instantaneity, so the time of physical movement, which cannot be increased beyond certain skilled speeds, remains an important index of value. The temporality of stitch gives to textiles the status of Winnicott's 'transitional phenomenon', marking the meaning of threshold experiences of change and transformation. Cloth, used in rituals, is attributed magical powers of causing change, or of representing the belief that such change is possible. The mystery of how human subjectivity is capable of transitional changes from states of sensory experience to abstract knowledge is given recognition in rituals of transition.

The stitch as signifier restores a sense of the embodied experience of temporal limitation, because actions require the discipline of acquisition through fine motor control, and because each repeated enactment of the movement reiterates the whole series of actions that are 'held' in the muscular control of the now automatic gesture. The years of apprenticeship to the acquisition of tacit knowledge, as noted by Sennett, find no record in written archives but are given memorial recognition in the haptic indexical level of the sight of the textile artefact.[13]

The capacity of stitch to indicate a tacit understanding of the significance of holding has many possible origins. For example, the Judeo-Christian culture finds in the biblical book of Genesis the story of the originary moment of culture that demarcates the pre- from the post-lapsarian periods of humanity. The act that opens the story of the fall is the gesture of the hand reaching for the forbidden fruit of the tree of the knowledge of good and evil, a gesture that symbolizes the co-ordination of hand as the executive organ of both eye and mouth. The gesture that is the cultural 'rhyme' or replication of this hand, that reaches out to pluck the fruit, is the hand (of Adam) that sews together leaves to make garments with which to clothe the naked body that has taken on the meaning of shame. Although Adam goes on to plough and tend the land 'East of Eden', and Eve is allocated the travails of motherhood, it is interesting that this narrative of mythic origin should cite stitch as the originary moment of human culture. The narrators of Genesis (and we know they were several, since the narratives within the book itself are multiple) were no documentary anthropologists, and they thus give no fascinating accounts of the origins of needles, tools or even of thread made from hair or fibre. The interest in the history of technology is modern. What was significant for thousands of years was the history of knowledge: the episteme, not the *techne*. The meaning of the stitching contains the same indexical significance of embodied knowledge then as it does now: namely, that of the mystery of tacit, bodily knowledge. The stitch pierces, punctuates, penetrates, as it unites the separate edges, and within a single gesture it combines both aspects of the paradox of destruction and creation. It also replicates the hand–eye co-ordination that, when articulated with oral appetite and instinct, was judged to be transgressive, and in place of the oral instinct to devour we are given the idea of 'making', by transforming nature into culture. If it was the feminine principle that embodied the instinctive appetites of nature, and was punished by means of the embodied pains of nature, then it is the masculine principle that is given the task of confronting the self cleaved between nature and culture, and his is the work of continuously transforming nature into agriculture. Sewing is the reflective act that enables self-consciousness to take the place of instinctive action, and we find the same morality present in the feminine rite of passage of sampler sewing across later generations.[14] For a girl to be occupied with her 'work' is to prevent the diabolical abuse that might otherwise occupy her 'idle hands'. It is not difficult to sense the latent presence of sexual ideational content, but this, although undeniable, is not the main thread of the narrative. At the level of the cultural meaning of textile artefacts, their cultural history in myth is one dimension of analysis. It is worth drawing attention here to the exhibition *The Fabric of Myth* (2008), which explored the significant use of thread, weaving and stitching metaphors in mythology, including the role of weaving in the Greek myths of Penelope, wife of Odysseus, and Arachne, who was turned into a spider; Clotho, one of the Fates, who spun the thread of life into existence; and Ariadne, who provided Perseus with the thread that enabled him to find his way out of the Minotaur's labyrinth.[15] These themes were all represented in the exhibition in ancient and modern imagery, from Greek amphorae to the more recent work of Louise Bourgeois and Elaine Reichek.

### Tenderness

The stitch has a reparative level of indexical meaning that also relates to this level of bodily presence implicit in fabric, particularly in relation to the hand and holding. Again psychoanalysis offers us two concepts that are useful here: Winnicott's concept of 'holding' and Wilfred Bion's concept of 'the container/contained', both of which refer to a relationship experienced in infancy that is internalized to become a capacity of the self, and a symbolic process that takes place within the 'representational world' of the ego.[16] The etymological root of terms associated with the hand can be found in all words with the 'ten' or 'tain' element, which indicates their ideational origins in the unconscious concept of holding. The concepts of tension, tenement, tenacity, tenable, attainment, pertain, maintenance, entertainment, containment, are just some of the terms with traces of the meaning of holding. The complexity of the textile's capacity to 'hold' meanings relates to the indexical trace of the hands and their movements in the making of textiles, and the unconscious symbolism of 'holding' and 'containment'. Not only is the unconscious fantasy present in the etymology of the language of concepts of holding but there is an affective register that is evoked by the haptic quality of textiles. The concept of tenderness is the affective level that corresponds to the pre-Oedipal states of the 'holding' fantasy. Hungarian psychoanalyst Sándor Ferenczi writes of the 'confusion of tongues between child and adult' where the 'language of tenderness' of childhood becomes misconstrued by the adult as the 'language of desire'.[17] The meaning of tenderness is experienced as a property of the textile itself rather than as a memory from childhood, or as a fantasy of regression to dependence. This semiotic quality is responsible for the attribution of a protective agency to cloth and textiles, including their use as magical materials in the history of medicine. Related to the superstitious or irrational belief in the curative power of touch, the haptic meanings contained by the semiotics of textile at an indexical level are significant.

Another dimension of the indexical significance of the hand–eye co-ordination that leaves its trace within the textile artefact is one with specific meaning in a post-industrial age. The stitch, like the hand-drawn line, the brushstroke or Barthes' 'grain of the voice',[18] is the trace of a movement that refers us to a time in which experience was tangible and available through the senses as guarantor of presence. The power of this indexical trace of a time of presence is both sensual and affective. When we urge a fantasist to 'Wake up and smell the coffee!', there is a gain of pleasure from the release of energy

that is used, in consciousness, to keep the concepts of time and smell separate, and the joke that conjoins different sensory registers is based on the idea
of smell as a sense of the experience of the present and the real. The relation
of memory to taste, smell and other sensory registers of visual and acoustic
representations is complex, but the absorbent qualities of the textile endow
it with both tactile and olfactory presence. Fabric, in its paradoxical transposition of sensory registers, restores to us the memory of an experience that
took the form of 'states of being' rather than organized separate sensory
modalities. This memory offers the promise of a return to a lost 'oceanic'
state of synaesthetic synergy, where boundaries differentiating self from other
have become fluid, permeable or mutable. The promise held by the fantasy of
the restoration of this state, from memory to actuality, is one of the elimina-
tion of affects of loss, suspension of anxiety, and a lifting of the burden of
sense used for reality testing and self-observation. It is a fantasy of the potential victory of the 'pleasure principle' over the 'reality principle'. The illusion
of a hyper-reality that is generated by the augmented virtual reality of new
information technologies is one in which embodied knowledge becomes dis-
connected from judgement and is channelled through the senses as perceptual rather than self-reflexive. The two meanings of the adjective 'haptic'
illustrate this clearly. In techno-speak the term 'haptic' refers to the production, through software, of the illusion of real, because embodied, actions.
The training in the gestures of surgery or in machine operation can take place
remotely through the science of computer 'haptics'. The other meaning of
'haptic' refers to the sensory relationship that exists between optical and tactile, or the muscular action of manual dexterity. Sometimes it is used to refer
more generally to the relation between optical and visceral senses, as in Laura
Marks' writing on film.[19] 'The haptic' is a quality that is strongly indicated
within the meaning of textiles, and it can give cloth powerful meanings of
relationality. It is one of the qualities of the haptic that it is not easily rendered
in verbal, symbolic or spoken language, but is closer to iconic and indexical
forms of signification. The haptic is not, therefore, subject to the rigours of
syntax, with its requirements of a triangulated relation between subject, object
and verb. If the subject of syntax is either passive or active in relation to its
object and its verb, this is not the case in the logic of the haptic, so that 'doing'
can have the meaning of 'being done to' in a way that combines active and
passive both simultaneously and indivisibly. The pleasures of the illusion of
such fusion offer endless horizons to narcissism by removing all focused sense
of agency and therefore of both frustration (failed agency), or responsibility
(agency realized).

## The agency of textiles

To bring the semiotic method to textiles is to acknowledge the potential of
textile as a complex cultural object of knowledge, as well as matter. This is to
acknowledge that the set of cultural practices comprising textiles are too inter-

esting and important to be overlooked in the interests of 'using' textiles as material. Although an essential element of textiles culture is material science, it is not a science that analyses textiles as inert matter. The frontiers of material science and textiles are acknowledging the agency of textiles as materials with interesting and powerful 'conformable' properties which have advantages in research fields where questions of scale, of mobility, of pliability and ambient surface are necessary. The potential for textiles to provide substrates for the growth of new neural tissue is becoming part of current medical research practice. The potential for textiles to give form to polymeric yarns with various degrees and types of conductivity is another indication of the importance of textiles for research into intelligent and smart fabrics in a material science context.[20]

This quality of being 'relational' or 'connective', which is an integral part of the meaning and matter of textile, is what gives it this power of 'agency', in the terms discussed by Alfred Gell.[21] As we work to secure the cultural recognition of textiles as a complex matter with agency, it is important not to overlook the valuable qualities, both of liminality and as a paradoxical 'subjective object', that are inherent in the haptic dimension of its materiality. This means that having secured its status as 'object' we now need, also, to further explore and understand textiles as a complex practice.

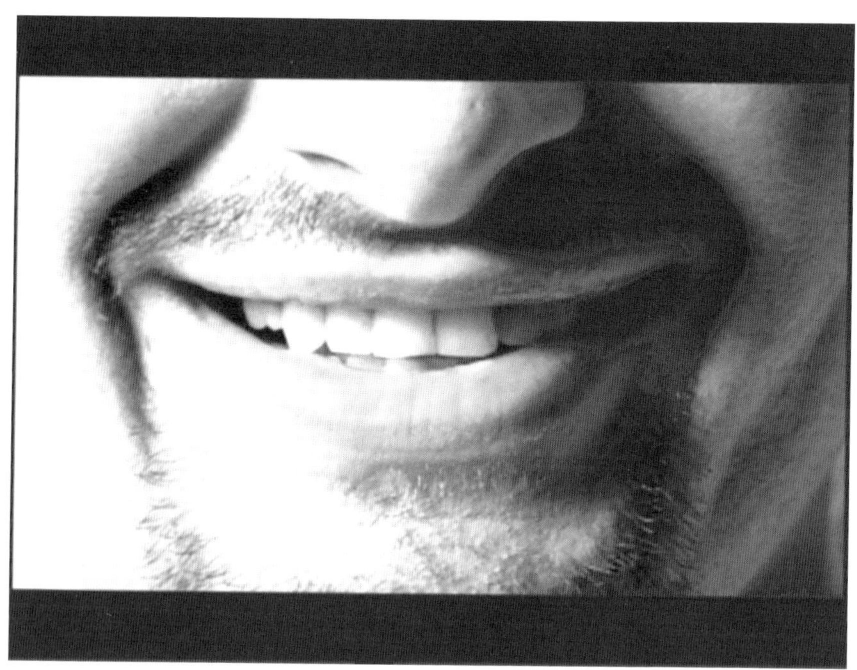

8.1–8.7   All images in this chapter are DVD stills from David Haines, *Three Months* (2004). Reproduced with thanks to David Haines. All images © the artist.

8

# LOOK, NO WIRES!
## Some Notes Around the Idea of a Sign (1, 2, Nothing)

*Adrian Rifkin*

'"Tis some visitor,' I muttered, 'tapping at my chamber door—
Only this, and nothing more.'

Poe, *The Raven*[1]

$$\frac{\text{queer}}{\text{gay}} = \frac{\text{signifier}}{\text{signified}} = \frac{\text{desire}}{\text{need}}$$

Donald Morton, 'Birth of the Cyberqueer'[2]

Plausible indices of a unicorn may be produced using a set of horse-shoes and a bull's horn, and do not testify to the existence of unicorns. A faked photograph of a unicorn, or whatever, may be assembled, using pieces of real photographs, processing them in a computer, or even creating them entirely by means of a computer program. Of course, the latter pictures are no photographs, and so no indices, but there is no way we can discover that from looking at them [...]. For all practical purposes, then, indices cannot testify to the existence of their objects.

*The Internet Semiotics Encyclopaedia*[3]

I found this third incipit—(the first will explain itself in due course; the second is refuted by the first which properly makes (un)clear the Lacanian relation of real and the imaginary, whereas the second believes that the imaginary (in this case the queer) can be seen or literally brought into view by a design rather than by a poetic)—on the internet, amongst the many linguistics and philosophy sites that crop up when we begin our daily grind with Google. And doubtless, in this case as in countless other cases, if the quotation does not point to an object, nor, according to its own argument, may it do so, then at least it is still safe to say that it emanates from a subject of sorts, individual, collective, corporate. That should be axiomatic, even though the nature of the subject remains an enigma or immaterial. The subject-enunciation of the internet works much as it does in daily speech, in academic lectures or in law courts, wherever—and in this respect the working papers of the European Graduate School, the sex chat rooms and gambling parlours, to take but three kinds of example, are up there on their websites in much the same way as origins of enunciation. The internet is but one historical formation of the process and, in the end, there may be nothing more or less interesting about it than the traces that it leaves in works of art or the accumulation of wasted time.

I was struck by this quotation as I thought that I myself had recently seen a unicorn or two, or some phenomenon corresponding to an index of some thing that certainly does not exist in the form that the indexical system represents it. This was 'in' the art work around which this essay circles, David Haines' video *Three Months* (2004), an acted out or performed version of the transcript of a three-month long exchange between two men on the well-known gay sex site, Gaydar. Here, even in an initial exposition, the problem is exemplified at the smallest element of terminology. Are the unicorns in the work, or is the work itself the set of a unicorn system? What is the invisible spare ground between a performance and an acting out, as the form of a possible referent for either the one or the other, the 'about' with which they are concerned? Is this anything?

The puzzling character of *Three Months*, which is not a blue movie, led me to think that, in respect of the theoretical questions of indexicality framed in this book, were I obliged to choose between competing theories of language, the model of Emile Benveniste in his discussion of pronouns would be a clear winner.[4] I am happy with it as it works at a practical level of allowing us have a speaker and, at the same time, gets along with and sticks nicely to both a Saussurean and a post-Derridian model too.

It makes for what we can call a mechanism of uncanny thinking around the enunciative character of the 'I', and permits a means of tracing a thought–subject relation in the art work rather than providing an explanatory model for it, an 'as if/what if' relation. With Benveniste the finally uninteresting question of the binary in Saussure versus the betterness of a tripartite system in Peirce falls away. In a world of cultural phenomena that can anyway be thought through *différance* and deferred action in their mutual excitation, the supposedly reductive function of the binary looks like something of a red herring, as is the Peircean model if it is adopted to assign a refuge from binary reductionism. We can rather concern ourselves with the inherent fragility of an enunciation, its evanescence, and its incoherence. The performance, which we find in this fragile time or moment, lends itself properly to the mutual interrogation of works of art of different forms and media amongst one another. It allows us to set aside questions of the medium, such as new versus old, virtual versus non-virtual, film versus paint, and to understand it as one element of signification amongst others. At the same time it gives us reason why we may, unashamedly, claim to be Cartesian subjects.

This is germane to what follows, as the iteration of 'I'—as a subject fully confident of at least fantasizing its goals—starts with the first tapping on the keyboard. Sometimes the mood of this procedure reminds me of aspects of Descartes' *Méditations*, especially those passages where he watches himself, observes his own physical being, but here it is not God that secures the subject, only wanting to desire and the text's scrolling as its figure. Any other deity is wanting.

Yet, having put all of that in order, what *Three Months* confounds is the very idea that the *énoncé* emanates from anywhere! Yet at the same time we see the *énoncé* as the iteration of a desire on the part of the other—I wish you to desire me in this way/to be desired by you in that way, and this iteration is who or what I am (at the moment of writing).

This cutting between the said and the seen as the men come to know or invent one another and a kind of self, generates a rhythm of image and sound,

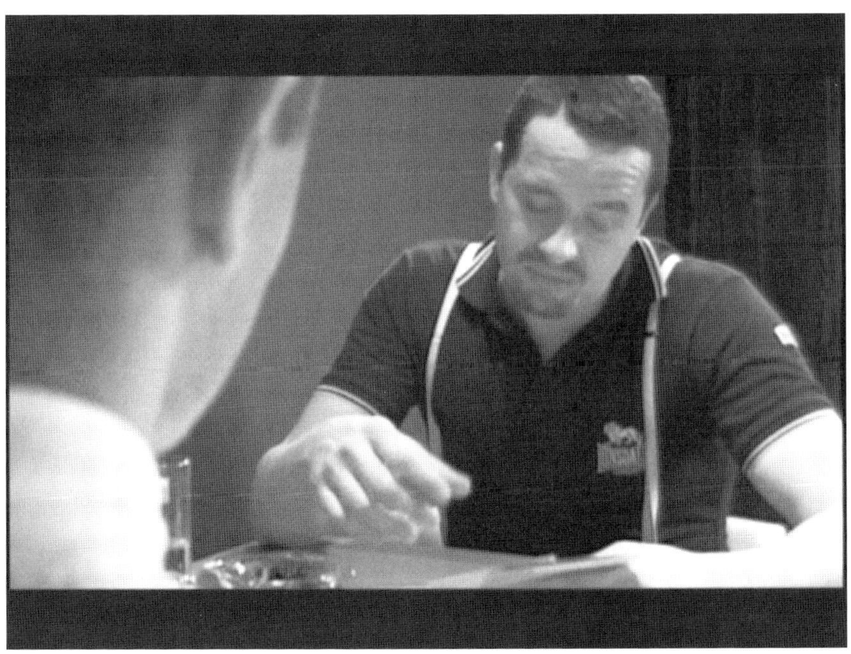

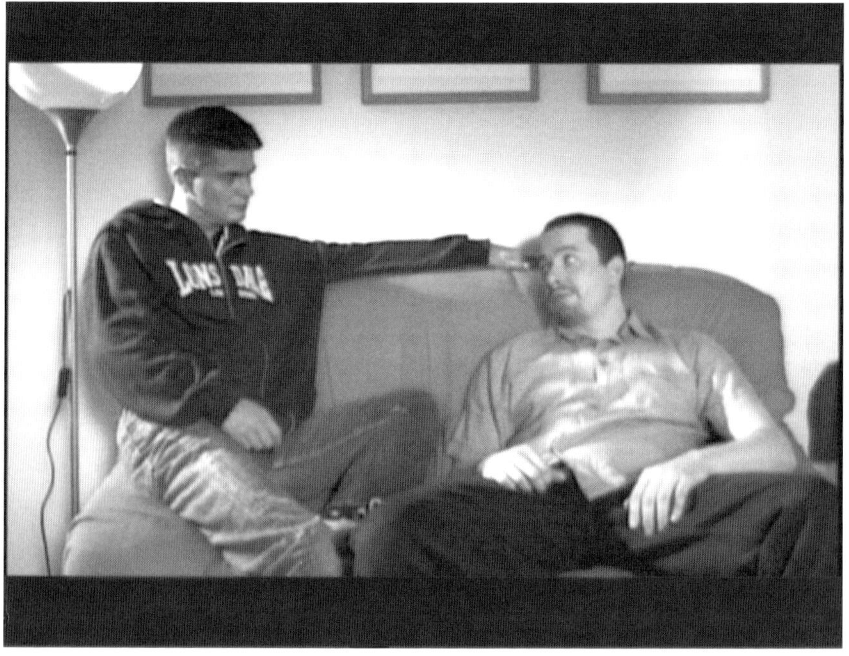

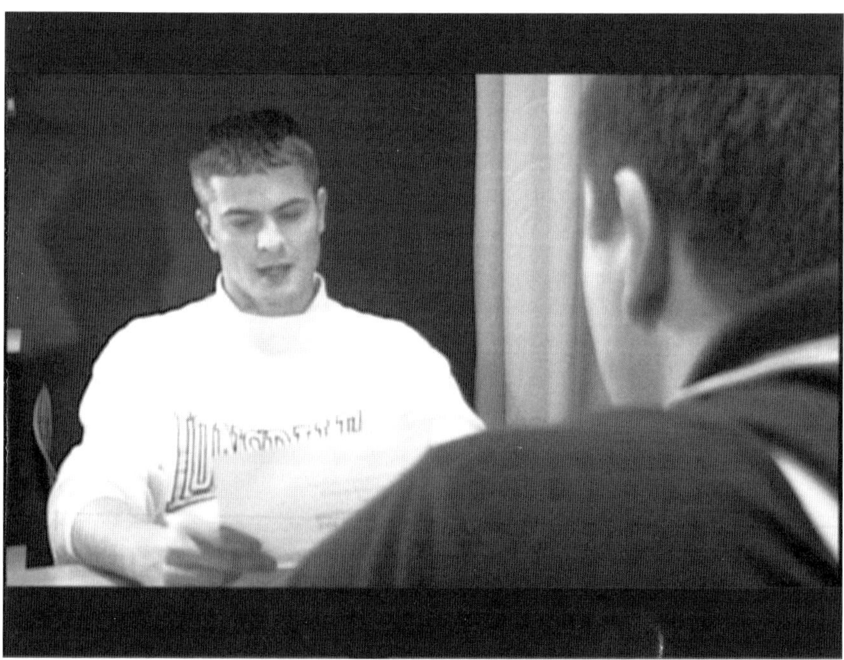

in which what is, in effect, voice-over is spoken as if daily speech. Is this what seen speech sounds like? These inner speculations concerning the heard separate the seen document from the probability of its existence other than in the disinterestedly aesthetic logic of the video as a text—which is yet not a fiction. It is not necessary to explicate this but rather to see where it belongs in the matter of meaning at all, or as *signifiant*. How do we attend to this?

If we take the distinctions between, for example, Henri Meschonnic's poetics of rhythm and Julia Kristeva's semiotic chora, we can see that these differences are about nothing other than the way in which we attend to an utterance and inhabit it. To go on to take this literally is to come to wonder if these differences really concern nothing, and the possible form of their unity, but a nothing that we might want to save for interrogation and play, which is a nothing of the text in the process, rather than as Benveniste supposes a nothing of the subject other than in enunciation. As I understand the 'being only in writing' of Meschonnic and the 'being in chora' (my phrases) of Kristeva, they both pose the emergence of *signifiance* in relation to something which is said/written, but which is neither its material nor its meaning, a commonality rather than a difference.[5] And this thing in common is indeed no thing at all and, at the same time, not Hegel's impossible nothing. But it might also be the nothing that unfolds in *Three Months*, a something that can happen only in the video or as the video, as its substance.

Nothing is both the precondition of the subject/text and the continuing absence that we hypothesize as a beginning, constantly played out in daily life and thought through concepts such as the unconscious or the *néant*. The concern with nothing, then, from the beginnings of Christian theology in texts such as Augustine's discussion of the Book of Genesis in the eleventh book of his *Confessions* to twentieth-century phenomenology and existential thought, is important enough to be brought into the play of reflections on the sign in the framework of contemporary technologies of vision and attention. The more so when we want to ask if something has happened, if anything. Poe in his *The Raven* and Eliot in *The Waste Land* are insistent on the matter as something in poetic language: 'What is that noise now? What is the wind doing?/ Nothing again nothing [...]' Or 'On Margate Sands/I can connect/Nothing with nothing [...]'[6] Obsessively, poetically the word nothing marks and remarks the point at which the work comes into being as if despite itself; despite its being nothing, in the first place and in the end it is these nothings that the poet connects: 'I *can* connect…'

This nothing, then, to which I will return, has a relation to negation and *néant(ization)* but it is by no means the same as these— which is a bold enough statement in a field of such speculative uncertainty. It is something we can postulate in, say, Giorgio Agamben's thinking of the *muselmann* in his *Remnants of Auschwitz*, which could be understood as a negative aesthetic and theology of the subject in extremis.[7] But a detailed and compelling account of the intricacies of these paradigms and histories of being a subject can be found in Kristeva, rethinking Sartre, Barthes, Freud and Aragon, in her *La révolte intime*.[8] Here her post-Debordian locating of these intricated theories to imagine the perhaps impossible survival of the unconscious in a hyper-mediated world underpins my eclectic devotion to Haines' video: in my own turn, in the hope of finding in my viewing of it the after-time of devotion, is a hope for the future of the work itself, the something that may come of it.

But if the crucial element of this methodologically fragmented attention is my learning from the video how I myself can think, then it is certainly worth imagining that this can also lead us to Laura Mulvey's understanding of the DVD still from Douglas Sirk's *Imitation of Life*.[9] This is in two senses the *néant* of the filmic sequence, in not just the way that it stops the film and drains it of its diegetic haste or concealment, but even more in the absence of a point of sound, the aural content of one frame; an absence that empties the still of its having been film at all. Following on from Mulvey's early lectures on the still, I began to stop-frame just about everything I watched; in the case of *Easy Rider* I found what I had could not have imagined—something uncannily close to *The Waste Land*, signifying spaces of emptiness and cluttered ruin rather than a rock-road movie. Haines' video again disturbs this unexpected quality of the stop frame and its rethinking as film. When *Three Months* runs it seems as if Mulvey's stills are brought back to movement, but no longer make the same film. To go back from the video to the script is to find noth-

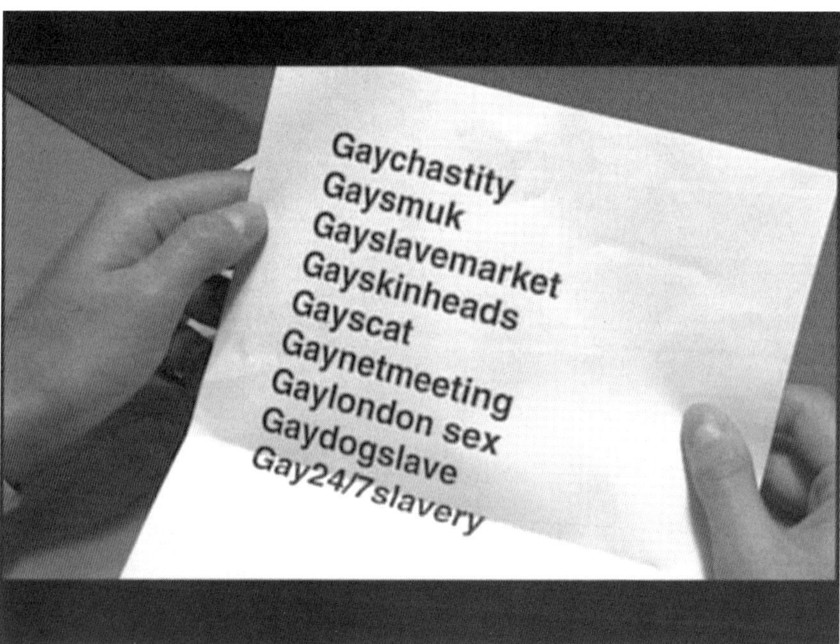

ing that really adds up to it, yet the text is not necessarily an open ended play-script, to be performed and redirected. It is a documentary record of something that never was, and in this it is an acting-out of a desire for something to be present, perhaps the necessity of desire, and nothing more. I only guess.

This juxtaposition of such radically separate and incompatible levels of significance as these models and that of Haines' work at the diegetic or semantic level, in effect leads me to hold to a notion of *significance* as a crucial step in aligning its procedures with those that are open to me in my reflections on the virtual and the sign. What now follows is more what jumped out of this box of secrets than it is an argument.

In effect, when I saw *Three Months* in 2004, shortly after it was completed, it put an end to the work that I had myself, like so many academics, being doing around the internet and the virtual. If in my case the course of this work was jolted and stimulated by Laura Mulvey's important essay 'The Index and the Uncanny' it was first and foremost a rationalization of my own unexpected addiction to the thing and the discovery of how many older activities it now stood in for, such as going to a library or waiting for economy hours to make phone calls overseas. I became concerned with a capturing of my attention by something in which some of the theoretical terms of the discussion of the image—gaze and object, screen and gaze—seemed to merge in a freedom that only imagines its own limits and delusions at the point when the interdiction of the remaining world falls like a shadow across the screen.[10] Or, the moment when another two words, 'real' and 'virtual' get to take a new turn around each other as the virtual begins to look more like the effective reality of the symbolic than like the real out of which the symbolic is made in a Lacanian schema: and precedent forms of the symbolic slide into the position of the 'real'.

While I can now see that this was part of an emerging discourse on the internet in which Margaret Wertheim's *The Pearly Gates of Cyberspace*, and the intense reflection that surrounded it had a played a determining role, I want here to restrain my discussion to a notion of the divine as a methodological issue rather than part of the larger description and analysis of cyberspace as a sacred space bearing the promises of Christian eschatology.[11] An article by George S. Hendry entitled 'Nothing', on an internet theology page, covers very much the same ground, from Augustine to Heidegger and Sartre (as well as Tillich), as does Kristeva.[12] Its presence on *Theology Today* underlines both the banality of virtual communication as a space of enunciation and as a vector of conventional and established discourse in which we can become all-too clear about how our discourse hardly belongs to us, as if we ourselves were nothing to do with it. So it is important to note that it is on the internet that doubts concerning the character of the new, in our days, and its possible newness circulate as well as speculations around its frail appearance as nothing more than the residue of something ancient. The very choice of such distinctions as that between the divine and the sacred, indeed, already implies a discourse more like that on and of Renaissance mysteries than one of contemporary street cultures or imaginary cities.

In my thinking I had focussed on the internet around a detailed textual analysis and 'real-time' tracking of my conversations in gay chat rooms, particularly in terms of how utterances misalign, get out of sequence and slip into becoming an unintended poetic on the one hand, and trying to approach the effect of this process as a perverse form of one's presence to one's self, at the same time as it becomes present to the interlocutor. This developed into a series of long and complex seminars pulling together theories of urban space since Maurice Halbwachs, to take just one reference point, with other paradigmatic accounts of spatial practice and psychoanalytic configurations of the formation and action of the subject. The replication of a city like London, imbricated in the world of virtual communication, generates a space of strange expansions and contractions in which the gazes of the street, the cruising gaze of another era, shifts from induction to deduction as its starting point. Rather than isolating a figure from the crowd as in the tradition honoured in Poe and Baudelaire, and inherited by gay cruising, the crowd is reassembled as a topographically constituted object of which certain coordinates may come to embody or congeal a crossing of general and specific desire with a geographical availability, itself conditioned by the weather (never indexed), time of day, degree of certainty that there will be a meet, and so forth.[13]

The images electronically exchanged, either as a lure or a gauge, as an offer or in response to a request, now bold and now coy or even timid, extend and elaborate the moment at which a kind of name falls on the interchange—a name like 'Yes, this' or 'no, not', or some other inner utterance that prolongs, ends or concludes the chat. The point at which a sexual encounter becomes impossible instates a cut in the phantasm; perhaps because it is raining, or you don't like the 'pics' or he yours, or you do but the guy is six zones away, or he or you cannot be bothered going out, in the end. And an even worse, more radical interruption of 'reality' can be that it is indeed possible, because he has a BMW and can actually cover those six zones in twenty minutes. Will I really like him? Or he me? And what if… ? The scenario is obvious enough and the scenarios of its prolongation are obviously endless.

But wherever it occurs, whenever, the cut is an intrusion in the daydream, much as arriving at a bus stop when you have fallen into a reverie on a long, hot journey in the city. It is a fleeting imposition of the law. 'Too strange to each other for misunderstanding […].'[14] Yet at the point in Haines' video where the two men are actually seen to meet, in the outside world, in the presence of other people to whom they are of no importance, misunderstanding is the very substance of this 'too strange…' and has brought it into being. At this point the decor of the encounter is no longer a kind of brightly coloured set, but the outside world, peopled with day-to-day activities. The everyday becomes uncanny or non-normal and, at the same time, the two modes of document ruin one another and with themselves the field of the indexical.

Here, as on the internet, once some shock has shattered absorption and distraction, which is here felt as absorption's involuted form, the state of mind diffused turns out to have been nothing other than one of devotion, caught in a devotional posture long prepared by the bend of the neck that is specific to the observation of a VDU. Here, in its arranging and rearranging the signs that the keyboard and the mouse articulate and summon up, this devotion might well point to an Other, but this Other is an effect of my acquisition and re-attribution of its names imagined as his making present—something like a unicorn, indeed, or an angel in Moses Maimonides' twelfth-century intrications of the presence of divine 'substance': it is not quite like anything else, this process of devoted naming of one's own desire as another's, unless it has something of a Flaubertian absence of metaphor and its fetishistic signalling of the presence of the world, as does Haines' video in its making present of this making present.

At the same time the purpose of my considerations before *Three Months* had been to counter the more trying sociological tautologies that populate the pages of SAGE journals and media studies books that have proliferated around the internet, full of propositions of the general order that 40 per cent of group X do Y because they like it, or feel lonely, or both, as well as to evade the somewhat more subtle discussions of a Lev Manovich, for example.[15] These kinds of academic project, however different, share the function of formulating the virtual, the electronic and their forms as an academic disciplinary object, and it was this general order of discourse that I wanted to evade in my making the terminal into an object of reflection or of devotional attention and myself into a kind of angry Saint Teresa, waiting for what in the end one would never know to have happened, the *jouissance* which will never have been. I wanted my messages to take on some of the poetics or rhetorical flavour of a Teresa or a John; the position I adopted was not the epiphany proposed to the reader of William Gibson's prophetic *Neuromancer*, for example, but the frustrated or deprived condition of the Saint who will have missed the epiphany exactly as a condition of having come to know of it.[16] To do that seemed like the best way of saving or recovering lost time—and I recall how much time we did lose, albeit with disinterested virtue and sublimatory projection, in our devotion to the cause of the Working Class. This was still the only categorical ethic available to a Marxist of the 1970s who was living at that hopeless end-point of the European and Asian social(ist) revolutions. Now I can be saved by this knowledge: that the mess of words and images that is left as a trace on my computer is a record of something that was never, or not as yet, to be. Or, cyberspace offers nothing (new), but in that it does offer a nothing of complex signifiance.

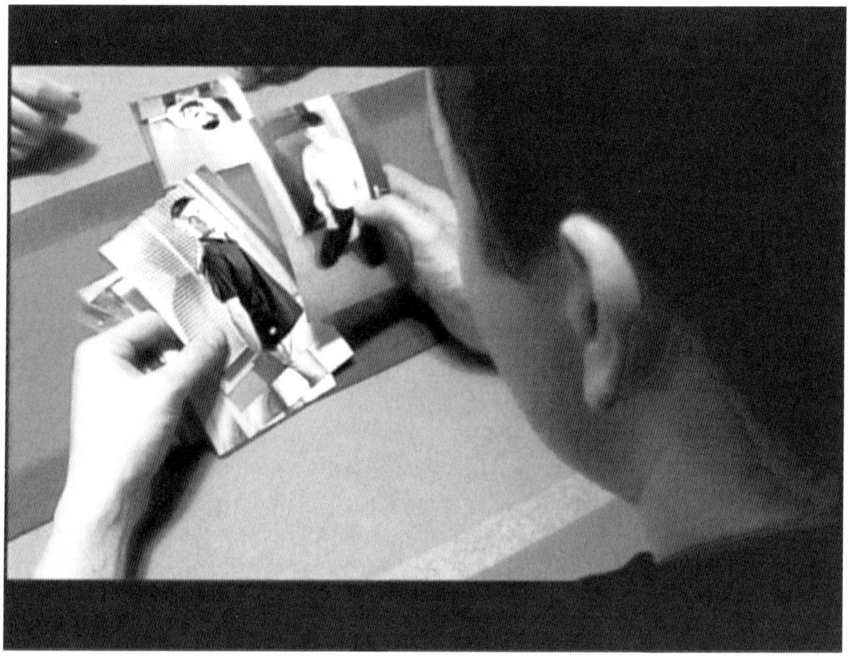

*Three Months* in effect accomplished what I would have wanted to achieve, and did so in a single but enigmatically complex gesture, suggesting the realization of a question that I had not even begun properly to formulate. It is, of course, something that artists can do from time to time, the kind of demonstration for which the Ascension of Jesus is such perfect material, the 'look, no wires' effect of Raphael's version in the Vatican. (Something much later to be refuted by Bruce Nauman in his *Failing to Levitate in my Studio* (1966), but who, in his failure, remains an artist, or becomes one.) The Ascension is a subject that shows what art can do, it is a matter of art rather than of theology and its representations, and offers a paradigmatic figure for the possibility of an impossible that is, finally, autonomous of faith. The matter of the unicorn and its indices is far more complex than my opening quotation could ever envisage and, at the same time, stunningly simple as the unicorn's many images—the Cluny Tapestries for example—testify. The unicorn is easily fabricated and made to point to something other than itself; allegory's allegory in that this is all it can do. If my chatting is, after all, allegorical, I have still to find of what it speaks.

The way in which the video performs this vanishing act is, I guess, as follows. Haines imagines the metaphorics of the internet back to front, as if they were an analogy or a documentary (denotation) rather than a metaphor. In a classic fictional manoeuvre he identifies 'as if' with 'what if' so that proposition and supposition justify one another in a curious tautology of 'this is'—which aimlessly drifts somewhere near to Ludwig Wittgenstein's classic formulations of language's aporia. But the men in the video—the actors—do not point to the chatters they represent, but to the scenario of desire already engendered by these chatters and now dissipated. In the chat room these forms of speech relate to each other in a fluid and inconsequential manner, according to the flow of the unfolding daydream *à deux*, and to the only approximate relation of one cell of chat to another as a statement or a question or a response. Above all there is no voice, other than that imagined or 'heard' by the chatter as he writes or reads a message, so the silence is bathed in a phantasmatically perfect sound generated by the figuring of desire.

In the above part-frame one man has offered to the other, across the table at which they are sitting, prints of the photographs that they have originally exchanged electronically, either voluntarily or at one or the other's request. Each in turn admires the other as if he was absent, and one then says 'I would really like to meet you'. In effect the idea of the chat room—whether it is on a governmental, academic, teenage lovers', gay or terrorist website—is a new one, and probably should have had a new name: it points to something that does not exist in our day-to-day life, while being a part of it, and can hardly be translated into its other forms other than by the no-strings faculty of art. It remains a 'space' where one goes to chat rather than to smoke or eat lunch, to chat as a separate and distinct function from simply speaking to each other over a sandwich or a cigarette, and it is truly becoming a generalized alternative to other forms of social relation, to the extent that some of us are even asked to put up a chat room alongside an academic syllabus.

Thus, though Haines' manoeuvre arises from a conversation in a particular gay cruising chat room, its findings could be extended in various ways back into the real—as distinct from the virtual in this restricted sense—and so virtualize the convention of a documentary reality of which the chat room is a particular and original abstraction. This, the chat room, is what sociability becomes as it is abstracted to certain of its functions—these functions are an always-already virtuality of the social as the articulation and projection of sexual desires—and queerly, while gay, precedes gender.

At the same time, one might prefer to leave this formulation close to Lacan's naming the formation of the unconscious, in his fifth seminar, as that of a virtual reality,[17] and so say that in the internet chat room, what stands outside it comes to play a role of the imaginary in its relation to the symbolic within—in a general Lacanian sense of contemporary cultural theory. Clearly this is open to a deepening and a more complex understanding as 'Lacan' becomes more fully read—each succeeding paragraph of the passage I have in mind would tend to virtualize my deployment of its predecessor, and this piecing together of something that is not an ensemble will be important in the unfolding of this work.

So what Haines does is to imagine a number of rooms, public and private spaces from the bedroom to the office to the park or art gallery—documentary spaces, so to speak, or ones that can be documented in a documentary convention—and to treat these spaces as those in which the little written exchanges of the chat room come to have been uttered. Two men (unicorns? Angels?) play an elaborate sexual game with each other, of desire and domination, spoken in the partial and contracted language of the message, with its imagined inflections—inflections which are, so to speak, the inner speech of these little utterances, their enunciative principle—but one that can only be made audible at the risk of sounding inauthentic, inappropriate and unconvincing. Sometimes the men terminate a phrase expressing quite specific desires—to be humiliated, to humiliate—with the shortening 'etc., etc.', something we rarely say in the street, while each exchange of smiles—of smileys in the text—is figured through only one repeated set of lips and teeth. The smiley transcends human particularity—and does so in silence, in a rupture of the diegetic flow by a detached mechanism of affect that does not quite adhere to the symbolic, which anyway is shattered in the speaking aloud of these written texts that are not a script.

This manoeuvre, the 'look, no wires' of the video, thus reverses figuration in either its accepted rhetorical or pictorial procedures; and for the length of its 37 minutes, in the almost crushing banality of its script—which is the complete transcription of the 'conversation'—the video sustains an uncanny sense that 'one' has not seen this or even this kind of thing before and that its reality is irreducible. Yet it is not a script in the theatrical or filmic sense, it has indeed already 'happened', it is a trans-script that is as if fixed in being otherly performed, but only after its meaning has been depleted. *Signifiance—nothing* indeed seems like the borderline activity that I imagined above.

One man says to the other that he wishes to be able to treat him violently, bondage, scat, etc., as and when he wishes, and the other replies that he would wish for this to be the case. In each demanded instance of a 'humiliation' he resists, but finally says: 'for you' I will do it. Not for my own pleasure, or me but *for you*. And here what we rediscover at the heart of the novelty of the banal is a memory of an immensely long term, almost like the bio-time of the uncanny, nothing more or less that the heretical Christian concept of pure love according to François Fénelon, as it phases into the Kantian categorical: 'if you, god, choose to destroy me I will love you for your choosing and do so without interest or the hope of recompense.'

Curiously and necessarily nothing is consummated in this scenario. At one point, as I have already noted, there is a careful re-enactment of a meeting that did take place, a lunch, shot in a different style of reality, or a lesser style of ideality, in which the lighting becomes conventional and *random* figures appear here and there. There is not sign of sex as a touching but rather its absorption into speech; as if there really is no sexual relation, other than there. But at the level of desire's daydreaming an ancient form of the absolute enters as a sexual relation with one's self in one's relation to the screen. There is a meet-

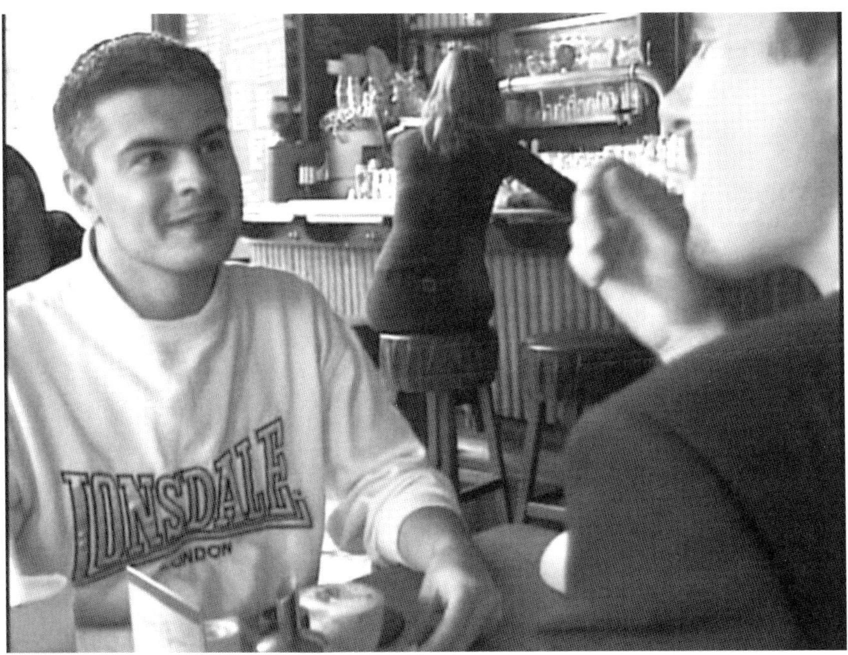

ing, and here I want to press on with other concerns, even though this meeting may turn out to have been the most pressing.

It was on account of this realizing—in an elaborate and protracted metaphor that, in Haines' film, becomes the substance of the screen, even in the film's absolute exclusion of metaphor as a figure—of the devotional character of the terminal and the modes through which it may be addressed, that my own work came to a halt, if only because the image points to more things than my arguments had been able to shape—unicorns you might say—for which there is no index. I had looked to the internet to form a version of some kind of a highly differentiated and fractured unity of the kind we call a 'self'—something on which J. B. Pontalis has written eloquently in his *Entre le rêve et la douleur*.[18] I had reached the following provisional conclusions before I gave up.

1. The interaction between the temporary self of the chat room (which might also be longer lasting than it seems or even a 'true' self) and its interlocutors represents a drive against the reality principle. This drive is either reversed as soon as a meeting is arranged between two chatters other than in the imaginary spaces of the web. For now the concrete spaces of the city, distance, cost of transport, weather all intervene to say yes or no, as does one's own diary that lies half-neglected on the desk with its already existing appointments, between them reinstating the law. More often a meeting must be deferred and, perversely as an outcome of this process desire itself is hypo-

statized as the very vector of deferral. Or, alternatively, the daydream-like structure of the relation with the gaze is more likely to be destroyed by the offer of a meet than by its refusal, as at that moment the promise of sexual pleasure becomes confused with *jouissance* as a wager won in advance of its own illusion. It becomes delusion.

2. As an outcome of these considerations as well as many others, it begins to look as if the relation of the internet to the individual in some way resembles Walter Benjamin's problematic of the new or the revolutionary having expressed itself in an old and inappropriate technology or cultural form: here the most contemporary culture of communication is one that is itself easily seduced by the formation of the subject and the conflict between Freud's systems Ucs., Pcs.-Cs. and so on; the unconscious nestles in this 'place' and nourishes it, overpowering or disempowering its newness. At this point chatting assumes the unicorn-like quality of becoming allegory's allegory.

3. Waiting itself becomes a sustaining structure for the subject of this enunciation—you might even say that waiting is the subject's medium, in which it is suspended and is nourished. It is in waiting that the non-correspondence of things and signification is anyway invested: then in this, in the being-subject of the enunciation, in waiting for the signs, icons, indices, and signifieds to stick together, something of the historical experience of the mystic begins to look like a matter of language in the everyday, at least in this new aspect of the everyday. Interestingly the times of waiting are highly differentiated from the most immediate, such as the now collapsed of photographic time for the taking of a picture and putting it on-line—which impatience may turn into an age—and the months it sometimes takes to arrange to meet someone. These times enter into each other through a mixture of languid patience and little epiphanies of visual pleasure in the process of exchange and reading profiles. The consumerist slogan of Gaydar, '*What you want, when you want it*', so similar to that of early credit cards, traps the individual in the promise of *jouissance*, but as if it were the threat of a privation, as if this were always acknowledged. At the same time the enunciation of the internet and its exchange of words and pictures teeter on the borderlines of the whole matter of the infinitesimal yet cataclysmic conflict between transubstantiation and consubstantion that shook European society in the sixteenth and seventeenth centuries, something that also concerned what you want and what you get, and when. This past is trapped in such a mesh, in the sieving process of a contemporary vernacular, and in turn takes hold of it and clogs it up. Whether the flesh and the word will coincide, and how and when is a pragmatic theology of the present.

4. Waiting at the monitor figures the screen as the collapse together of the object and the gaze, as if they have ever really been so highly differentiated, something which is embarrassingly obvious, a purloined letter, in its shiny luminescence, in the literalness of its screenness, the text lying just behind it,

and so forth. Another way of putting this, that would relate to the work of critics who have recently thought through the implications of Lacan's later work and the concept of the *sinthome*, is that this whole process and relation is something that teeters on and shows the edge of the 'real'. Somehow we see over the excluded or negated matter out of which the symbolic has come to be made, at the point where its functions are put into doubt.

A preliminary conclusion must be, then, that not much has happened, and maybe nothing and that this nothing is germane to the question of the index. In one sense, if we were to think of the process of producing signs as god-like, then we can begin to borrow from an old theological language—not so much concerning the presence of the body, transubstantiation, consubstantiation and so on, which are indeed concerned with the index—but rather the inscription of signs in Philo of Alexandria:

> God is continuously ordering matter by his thought. His thinking was not anterior to his creating and there never was a time when he did not create, the Ideas themselves having been with him from the beginning. For God's will is not posterior to him, but is always with him, for natural motions never give out. Thus ever thinking he creates, and furnishes to sensible things the principle of their existence, so that both should exist together: the ever-creating Divine Mind and the sense-perceptible things to which beginning of being is given.[19]

In the end the best way to set out and maybe even conclude this essay is to set out the phases in which it might see a completion, which is not necessarily desirable. I had wanted to start with two gestures, one of which is the trying to think about this at all and admitting a failure, and the other of which is dramatizing the way in which this was brought to a halt by something which in itself represents all the questions we pose to the index and the virtual—the video in question.

A guide through the phases that set up the space of my discussion could then look like this, and they are archival and theoretical:

1. The argument of the old timer and the Preacher in *Ecclesiastes* (Qohelet), Solomon, or whoever it was: There is nothing new under the sun. Suppose we take this as a phrase to be heard, something which for me is always important in relation to writing, and that which writing can too easily take back from speech in its graphocentrism. Where will the emphasis fall? The phrase could be uttered in such a way that what we believe to be new under the sun is, exactly, nothing, despair, resignation. Or, the nothing is what is new, and we need to ask what is the character of this nothing that the new is? You can see that these tonalities can be strung out on reflection, the reflection of uttering and audition.[20] If, in Benjamin's formulation, that I have already mentioned, the new eventually finds an appropriate technology, at the point it becomes

fully visible it is no longer new; so it is an as if: a nothing of this new technology on which it has taken hold and at the same time renders the something new as if nothing. The relation of futurism and the cinema might be something like the relation of the unconscious and the internet, so that the virtuality is something that occurs elsewhere, as if before the internet and the loss of the indexical: nothing in turn will point somewhere; it will become a negation or a negative index.

2. One form of this negation that may be useful for us is something that Hannah Segal said in a conversation at a public seminar of the performing arts group RESCEN, in reply to a request to repeat what she had said at a preceding workshop (to paraphrase): 'everything I say is new and very old.'[21] This can be heard as a way of saying that the new is an epiphenomenom of something that might have already happened; and another might be André Green's discussion of 'rien' in his essay on King Lear, which is not about the famous phrase 'nothing will come of nothing', but that exchange where Cordelia tells Lear that she can give him nothing back, without which denial, Green asserts, nothing more can unfold: 'Cordelia ne peut rien rendre'. There is nothing to return in return for a gift or heritage, and it is this necessity that sets the symbolic in crisis, or loosens Lear's position within the chain.[22]

3. All of this is germane to a question of waiting for the sign, once brought into being, to adhere: to a historical body of material, in a way that seems to articulate the insight of deferred action as a temporality—an affect that now haunts *Nightcleaners* (Berwick Street Film Collective, 1975). Is this nothing what is new, or is this new actually a 'nothing new'. Does the experience of the virtual as it happens in the internet, before this gaze and object that is the screen, reinstate the subject as a monad at the point where we had critically and theoretically achieved the dispersal of the self? Or does it point to its intensified dispersal just at the point where the seduction of current fields of dispersal and distraction—portable phones, internet and so on—could make us wish to resort to the monad as an idyll, a resistance, political and economic, to this hardly voluntary process of being networked? I don't think that these things are known or decided, but they seem important in taking an account of what might have happened and what it is that we have done.

Since I am here tracking something that looks like a non-dialectical relation of what we call old and new in a complex process of small negations, and looking for the substance or materiality of signification, it has already come to seem strategically valuable to track the whole question only through texts that distance us from contemporary thought. Here I would like, as a further possible alienation, to propose the Judeo-Aristotelian discussions of the unity and incorporeal nature of god written by Moses Maimonides in his *Guide for the Perplexed* and his *The Laws of the Basic Principles of the Torah*, or the related discussion of the different types of angel found in both books. It's interesting too for me to do this, as nothing could be less gay than this great scholar.[23]

Taking the following quotation, this time from his Thirteen Principles, as a base we could think about how its certainty haunts contemporary descriptions of the virtual and the internet as an unnameable set of sets in distinction to previous forms of communication:

> *The Third Fundamental Principle:* We are to believe that He is incorporeal, that His unity is physical neither potentially nor actually. None of the attributes of matter can be predicated of Him, neither motion, nor rest, for example. They cannot refer to Him accidentally or essentially. That is why our sages denied Him composition and separation, and said: 'On High there is neither sitting nor standing, neither want nor weariness' […]. The prophet asked: 'To whom can you compare God, whom might He resemble?' […]. If He were a body, He would be like other bodies.[24]

This opens a flaw in our post-Foucauldian modes of thinking-comparison (*Les mots et les choses*, for instance), for us to imagine ways of arguing about incomparability in the bodiless sameness of the virtual as well as about the body as a ground of signification.

I would like to underline the discussion of trans- and consubstantiation and other theological discussions, such as the identification of the living flame with Jesus or the Holy Spirit, something that has recently received a compelling exposition in Derrida's late work, especially in his *Le toucher: Jean-Luc Nancy*. This seems to be of some urgency in reviewing any theory of the sign, not least in relation to the insistent *mise en scène* of Catholicism and mysticism in Lacan's work. This has recently been discussed in Jacques Lebrun's *Le pur amour de Platon à Lacan*, while Jean-Louis Vaysse's magisterial study, *L'inconscient des modernes* traces the evolution of a space that we come to call the unconscious.[25] All of these three foreground the complexity of the old–new relation and its discursive fields and the slow, uneven and non-self possessing character of the unfolding of our thought. What is new of the internet is that, in the endless superposition of words and images and even of word and image, it reminds us that the 'problem' of such relations is ongoing and has never been of itself very important. It shows us something old but in a new way and for now. This newness is the medium of the artist David Haines, and not video.

*       *       *

After simply sketching a few possible displacements of our subject, ones that become really possible in the space of virtual combination, and evacuating any sense of progressive time from it, I would, were I to complete this essay, be concerned simply to speak to the value of some of these sources as a practice of estrangement, as a mimesis of a certain moment in the belief system of modern radical or avant-garde art and its theories. That is, to treat this looking back, or giving in to the re-emergence of the old, as a radical thing to do that is consonant with the onetime ambitions of radical and political academic theory. As for the question of the relation to the working class, I would hazard that our relation to this class was already, always perhaps, in spite of the desire for justice, a devotional one to a virtuality, and as good an example of pure love as I could find, the resolution of which will do or undo what I have said above. For it will return us to other questions of liberty and justice, for which this work is an allegory.

Nothing is what we make, not of the thing in itself.

9

# AIRPORT

Martha Rosler

Airports and air travel are much on our minds these days, or more properly, perhaps, at the heart of core anxieties of the age. One of the iconic images of the new millennium in the West was of the New York City towers burning and falling, brought down by commercial airliners used as guided missiles. In respect of a more chronic, slowly evolving worldwide catastrophe, namely, global warming, a critique of air travel has recently been mounted for its alarming levels of $CO_2$ emissions. This criticism is especially strident in countries like Britain whose powerful carriers, like British Airways, are most affected by the rise of very low-fare European airlines that have led, over the past decade, to a great expansion of tourist travel. Flying also engages some of our deepest fears of sudden death (not to mention claustrophobia, agoraphobia, and acrophobia) alongside our fantasies of effortless flight. Air travel is the premier and most highly capitalized mode of transportation—though very far from being the most commonly employed—and represents a critically important node in national and international transportation networks. The continued stratification of air passengers into travel classes, with their graded comforts and discomforts, echoes the increased stratification in the industrially advanced societies. The centrality of air travel (and document transfer and communications) to the present round of economic and cultural 'globalization' is obvious; still, I want to call attention to the central, and growing, role of air travel in the aggressively internationalizing art world. Not only

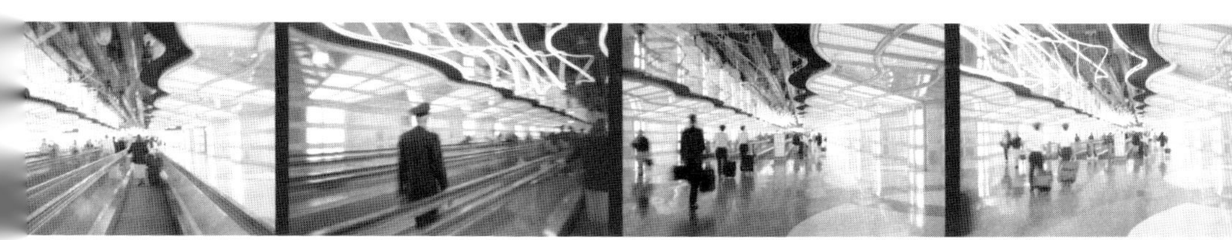

9.1    O'Hare underground tunnel. All images © Martha Rosler.

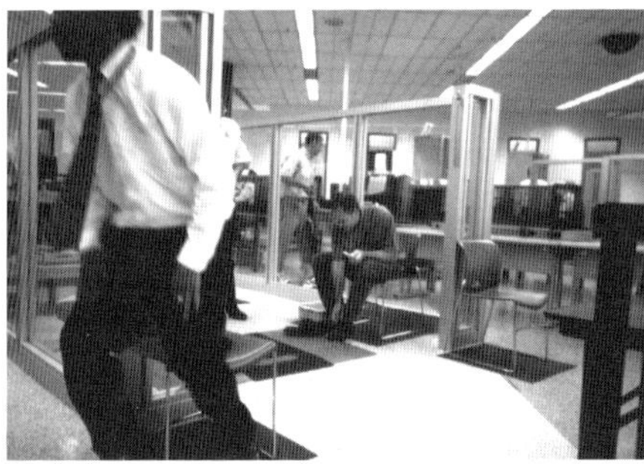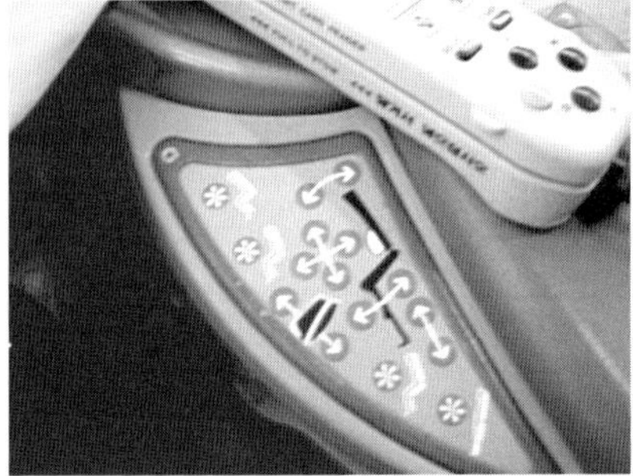

9.2      (left) Cincinnati security check. (right) First-class bed/seat adjustment
         panel.

the art works but the artists (often irrespective of exhibitions) are urgently
invited or required to show up from afar, as the physical embodiment or totem
of the 'work-of-art enterprise', to coin a phrase. This state of affairs, now
well remarked on, has been long a-building.

     For 25 years I have been flying on ordinary, scheduled commercial flights,
as a result of art-world invitations, often travelling long distances, at first pri-

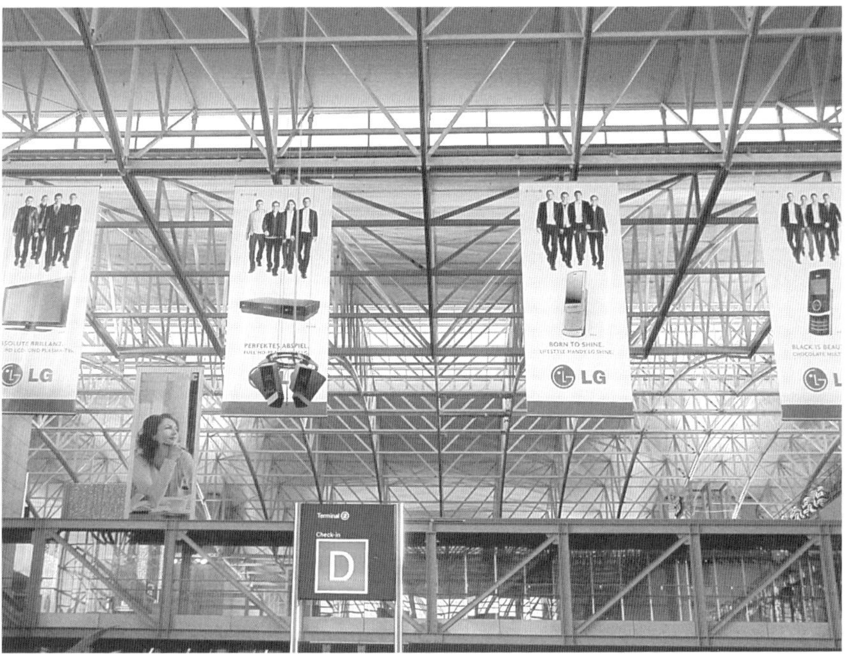


9.3      Frankfurt/Main airport.

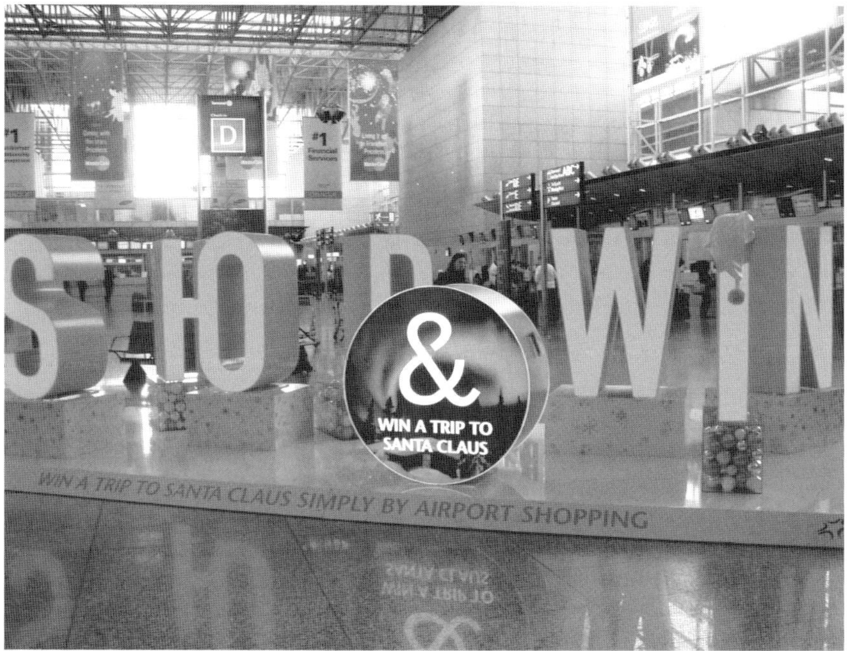


9.4    Frankfurt/Main airport.

marily within North America—where I live—but subsequently to and from
Europe. This has given me, a business traveller in economy class, a great deal
of time to observe a system at first mystifyingly new to me, a person initially
more likely to drive or to take the bus to get around. I felt that 'intern-
odal'/intermodal transfer, from one neutered, bewildering corporate space
to another, could be taken as representative of a newly established paradigm
of transportation. Because of the systematic loss of specificity (and thus of
historicity) as to place and time through 'dis/placement', it seemed reasonable
to refer to the system and structure of air travel as postmodern—not so much
to invoke a definitive historical periodizing but in response to the prominence
of characteristics identified with 'postmodernism', among them the flattened,
depthless rendering of space and time and the reimagining of experience into
a set of trajectories. Rapid spatio-temporal dislocation often produces in the
traveller a sense of being cast free—rather too abruptly, perhaps—of the
ordinary narrative nets of daily life; in the air terminal and aboard the plane,
the links to everyday life are provided by simulacra and distractive media as
the leading face of commodity and commerce. The corporations that determine and define this experience try to keep us firmly within the logic of consumption: docile even in the face of discomfort, accepting of fare-based/
class-based inequalities, and atomized, but in the first and final analyses still

tied to them through the bonds of both necessity and choice. The air terminal, and the system for which it is the primary *mise en scène* on the ground,
properly if idiosyncratically ensconced within national boundaries, form a
microcosm, then, of our collective though partial projection of the world system. I have earlier written that:

> as production in advanced industrial societies is increasingly character-
> ized by metaphors of transmission and flow, I am interested in the
> movement of bodies through darkened corridors and across great dis-
> tances but also in the effacement of the experience of such travel by
> constructs designed to empty the actual experience of its content and
> make it the carrier of another sort of experience entirely. This totalized
> industrial representation of air travel and its associated spaces as 'a world
> apart' is different from that of any other form of mass transport.[1]

Our civilization continues to require the circulation not only of commodities but of ideas, and not only of ideas but of people. But in the dozen
years I have been writing about airports and air travel, many of the conditions
I observed have evolved or intensified, notably the sense of risk and the centrality of individualized surveillance especially after 11 September 2001 (see
above). Structures, both architectural and economic, have changed. But in

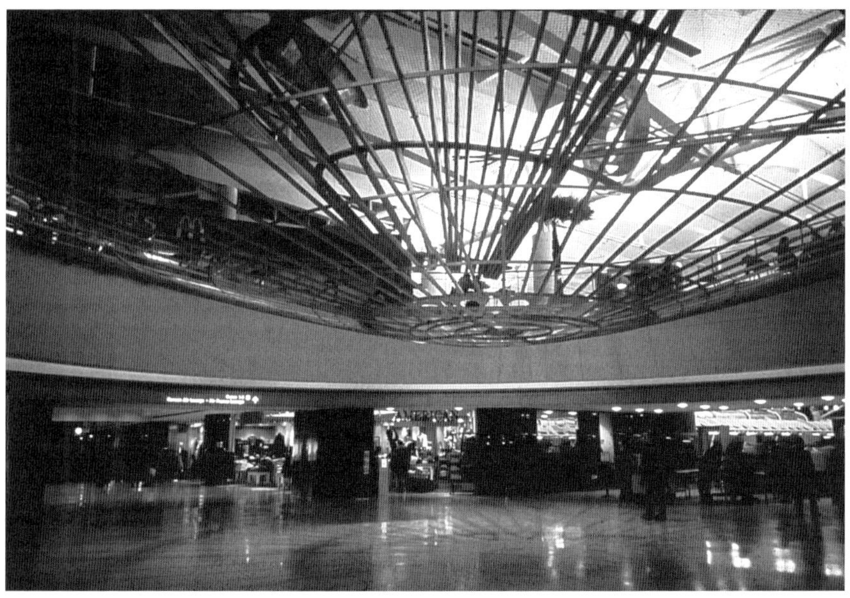

9.5     Terminal 2, John F. Kennedy airport, New York.

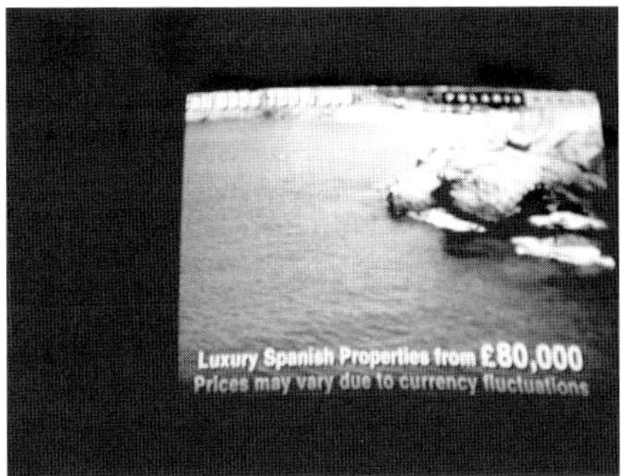


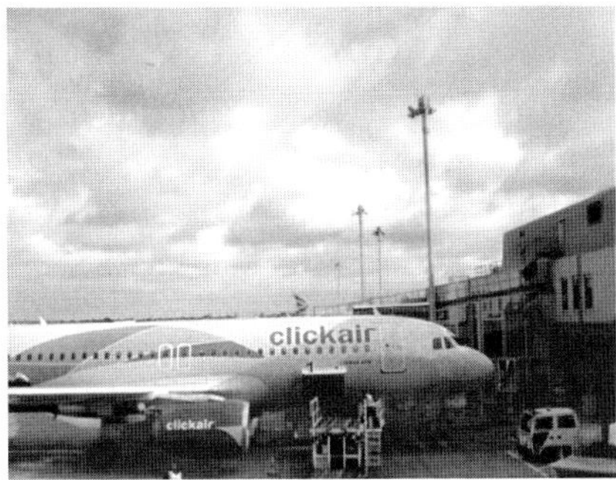


9.6    (left) Luxury Spanish properties for Britons. (right) Low cost airline for British–Spanish commuting.

talking to a new acquaintance about this project of mine, I didn't get very far before he started in:

> Airports? Airports! My family just took a trip, and the planes were so crowded and the airports—they were all the same! And they're not even in town, they take so long to get to. And one of the worst things was the TVs playing really loud everywhere. We asked the gate agents if we could turn them off and they said, 'Now, that would be something'—because you really can't turn them off.

He added a few more disgusted remarks, and during that brief outpouring, I was brought back to the ground floor of immediacy that had led to my photographic project and to my observations that still seem to touch upon a widely shared experience.

In my milieu, the art world—an imagined community in Benedict Anderson's sense—the physical circulation of art objects, and their associated professional populations, is an escalating principle; in this the art world is taking part in the globalizing momentum of this moment of 'flexible accumulation' (a term preferred by some to 'postmodernism').[2] The art world, after hesitating over the new global image game (largely dominated by mass media/pop culture images, of course) has responded by developing several systems for regularizing standards and markets for their high-end products and their associated ideological frameworks. Three prominent means were adopted by the art world to raise the visibility and drawing-power of its contents under the new global imperative. The burgeoning biennials of the 1990s, of which there now appear to be hundreds, have elicited some degree of derision on the part of observers, but they serve to insert or incorporate an urban, and often a national, locale into the international circuit, creating a physical space to attract

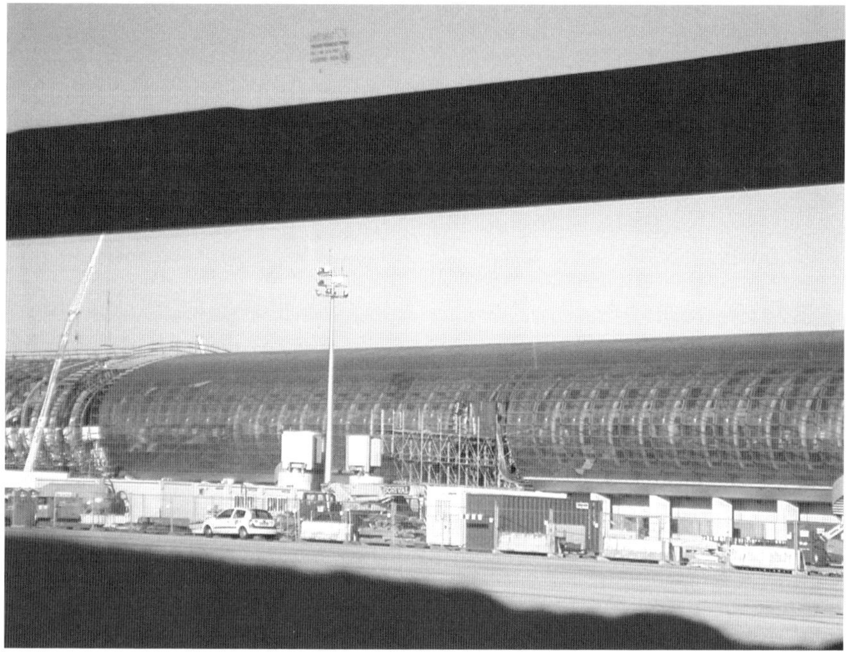

9.7     Charles de Gaulle construction.

art and art world members, including museum professionals, journalists, and
of course artists, as well as ordinary tourists alongside art tourists. That the
local audience is educated about international styles and mores is important
but the effect is only secondary to the elevation of the local venue (in the
wider sense of local city and art institutions and art economy) to top-rank
global ('world-class') status, which means in principle that the important audience must arrive from elsewhere. The biennial model provides not only a
physical circuit but a regime of production and normalization. In more
peripheral venues, it is not untypical for artists representing the local or home

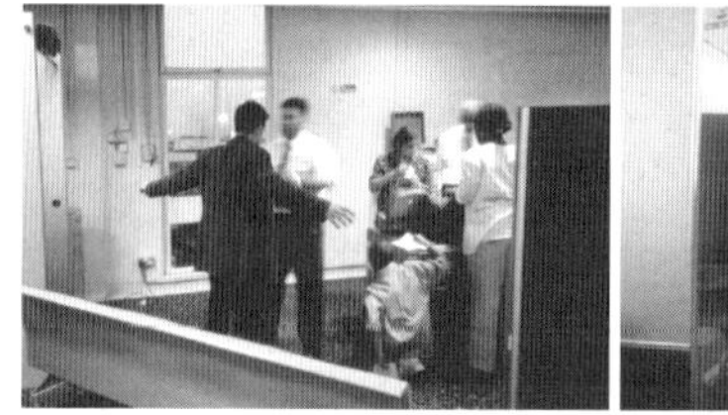 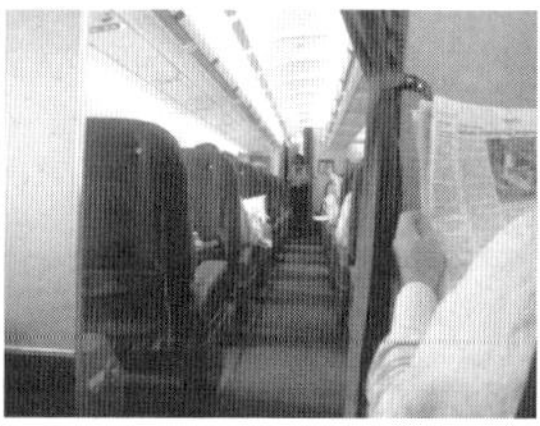 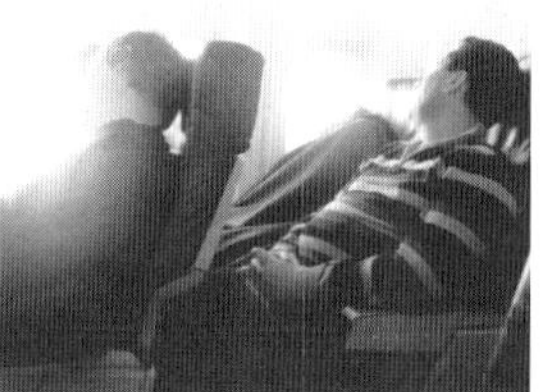

9.8     (left) Heathrow security inspection. (centre) European business flight.
        (right) Passengers.

culture to have moved to artist enclaves in fully 'metropolitan', first world cities as the portal to the global art market/system before returning to their countries of origin to be 'discovered'. The aeroplane saves the day, allowing a continued relationship with the homeland and home culture; expatriation can be a prolonged stay away that is punctuated by time back home. This condition, of course, defines all migrant and itinerant labour under current conditions: needing to cross (or if possible effectively ignore) borders, just like the flow of capital.

Localities have also sought to capitalize on art world holdings and institutions by commissioning 'signature' buildings by celebrity architects, much as they have sought to differentiate their air terminals from all others by hiring celebrity architects to build them, inevitably producing a new circuit of accommodation to normative standards. High-profile architecture is a small-scale (building size) intervention. It increases traffic—'architourism'— dramatically in some cases (the famous, and signal, example being the Guggenheim branch, designed by Frank Gehry at industrially dilapidated Bilbao in Spain's Basque Country) but probably not on the scale of the other efforts. Unlike them, however, architecture has some degree of structural permanence and continues to cast an aura of importance over the changing exhibitions within.

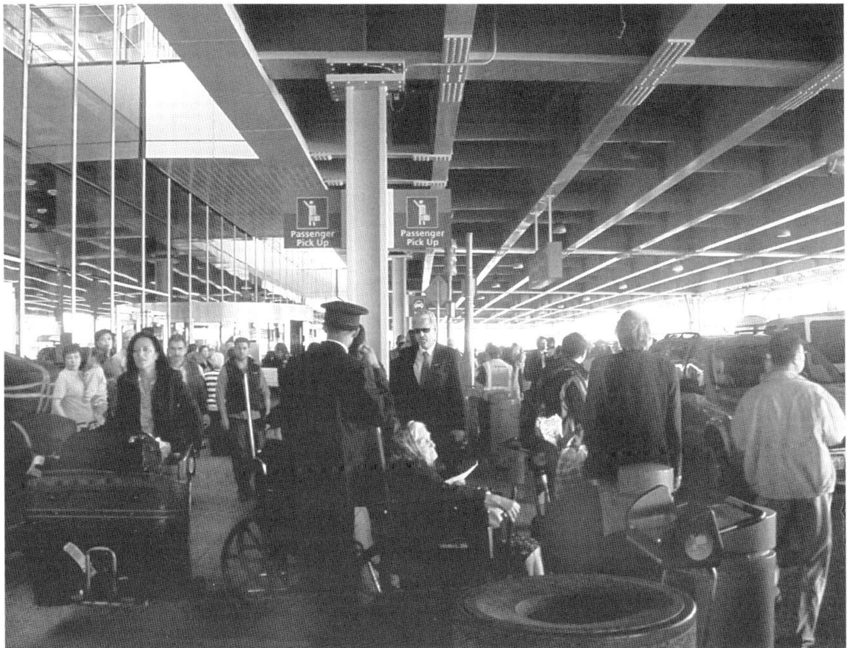


9.9    Busy concourse.

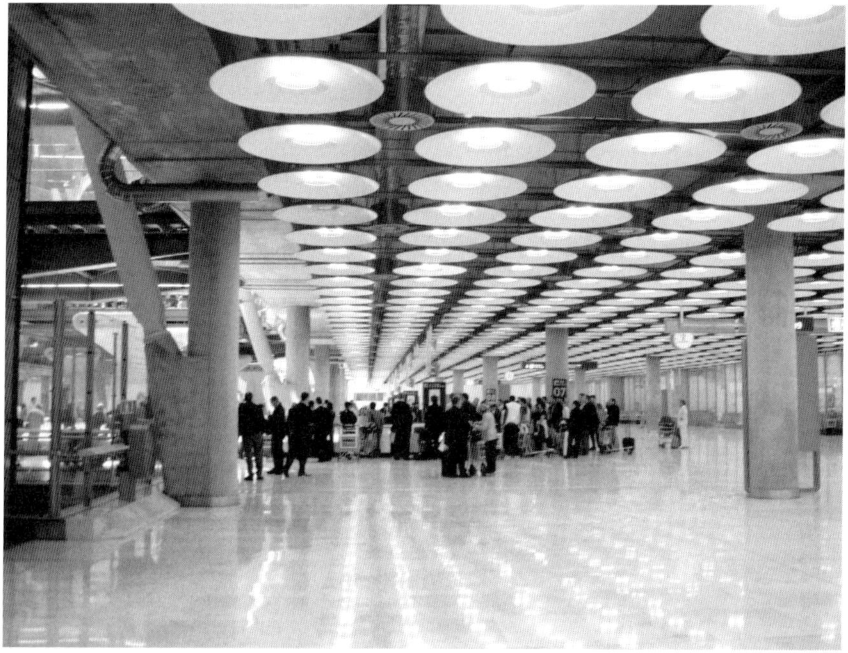

9.10   Madrid.

A third, most recent method of global discipline, one that has trumped
the others and changed the big picture, has been the great increase in the
number and location of commercial art fairs in a very short period. The pre-
eminence of the art fair (an often enormous array of temporary booths of
art dealers, each of whom pays a small fortune to exhibit their wares) represents the art world's rapid monetization; the art world has impatiently shaken
off the need for internal processes of vetting and quality control in favour of
speeded-up (exchange value) production and multiplication of financial and
prestige value. A wider prestige, however, is of little moment in comparison
to the astounding price inflation. Some of the most important fairs are satel-
lites, colonies that have come to out-shine their original venues (often with no
negative effect to the parent) and to jump from the periphery of the art
world's institutionalized vetting circuit to centre stage. As the main art fairs
have grown in dollar (or euro) receipts, they have expanded beyond the simple sales-booth format, adding legitimating features. Curatorial efforts, including 'project rooms' and small monographic exhibitions, as well as lectures by
artists and members of the international intelligentsia, have become the norm
at art fairs, mimicking the more established institutions. In reality, however, no
discursive matrix is required for participation. Visitors need only a travel agent
(or a flight plan for one's private jet) plus hotel accommodations, since the pri-

mary determinant of the success of these fairs is that hoary real-estate prescriptive line, 'location, location, location!' Here artworks are scrutinized for portfolio suitability, while off-site fun (parties and dinners), fabulousness (conspicuous consumption), and shopping for local luxury goods are the selling points for the best attended fairs, those in Miami, New York, and London (staid Basel, the 37-year-old parent of the Miami fair, which is called Miami/Basel, remains vitally important, an originary event that remains well-funded, well located, and well-attended) and the celebrity spotlight has begun shining at least as brightly on fairs as on museum exhibition openings.

All three of these adaptations of the art world and art market are, as noted, dependent to a greater and lesser degree on accelerated expectations of air travel as ordinary and normal. It might be objected that art professionals have long been required to travel to distant exhibitions. It is artists, at every stage of their working lives, who are now increasingly drawn into the distance-travel net (and not just to install works in exhibitions) as the circulation of information has become ever more central to social exchanges. Indeed, is frequently placed at the heart of the 'museum experience' by those in a position to define it. Collectors, we may assume, fly in comfort. Many upper-level museum professionals also fly in the expensive seats. But most artists, aside from those at the highest echelons of acclaim, do not. The fact that virtually

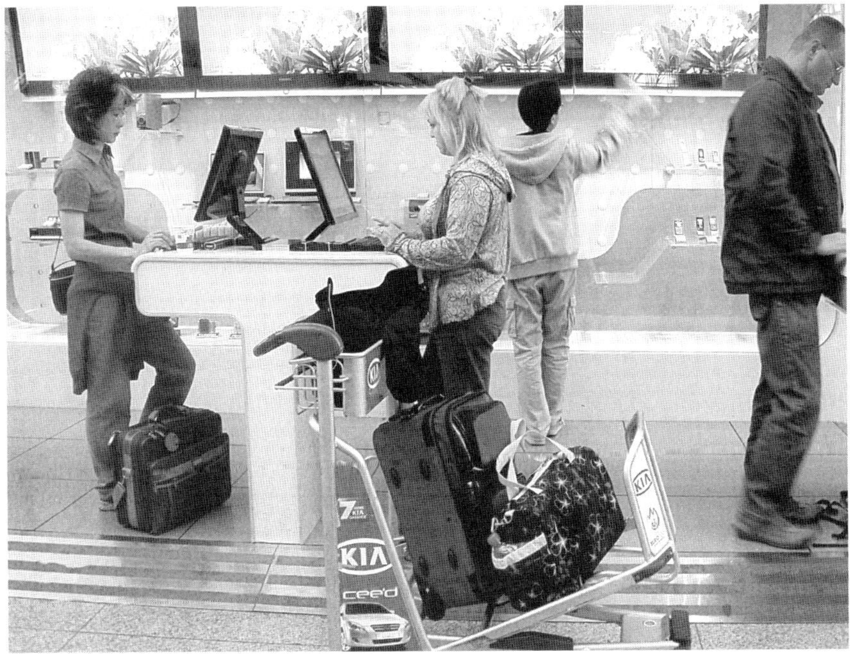

9.11   Free internet with man cleaning.

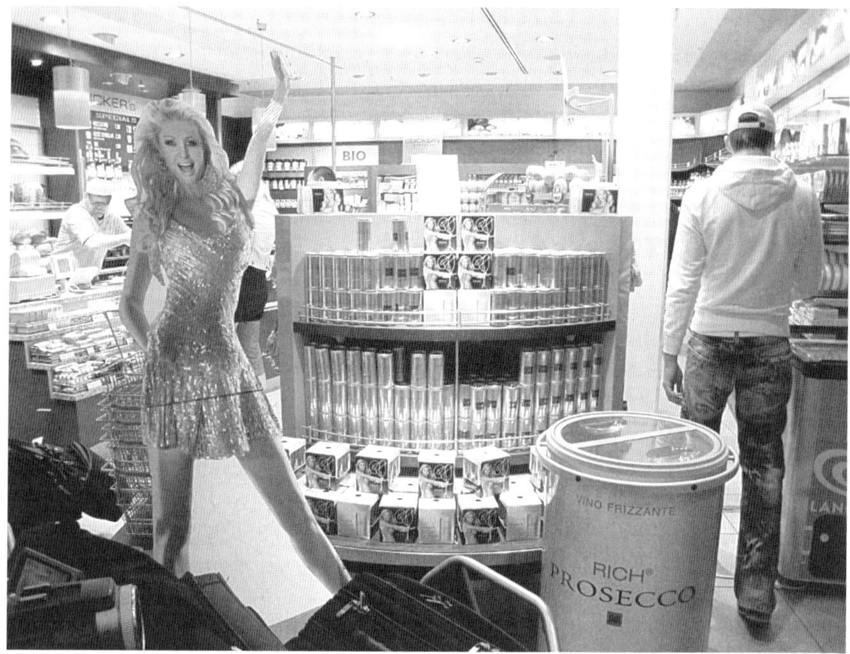

9.12    Charles de Gaulle airport, Roissy.

all major museums not only pay artist-speakers a tiny amount of money but also plead poverty when it comes to paying for air travel—even for most artists having solo exhibitions or screenings—is less astonishing when one notes that the artists are being treated as what they are: the work force. But even for those travellers, including celebrity artists, who fly in luxury, the process itself may be hardly more than tolerable.

In an old issue of the Sunday *New York Times Magazine* devoted to business-class flying, nary a good word could be found about the experience (the cover proclaimed: 'The borderless economy has created a new elite of glazed nomads with all their needs catered to—except those that really matter').[3] Yet many airlines advertised therein, for the obvious reason that for business travellers flying is obligatory, not optional; airline advertising centres on the marginal betterment that their particular brand offers the discomfited high-end traveller. For the rest of us, air travel gets us where we need to go, and often where we *want* to go, but the ritualized (and ever-increasing) discomfort is treated as inescapable. By and large, the physical discomforts of flying result from poor food, inadequately refreshed air, and above all the cramped seating accommodations (as well as, after the flight, the stresses of jet-lag), and airlines have attempted to step up distractions by increasing the entertainment program. Recently, and scandalously, when thousands of travellers were

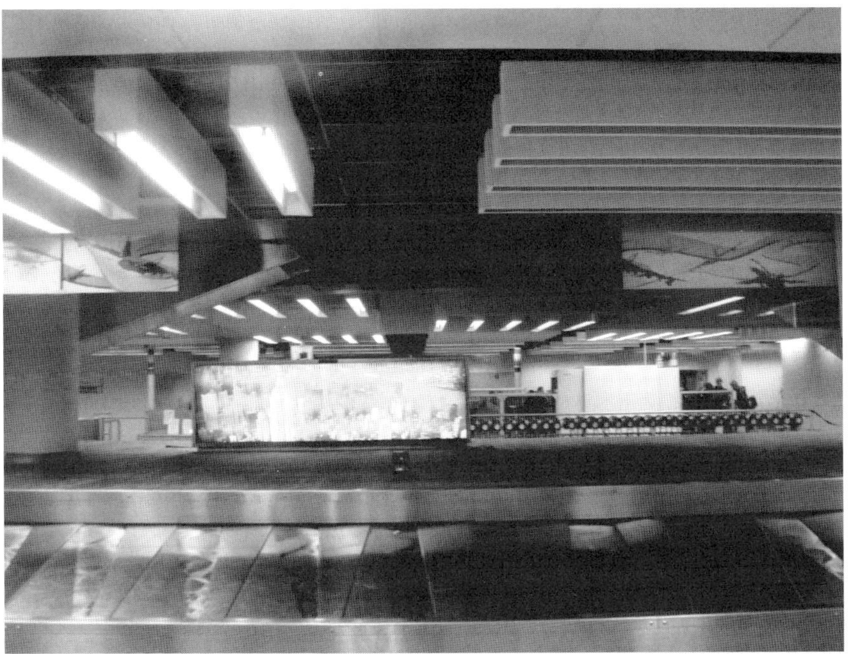

9.13  John F. Kennedy airport, New York.

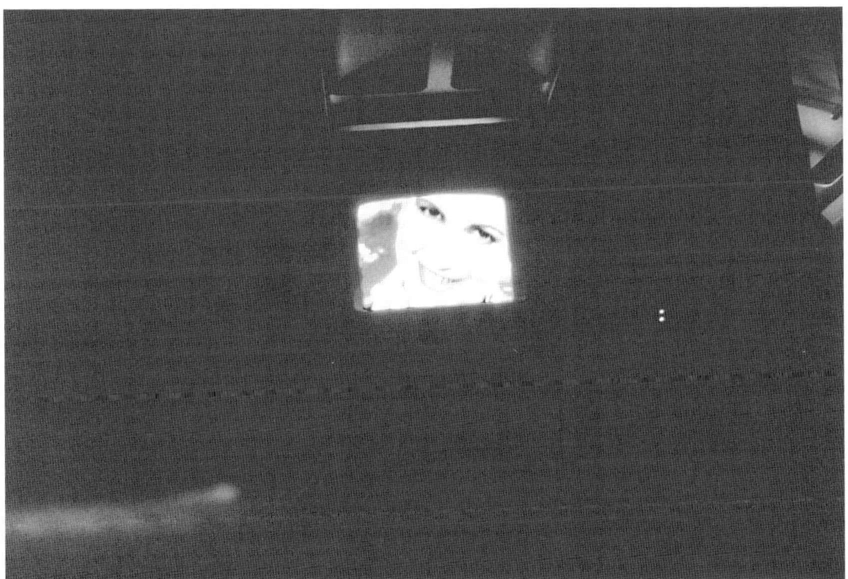

9.14  Kuwait Airlines.

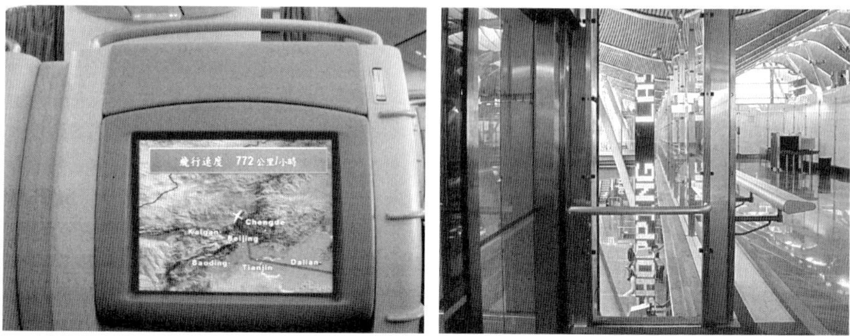

9.15    (left) On-board map. (right) Madrid.

kept for as long as fourteen hours without food or air conditioning on the runways in a US East Coast blizzard aboard planes of a 'no frills' airline, Jet Blue, a young bystander opined scornfully for the cameras that the passengers 'knew what they were in for' when they bought cheap tickets. This sort of inconvenient and inconsiderate behaviour on the part of airlines has long plagued mass airline travel, no matter what the young man, with his repre-

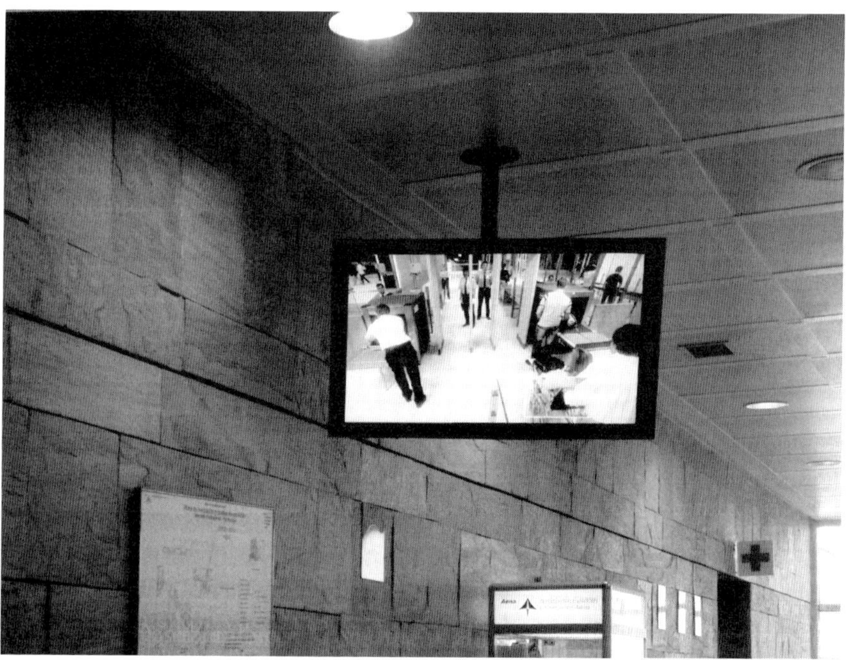

9.16    A Coruña airport.

sentative attitude, may imagine. Still, airlines such as Ryanair and Jet Blue have paved the way for even some flagship carriers to offer fewer services, and in particular to cease offering meals (and in some cases beverages) on flights of any distance, to remain 'competitive'. (Jet Blue offers many television programmes viewable on the backs of its comfy leather seats and accompanied by cheap biscuits, but even this is more than is provided by the infamously chintzy Ryanair, whose founder has boasted that not serving water in flight—considered medically necessary to maintain health—has lessened the need for servicing on-board toilets.) This adds to the burden of discomfort (passengers complained about the food, until there was no longer any food to complain about) but is incorporated into the assumed privations of the cheap-fare bargain, even when the fares are not, after all, so cheap.

The psychic dislocations of flying, however, are endemic to modernity (and presumably postmodernity) and long precede air travel and even motor travel. The acute anxieties, and chronic stress reactions, associated with rapid movement in conveyances were first remarked on in relation to mid-nineteenth-century train travel. But the advent of commercial aviation made control of the problem of the frightened or unruly passenger a matter of central concern and explicit, if unannounced, planning, for orderliness aboard an aircraft brooks no smallest interruption. The need for pacification of passengers in 'cattle class' (in German *Holzklasse*, or wood class) produced a regime of dual, but related, regimentation: a soft militarization and infantilization.

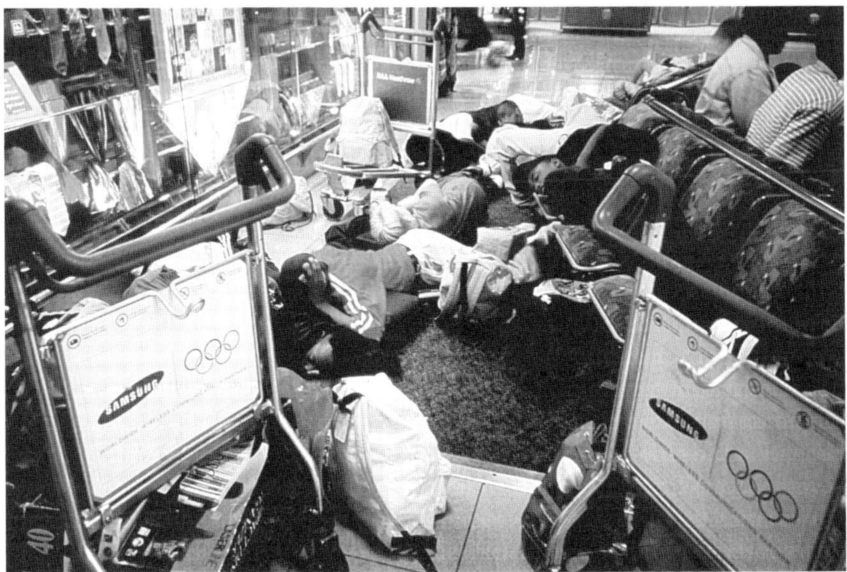

9.17   Boy sleepers, Heathrow.

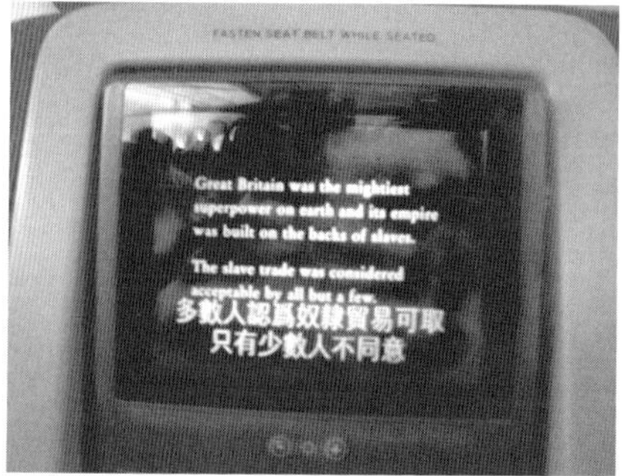


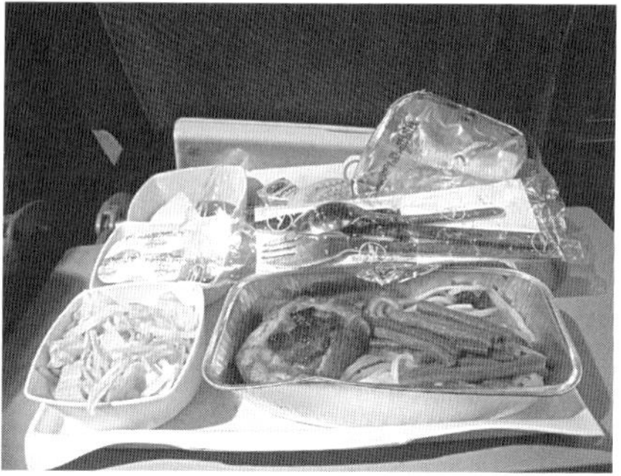

9.18   (left) On-board entertainment. (right) Airline food.

Guardians of tranquillity and order have metamorphosed from railway attendants and engineers (clearly identifiable as servants and workers) into, on the one hand, a professionalized cabin crew, outfitted as nannies in quasi-military uniforms and, on the other, a flight crew in uniforms drawn directly from the military (as are many of the pilots wearing them). Infantilization has centred on gratification through food and drink, including alcohol (or what I have also referred to as a hospital regime of feeding, sleeping and waking) and entertainment, which has increasingly become the focus of most airlines' efforts (see Jet Blue's solution, above). A new universe of electronic distractions in every form—except the internet and cell phones (so far)—is now offered, and the choice is individual. Canned entertainment is more effective than food and drink: one can eat only so often, and alcohol may cause more problems than it solves; moreover, poor entertainment choices, unlike poor food, are likely to cause only diffuse complaints. The unsettling reservoir of unconscious or suppressed fears and anxieties that accompany air travel and ventures into unknown territory is never directly addressed. For those individuals who suffer anxiety and fear, medication obtained before the flight is indicated.

The plane interior itself is a bland corporate enclosure whose design stems from early utopian visions of the aircraft as a streamlined 'flying house' (in Le Corbusier's formulation). The stripped down functionalism was deemed beautiful, representative of the modernity of flight, which from the beginning was focused on the business traveller and thus on the plane as flying office (with upholstered reclining seats whose 'tray table' appears copied from a student desk). This vision similarly informed the conception of the modern air terminal, gateway to the future. The characteristics of the high-rise steel-girdered office building, with its decentralized suites and a soaring atrium, remain. The effect of this standardization, with at best token references to the actual locales, is to produce the feeling of anomic displacement I mentioned at the outset. More recently, cities and airport authorities that can afford to do so

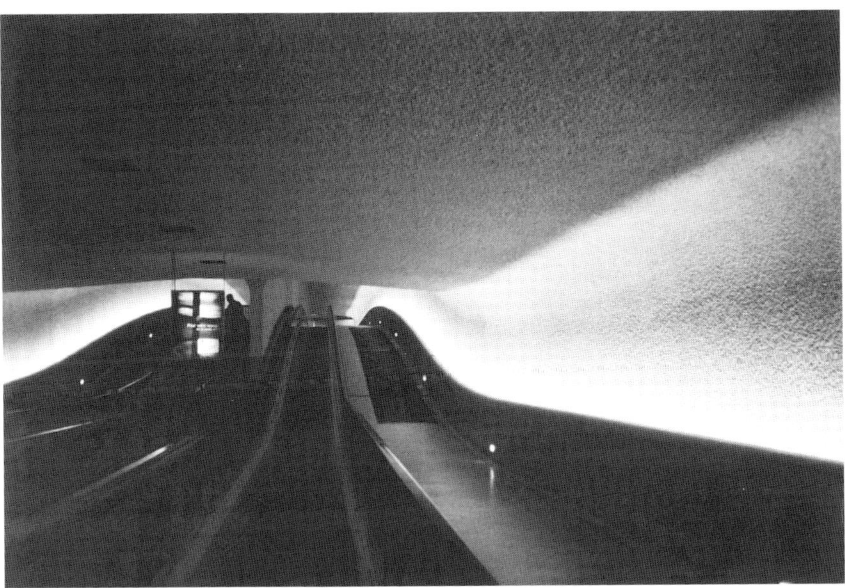

9.19   Charles de Gaulle airport, Roissy.

have invested in airport complexes with important architectural statements by famous architects. Many, as in Asia, are doing so to help foster their expanding and internationalizing economies. Others are simply hoping to have their air terminals become 'destinations', as some were in the early postwar era; now, rather than optimistic futurism, the draw of the terminal complex (despite the wishes of the architects) is as an enclave devoted to high-end retail shopping and other pricey pleasures, a mirror of the out-of-the-office imaginary of the increasingly rich international middle class. Spaces not occupied by retail shops and services are likely to bear large, illuminated advertisements promising dislocation and connection at one and the same time, based on the latest electronic gadgets suitable for use in distant and exotic locales. There is no longer the rush of elation that might arise from sensing oneself part of a grand social endeavour, a feeling of participation in the future that the grand railway terminals and early airline terminals (Sagebiel's Berlin Tempelhof, Saarinen's TWA terminal in New York) meant to invoke. The increased security measures are an accepted part of the discomforts of commercial flying (although the passage of high-fare-class travellers is expedited), and they also mirror the dystopian surveillance societies outside. We art world denizens and other members of the 'knowledge class' who find our validation and our work within the international circuit, are likely to be regular participants in this system, at every level of privilege, for the foreseeable future.

10.1  (facing page) Mary Kelly, *Circa 1968*, installation, Whitney Biennial 2004, projected light noise on compressed lint, 256.5 × 266.7 cm.

# 10

# DOSSIER
## Mary Kelly *Circa 1968*

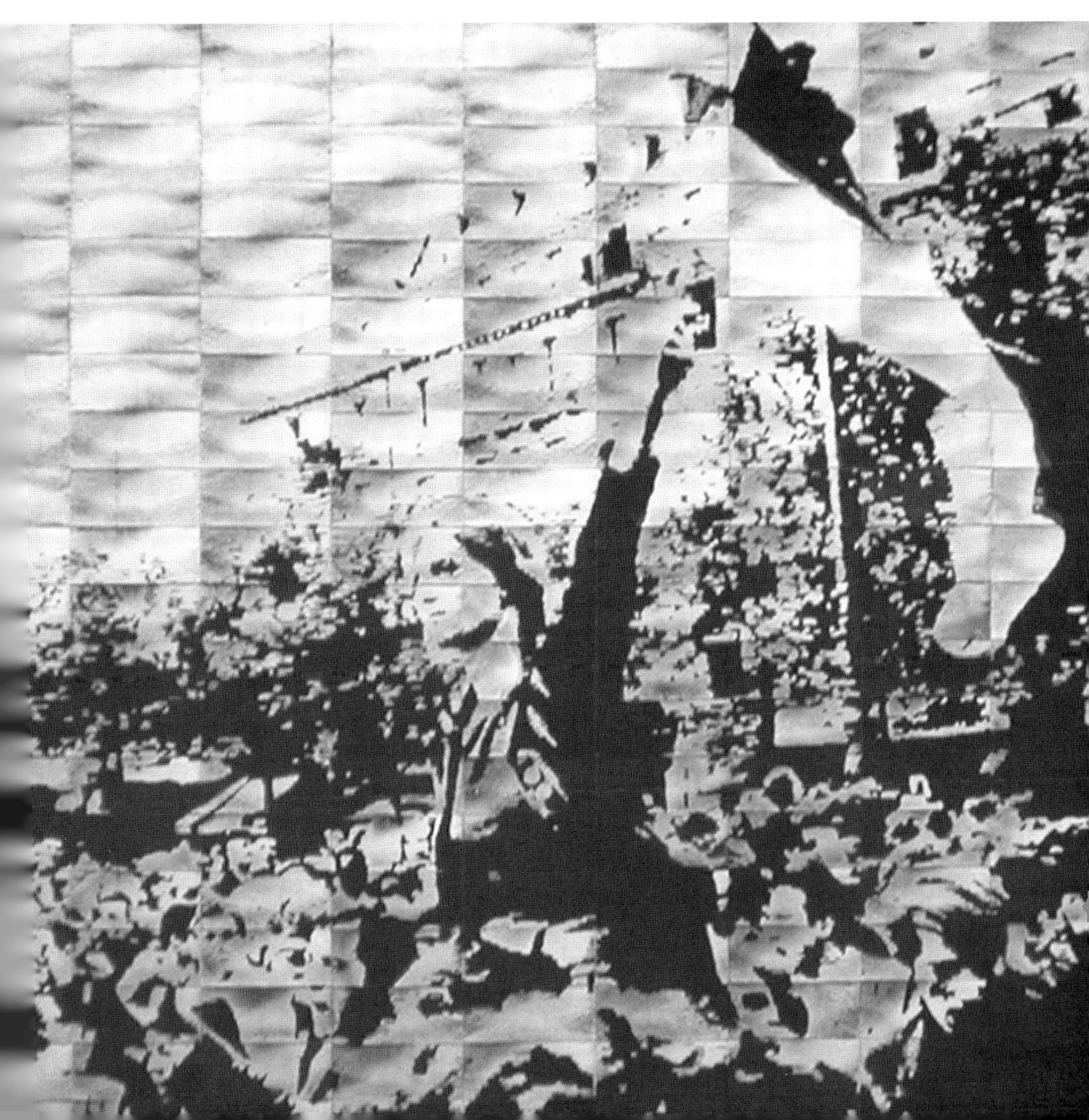

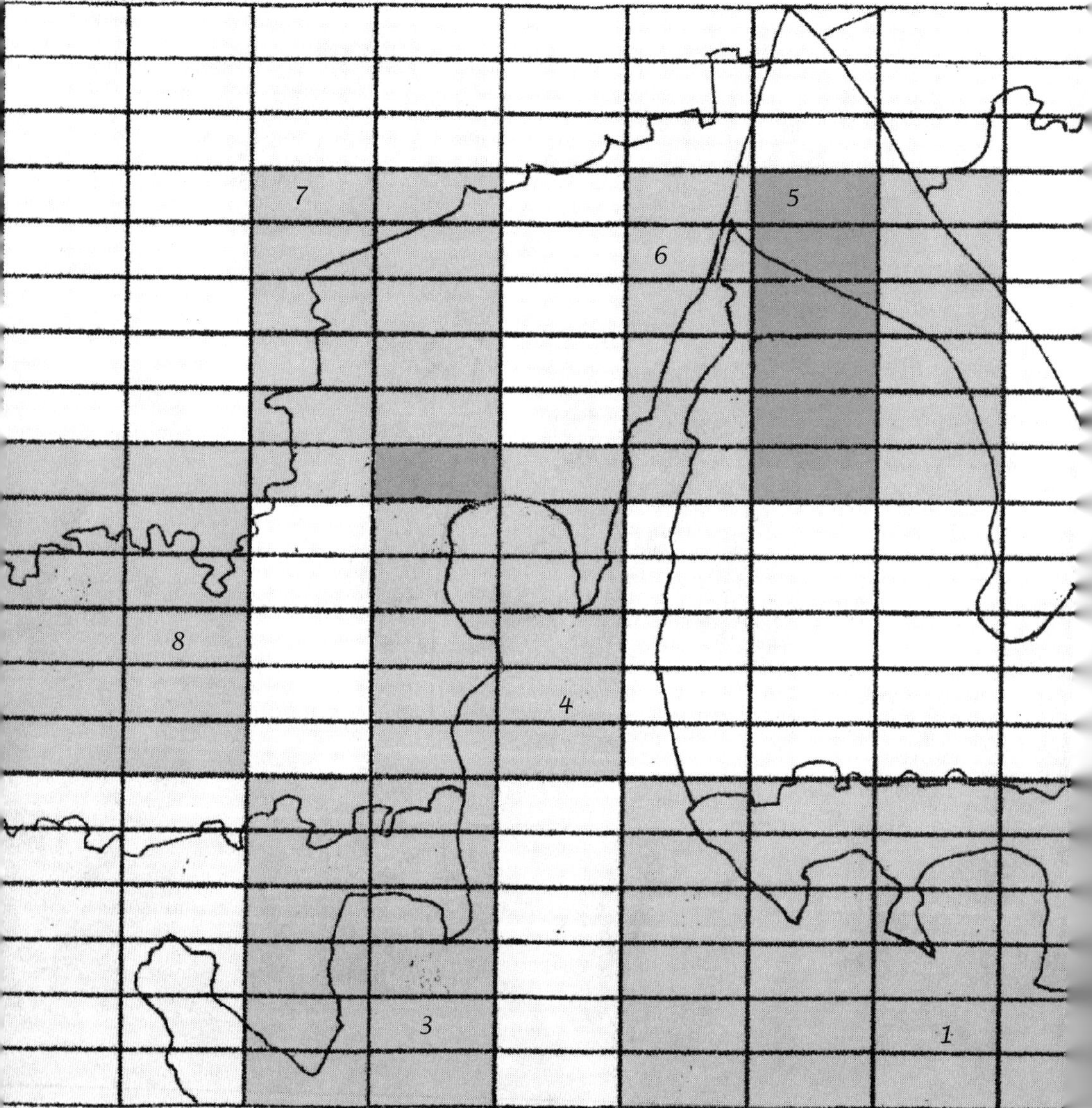

1.  You are here, next to a young man with beautiful hair, en route to the Bastille, May 13, one day before the general strike, two days after the Sorbonne reopens, ten days since the police occupation, four months following the riots at Caen, in the wake of wildcat strikes in Lyons, longer since the *matraquage*: October 17, 1961, Algerian workers, clubbed to death, thrown into the Seine from Neuilly Bridge.

2.  Behind you, the photographer, seconds before the shutter clicks, immuring the moment, not long before you are born.

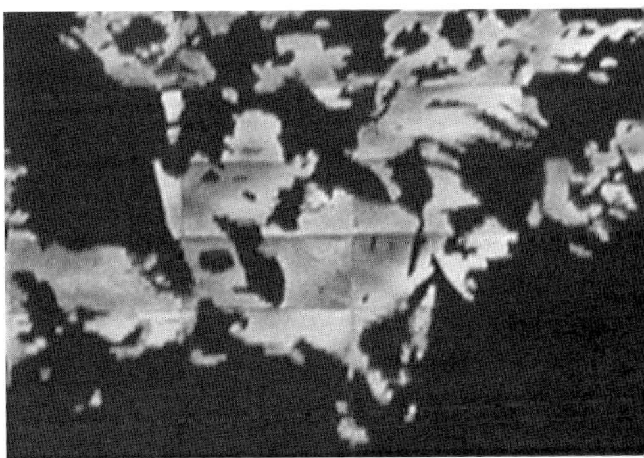

4.  *La Marianne de mai: 'Des tas d'idées me passent par la tête. Je
pense même à la Révolution française. Moi, la jeune fille d'une
bonne famille anglaise. Je commence à poser. Mon corps se raidit. Je
tends mon bras. Mon visage devient plus grave. Alors, je suis piégée
par le rôle que j'essaie d'incarner.'*

3.  Straight ahead, the shoulders of an artist,
supporting his companion who has *mal aux
pieds*.

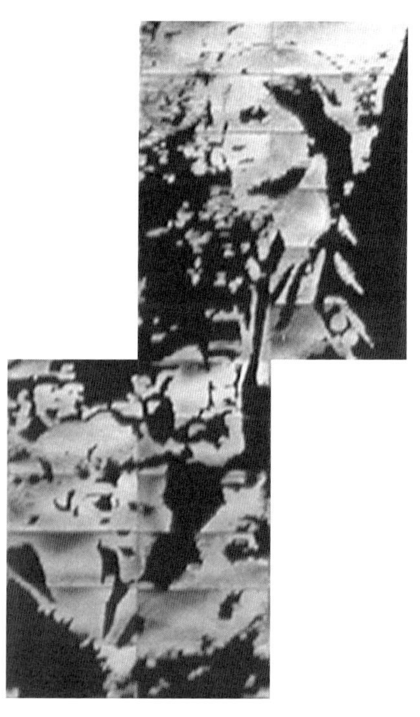

5.  Above, a flag, neither
communist, nor anarchist, but
Vietnamese, two years after the
bombing of Hanoi, Chicago
and Kent State still ahead. Now,
'We are all German Jews.' 'We
are all *la pègre.*' '*On a raison de se
révolter.*'

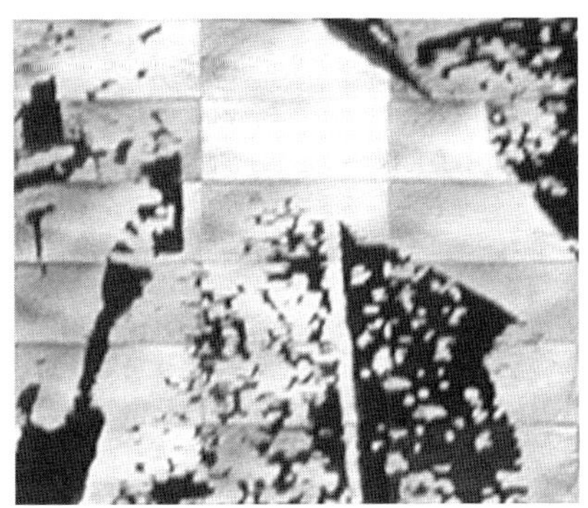

6.  On the balcony, a banner:
USINE-UNIVERSITÉ-
UNION. No separation, no
delegation, no right to speak
without *les enquêtes.*

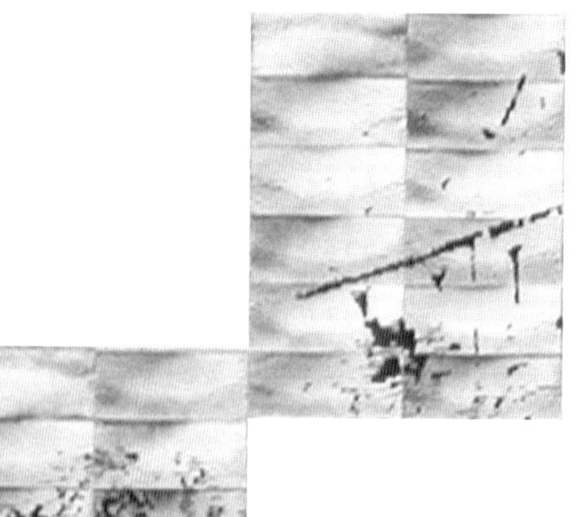

7.  To the left, 'We want more time to live!' More time…more…everything…'Everything, right now!'

8.  Below, *les marronniers*, in bloom perhaps. The smell of exaltation, exhaustion: ten dead, 1500 injured. More than a cultural revolution, yet less than expected. Beneath the paving stones, more than the beach.

# On Fidelity: Art, Politics, Passion and Event

*Mary Kelly*

Artists generally think of themselves first of all as practitioners and then, perhaps reluctantly, as educators. But, over the years, I have found the two practices more deeply imbricated than I could ever have imagined, not by an institutional imperative, but as a consequence of lived experience. Let me start with an anecdote concerning the recent anti-war protests at the university where I teach. While crossing the campus, I encountered a sprawling slogan on the pristine wall of a newly renovated building which read: 'stop the war, have sex!' For those of us who are old enough to remember the original—make love, not war—it would appear that the unimpeded bliss of our sexual revolution in the sixties looks decidedly more mundane to this generation through the keyhole of the present.

Those who were born around 1968 have a peculiar fascination with its significance. I would describe this, not as nostalgia, but rather, as a form of intuitive knowledge forged from the words, gestures or silences of familial interactions and decoded as parental desire. Insofar as it concerns the mystery of conception in the social and historical sense, I have come to call this psychic disposition *the political primal scene*.

Although Freud cautions us against digressions that foster the 'phylogenetic heresy', he finds it reasonable to suggest that after analysis has thoroughly excavated the psychic strata acquired by the individual, traces of what has been inherited are visible in the form of symbolic connections that reach beyond the analysand's experience. The primal phantasies—scenes of observing parental intercourse, being seduced in childhood and threatened with castration—are exemplary in this regard because they are both prehistoric or pregiven and contingent. The primal scene, in particular, displays its somatic meaning in the anal-sadistic stage, but reveals its structure in the child's question: 'where did I come from?' The answer invades the child from the adult world as an already given schema in which Oedipal identification mediates love relationships and desire subordinates satisfaction to the conditions of phantasy. Hence, the libidinal charge of an infantile sexual experience remains shrouded, and the adult is subject to 'retrospective phantasying', as Freud calls it, long after the event. In the meantime, he notes that a child catches hold of the phylogenetic experience to 'fill in the gaps' in his own, replacing occurrences in his own life with those of his ancestors.[1]

In another way, this fills in the gap between Freud's image of the analyst as archaeologist excavating the unconscious strata of events in chronological time and his invocation of a linguist deciphering hieroglyphics according to the logic of determining absences and simultaneity in time. His description of the psychical apparatus as a series of inscriptions is reiterated in Lacan's now well-known assertion that the unconscious is structured like a language. And, if the symbolic order precedes the subject's entry into it, then the unconscious is already outside the limits of a singular subjectivity. Before you were born your parents desired a child, or perhaps not. They wanted a boy or a girl. They gave you a name and the rest is history, that is, the history of the unconscious as the effects of the speech of the Other on the subject. At this point, we are returned to the exogenous import of the primal scene understood as the child's traumatic encounter with the enigma of parental desire. According to Lacan,

> In the intervals of the discourse of the Other, there emerges in the experience of the child something that is radically mappable, namely, *He is saying this to me, but what does he want?* […] The desire of the Other is apprehended by the subject in that which does not work, in the lacks in the discourse of the Other, and all the child's *whys* reveal not so much an avidity for the reason of things, as a testing of the adult, a *Why are you telling me this?* […][2]

Since the process of symbolization circles around a void, the subject fills it with symptoms that form an archive of unconscious transmissions. I would like to propose that buried in that archive there is something that makes the socio-political as well as sexual interrogation of the enigma mappable. Here, I am thinking not only of the girl who complains that her father wanted a boy, or the young man who insists that his paternal grandmother never held him because his mother was Polish, but also, of a student who told me, 'I'm a flower child, so I've been a feminist since I was born,' and another who said, 'I *wish* my parents had been part of the student movement.' It appears that identity is shaped by filling in the gaps in what our parents say with the imagined failures and aspirations of our ancestors. The question of origins, or where we come from, includes not only the family saga, but also the grand narrative of social change, and for both, the answer revolves around something missing; a lack in the past that makes a claim on the present and the future.

Possibly, this is what Walter Benjamin means when he refers to 'a secret agreement between past generations and the present one'. But his thesis, which goes beyond the psychoanalytic scenario of repetition and failure, introduces the idea of redemption, or ethical possibility, and he links it, famously, to the dialectical image.

> [W]hile the relation of the present to the past is purely temporal, the relation of what-has-been to the now is dialectical: not temporal in

nature but figural [*bildich*]. Only dialectical images are genuinely historical—that is, not archaic—images. The image that is read—which is to say, the image in the now of its recognizability—bears to the highest degree the imprint of the perilous critical moment on which all reading is founded.[3]

In part, I believe what he is proposing here concerns the archive of symptoms as a collective formation, one which becomes legible in objects or images when they register a moment of crisis. This, I would also suggest is what broadly defines a generation, not in the anthropological sense, but its historical meaning. For instance, for my generation, the political primal scene would be World War II and for the current generation the 'events of 1968'. The political primal scene, perceived as a violent act, induces a certain amnesia, but the memory trace remains, and later it may be revised and endowed with psychical affect through the coincidence of predisposition and historical accident. For example, the failure of our parents to prevent the Holocaust was inscribed in the shame we felt during the Vietnam War. This in turn, imbued the current protest against the war in Iraq with the psychic aura of deferred action. However, ethical possibility, in my view, entails a disruption of the unconscious order; a break or new way of thinking that shatters the compulsion to repeat. This possibility, I think, is the compelling absence in the oppositional politics of our time. With reference to 1968 and after, students, now, most often say, 'I missed a moment of clarity … of decisive action … of collective aims.' Is this imagined plenitude the secret agreement between our generation and theirs? And are they really saying, 'Why did you fail us?'

My encounter with, rather than answer to, the question is, first of all, figural, in Benjamin's sense, that is, an image, although I cannot claim the result is dialectical. Here, I want to return to the archive, in a literal sense, my archive, where there is a group of photographs documenting what we now refer to as 'the events of 1968'. I have returned to them often, but one, in particular, has become emblematic of that moment. Jean-Pierre Rey, in Paris, took it on 13 May, the day before the general strike. He has captured an extraordinary image: Caroline de Bendern, on the shoulders of an artist, Jean-Jacques Lebel, hoists the flag in a photogenic gesture of revolutionary zeal. At the same time, he has exposed a certain vulnerability; the vulnerability of a woman as 'image', her precarious position, above the crowd, visible but largely excluded from the grand narrative of social change. Then, there is the vulnerability of the emergent movement itself, implied by the undecipherable flag. Was it Communist, Anarchist or Vietnamese? All, and none of these, it appears. As an empty sign, it marks a collective aspiration, endlessly deferred, rippling in anticipation of a utopia not yet named, 'beneath the paving stones'.

This less visible trace of the past is what interests me and the work I made in response it, *Circa 1968* (10.1), was an attempt to capture the affective force of the photograph, both as a material process and as a time-based installation, by filtering it through two grids—one indexical and the other virtual. For Roland Barthes, the photographic image has 'two times': the cinema, which propels us into the here and now, and the still that clings to the past. But in *Circa* this is reversed. The grid of lint units, which reproduces the still, also 'doubles life' insofar as it marks duration, that is, the making of the piece in real time, while the pixellated light noise projected onto the lint image as an endless loop goes nowhere, immobilized or 'brushed with death'.[4]

The vulnerability of the woman in Rey's photograph and its iteration in the ephemeral medium of *Circa* touches on the symptomatic archive, that is, my subjective investment in the image and a particular narrative of its relevance. The legacy of 1968 includes the rise of feminism, more accurately the second wave, and the formation of a movement in England in 1969. For me, this took on the significance of an 'event' in Alain Badiou's sense of the term, although his emphasis is certainly more heroic than mine. Something breaks with the ordinary, he argues, and instigates a truth procedure; not a search for objective truths, but a much less logical process of 'holding true' to the consequences of the event. In that process, there is the possibility that a new way of thinking will emerge. Although an event has no specific content and he names art, science and love as well as politics in the fields of truth, perhaps, the emergence of psychoanalysis in the field of politics could be considered as an instance of the kind of enquiry that proceeds by exposing the absences in the established particularities of the known. In the women's movement, we used to talk about reading between the lines of the *German Ideology* and finding Freud there. Filling in the gaps in a theoretical enigma was propelled by fidelity to the event, and infused with a passion to make sexuality pass into the discourse of radical politics that prevailed in the sixties.

At the same time, the feminist enquiry informed by psychoanalysis became an integral part of my practice as an artist. In the context of conceptualism's resistance to a theory of subjectivity, I argued that if medium comprised not only a physical support, but also a technical one with a set of procedures or rules, then in my case, the rules were generated by a method of free association in which material indexicality was the privileged means of translating psychical affect into form.

Above all, for a generation of artists who witnessed the events of May 1968 as participants, (Lebel, for instance, led the occupation of the Odeon), or simply by coincidence, the slogans emblazoned on the startled monuments of Paris have left a trace in the archive of unconscious transmissions that reappear in the present as the lost object. I am thinking, in particular, of 'No right to speak without *les enquêtes*', that is, the interrogations. (I admit, interrogation has acquired a sinister reputation and is badly in need of redemption.) Remember, for instance, conceptualism's two paradigms of interrogation: first, with respect to the object and then, the interrogation itself.

Also, consider the far-reaching consequences of these paradigms in the discourse of the university; notably, with regard to art, the concept of research as practice, which implies the production of new knowledge, not as an end, but as a means or, more exactly, an encounter with the question.

In their persistent curiosity about where they came from, this generation has excavated strata of my own practice that concern, not the method informed by psychoanalysis, but the etiology of the enquiry itself. Here, all roads lead back to *les enquêtes* because, at one level, this process exposed the gaps in our narrative of political origin and at another, it addressed the urgency of 'a project'. Certainly, a project that is historically determined and transformative requires more than the reinvention of an imagined moment of clarity, yet, I would say that for many students, this aspiration sustains a medial, ethical and dialogical engagement with their art practice now, at a time when the boundaries between the institutions of education and those of the entertainment industry have been obscured. The exhibition as a system of meaning, once aimed at educating the 'good citizen' has been replaced by the aim of entertaining him. Often, the museum replicates cinematic space in the guise of installations or alternatively, promotes the architecture itself as spectacle. Increasingly, the art fair displaces the biennial and the collector's influence out-bids that of the critic. Perhaps, these observations signal a wider crisis: how to rescue the utopian legacy of entitlement in the form of global civil society rather than one of control. I see a certain resistance to the later in the current preoccupation with the social movements of the sixties. While the desire for a project, in terms of its unconscious meaning, resides neither in a scenario of failure nor in fulfillment, but in the gap where the question of origins is posed, its political significance, accrues in the trajectory of another query, vividly described by Alain Badiou, to whom I give the last word:

> We are living through the revenge of what is most blind and objective in the economic appropriation of technics over what is most subjective and voluntary in politics. [...] To change what is deepest in man was a revolutionary project, doubtless a bad one; it has now become a scientific problem, or perhaps merely a technical problem, in any case a problem that allows for solutions. We know how, or at least we will know. Of course, we could ask: What is to be done about the fact that we know how? But to reply to this question we require a project. [...] And since there is no project, or as long as there is no project, everyone knows there is only one answer: profit will tell us what to do.[5]

# Legacies of Resistance

*Juli Carson*

You are here, next to a young man with beautiful hair, en route to the Bastille, May 13, one day before the general strike, two days after the Sorbonne reopens, ten days since the police occupation, four months following the riots at Caen, in the wake of wildcat strikes in Lyons, longer since the *matraquage*: October 17, 1961, Algerian workers, clubbed to death, thrown into the Seine from Neuilly Bridge.

Behind you, the photographer, seconds before the shutter clicks, immuring the moment, not long before you are born.

Mary Kelly, Circa 1968

In a photograph taken by Jean Pierre Rey published in *Life Magazine* on 24 May 1968, we are given the following scene: a demonstration in the streets of Paris on 13 May 1968. The photograph definitively marks the moment. It serves as an eyewitness to the event. And yet, when Mary Kelly appropriates this image for an artwork, she adds the word 'circa' to the date. The word 'circa' means literally 'about'. When a date appears in historical writing without the word 'circa' preceding it, we assume to know the exact date with certainty. What, then, should we make of Kelly's use of the word 'circa' vis-à-vis a famous photograph that unequivocally documents an historical event? Indeed, there is a mystery at the heart of Kelly's *Circa 1968* (10.1), a mystery unfolding in the 'scene' between the date Rey took his photograph and the date the depicted event returns to us. This scene constitutes the ellipsis of cultural legacy—the productive space between one generation and the next through which historical memory is made. And since history is always a question of that un-traversable divide between an event that happened 'then' and our recollection of it 'now', history is at once a question of *longing to be where we are not*. It is precisely this question of desire in the space of critical analysis that's at stake in *Circa 1968*, a stake that has characterized all of Kelly's artwork since 1973.

On this question of longing, Jacques Lacan's comment at the end of *Seminar XI* is useful here: 'When, in love, I solicit a look, what is profoundly unsatisfying and always missing is that—*You never look at me from the place from which I see you*. Conversely, what I look at is never what I wish to see.'[1] In love, there is thus the problem of an un-traversable divide; a gap initiated by the primordial instance of the infant grasping sight of him/her self, which, in turn, initiates the simultaneous identification with, and alienation from, oneself as Other. Forever after the subject will try to close this gap. It is this 'scene' that the historian analogously faces vis-à-vis his object cause of desire in the form of a 'lost' past event. According to Lacan, on the matter of the subject never being able to complete himself romantically by way of truly coalescing with the Other, *there is no sexual relation*. His claim may be extended, allegorically, to the historian and his event when we say: *there is no historical relation*. There is simply no way to close this gap, though the subject may try insistently to do so. And necessarily so. While there exists the conscious wish to be closer to the loved object or to the historical event, there is concurrently an unconscious pleasure at work in never obtaining it. In the right artist's hands this question of the unconscious does not mark a critical blind spot nor an analytic quagmire but an opening to an ethical space of self-reflection on the question of historical memory in relation to contemporary art. We are then left to unpack the following question: *to what do we return and why?*

Let's return to Kelly in conversation with a young curator about *Circa 1968*:

> *In terms of returning to this moment for those born between 1963 and 1973, May '68 was what I would call the political primal scene—the mystery of conception in the social and historical sense* [...] *My generation was preoccupied with our parents in the context of WWII* [...] *I might say, well how could my parents have allowed something like the Holocaust to take place, and your generation might think, why wasn't the Cultural Revolution ever realized?*

Jean-Luc Godard raises these same questions in his 2001 film *In Praise of Love* (*Éloge de l'amour*), where he causes the sites of historical analysis, political resistance and the scene of 'love' or desire to collapse. Edgar, the film's protagonist, is an intellectual trying to make a film about three couples representing three generations: young, adult and elderly. Their love stories, in turn, are staged as allegories of three historical events: 9/11, 1968 and the Holocaust. Each of these moments is further comprised of four stages (in love as in history): meeting, passion, separation and reconciliation. In life, though, these four moments always arrive either too early or too late for the subject—what Freud called 'deferred action'—thus producing a crisis of historical agency for the actors and their real-life referents. To invoke this crisis in the love story one needs to collapse the operation of historical time onto the narrative arc of love. Edgar warns his young actress: *It is not Eglantine's story, but a story of history moving through her ... it is the moment of 'youth'*, though this is not Eglantine's conscious experience of the love-event. At the other end of the generational spectrum, Edgar follows the older couple, both Resistance survivors, in the process of selling their story to a Hollywood film director. The couple's historical moment is one lived before the story that will be sold to Hollywood, and, paradoxically, one that will lived by others (and by them) only *after* its Hollywood re-presentation. Caught in the middle, finally, is Edgar who tries unsuccessfully to be an 'adult'—to experience the political presence of 1968—between the moments of youth (today) and old age (then). But adulthood, like the historical event itself, is a very slippery, fleeting object because the adult is neither in the primordial moment of youth (pure experience) nor in the elderly space of reflection (pure representation). And as we introduce the idea of the photograph, this question of 'presence'—allegorically the question of 'adulthood'—becomes even more elusive.

Which brings us back once more to *Circa 1968*.

What's so compelling about *Circa 1968* is that the clues to unravelling this mystery of time, memory and the unconscious are actually embedded in the artwork itself. The 'meaning' of *Circa 1968* springs from the material technique Kelly employed in its making, an intentionally outmoded procedure that underscores the non-distinction of the work's form and content. Using the lint trap of her household dryer as a ready-made mould, the casting process required six months of washing and drying more than ten thousand pounds of laundry. Kelly began by reducing Rey's photograph to a line drawing and then breaking the drawing into a grid, each section of the grid corresponding to the dimensions of her dryer's lint trap. By inserting vinyl graphics based on the line drawing into the trap, Kelly produced a re-presentation of Rey's photograph through the ready-made process of lint collection. The original image was then re-established by arranging the sections to form a single panel measuring 256.5 × 266.7 cm. On the surface, the finished work tonally simulates the look of photography, which circles us back to the original photograph and the more general tradition of photojournalism, the very medium of the historical event. And yet, in *Circa 1968*, both the original historical event and the photograph continue to slip from our grasp. If we think of the 'event' in terms of something one can't directly encounter or discern, then it's especially meaningful that the bits and pieces of Rey's image are pressed into something as non-substantive as lint, through which a filtering process posits a symbolic yet enigmatic trace in the place of a representable event. In terms of 'filtering', the lint trap can thus be likened to what Freud called the preconscious, that which paradoxically produces something in the process of its effacement or censorship. Mirroring the viewer's own subjectivity, the primordial event in *Circa 1968* is simultaneously *there* and *not there*. Something in the picture is thus *out of place*, but it is precisely this 'something' that drives our cognitive experience of the picture.

Roland Barthes derives that the thing 'out of place' in all photographs, that thing to which his famed notion of the 'punctum' guides us, is time itself. He clarifies this point in the following passage from *Camera Lucida*: 'This new *punctum*, which is no longer of form but of intensity, is Time, the lacerating emphasis of the *noeme* ("that-has-been"), its pure representation.' Barthes saw this *punctum* clearly in the Alexander Gardner photograph of a young Lewis Payne, the man who tried to assassinate Secretary of State W. H. Seward in 1865, photographed in his cell as he was waiting to be hanged. 'The photograph is handsome, as is the boy: that is the *studium*,' Barthes remarks. 'But the *punctum* is: *he is going to die*.' As a result, we read two things at the same time: '*this will be* and *this has been*.' We experience the uncanny horror of an 'anterior future of which death is the stake'.[2]

Again, the intellectual paradox of an 'anterior future' is laid bare in the materiality of *Circa 1968*. By recessing the reconstructed image into the wall and projecting a two-minute fade of light noise onto the surface, the compressed lint image resembles not just a photograph but also a screen. In his essay 'Screen Memories', Freud responds to the question 'Do we have any memories at all from our childhood?' with the answer that we only have memories *related* to our childhood. Which is to say, the nature of childhood memories—the manner in which they suddenly appear and disappear in simultaneous modes and forms—demonstrate that one's earliest experiences are never remembered *as they were*. Rather, these past moments are paradoxically experienced in the present as a *screen*, triggered by related events taking place at the time of the memory's (present) formation.[3] Standing in front of *Circa 1968*, what the viewer thus 'remembers' about the Paris demonstrations is thus screened through the present conditions of his/her reception of Kelly's work. And as the white noise pulses over the lint surface, one's gaze pauses on the various details of the image, details that Kelly diagrams separately with accompanying captions. In the picture, is it the 'shoulders of an artist, supporting his companion who has *mal aux pieds*' that touches us? Or is it 'a flag neither communist nor anarchist, but Vietnamese' that makes us pause? Perhaps it is the lyrical slogan 'We want more time to live!' combined with the smell of '*les marronniers*, in bloom' that stays with us. What we locate in the image relies as much on where one was there in the moment of the picture *then*—was I even born yet?—as it does on where one is here in the moment of looking at this image/event *now*.

Bertolt Brecht's observation from 'Popularity and Realism' is helpful: 'Reality changes; in order to represent it, modes of representation must also change.'[4] However, as we see in both Kelly's and Godard's work, reality is not just the progression of events as they unfold in time, but the events themselves as they change upon our continual re-encounter with them. In normative realist representations, such as photojournalism, the following question arises: How does one maintain fidelity to the cultural moment of an event that has passed but nevertheless returns within a different set of cultural and ideological conditions? Moreover, what are the means of representing the event as *defined* by this temporal paradox; a paradox that mirrors the viewing subject's own historical position? The lessons of *Circa 1968* suggest that we must continually go to work on the very *means* of representing an event, which is to say that the artwork must *re-enact* the dilemma of the subject's divide such that one is forced not only to confront the moment of the sixties cultural revolution, in this case, but also to consider his/her *relation* to it in contemporary terms. For any authentic return to the sixties is as impossible as any dismissal of its inevitable return. In this way, the questions that *Circa 1968* ultimately leave us with are these: What is the legacy of the sixties cultural revolution today between the generations that Godard allegorically indicated as the young and the elderly? Moreover, who are the so-called 'adults' that will critically negotiate this divide for us? *Circa 1968* does not presume to answer these questions. Rather, it beckons us all to ask them.

11

# MARY KELLY'S
## *BALLAD OF KASTRIOT REXHEPI*
### Virtual Trauma and Indexical Witness in the Age of Mediatic Spectacle

Griselda Pollock

On 11 December 2001, the Santa Monica Museum of Art, Los Angeles, opened an exhibition that included a chamber orchestra and singer. The American artist Mary Kelly (1941–) created the dual event under the title: *The Ballad of Kastriot Rexhepi*.[1] Kelly's artwork was snaked, about head height, around the vast chamber of this cavernous gallery (11.1) in an almost continuous movement of 61.8 m of black-edged, Perspex-framed, grey lint. The lint—the fluff that comes off clothes and is caught in a filter in a domestic tumble dryer, whose simple industrial shape became the formal unit for this work—was mounted in alternating curvilinear sections. This pattern of repeat and inversion evokes both a visual register of sound waves and images of pulse and flow as well as recalling the structure of biological life, the helix. These associations work to generate in the viewer, at the level of already abstracted systems of representation, a sense of sound and movement while none is directly part of the work's effect. A running thread of black text— what one critic called her 'rhythmic prose'[2]—holds a constant line either just below or just above the median point of the curved sections created by the exact shape of a large domestic tumble dryer in which, by the washing and drying of 18.8 kg of specially selected black and white clothing, Kelly created the material that is the evocative medium for this work: compressed lint, the blown residual tissue or the waste and relic of daily domestic rituals, whose complex imbrication with social and psychic life have been the substance of her whole career's faithful investigation.

Thus between the given or ready-madeness of the conceptualist's favoured choice of industrial form—the filter's shape and screen, and the registering

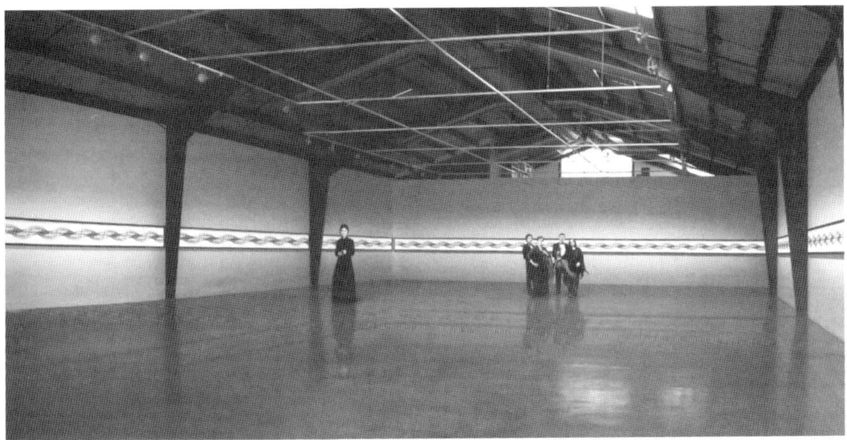

11.1   Mary Kelly, *The Ballad of Kastriot Rexhepi*, 2001, compressed lint, 49 framed panels 42.5 × 120 × 2 cm, overall length 6180 cm. Installation view, Santa Monica Museum of Art, Los Angeles. Reproduced courtesy of the artist.

from domestic labour of a fragile substance that has a tenuous link with the human body which these textile fibres once touched and yet is colourless, shapeless and discarded (11.2, 11.3)—Mary Kelly has created a material as medium that is both virtual and indexical, both matter and nothing, onto which to impress in painstaking manufacture with a simple printing process the blown words of historical tragedy that she wants to embed in the moving track of cultural memory and personal affect. Finally, lint's curious variations of tone with its prevailing greyness gives a photographic effect from a distance—the photograph being both substitute for direct witness and index, as Barthes declared of trauma in photography:

> Truly traumatic photographs are rare, for in photography the trauma is wholly dependent on the certainty that the scene 'really' happened: *the photographer had to be there* [...]. Assuming this (which, in fact, is already a connotation), the traumatic photograph ([...] captured 'from life as lived') is the photograph about which there is nothing to say; the shock-photo is by structure insignificant: no value, no knowledge, at the limit no verbal categorization can have a hold on the process instituting the signification. One could imagine a kind of law: the more direct the trauma, the more difficult is connotation; or again, the 'mythological' effect of a photograph is inversely proportional to its traumatic effect.[3]

By this same token, the photograph's impossible relation to the trauma that founds it becomes virtualized in transmission, becomes for everyone else a

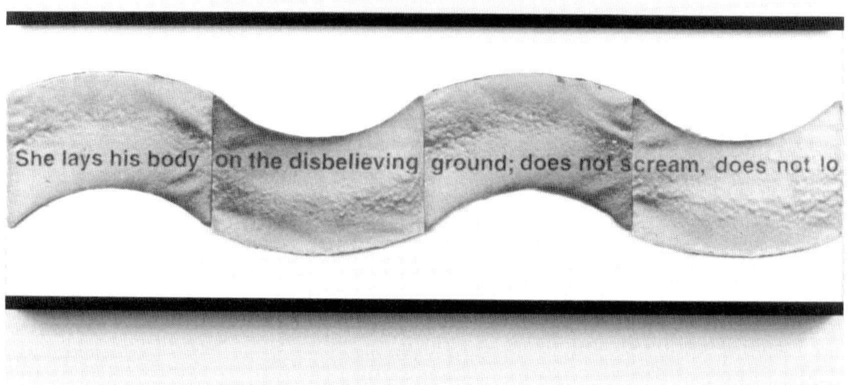


11.2    Mary Kelly, *The Ballad of Kastriot Rexhepi*, 2001, compressed lint, 42.5
        × 120 × 2 cm, detail. Reproduced courtesy of the artist.

kind of spectacle since that guarantee of the indexical witness, the photographer was there, cannot be repeated and raised to the level of signification.
Thus Mary Kelly's production of a substance that, in its minimal materiality
evokes the photographic visual effect while yet bearing no image, and staging
no sight again, performs a constant Kelly move: to stage in a created art work
a commentary on the modes of seeing and knowledge typical of our cultures
and media, one face of our creation through the interface with these signifying systems as social subjects. From the an-iconic materiality freighted so economically with the traverse of public and private, labour and spectacle, the
work once again probes who we are when we look, hear and see our world.

A small orchestra briefly occupied the centre of the large exhibition space
at the opening event (11.1), that performed a score specially created for this
work by Michael Nyman. Words that were intaglio-printed onto the wave-
forms of domestic lint which circled the musical ensemble were sung by Sarah
Leonard, whose earlier performance of Nyman's composition for Peter
Greenaway's *Prospero's Books* (1991) with Nyman's setting of the poetry of
Paul Celan, *Six Celan Songs for Low Female Voice*, had led Mary Kelly to invite
the composer to participate with her on this new project 'by writing a score
for an exhibition, rather like music for a silent movie'.[4]

In his 2002 review of this installation/event, Ernest Larsen astutely suggests that all Kelly's major artistic projects 'in one way or another investigate
the processes by which the subject intersects with a wider history'.[5] Maurice
Berger's essay in the 2001 catalogue phrases this slightly differently: '*The ballad* [...] is the latest instalment in her thirty-year aesthetic inquiry into the
question of subjectivity and historical memory.'[6] This work, however, takes on

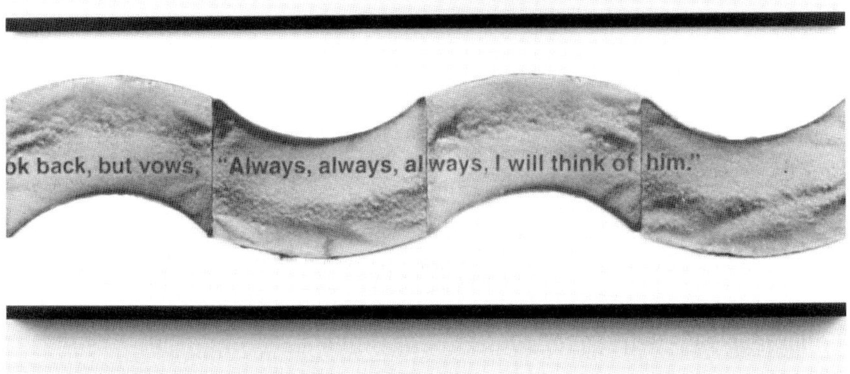


11.3   Mary Kelly, *The Ballad of Kastriot Rexhepi*, 2001, compressed lint, 42.5 × 120 × 2 cm, detail. Reproduced courtesy of the artist.

the current understanding of the subject's encounter with history as 'traumatic'. Through the distilled economy of a profoundly reasoned conceptual aesthetic (if this is not contradiction in terms) that secretes the depth of its theoretical insight that *trauma is a transmitted effect* in its minimal gesture, Kelly's work catches us in unexpected encounter not with the real, but with an ethical art making and viewing that reframes us as witnesses. Art here reworks the current theorizing of trauma, delay and belated witness, shaping it through an aesthetic economy that is simultaneously a site of art-thought: *theoria*.

Since her arrival in London in the early 1970s after several years' teaching in Beirut, during a particularly intense period of Middle Eastern history in the later 1960s, Mary Kelly has made major cycles of artwork that have consistently pushed at the limits of Lacanian accounts of the subject to accommodate both feminist and Marxist concepts of sociality and history. At the point of intersection between the social determinations of the subject within terms of class, gender or race, there is what psychoanalysis uniquely introduces into cultural theory: both a theory of the mechanisms and processes of subjectivity itself, and a theorization of the recalcitrance of what is, psychically, irreducible to social determination of the subject precisely because there could be no subjective impact of social determination without the processes and mechanisms of subjectivity that are partially autonomous of and excessive to the social.[7]

The subject is logically always-already historical, situated, generationally and geographically located and overdetermined, predisposed, as it were, through its arrival in the cultural framings that anticipate its becoming and accessing to a symbolic order. Yet elements of subjectivity are always in excess of these socio-economic and linguistic dispositions by virtue of what has to be incited in the human person to become a subject: lack, fantasy, desire, sexuality, the unconscious, and what remains from these processes, death drive, abjection, affect, melancholia and so forth. As Jacqueline Rose wrote many years ago:

> Like Marxism, psychoanalysis sees the mechanisms which produce those transformations [of ideological processes into human actions and beliefs] as determinant, but also as leaving something in excess. If psychoanalysis can give an account of how women experience the path to femininity, it also insists, through the concept of the unconscious, that femininity is neither simply achieved nor is it ever complete. The political case for psychoanalysis rests on these two insights together—otherwise it would be indistinguishable from a functionalist account of the internalisation of norms. [...] The difficulty is to pull psychoanalysis in the direction of both insights—towards a recognition of the fully social constitution of identity and norms, and then back again to that point of tension between ego and unconscious where they are endlessly remodelled and endlessly break.[8]

What is of interest in Kelly's *The Ballad*, however, is not the processes of subjectivization 'as usual'. It is those moments of exceptional encounter not between the subject and its histories, but between the subject and history, that marks the current intellectual interest in trauma which has formed the focus of Mary Kelly's work since *Mea Culpa* (1999), which itself followed on from work on masculinity and war during the first Gulf War, *Gloria Patri* (1992).

The event that triggered the making of the large work, *The Ballad*, was an article and photograph in the *Los Angeles Times* on 31 July 1999. Under the banner headline 'War Orphan regains Name—and Family', the article reported the reuniting with his parents of a 22-month-old Albanian child, who, at 18 months, had been left as dead when his parents escaped a Serbian attack during the Kosovan war of 1999.[9] Kelly's oral/textual *Ballad* starts:

> Unnatural spring;
> Metal seedpods germinating bloody flora,
> Anticipating the 'expulsions'
> Men in uniforms of blue and green
> Faces masked,

And having described the terrors of hiding, starving, watching their child grow weak, stop breathing, lie still, it continues:

> She lays his body on the disbelieving ground;
> Does not scream, does not look back, but vows

'Always, always I will think of him.'
His downy crop, his coral mien

Found on the battlefield and given a Serbian name, Zoran, the child was again abandoned as the Serbians retreated. Kelly's version:

Kastriot is found sitting in a field,
Battle in full thrall, a body sprawled nearby,
Severed head at its side.
He speaks not a word.

Reclaimed by Albanians, he was renamed Lirim, before he was finally reunited with his grieving parents for whom he was their lost son 'Kastriot'. The report of this extraordinary story, with its 'happy (?) ending' amidst the traumatic devastation of 'a nation razor-wired to loss' (Kelly),[10] was accompanied by a staged photograph of the tiny blonde child being kissed on both cheeks simultaneously by his parents—'*pater, mater, familia*'—whose large adult heads create a dark frame around his smiling but bemused face (11.4) in one of those classic images that, in capturing the most banal of news photographers' clichés,

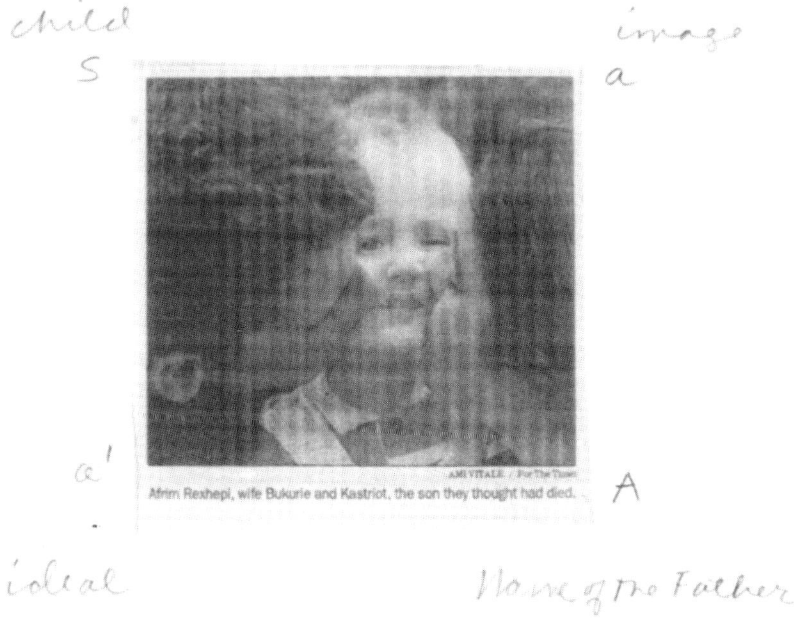


11.4   Untitled photograph from *Los Angeles Times*, 31 July 1999, with notes by Mary Kelly (Mary Kelly Archive). Reproduced courtesy of the artist.

unwittingly stages/images the clamp of the Symbolic that this child had almost missed: his first and Kelly's work's final word is 'Bab'/Dad.

Kastriot Rexhepi endured a trauma to which perhaps he will never be able to give testimony. The event of almost-death, resurrection, claiming and naming, loss and abandonment, reclaiming and renaming, and finally 'coming home' as another reinsertion into name and family marked by the first word he spoke 'Bab'—Albanian for 'Dad'—all these highly significant and decisive moments occurred between 18 and 22 months. The artist who had made *Post-Partum Document* (1973–79) as a study of the mutual subjectivization/socialization of maternal and infant pair could not but notice the psycho-symbolic significance of this time scale which raises the child's story from within the events of the Kosovan war and the scourge of ethnic cleansing to a mythic status, without losing its historically specific clothing. It is the artist's work to hold the double frame of psycho-symbolic and historical time before us, the space of the social subject and the psychic space of the subject:

> [...] I looked at the story closely: Kastriot was only eighteen months old when he was left for dead, then found and renamed by the Serbs. So he was literally learning to speak at that moment, entering into the order of language and culture, you could say, taking on a sexual identity, and in this case, a very confused ethnic identity. When he was reunited with his Albanian parents, Kastriot was twenty-two months old, usually the age when a child can put words together in an elementary syntax, and, psychologically, can project an image of himself as 'I'. Significantly the first word Kastriot said, according to the reporter anyway, was 'Dad.'[11]

It was Kelly's politically acute and theoretically informed 'reading' of the everyday news report of *fin-de-siècle* near-catastrophe and good news in the Balkans that revealed the deep structure of myth at work in the story: 'For me the story became less literal and more generic as I got into it. It has the structure of myth—can be told many ways without altering the underlying themes—and I wanted to reflect this in my writing.'[12] Pared down to phrasings that poetically expose the mythic armature within this single story of political barbarism and genocidal atrocity, the work makes us hear the rhythm of, or register acoustically, the affect that is trauma in contemporary history which disseminates to other bodies and other homes via the immediacy and inscription of the media.

In one sense, the newspaper or news programmes make us all witnesses to catastrophic events. The instantaneous beaming back of on-site footage and reportage brings the traumatic event directly into homes and countries far distant from the actual occurrence. Transmission occurs at several levels. Unlike the shock of discovery that attended the American and Allied troops as they entered concentration camps in 1945 and began to send home first verbal and then photographic reports that seared their viewers—remember Susan Sontag's powerful witness to the impact of seeing these images as dividing her life into a before and an after—we have no delay in the age of satellite and digital communications.[13] Embedded journalists at the centre of war as it unfolds make every day's news bulletins as potentially traumatizing as that first time in 1945—yet the constant stream renders even outrageous atrocity just another news item. Sontag has long since argued that shock wears off, that 'images anesthetize' and 'repeated exposure only makes the event less real'.[14]

Even with these apparently immediate floods of digitized information to which we have access, the mythic structuring of the material into narratives and stories that service deep, ideologically and culturally charged interests is inescapable. Thus the potential witness created by the image is subtly, or grossly, supplanted by a fabricated consumer patterned to receive the mythically familiar. The Barthesian analysis of myth as 'depoliticized speech', as the naturalization of the historical through the process of ideological re-inhabiting of the borrowed and denuded signifiers of historical events, raises important questions for theories of witness which are addressed in significant ways by the theorization offered through artistic translation.[14] As with all Mary Kelly's work over the last 30 years, *The Ballad* triangulates the question of aesthetic form, the traumatic/subjectivizing event, and the mode of subjectivizing encounter that invokes the question of *theoria*. *Theoria*—to look at, to view, to travel to see, to be sent to visit an oracle, to judge one thing by another, to contemplate, consider, theorize—is a seer. Hence theory is itself a kind of witnessing, a mode of seeing, considering, thinking that involves the real or metaphorical experience of sight/insight and—of course—its opposite blindness.

In *The Ballad*, Mary Kelly seems to offer nothing to see—in the form of image or representation. What she offers is not the story but an architecture for the transmission of the affective residue of trauma precisely in order to create an order of theoretical seeing, insight, into that which we are called to witness, but which the mythic translation by our media and cultural apparatuses of daily exposure render so already known that it ceases to instigate reflection or affective response. The family under stress in the crisis of war is the very symbol of destruction, as Picasso suggested in his response to the sight of the first photographic images of the German death camps. His painting *Charnel House* (1946), deployed the artistic handwriting created for his visual scream, *Guernica* (1937)—monochrome Cubist faceting—to depict the father, mother and child of a shattered family home, recuperatively centring the entire Nazi project to destroy all humanizing structures, and particularly the affective bonds of family, precisely on its most sentimental antithesis. In the newspaper photograph that serves visually to anchor the sentimental resolution of the fairy tale of a lost child returned to its proper parents, coun-

208 | 

try, name, identity, Mary Kelly catches a more troubling ambivalence. She registers another resonance or tone that can be aesthetically explored, as she has so often done, by abandoning the iconic site of mythification—the mother/child (*Post-Partum Document*), the older woman (*Interim*, 1984–89), the hero (*Gloria Patri*)—for the registers of sound and substance that work together between abstraction, formality and conceptualism to hold both affect and understanding.

The signifying economy created by the now embedded legacies of Minimalism and Conceptualism exceed the museal narratives of a succession of styles to register the battle with, and distance from, the dominant registers of visual representation and popular narrative that enclose us in the mediatic spectacle of global information and entertainment. These show us things before which we are made spectators—or worse, consumers—but never witnesses. To wrench the encounter—the traumatic event—into a relation of humanizing knowledge, what Bracha Ettinger might call co-affection, requires a calculated impoverishment at the level of spectacle and a displacement of the mythic to other registers of acoustic and visual memory that can use affective response to generate understanding.

In a work of 1999 that initiated the use of imprinted pressed lint, *Mea Culpa* (11.5), Mary Kelly showed four works comprising 16–20 units combined to form one panel assembled from four to five sections, 43.2 × 482.6 × 5.1 cm (four sections), or 43.2 × 596.9 × 5.1 cm (five sections). The process is printmaking (monotype) using the filter screen of a domestic dryer on

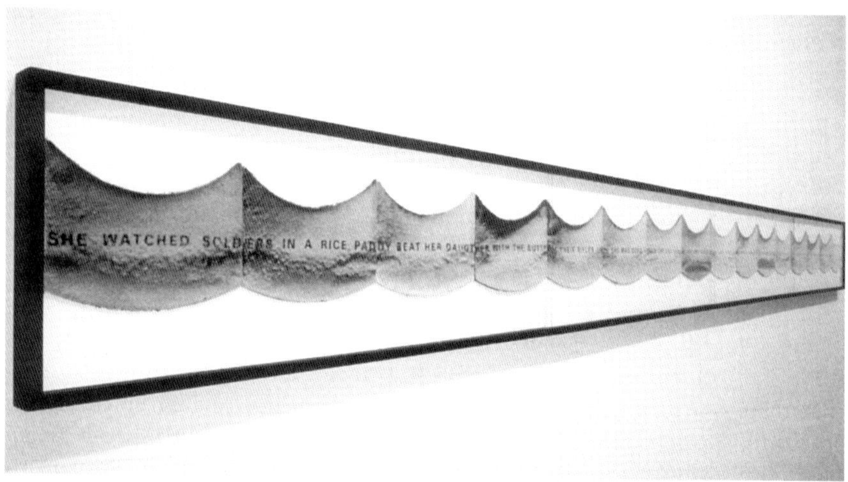


11.5   Mary Kelly, *Phnom Penh, 1975*, compressed lint, 43.2 × 482.6 × 5.1 cm, from *Mea Culpa*, 1999. Reproduced courtesy of Postmasters, New York.

which, in low relief intaglio print, a line of words is placed so as to be impressed onto the lint as it accumulates in a drying cycle. The four sections deal with four major traumatic events:

1. Khmer Rouge massacres in Phnom Penh 1975.
2. The bombing of the refugee camps Shatila and Sabra in Beirut by the Israeli air force in 1982.
3. The massacre of Muslim refugees in Sarajevo by Bosnian Serbs in 1992.
4. The Truth and Reconciliation Commission in post-apartheid South Africa in 1997.

Each historical trauma or event is marked by a cryptic line of words that runs just below the centre of repeating curved shapes created by the filter's ready-made form. These are grouped in what the artist names a musical form of four-four time: 'a beat which holds back on both the speed and lyricism of the piece. You might have noticed that a work always ends on four, even if the narrative stops before then. The rhythm determines how the spectator walks through it [...]' To which the interviewer adds 'Four-four being a march time as well'.[16]

Each of the narratives printed onto the compressed lint, apart from the confessional South African report, focalizes through the use of a third person pronoun: 'she'. In each case this 'she' sees or hears something. In *Phnom Penh 1975*:

She watched the soldiers in a rice paddy beat her daughter with the butts of their rifles until she was dead. Then she had headaches and trouble with her eyes. To distract herself, she worked at the bridge of her nose with a knife. When the pain subsided, she could no longer see.

*Sarajevo 1992* reads:

A few bathroom tiles and the smell of burning: nothing else left. Probing the ashes she retrieved a family photograph, their faces scratched out with a drill bit. She rocked back and forth on her heels. What shall we do? Slit their throats said her four year-old son.[17]

These abbreviated narratives carry the mark of their origin in newspaper or television reports stripped of all sensationalism and sentimentalization with an analyst's understanding of the psychological import of casual utterance. Mary Kelly tells interviewer Juli Carson that her work often begins with a photographic and verbal archive, a kind of cultural ethnography in which both what is said around her is listened to as an analyst might for the core elements, the trigger phrases, the deep psychic valences. But she is also 'on the couch' responding to the noise of her archive with the selective attention that marks it with her own desire and psychic urgencies. In this case, Kelly collected material on war-related atrocities, which themselves lured the artist's personal rather than dispassionate interest, and activated her memory perhaps of time in Beirut and growing up through the Vietnam War, the first war that was so daily brought home to American televisions.[18] But also her attention was drawn to aspects of intense experience: fear of losing one's child.

The mutilated family photograph came this way from an accumulated archive, but the South African episode was prompted by a report from the Truth and Reconciliation Commission overheard on the television from another room. It is this relation of chance encounter—overhearing—with the trace of the traumatic events occurring somewhere else and to someone else, that marks the distance between the failure of witnessing that is reportage and the new creation of the conditions of witnessing that is the art work in order to refute the current overemphasis on authenticity and testimony. Reflecting on the theoretical underpinnings of this position, Juli Carson pointed out that Mary Kelly is not intending to present the 'reality' of war atrocities and thus fall prey to the ethical dangers of representation. Mary Kelly tells her:

> I think there is a mistaken idea that trauma has to do with an immediate experience—when something happens to you. We usually attribute a certain authenticity to the accounts of survivors, although the 'accident' is shaped in tandem with a person's particular sexual disposition or phantasy life. Following Freud's contention that it isn't the real event, but the psychic *effect* that produces trauma, I started to think about the impact that atrocities have even when they are received secondhand through the media. The way they seem to induce different forms of identification with the victim, whether they are hysterical or megalomaniacal, I'm not sure, but I couldn't deny the traumatic effects of these representations and how they filter into the everyday.[19]

Mary Kelly describes how as part of the long gestation of the work *Mea Culpa*, she herself staged a photograph of her own body as if dead, shrouded in sheets: 'I needed to act out this tendency to experience the unimaginable vicariously in order to get some distance from it.' Juli Carson glosses this:

> That's exactly how Lacan describes trauma, as a *missed* encounter with the Real. To actually have that encounter would, of course, be the death of the subject. What I mean is, to look beyond the spectacle of representation, of language, behind that screen on which we project every one

of our life-sustaining (traumatic) phantasies, is to encounter that, in fact, 'nothing' is out there. Contrary to claims made in some recent cultural theorizations of the Lacanian Real, that's an encounter you don't walk away from as a subject.[20]

Mary Kelly speaks of the displacement from the body in the image, the identification with the image of the victim which renders death a mere performance rather than this brush with 'nothing', the annihilation of the subject, and talks about wanting to find a means to 'translate' the material onto which the issue is displaced into a process of making the non-iconic image. I cannot emphasize enough the import of this stress on the relations between coming to terms with the process of making and its materiality which forms a typical part of any engagement with conceptual post-minimalist art practice and the ethical dimension of her practice in its social and historical engagement. It is here that the possibility of an indexical relation to a historical real—that bypasses all 'realism', authenticity and immediacy, which have been virtualized to such a degree that what we might, in old fashioned terms, call an ethical rather than a social realism—is transferred in potential at least to the most conceptual and depleted modalities that can still promise, but never guarantee, the necessary affectivity, or co-affectivity, that marks the transmission of the traumatic effect sufficient to create a work of political witness.

Kelly's process produces something anamorphic: for the viewing subject in the exhibition hall cannot master or grasp the whole work from any single position, but becomes a subject in and of the space whose rhythmic prose 'narrativizes' events for that decentred subject. The complex aesthetics of making use of a domestic industrial machine associated with cleansing to stage affective encounters with the atrocities of war and ethnic violence functions at yet another level of challenge to and interruption of the mediatic, which, as I am suggesting, virtualizes the event. Mary Kelly says:

I think human rights legislation—which was actually launched in 1948 by Eleanor Roosevelt—will become the major issue for democracies in the twenty-first century. More specifically, I'm interested in the way artists like Shirin Neshat and William Kentridge import cinematic devices into the gallery space without the aspect of spectacle.

But I wanted to go in a very different direction—to explore the possibilities of material indexicality as a visual experience, as a pleasure really, compatible with the archaic nature of the gallery space—archaic in relation to dominant cultural forms like film, television, and technology-driven entertainment. That's why it seemed so appropriate to invent an outmoded medium—washers and dryers, after all, belong to the industrial rather than the information era. I find Walter Benjamin's suggestion that there is a redemptive aspect to the outmoded more and more meaningful [...] I do think it's important not to forget the kinds of social relations embedded in past events—simple ones like reading a book, as well as complex and traumatic ones, like war.[21]

Drawing on these terms, I propose that beyond the problematic of representation, which is so complexly virtual and virtualizing, the now archaic forms of modernist-made art, historically freighted with its own social relations and memories, perform the indexical relation not via the icon but the material as a transport medium capable of inciting a trans-subjectivity that is not voyeuristic or identificatory. To bring this finally back to the theory of witness, I want to introduce one of founder thinkers of witness: Dori Laub. In his study of Holocaust testimony, 'Bearing Witness'—which involves both the survivor giving testimony and the witness who was missing at the time of the event, absence compounding the traumatically dehumanizing event— Laub typifies the dangers of witnessing, as the receiver defends him or herself from the invasion of the other's trauma. He notes a range of defensive responses: a sense of total paralysis or fear; fear of merger with atrocities being recounted; a sense of outrage or anger directed at the narrator; a sense of withdrawal and numbing; a flood of awe and fear leading to a fake sanctification of the victim; obsessive interest in facts to foreclose the affective charge; hyperemotionality that looks like compassion but floods out the testifier with the listener's defensive affectivity.[22]

Held by the fineness of calculated aesthetic forms addressing the rhythms of seeing and hearing in narrativized space inviting the viewer's work upon its materials and forms, Mary Kelly's recent work since 1999 brings a still deeply feminist perspective to bear on the question of history as trauma. Deeply feminist in its fidelity to the exploration of the complex hinge between subjectivity and the social and historical, this work swings around from the original refocusing of attention onto the domestic site of labour as one key locale of socialization and subjectivization within class and gender relations back onto the public space of war and violence. Yet, in its relay of current events to the intimacies of our homes, the media itself corrupts such distinctions, investing our homes and domestic spaces with the social and historical. When, as at the end of the last century, the fiftieth anniversary of the full exposure of the Nazi genocide found Europe riven once again by ethnic violence and atrocity, traumatic delay retriggered by traumatic repeat raised the theorization of history as trauma to the headline of theoretical research. The enormous volume of work on the Holocaust as the traumatic shadow-stain on twentieth-century Europe opens out to events which find traumatic resonance in almost every post-war society from Taiwan, to Korea, almost all of Africa, throughout Latin America and then the Balkans. Our relation to the scale and depth of human suffering must be one of the critical questions of our time, when older frames of political formulation have been smashed and globalization—the latest and most spectacular of the phases of capitalism—unravels most of our existing structures for the management of its terrifying forces of transformation.

*The Ballad of Kastriot Rexhepi* becomes an interesting theoretical event, creating a space in which to reflect upon who we are summonsed to be in relation to another, not in the age of mechanical reproduction but of digitized virtuality which screens (in both senses of the word) the nature of brutal and violent physical reality for most of the world's populations whom development, neo-colonialism and greed have reduced to levels of such atrocious and traumatic suffering that the whole of modernity's dream lies indicted. The arcane and esoteric exercise of conceptual art-making in an advanced Western nation, whose conditions of existence involve galleries and orchestras and art magazines, seems utterly irrelevant to the scale of trauma that we now witness worldwide. But that is not so. For embedded in this archaic practice of made and viewed art is the complement to the necessity for synthetic, sociological knowledge of globalization and violence, namely aesthetic knowledge, knowing for yourself, knowing in yourself, knowing at the level of human witness.

For many years the focus of one area of my teaching and research has been the passage from trauma to cultural memory. In the time scale of that work (1990–), these terms have become major areas of investigation in cultural theory, acquiring an awesome bibliography that does some justice to the significance that each term, trauma and cultural memory, hold for a world repeatedly traumatized and increasingly seeking to grasp/create meaning in events that traumatically knock it out. At the intersection with work that has largely focused on the trauma and cultural inscription of the memory of the Shoah/Holocaust, I have continued my other intellectual project as a feminist art historian and cultural analyst, working on interventions in art's histories from theoretically informed feminist analysis, the latter term invoking, hopefully, both a legacy of critical thought and psychoanalysis itself. Central to both projects has been the aesthetic: not as the beautiful or the best, but rather as a practice that articulates thought and affect through material and semiotic processes. I ask myself: what can art historical work contribute to the philosophical, literary and psychological/psychoanalytical literature on trauma and cultural memory? What is the role of art?

In introducing the course on trauma and cultural memory in relation to the Shoah, I ask my students: who/what we shall be when we look back at this historical moment, that, in the character of trauma, happened in historically determinable dates within which its effects are not confined and thus returns with the force of the repressed out of time and out of place? I have written elsewhere of the danger of what I call the Orphic gaze, the second look that kills again.[23] The danger of voyeurism, abjecting the other, recoiling from their dehumanization in horror, and many other inappropriate but inevitable responses need to be considered before we even begin. So I propose the now well-known suggestion of Dori Laub that we are called to become the belated witnesses eradicated from the genocidal process, which he characterizes as 'an event without a witness'.[24] Thus we restore to the testifying victim/survivor the human ear and subjective affirmation destroyed as part of the calculated violence of the planned destruction of entire peoples. But this is based on the model of testimonial exchange that forms its own new models of literature and historical writing.

It is a difficult proposition that bends time and place and raises difficult questions. Laub's concept of the event without a witness has been taken up by Bracha Ettinger and transformed into a general proposition about the belatedness inherent in trauma in which the impact of the traumatic effect may be deferred or even transmitted across generations and beyond the boundaries of the discrete subject. Ettinger also pushes this implicatedness to include the viewer of the artwork, who is, by definition, also a witness without an event. That is to say, the event, the experiential or other cause of the art work and its making is not the experience of the viewer. Yet the viewer is called upon to participate affectively in confirming the human significance of the trace of that now missing event: the making or even the maker, to raise the objective materials to the level of signification, communication, subject–subject relay. We respond with our own emotions or thoughts to what is not ours while we are in turn transformed by the affect of the other within us. Thus witness ceases to be a mere legal or even a psychotherapeutic condition; it is an ethical relation to the suffering of what is no longer the other, but a co-affecting trans-subjective dimension of subjectivity that is particularly operative in certain moments of engaged aesthetic practice. But Bracha Ettinger will take this one stage further and expose what had seemed at first— in the idea of witness—an ethical and affirming point of meeting, of mutual confirmation, as something that still leaves a gap. Thus, to define the specific moments or elements of non-psychotic transitivity that may be incited in the aesthetic experience (of making as well as of viewing) she alters the word *witness* visually to create 'wit(h)nessing'. Introducing the letter 'h' from the word *with* breaches the dominant formulations of the conditions of subjectivity in which the subject only emerges when it ceases to be with an other, separates itself, defines its boundaried ego through a scarifying gap through which hole will whistle the subjective engine of desire. To be too much with, to over-identify, to fail to maintain clear boundaries between self and other is to fall prey to a host of psychological problems verging ultimately on a psychotic disintegration of the self, an alienation so profound that intersubjective exchange becomes impossible. Thus the moment of balancing the varying potentials of subjectivity for its contact or collapse must be negotiated and staged. While there is a gulf of considerable theoretical significance between the Lacanian underpinnings of Mary Kelly's work and the post-Lacanian feminist matrixial theory formulated by Bracha Ettinger, it is possible to allow the latter to reflect upon the contribution to the relations of aesthetics, trauma and witness because the work of Mary Kelly must itself be in excess at the affective level of its own self-understanding that generated the practice. The combination of the visuality of rhythm and the collaboration between Kelly's word poems and Nyman's music staged at the opening of each of the three venues for *The Ballad* suggested to me a third part to this exchange in the form of this theoretical statement:

> A rhythm of swerving in rapport of transmission and transference, conducting toward an unforeseen home while creating it, bypasses the off/on beat. This rhythm never [reaches] total 'on' or total 'off' [...]. Co-in/habit(u)ation is primarily affective, not visual, and it destabilizes visuality by transgression of affect that causes infiltrations of invisible trauma into appearance.[25]

Suspended between the inherent virtuality of subjective processes (fantasy and the unconscious), the indexical trauma that founds the subject who never knows it, and the virtuality of the socio-economically conditioned media/information systems and the historical trauma they report but mythify, art-making and its specific aesthetic processes and practices (in a Kristevan not a Kantian sense)[26] may create both witness and *wit(h)ness* that 'cause infiltration of invisible trauma into appearance' and audibility, to create witness-subjects, which is not only an ethical but a deeply political effect.

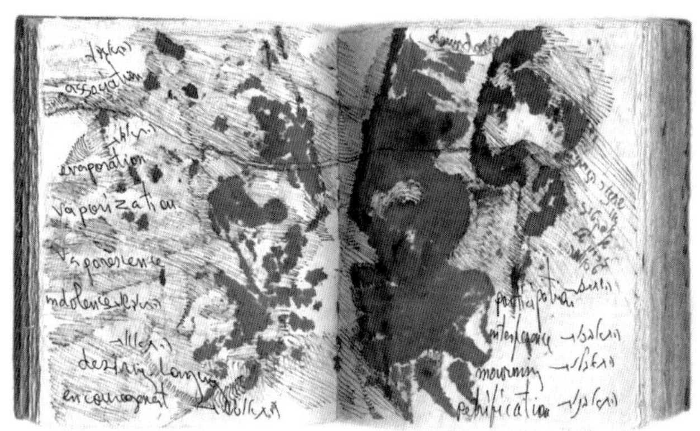

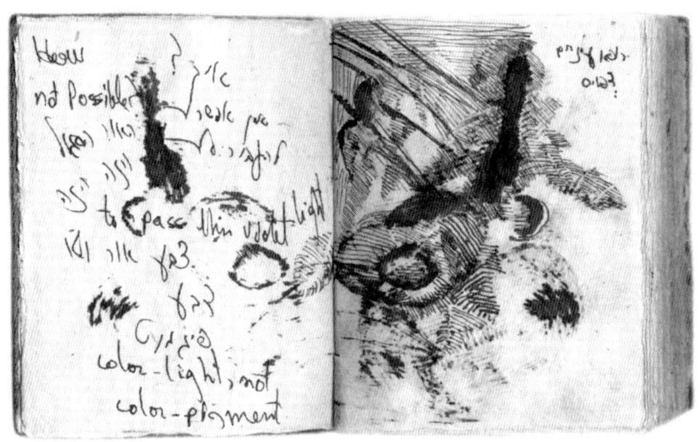

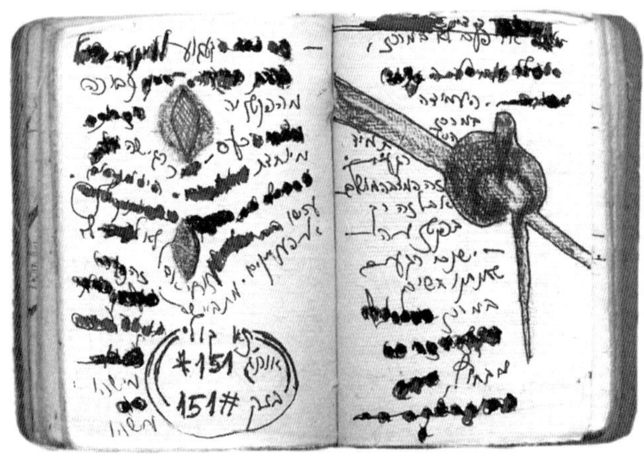

12.1   Bracha L. Ettinger, Scannographs from *Notebook 2006–7* (2009). ©
Bracha L. Ettinger. Reproduced courtesy of the artist.

# 12

# NOMAD-WORDS

*Anna Johnson*

A specific aspect of the Deleuzian idea of the virtual underlies the concerns of this essay: that of its actualization. If the virtual can be understood as the immanent ground of the genesis of thought, my preoccupation here is precisely with the process of that genesis. The virtual in this sense is nothing new; its associations with the ultramodern, the digital and life abstracted from the material real are only the present guise of something much older. The virtual is as old as writing itself; it is nothing new, but it drives the new; it is that which compels the generation of thought:

> The act of thinking does not proceed from a simple natural possibility; on the contrary, it is the only true creation. Creation is the genesis of the act of thinking within thought itself. This genesis implicates something that does violence to thought, which wrests it from its natural stupor and its merely abstract possibilities. To think is always to interpret—to explicate, to develop, to decipher, to translate a sign. Translating, deciphering, developing are pure creation.[1]

In the present essay, the thing implicated, the generative sign that provokes the act of thought is writing, but writing in a specific sense—the closest example of which is the hieroglyph—in which any absolute distinction between image, word or letter is unsustainable, and which both demands and resists an ongoing work of translation.

The object of this essay is the work of Bracha Ettinger, an artist and psychoanalyst whose formulation of the 'Matrix' and its surrounding conceptual and aesthetic constellations posits itself as an instance of a new mode of thought, radically expanding the horizons of psychoanalysis, subjectivity and affectivity to include a non-phallic feminine 'in itself', one that is not relative to, or the complement of, the masculine.[2] A major virtue of Ettinger's work in this context is that it positions itself in-between the fields of visual art and psychoanalytic theory and in so doing it offers us a rare material means of grasping some of the routes through which this ostensibly new theory has emerged, and—just as interestingly—of coming to an understanding of the particular nature of its newness. This positioning is at once practical and theoretical: Ettinger's intervention in the psychoanalytic understanding of subjectivity has an explicit stake in the possibility of transition or transmissibility between 'art' and 'theory', in the sense that her art practice is self-consciously given as the locus of the act of thinking behind her theoretical hypotheses. Her project as a whole is heavily dependent on metaphor as transport or carrying-over—the defining move of her theoretical intervention is metaphorical in more ways than one: 'I have transported the vague ideas of *matrix* and *metramorphosis* from art into psychoanalysis'[3]—but Ettinger is rarely explicit about how she understands the concrete processes of this transport. One early comment, however, articulates the ground of this transport through the idea of the *covenant*:

> The most graceful moments in the covenant between art and theory occur when theoretical elements, only directly or partly intended for particular works of art, and visual elements which refuse theory, collide. In doing so they transform the borderline between the two domains so that art is momentarily touched by theory while theory takes on a new meaning.[4]

The idea of a covenant between art and theory indicates a relation of mutuality or contract between heterogeneous fields, one (for the sake of argument) constituted around the singular and the affective, the other around the general and the communicable. There is, however, an unstated third term at play: insofar as a covenant is a contract guaranteed by a signature or mark—God's covenant with Abraham is, after all, a mutual agreement signed by the mark of circumcision[5]—to propose a covenant between art and theory inevitably invokes writing. What is the agreement between art and theory, this covenant? Does art agree to submit to the law of language, and to be marked by this agreement with the cut of writing? Or, more significantly, on the basis of a later agreement between God and Moses, is this a covenant in which, on the promise of a future plenitude, theory submits to wandering in the desert—and to bearing the marks of this wandering—following the name of that which will not show its face?[6] Rhetoric aside, the reason I evoke this second biblical covenant is to indicate an opening onto an understanding of theory as constitutively provisional, but which, in so being, is not unfinished as such, but enfolded around a series of points where the flow of theoretical communicability is sharply arrested; not conceptual aporia but material disturbances in writing.

In a less abstract sense, I wish to draw attention to the centrality of writing and language within Ettinger's combined artistic-theoretical project. In basic terms, and partly because her theoretical proposition is situated within a psychoanalytical field, she inherits the tradition of Freud's *Wunderblock* in her reliance on the image of inscription to account for memory and the registration of affects and events in the psyche. While the consequences of this inheritance for her positing of a 'beyond-the-phallus' dimension of subjectivity require investigation, for now they will have to remain unexplored. One avenue in need of attention in this regard is Ettinger's use of a metaphorics of writing—her texts abound with scriptural metaphors, notions of inscription, 'trans-scription' and 'cross-scription', as well as a persistent emphasis on the trace and tracing—but in conjunction with a claim to rethink the unconscious away from repression; that is, she retains an idea of an unconscious writing, but leaves open both the question of the topography of that writing, and its mechanisms.[7] In spite of these theoretical questions, however, my focus here will be more concrete: the function of writing in the transposition between different registers of thought, in this case between art and theory.

Ettinger's art work itself visually and materially explores ideas of transposition, translation and untranslatability; her paintings are built upon work with reproductions of found images and text, which are halted in the process of reproduction by photocopier, before the transport of the image by toner-dust can be fixed. Although more attention has been paid to her interruption and painterly reworking of documentary images (especially those of the Holocaust and the Łódź ghetto),[8] I suggest that the printed 'underlay' of images from the *Mamalangue* and *Eurydice* series (12.2–3), also present in several other works, is representative of another current in her visual practice. The appearance in these images of a fragment from a Hebrew–French lexicon also points to a motif repeated elsewhere in her work of the relationship between Israel and Europe, and between European languages and Hebrew, which in some senses estranges French and English as 'phallic' languages, Hebrew carrying the promise of access to a mode of 'non-phallic' language-work.

Before turning to Ettinger's visual engagement with writing, however, it is not her painting itself that will initially be the most helpful in understanding the role of writing in the concrete manifestation of a transport between art and theory in her work. Since the early 1980s, her day-to-day practice of making paintings has also been accompanied by a writing that is fragmentary in both form and process (12.1, 12.4), but which extends far beyond received notions of the artist's notebook.[9] Ettinger's notebooks are, firstly, a testament to the primary involvement of her work with writing and thinking on language: the notebooks date back to at least 1985, six years prior to her first conference presentation of a distinct 'theory' of the matrixial.[10] Their presence throughout her career—and their growing significance as works in their own right in more recent years (since 2006)—suggests that her painting can-

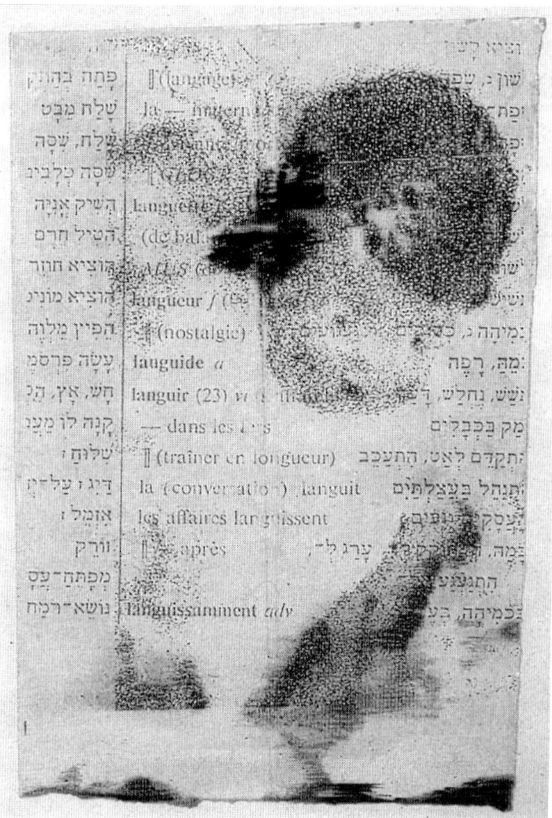

12.2   Bracha L. Ettinger, *Mamalangue* 1, 1992. Oil and mixed media on paper mounted on canvas. © Bracha L. Ettinger. Reproduced courtesy of the artist.

not be said to precede or stand separately from writing. This in turn inflects how we might understand the relation between her painting practice and her theoretical intervention in psychoanalysis. For example, to ask how we get *from* Ettinger's painting *to* her theory would be to miss the complex temporality of her practice: *with* painting (as present participle), and *in-between* painting and theory, there is writing.

More specifically, beyond attesting to the importance of writing for her project as a whole, Ettinger's notebooks continue the figuration of translation legible in both her art work and theory: although published extracts are in French or English, or a parallel text of both, the 'raw', unedited notebooks are an interweaving of English, French and Hebrew; literally a writing and thinking *between* languages. They also link the process of non-signifying mark-mak-

12.3 Bracha L. Ettinger, *Eurydice* 4, 1992–4. Oil and photocopy toner on paper mounted on canvas. © Bracha L. Ettinger. Reproduced courtesy of the artist.

ing in her paintings with the emergence of a developing conceptual vocabulary: what appears as a doodle in 12.4(c–d) is repeated in several early paintings as an inscription of the Greek letter *omega* (Ω) (12.5–6), and formally lends itself to a series of reflections on encirclement, enclosure, estrangement, the centre and absence.[11]

Although depicted here in their unedited form, edited versions of Ettinger's notebooks have been published in various forms over the past two decades, most extensively as *Matrix Halal(a)—Lapsus: Notes on Painting* (1993). These edited fragments have initiated much of my analysis here: the reflections on language they contain, particularly concerning Hebrew etymology, can be used at once to shed light on the nature and status of Ettinger's theoretical writing, and to help to understand its peculiar difficulty, characterized as it is by a

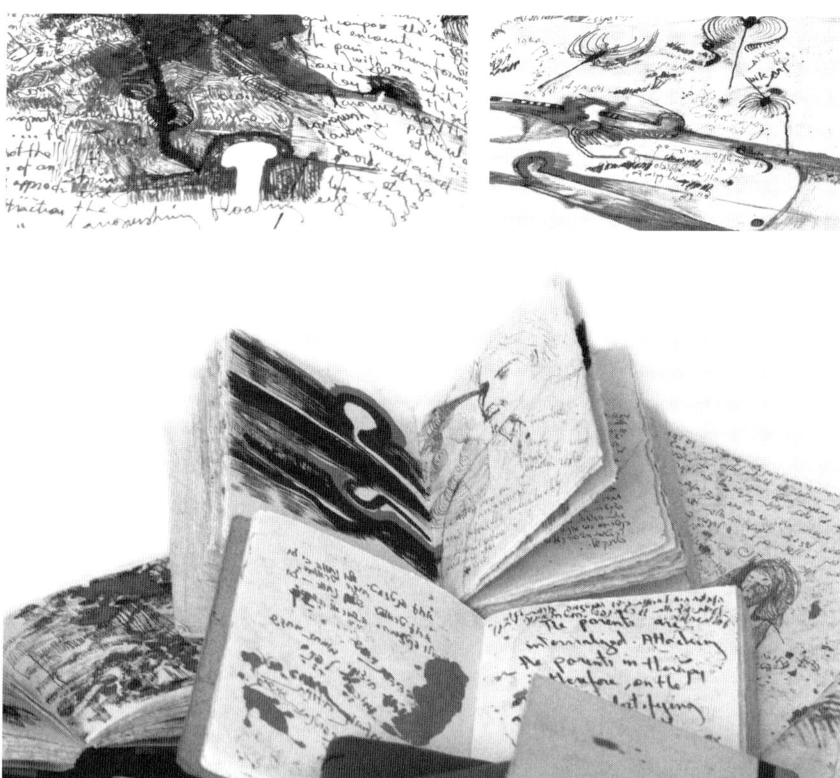

12.4    Bracha L. Ettinger, *Notebooks*, 2005. © Bracha L. Ettinger. Reproduced
courtesy of the artist.

proliferation of naming and neologism. An important element I will draw
attention to in this context is the potency it attributes to the *word*, although I
hope to show that this *word* is not necessarily complicit with *logos*:

> One must be endowed for the signs, ready to encounter them, one must
> open oneself to their violence. The intelligence always comes after; it is
> good when it comes after; it is good only when it comes after […] *There
> is no Logos; there are only hieroglyphs.* To think is therefore to interpret, is
> therefore to translate.[12]

To return to the idea of the covenant, I would like to propose a level of
reading that can be open to the letter of Ettinger's writing in order to show
that it enfolds a material dimension, demonstrably marking its mobilization by
forces beyond and beneath the ostensible clarity and communicability of the-

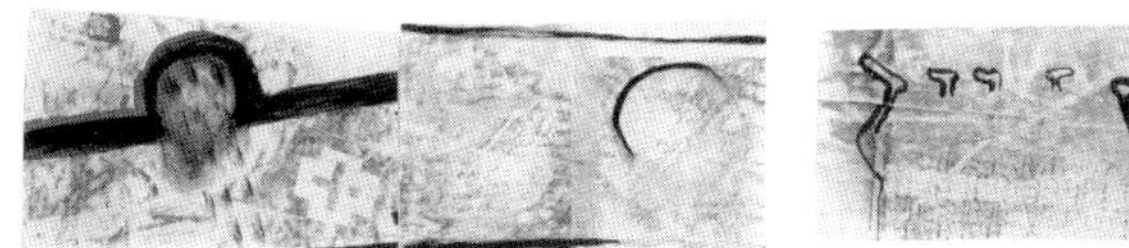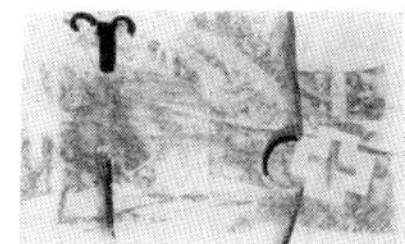

12.5 Bracha L. Ettinger, *Family Album—Means of Transportation*, 1988–9. Mixed media on paper. © Bracha L. Ettinger. Reproduced courtesy of the artist.

ory. What I aim to demonstrate here supports Ettinger's idea of a collision between 'theoretical elements' and 'visual elements which refuse theory', but also seeks to indicate that such a collision, rather than taking place outside what is proper to theory, actually operates *within* Ettinger's theoretical writing and is the very means by which her theory *works*.

My attention to Ettinger's engagement with language will focus on two areas. The first is through the idea of 'nomad words'—metaphorical enactments of formal characteristics of the Hebrew language—with which I aim to enable previously undisclosed modes of transport to become visible. Following from this, I will then raise some important questions concerning the nature of grammar and syntax, which will allow a repositioning of the singularity of Ettinger's theoretical writing as a matter of subterranean language-work, operating at a level imperceptible within the conventional registers of sense and reference implied by its overt (sentence-level) syntactical structure.

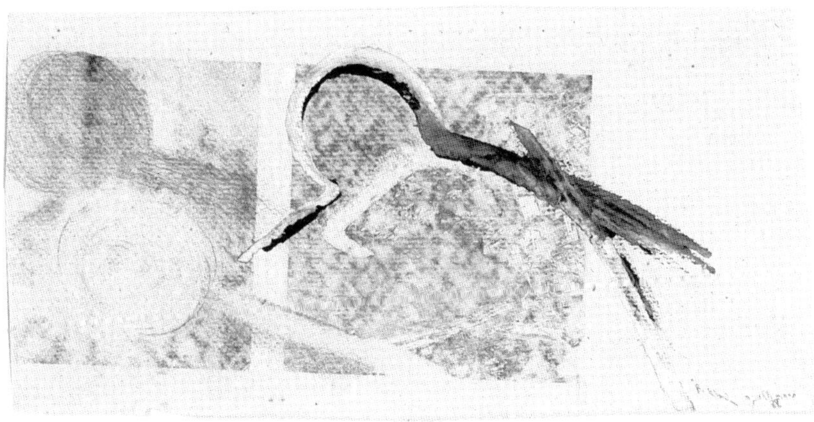

12.6 Bracha L. Ettinger, *Aerial View*, 1988. Mixed media on paper. © Bracha L. Ettinger. Reproduced courtesy of the artist.

This mode of reading will not displace the higher-level theoretical structures she claims; rather, by bringing out a combination of scriptural, etymological, morphological and syntactical considerations, I will indicate a shifted understanding of the relationship between her higher-level theory and the aesthetic/affective dimension it articulates.

## Metaphorization of Hebrew

Connected to a series of fragments concerning language, translation and the trace, Ettinger's treatment of the Hebrew language in *Matrix Halal(a)—Lapsus* appears to have a critical role to play in informing her theoretical methodology, in so far as it supplies tools to work upon words; to analyse, associate and synthesize meaning. Hebrew is valuable to Ettinger in this context because its derivation of words through variations on a three letter root form facilitates an idea of words as *materially* multiple in their meanings—and thus, for one thing, irreducible to the one-to-one correlation of signifier and signified in the Saussurean sign.[13] In an early theoretical text Ettinger elaborates on her understanding of Hebrew etymology, arguing that within Hebrew, words themselves *mean*, not only through the vertical and horizontal movements of signification, but also via a third dimension—the association given in the formal characteristics of the root form, the 'scope' of the signifier. She uses this to suggest a latency, a dimension of the virtual, within words:

> In Hebrew, because of opened passages between words and their roots, each word quivers, trembles and ejects several meanings, even before insertion into a context. […] The links between the different possibilities offered by the signifier operate whether we cast light on it or not.[14]

In Ettinger's hands, Hebrew is also given a specific role to play in relation to failures in language, and within reflections on the relationship between Israel and Europe.[15] An early notebook fragment (from 1985), describes one of several autobiographical scenarios that chart the afterlife of the Holocaust in 1950s Israel, and associates a combined failure of translation and maternal estrangement with a drive to acquire words. She writes:

> My mother didn't speak Hebrew at the time. My parents spoke Polish to each other. My brother and I didn't understand. I needed words. I took them from books. Nomadic words. I liked taking words that meant nothing to me.[16]

The themes carried in this short passage—a rupture between Polish and Hebrew, the idea of an acquisition of words to fill intervals in meaning and communication, as well as the use of words *without* meaning—run throughout *Matrix Halal(a)—Lapsus*. The initial discontinuity between Polish and

Hebrew is later (1987) broadened into a consideration of the 'moulting of meaning' in translation,[17] not only between languages, but also between different dimensions of experience, especially 'painting' and 'language'. Translation, for Ettinger, is in many senses discontinuity and loss, yet such loss is not an inevitability. The idea of 'nomadic words' in the above passage, although not 'theorized' as such, later reappears as a coined phrase-word: the 'nomad-word', and can be usefully deployed in understanding Ettinger's approach to translation, coinage and theorization, especially where it is clearly echoed in the acquisition or creation of terms—such as *Matrix* and *metramorphosis*—to repair the cultural blanks that over-write the traces of a non-phallic feminine.

It is my view that a necessary (if not sufficient) condition for Ettinger's *matrixial* intervention in the symbolic is a latent theory of language, which includes, among other things, an idea of the power of the word—*a* word in the first case: *Matrix*—in effect, to alter the 'reality' of cultural meaning. The word *Matrix* is put forward as a symbol for processes that have always played out—Ettinger contends—in the *infra-* of experience, but which are excluded (foreclosed) from cultural processing, history and memory, because they are unnamed or unsymbolized; Ettinger frequently deploys Christopher Bollas's phrase the 'unthought known' to characterize this domain. Gathering together these unthought, although 'known' experiences under the symbolic umbrella of the word *Matrix*, she hypothesizes, opens the way for them to have a symbolic presence and thus a cultural voice. This is, then, her estimation of the power of the word: 'The Matrix gives meaning to a Real which might otherwise pass by unthinkable, unnoticed, and unrecognized [...]'.[18]

Within Ettinger's theory, words are created and re-created to 'give meaning' to that which lies outside language ('give meaning to…' is a key refrain in *Matrix Halal(a)—Lapsus*).[19] The initiating appropriation of *Matrix* to fulfil a lacking symbolic function is only one instance of an 'additive' approach to language—which carries over into Ettinger's bricolage of other theories[20]—that uses word-modification (by standard and non-standard means), zero-derivation (derivational shift without prefix or suffix) and neologism as major processes of theoretical intervention. This approach to language also concerns writing, as well as the overlap between writing and drawing as mark-making practices: the 'donation' of meaning doesn't lend itself to transparency, since Ettinger's coinages also conscript silent, graphological elements—non-signifying, and often inaudible in speech—in an ongoing working and re-working of the materiality of words as the tracing not of the image, but of the non-representational force of affect.

In this context, the idea of words as nomadic has a particular significance. 'Nomad-word' appears to indicate a signifier without determinate signified, a word that within conventional signification can potentially 'mean nothing', but is credited with a generative power. 'Nomad-words,' Ettinger writes, 'can create (*leholel*) and dance (*leholel*) in the real'.[21] In their ability to travel, it seems, some words are better vehicles across lines of discontinuity or rupture than others, in the sense that the more a word can carry, the better it is able to withstand loss in translation. Describing 'nomad-words' through a repetition of *leholel* doubles this implied meaning, metaphorically enfolding the operation of the nomad-word within its description: *leholel* as a whirling or circular dance is thought to be derived from a root form, ל ל ח (HLL),[22] also the root of *halal*—which carries a wealth of other derivatives relating to desecration, profanity, piercing, wounding and hollowing,[23] all of which are central to Ettinger's etymological considerations. In describing the nomad-word, that is, she also enfolds a metaphorical demonstration of its operation. Such poetic analysis extends throughout *Matrix Halal(a)—Lapsus*; as well as HLL, Ettinger also uses Hebrew root-forms to connect a series of other concepts, for example end and threshold, as well as interiority, anteriority and faciality.[24] Most extensive is the analysis of the root ר (resh) ח (chēth) א (aleph), transliterated as a. ch. r, from which she derives a series of words relating alterity, finality and causality, that have become central themes within both her theory and her art work:[25]

| | |
|---|---|
| other (*acher*) | alterity (*acherout*) |
| otherwise (*acheret*) | responsibility (*achariut*) |
| beyond (*achar*) | last (*acharon*) |
| behind (*[me]achor*) | after, follow (*acharei*) |
| because (*meàchar shê*) | |

The nomad-word, in sum, is specifically connected with metaphors of passage and transformation, but also with *naming*:

> The named words, the nomad-words; those that travel well and those that travel poorly between two tongues. [...] There are others that suffer during the journey and hide out. [...] Named-words, nomad-words hide out and protest. They have the force of motion, of alternance [...].[26]

The analysis of Hebrew root-forms combined with the elaboration of the nomad-word are indicative of Ettinger's attitude to language in her theoretical texts. That is, the idea of Hebrew words as in themselves sites of the virtual, carriers of multiple and heterogeneous meanings—nomad-words—is something that Ettinger's writing seeks to metaphorize in English and French (which, however problematically, she appears to consider more rigid, or 'phallic' in their modes of meaning).[27] I will shortly show how a significant proportion of the words and phrase-words she creates within her theoretical 'matrixial' framework have formal characteristics comparable to those she draws from Hebrew: formation of terms that join together distinct and even oppositional meanings, and/or the modification of words through the varia-

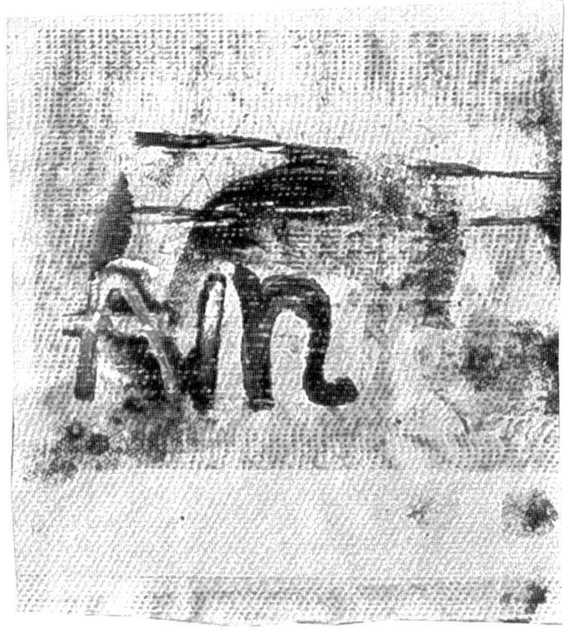

12.7   Bracha L. Ettinger, *Borderline Conditions and Pathological Narcissism* 4, 1989–91, detail. Mixed media on paper mounted on canvas. © Bracha L. Ettinger. Reproduced courtesy of the artist.

tion/addition of a single letter to a grounding root-form, as in her central neologism *metramorphosis*. This, I believe, attempts to mime the capacity she perceives in Hebrew, for ('nomad') words to carry undisclosed or indeterminate freight.

Before going too far in the direction of this work being something particular to Ettinger's writing—forged in her notebooks and simply carried into her theory—it is essential to pay some attention (albeit brief, at this point) to a visual registration of writing, which I have already noted with regard to the appearance of the letter *omega* in *Matrix Halal(a)—Lapsus*, her unedited notebooks (12.4–6) and her early paintings. A further example can be found in a detail from an early work in the series *Borderline Conditions and Pathological Narcissism* (1989–91) (12.7). This deceptively simple fragment is in fact an extraordinary intertwining of several registers of meaning, referring simultaneously to a word, a letter, an absent image of vision, and to the impossible origins of language.

At first glance, this fragment is difficult to decipher. To an English-, French- or German-speaking viewer it will mean very little, suggesting at most a word fragmented, incomplete or alien. Indeed, this is an assemblage of letters constitutively estranged: although in Latin script, its actual reference is to Hebrew; its three letters *a-i-n* spell out the *sound* of the Hebrew word for 'eye': ן י ע ('*ayin*). How might we explicate the knotted figurations of translation this fragment carries? At second glance, we might detect a metaphysical or logocentric attitude to writing: *a-i-n* spells out the sound of a spoken word, and so uses writing merely to transcribe. Things, however, are not quite so simple: as well as spelling out the sound of the word 'eye', *a-i-n* also spells out the *name* of its initial character, the letter ע (again pronounced '*ayin*). Thus, where we might see Ettinger's phonetic spelling as positioning writing in the place assigned it by Rousseau (as the transcription of speech), this work also undertakes a reversal, spelling out the name of a silent letter, writing down sound to refer to a prior mark that is, on its own, unpronounceable. I say this because although the letter ע is *named* by the sound spelled out by *a-i-n*, in speech it lacks a straightforward pronunciation as a phoneme. Ernest Klein indicates that the pronunciation of ע is either a 'strong guttural sound', or is more usually treated like an aleph, which is 'silent in the middle of words if it has no vowel; otherwise it is pronounced according to the accompanying vowel sign'.[28]

To add a final, visual layer to this already complex *mise en abyme* of speech and writing, there is a further enfolding of word and letter in this fragment.[29] As well as homophonically evoking the *word* for eye, the letter ע also carries an archaic *visual* meaning—the image of an eye—by allusion to its ancient pictographic form ◉, which has the same name (*Ayin*) and is thus also phonetically written by Ettinger's three letters *a-i-n*.[30]

Here, then, we have an example of an additional characteristic of Hebrew not directly discussed in Ettinger's notebooks—its archaic pictographic history—but which is by no means an isolated instance of visual play;[31] indeed, this piece of work indicates a crucial further characteristic of both of her approach to theoretical writing and the metaphorization of Hebrew: an engagement with the word as *visual* form. The complex interplay here between the material word as both letter and sound, between different meanings registered by that materiality, and between thinking 'in painting' and in writing, also makes itself felt in her theoretical texts. Where, for instance, this fragment plays on the absent materiality of an unpronounceable letter, I will shortly show how this is echoed by the insistence of the unpronounceable mark of punctuation *within* words in Ettinger's theoretical neologisms.

## The writing of the matrixial

Before reaching the specificities of Ettinger's theoretical word-formation, it will be useful to say a few general words on her theoretical writing. In tone, this writing is surprisingly flat, apparently displaying little of the reflexivity, rhetorical flourish or play so evident in other post-structuralist works.

Ettinger's texts are often (broadly speaking) divided into two modes: classical rhetorical structures of hypothesis, claim and counter-claim: Lacan claims *x*, I propose *y*, and so on. Notable within this first mode is the frequency of formations such as *I call, I name, I term*, and *I have named*. Time in this mode is also simple—rare deviations from a coincidence of the authorial *I* and the present indicative are the present perfect, almost exclusively limited to an indication of prior naming (*I have called*) and simple future (*I will discuss*). The subject of this *I* gives nothing away, however; its function could be interpreted as one of (with all its paradoxes) a deictic positing of an authorial *here and now*, perhaps an authorial 'guarantee' of the ostensible referentiality of the text.[32]

Beside the bare first person, the second mode is also relatively anonymous and syntactically simple, at least at the level of grammatical sentence construction or phrasing. Where positive descriptions and statements are articulated regarding Ettinger's hypothesized theoretical framework—the matrixial—these have a remarkably impersonal tone. The following is a representative example:

A matrixial covenant zooms-in by chance and fades-out by/with-in asymmetrical metramorphosis. The series of encounters between the co-emerging *I* and *non-I* via conductible links on the trauma/phantasy level and on the phantasy/desire level, along with the connections between the *I* and the *non-I* and their hybrid *objet(s) a*, shared beyond time in a series of conjunctions beyond place, shape a unique borderspace that gives birth to co-meanings of I-with/for-Other […].[33]

Briefly, this passage gives us two sentences, the first a simple subject description, 'a matrixial covenant does *x*'. The second, although a more complex compound of sub-clauses and qualifications, is nevertheless built around a very simple statement: 'the series of encounters between […] *I* and *non-I* […] shape a unique borderspace that gives birth to [meaning]', grammatically very similar to the first. The extreme difficulty of this passage, however, a difficulty that pervades a great deal of Ettinger's writing, resides at the level of *word-formation*, not grammatical sentence structure. Its density lies in a proliferation of apparently descriptive terms that link themselves to conventional signification, but in their use of unusual juxtaposition, punctuation, prefixing, metaphor and coinage, *resist* the description or reference implied by the syntax. Indeed, Ettinger's work often appears to leave syntax unexamined, a characteristic that could distinguish it from other (post-) psychoanalytic, 'feminist' thinkers, especially Luce Irigaray and Julia Kristeva, for whom it is specifically syntax that is disrupted in the movement towards *parler-femme* or the irruption of the semiotic in poetic language. In *This Sex Which Is Not One*, Irigaray presents the idea of a hypothetical future 'feminine' syntax that is distinctly at odds with Ettinger's '*I call*', '*I name*':

what a feminine syntax might be is not simple nor easy to state, because in that 'syntax' there would no longer be either subject or object, 'oneness' would no longer be privileged, there would no longer be proper meanings, proper names, 'proper' attributes … Instead, that 'syntax' would involve nearness, proximity, but in such an extreme form that it would preclude any distinction of identities, any establishment of ownership, thus any form of appropriation.[34]

It is important to be clear at this point that I am not suggesting that Ettinger's theory is somehow undermined by this aspect of its writing, nor that the only authentic inscription of a non-phallic feminine is via the means Irigaray suggests. Ettinger's aims in theorizing the matrixial, and her methodology for doing so, are entirely distinct from Irigaray's utopian *parler-femme*, which privileges the immediacy of speech and proposes a too forceful bond between *the feminine* and *women* as a group, something to which Ettinger does not subscribe. Rather, my point is to draw attention to the importance of syntax, and its disruption, for other thinkers with whom Ettinger's work has significant connections, and to note her apparent silence on the subject. With these issues in mind, what is it possible to say about Ettinger's writing, which appears to leave syntax intact, and works instead on *words*? Gilles Deleuze also identifies syntax as the object of writing, and as the site of transformation in language: 'syntactic creation or style—this is the becoming of language', and, even more significantly, explicitly places syntactic creation as the antecedent condition of coinage: 'the creation of words or neologisms is nothing apart from the effects of syntax in which they are developed'.[35] While this might be troubling with regard to its apparent inversion in Ettinger's writing (at first glance free from syntactical peculiarities, but peppered with neologisms), there is a brief suggestion in Jakobson's 'Two aspects of language and two types of aphasic disturbances', which clearly recognizes a lower, if uncommon, level of syntactical operation—below sentence structure—in the form of the *phrase-word*:

> In any language, there exist also coded word-groups called phrase-words. The meaning of the idiom *how do you do* cannot be derived by adding together the meanings of its lexical constituents; the whole is not equal to the sum of its parts. Those word-groups which in this respect behave like single words are a common but nonetheless only marginal case. In order to comprehend the overwhelming majority of word-groups, we must be familiar only with the constituent words and with the syntactical rules of their combination.[36]

The idea of such a level of syntax, I suggest, could be put forward as the locus within which Ettinger's work on language in fact operates: following on from the idea of the 'nomad word', drawn from the formal characteristics of

Hebrew etymology, it is possible to argue that there *is* a syntactical disruption operative in her theory, but *beneath* sentence structure, taking form instead in coinages and assembled phrase-words.

Within this level of syntax, the scriptural will have a key function, in the sense that the use of punctuation—as that which is most specific to writing in distinction from speech[37]—is a defining characteristic of Ettinger's theoretical writing. This is marked first and foremost by a proliferation of the hyphen, which, in this respect, takes on two main functions. The first is what appears to be a commonplace word-joiner, but is used by Ettinger in the formation of compound phrase-words, functioning as coined substantives. The following key examples are all terms that Ettinger uses to rearticulate relation as trans-subjective:

distance-in-proximity
shared-in-difference
differentiation-in-co-emergence
fading-in-transformation
touching-in-separating

The -in- takes on two linked operations within such phrases: the synchronic 'reconciliation' of markedly heterogeneous or opposed terms, and the figuration of diachronic heterogeneity within movement. Both can be seen to mime Ettinger's idea of Hebrew words as 'nomadic' carriers of multiple meanings. This resonance with Ettinger's references to Hebrew in *Matrix Halal(a)—Lapsus* continues into another class of hyphenated phrase-word. In addition to the -in- copula, there is also -as-, which forms phrase-words not around simile (which would be suggested by the *as*), but through conceptual transformation. *Subjectivity-as-encounter* and *before-as-beside* are constructions which function to provoke the reader to reconceive subjectivity and temporality by expanding them to include contradictory concepts.

I will only note the second distinct function of the hyphen, as it should already be reasonably familiar, having a strong pedigree in Continental philosophy and Lacanian psychoanalysis—the *insertion* of hyphens into given terms to re-configure their meaning. The proliferation of this hyphen in Ettinger's work, however, as well as its scope—far beyond prefixes and suffixes, beyond simple defamiliarization, or analysis of words into standard morphemes—indicates a radical disruption of given language. For example, *within* becomes *with-in* (emphasizing the alterity of 'with' disrupts any sense of interiority, unity or closure), *outside* and *inside* are hyphenated to emphasize 'side' as surface (loosening their connection to the closure of exteriority and interiority), *impure* becomes *im-pure*, deconstructively drawing attention to the dependence of purity on a defiled other.

Within the idea of work on word-level syntax as a prime mover in the creation of Ettinger's theoretical vocabulary, the interruptive hyphen can be considered but one example of a broader operation, one which follows in the tradition of Derridian differance[38] inasmuch as it often plays on a written difference inaudible in the spoken word. The difference from Derridian differance in Ettinger's word-work however, lies in a more forceful resistance to speech: the rupture of verbal consistency and/or unity by punctuation—closer perhaps to 'differ( )nce' than differance.[39] In Ettinger's writing, that is, the silent *mark* has a critical role to play, not only by opening words to each other in the formation of new phrase-words, but also (and especially) by punctuating the word in a material inter-ruption of meaning. That is, her introduction of punctuation *into* words lies below even phonetic analysis—the solidus, the parenthesis and the hyphen being frequently used as scriptural disruptions of verbal unity. Significant examples of this are the terms:

wit(h)ness
co/in-habit(u)ating

These are (a) verbally unpronounceable, and (b) highly resistant to a definitive attribution of meaning. Wit(h)ness in particular behaves in a peculiar manner in Ettinger's texts, when further modified with the suffix -ing, invisibly transforming an abstract substantive—*withness*—into a deverbal noun (i.e. derived from a verb) or present participle, *withnessing*, whose meaning is not clear. Wit(h)nessing, I will now show, is a prime example of the nomad-word: to repeat, a signifier without determinate signified that, within conventional signification approaches non-meaning, but which is credited, within Ettinger's theory, with the power to 'give meaning to' an otherwise occluded mode of (ethical) relation.

*Wit(h)ness*

If we test out the nature of wit(h)ness as a word, to examine it grammatically quickly reveals some unusual behaviour. A combination of *witness* and *withness* (a rare term, lit. 'the fact of being with some one or something; collocation, association'), wit(h)ness transfers characteristics of the former (a word with an already complex etymology and meaning; for example, the zero-derivation of the verb 'to witness' from the noun 'witness' makes its meaning heavily context-dependent) to the latter, more stable and straightforward term. In simple terms, the emergence of the verb 'to witness', appears to have taken the following course:

*witness:* testimony (derived from *wit:* 'knowledge')
   ↓
*a witness:* a person bearing witness
   ↓
*to witness:* the act of bearing witness.[40]

Combined in wit(h)ness, the word with greater fixity (*withness*) seems to 'piggyback' on the flexibility of *witness*. Thus, when *wit(h)ness* becomes *wit(h)nessing*, the meaning of being-with carried within this combined term shifts in a fundamental way: an abstract noun (the state of being-with) appears to become a present participle or a deverbal noun, both of which, of necessity imply a verb—*to withness*. For example:

> We are wit(h)nessing—witnessing and withnessing the others: my withnessing in a Thing-encounter permits my witnessing the Thing-event of my non-I(s), which is, in fact, a witnessing without event. Such non-cognitive wit(h)nessing transgresses the domain of aesthetics.[41]

Given that zero-derived denominal verbs can be understood to have the meaning of verbalized sentences (I witness = I am a witness),[42] the move from straight *withness* to *withnessing* skips a derivational move, eliding the meaning of its verbal form. That is, a hypothetical derivation of the verb *to withness*, following the course of *witness*, would be:

> *withness:* the quality or state of being-with
> ↓
> *a withness*
> ↓
> *to withness*

Thus, at least within a conventional grammatical framework, there are two levels of coinage at play in *wit(h)ness*: the formation of the word itself, and the hidden invention of a *personal* substantive, *a withness*, which appears to mime the peculiar metonymical relationship whereby the act of bearing witness gives rise to the identification of the *person* as a witness. I will not be able to elaborate on this without going into detail on the impossibility of an *individual* subject within the matrixial stratum, but, even regardless of the question of what 'a withness' could mean, since this proposes a single subject determined as *a* withness the idea is actually counter to the logic of the matrixial, constituted as it is on ideas of partial subjectivity, severality, and 'the impossibility of not-sharing'.[43] This peculiarity is lost in French translations of Ettinger's texts, where wit(h)nessing is rendered as *en (co)témoignant* (approximately (co)testifying, or witnessing(with)). Because the French rendering is closer to ordinary prefixing, and is thus more easily partitioned into *witnessing* and *with*, this substantially weakens the semantic concentration of *wit(h)ness*, materially watering down the ethical implications carried by its inextricable non-fusion of witnessing and being-with.[44]

Beyond questions of grammar and/or philology, another approach to both wit(h)nessing and co/in-habit(u)ating would be to see them not only as grammatical constructions—as words that mean in a *conventional* sense—but as visual/scriptural assemblages based on a treatment of words as images or even as *things* (to return to Freud), recalling Ettinger's trans-scription of ע shown in 12.7.[45] With reference to the process of condensation in the Freudian dream-work, wit(h)nessing and co/in-habit(u)ating could be seen at once as grammatical words, and figurations of the action of metaphor:

> The work of condensation in dreams is seen [at] its clearest when it handles words and names. It is true in general the words are frequently treated in dreams as thought they were things, and for that reason they are apt to be combined in just the same way as are presentations of things. Dreams of this sort offer the most amusing and curious neologisms.[46]

On top of this, Freud also describes an aspect of the dream-work that has a surprising resonance with Ettinger's overlay of distinct words to form composites:

> I did not combine the features of one person with those of another and in the process omit from the memory-picture certain features of each of them. What I did was to adopt the procedure by means of which Galton produced family portraits: namely by projecting two images on to a single plate, so that certain features common to both are emphasized, while those which fail to fit in with one another cancel one another out and are indistinct in the picture.[47]

Although visually, wit(h)nessing emphasizes the one feature *not* shared by both words—the 'h' (without the parentheses, *witness* would be obliterated)—grammatically those features 'which fail to fit in with one another', that is, the fundamental grammatical differences between *withness* and *witness* undoubtedly 'cancel one another out' and become indistinct.

### *ffAm*

I have indicated the importance of naming for Ettinger's theoretical intervention and its underlying theory of language, *Matrix* indicating the fetishistic power given to words in her work, which is marked by a wealth of assembled and invented neologisms. By way of closing this essay, I will approach a final invention that brings together almost every element I have discussed: neologism, the attempt to transpose into French and English the capacity for carriage of latent meaning given in the Hebrew root-form, and the insistence of the scriptural in Ettinger's theoretical vocabulary. The term that draws all these threads together is *ffAm*, coined c.2001.

Ettinger introduces this term in an analysis of Marguerite Duras' *The Ravishing of Lol Stein*, of Lol's enraptured immobilization (and subsequent breakdown) at the scene of her fiancé's abandonment of her for a seductive stranger. This scene, Ettinger argues, is a matter of an (interrupted) encounter with an-other, matrixial, femininity, which she specifies in the following terms: 'That which Lol finds ravishing at the same time as it ravages her, is the blind desirability within the fatal-woman-Other-mother (phonetically in French, femme, i.e. woman; ffAm (*femme-fatale-Autre-mère*))'.[48]

Two questions that immediately come to mind on first reading this passage are: why specify a term in French when its sense is adequately given in English? And why the instruction to move from a combined phrase-word to a phonetic enunciation of initial letters? I would argue that the only sense that can be made of this scriptural creation is in the terms discussed in this essay, as an example of the transposition of a resistant exterior *into theory*, through a material working and re-working of language.

The first point to note is the peculiarity of this 'word' as a word: its shape, written down and unspoken, is difficult to reconcile with conventions of sense or reference. The opening of a word with a double *ff* is already an estrangement—the non-existence of a corresponding phoneme in either English, or the phonetic 'French' indicated as its milieu, means that enunciating *ffAm*, as its explanation impels us to do, is inevitably a truncation of the written word. But, because the difference between the two terms *femme* and *ffAm* lies in the written word, the written *ffAm* has priority over speech, in the sense that it does not transcribe a phonological presence, but *vice versa*: again recalling Ettinger's work on the letter ע (12.7), speech *translates* a scriptural form.[49] *FfAm*, as with differance, indicates that the self-presence of the spoken word as *logos* is disrupted by the insistence of writing. The enunciation of the term in French—*femme*—undertakes an erasure of the specificity of writing by speech at the same time and in the same moment that speech is called into the service of a non-phonetic writing. As written *ffAm* evokes speech: we are encouraged (instructed?) to form the French *femme*; as spoken it calls upon writing (the letter) as the mark of its specificity.

Because French already has the phonetic term /fam/, to which *ffAm* is phonically identical, using an estranged *French* speech to underwrite it points to an act of supplementation. That is, English is unable to provide the resources to sufficiently articulate this term (and so is lacking), and French is the exterior source of the additive solution. French, also, is lacking, as neither the 'proper' *femme*, nor the unabbreviated *femme fatale Autre-mère* is sufficient to present the other femininity Ettinger seeks. The resulting term is thus a nomad-word, a combination of inscription, abbreviation and coinage that belongs to neither of the languages through which it is articulated.[50]

*          *          *

By way of a provisional conclusion, the relationship of the characteristics outlined here is such that Ettinger's writing may be considered to be suspended between the 'presence' of the authorial *I* that organizes much of her theoretical work, and the withholding of logocentric presence in the material insistence of words and writing. Through such suspension this theory at once refers to the aesthetic field of the matrixial as an opaque exteriority, while transporting that resistance within its own work on language. The persistence of a work on words within Ettinger's theory means that its referentiality and descriptiveness, even at times its logic, is disrupted. Such disruption, however, does not undermine the higher-level theory she proposes, but rather gives the strongest indication of the import of her work, since it is, to my mind, the effect of the covenant she proposes between art and theory, a legible mark of the paradoxical appearance of the matrixial dimension *within* theoretical language. Perhaps even more than Ettinger's conceptual-theoretical rigour or poetic 'performance' of matrixiality, this mark is a clear testament to the profound seriousness of her matrixial proposition.

# NOTES

The editors have sought to ensure that all URLs for external websites referred to in this book are correct and active at the time of going to press, unless otherwise stated.

**Series Preface**

1    Mieke Bal, *Travelling Concepts in the Humanities: A Rough Guide* (Toronto: University of Toronto Press, 2002).
2    Mieke Bal, *The Point of Theory: Practices of Cultural Analysis* (Amsterdam: University of Amsterdam Press, 1994); Mieke Bal, *The Practice of Cultural Analysis: Exposing Interdisciplinary Interpretation* (Stanford: Stanford University Press, 1999).
3    Bal: *The Practice of Cultural Analysis*, p. 1.

**Editors' Introduction**

1    Hannah Arendt, 'Prologue', in *The Human Condition* [1958] (Chicago: University of Chicago Press, 1998), p. 1.
2    Louis Althusser famously adapted Jacques Lacan's psychoanalytical reconceptualization of the Sartrean Imaginary (the study of the imaginative faculty as the site of human creativity and freedom) as one of three registers of subjectivity: the Real (traumatically unthinkable), the Imaginary (the register of misrecognition, fantasy and the image) and the Symbolic (the register of thought and words). Althusser used it to redefine ideology not as false consciousness but as a structure of misrecognition that determines as imaginary the way in which we live our relations to the real conditions of existence. Louis Althusser, 'Freud and Lacan', *New Left Review* 1/55 (1969), pp. 49–65.
3    Karl Marx, 'The Fetishism of the Commodity and Its Secret', in *Capital*, vol. 1, trans. Ben Fowkes (Harmondsworth: Penguin, 1976), pp. 165–6.
4    Paul Hirst and Penny Woolley, 'The Social Formation and Maintenance of Human Attributes' in *Social Relations and Human Attributes* (London: Tavistock, 1982), p. 42. Emphasis in original.
5    Donna Haraway, 'A Cyborg Manifesto: Science, Technology, and Socialist-Feminism in the Late Twentieth Century' [1985], in *Simians, Cyborgs and Women: The Reinvention of Nature* (New York: Routledge, 1991), pp. 149–81.
6    Walter Benjamin, 'The Work of Art in the Age of Mechanical Reproduction'[1935], in *Illuminations*, ed. Hannah Arendt, trans. Harry Zohn (London: Fontana, 1973), p. 220.

7   Manuel Castells, *The Informational City: Information Technology, Economic Restructuring, and the Urban Regional Process* (Oxford: Blackwell, 1989), p. 149; Manuel Castells, 'Informationalism and the Network Society', afterword in Pekka Himanen, *The Hacker Ethic and the Spirit of the Information Age* (New York: Random House, 2001), pp. 155–78.

8   Philip Rosen, 'Old and New: Image, Indexicality, and Historicity in the Digital Utopia', in *Change Mummified: Cinema, Historicity, Theory* (Minneapolis: University of Minnesota Press, 2001), p. 309. Digital imagery may be formed from a physical scene, or it may be obtained from other kinds of photographic imagery through scanning. Finally it can be generated, which is known as 'image synthesis'.

9   For a searching analysis of the complex discourses around photography in Britain in its first decades see Steve Edwards, *The Making of English Photography: Allegories* (University Park: Penn State University Press, 2006).

10  André Bazin, 'The Ontology of the Photographic Image' [1960], trans. Hugh Gray, in *What is Cinema?*, vol. 1 (Berkeley: University of California Press, 1967), pp. 9–16.

11  Roland Barthes, 'The Photographic Message' [1961] and 'Rhetoric of the Image' [1964] in *Image-Music-Text*, ed. and trans. Stephen Heath (London: Fontana, 1977), pp. 13–52. See also John Tagg, *The Burden of Representation: Essays on Photographies and Histories* (Basingstoke: Macmillan, 1988).

12  Roland Barthes, *Camera Lucida* (London: Vintage, 1993), p. 5.

13  Laura Mulvey, 'The Index and the Uncanny', in Carolyn B. Gill (ed.), *Time and the Image* (Manchester: Manchester University Press, 2000), p. 141.

14  Mulvey: 'The Index and the Uncanny', p. 147. Emphasis in original.

15  Mary Ann Doane, *The Emergence of Cinematic Time: Modernity, Contingency and the Archive* (Cambridge: Harvard University Press, 2002), p. 91.

16  Barthes: *Camera Lucida*, pp. 94–7.

17  Doane: *The Emergence of Cinematic Time*, p. 227.

18  Mary Ann Doane, 'Indexicality: Trace and Sign: Introduction', *Differences: A Journal of Feminist Cultural Studies*, 18/1 (2007), pp. 1–6.

19  Trinh T. Minh-ha, 'Still Speed', interview with Elizabeth Dungan, in *The Digital Film Event* (New York and London: Routledge, 2005), p. 3.

20  Trinh: 'Still Speed', pp. 3–4.

21  The debates about photography as evidence reach back into the nineteenth century. In order to combat the problem of digital manipulation without proof of origin in time and space, photojournalists are required to tag the first image with the code RAW so as to enable to forensic verification. But this is itself problematic since there is no equivalent to the photographic negative in digital processing as each manufacturer produces its own proprietary and sometimes undocumented formatting. On 'practically infinite manipulability' see Rosen: *Change Mummified*, pp. 319–33.

22  The Paramount DVD release of *Forrest Gump* in 2001 contained a special item on the visual effects titled 'Seeing is Believing'.

23  'Reuters drops Beirut Photographer', *BBC News*, 8 August 2006, <http://news.bbc.co.uk/1/hi/5254838.stm>. See also 'Reuters Doctoring Photos from Beirut?', *Little Green Footballs*, 5 August 2006 <http://littlegreenfootballs.com/article/21956/>. For a discussion of a series of examples of unethical photo-

journalism in the context of Israeli incursions into Lebanon in 2006, see 'Framing the Story', *Washington Times,* 9 August 2006, <http://www.washingtontimes. com/news/2006/aug/09/20060809-090136-3068r/>. For a fuller analysis see Stephen D. Cooper, 'A Concise History of the Fauxtography Blogstorm in the 2006 Lebanon War', *American Communication Journal* 9/2 (2007), <http://www. acjournal.org/holdings/vol9/summer/articles/fauxtography.html>.

24  David D. Perlmutter, 'Photojournalism in crisis', *Editor and Publisher Online,* 17 August 2006, quoted in 'Perlmutter: Photojournalism in crisis', *Little Green Footballs,* 18 August 2006, <http://littlegreenfootballs.com/article/22168_ Perlmutter-_Photojournalism_in_Crisis>. See also D. D. Perlmutter and John Maxwell Hamilton (eds), *From Pigeons to News Portals: Foreign Reporting and the Challenge of New Technology* (Baton Rouge: Louisiana State University Press, 2007).

25  Unfortunately it has not been possible to provide a reference to the radio programme on which this item was heard, but I made a note of the anecdote as it was so striking in relation to my current work on photography and the Holocaust [GP].

26  William Gibson, *Neuromancer* [1984] (London: Harper Collins, 1993), p. 67.

27  Jack Womack, 'Afterword' to the twentieth anniversary edition of William Gibson, *Neuromancer* (New York: Ace, 2004).

28  Jacques Ellul, *The Technological System* [1977], trans. Joachim Neugroschel (New York: Continuum, 1980), p. 86.

29  Ellul: *The Technological System*, p. 86.

30  Jürgen Habermas, *Knowledge and Human Interests*, trans. Jeremy J. Shapiro (London: Heinemann: 1972).

31  Raymond Williams, *Television: Technology and Cultural Form* (London: Fontana, 1974).

32  Williams: *Television: Technology and Cultural Form*, pp. 11–12.

33  See Manuel Castells' The Information Age trilogy: *The Rise of the Network Society*, The Information Age: Economy, Society and Culture, vol. 1 (Cambridge and Oxford: Blackwell, 1996);*The Power of Identity*, The Information Age: Economy, Society and Culture, vol. 2 (Cambridge and Oxford: Blackwell, 1997); *End of Millennium*, The Information Age: Economy, Society and Culture, vol. 3 (Cambridge and Oxford: Blackwell, 1998).

34  Warren Sack, 'Social Networks', lecture at University of California, Santa Cruz, 24 January 2005, <http://dmedia.ucsc.edu/FDM20c/Winter2005/Lectures/24. 01.2005/lecture.ppt>.

35  Maggie Shiels, 'The US Virtual Economy is Set to Make Billions', *BBC News*, 29 December 2009, <http://news.bbc.co.uk/1/hi/technology/8425623.stm>.

36  Freud defined *phantasy* (spelt thus to distinguish it from the ordinary usage of the word fantasy) as the mode of what he called psychical reality. Psychical reality designates 'whatever in the subject's psyche presents a consistency and resistance comparable to those displayed by material reality; fundamentally what is involved here is unconscious desire and its associated phantasies'. Jean Laplanche and Jean-Bertrand Pontalis, *The Language of Psychoanalysis* [1967] (London: Karnac, 1988), p. 363.

37  Gilles Deleuze, *Difference and Repetition* [1968], trans. Paul Patton (New York: Columbia University Press, 1994).

38   For a discussion of virtuality and aesthetics see Simon O'Sullivan, *Art Encounters Deleuze and Guattari: Thought Beyond Representation* (Basingstoke: Palgrave Macmillan, 2006).

39   Elizabeth Grosz, *Architecture from the Outside: Essays on Virtual and Real Space* (Cambridge: MIT Press, 2002), pp. 78–9.

40   Brian Massumi, *Parables For the Virtual: Movement, Affect, Sensation* (Durham and London: Duke University Press, 2002), p. 4.

41   Scott Bukatman, *Terminal Identity: The Virtual Subject in Postmodern Science Fiction* (Durham: Duke University Press, 1993). On the virtual gaze, a mobilized gaze mediated by representation, see Anne Friedberg, *Window Shopping: Cinema and the Postmodern* (Berkeley: University of California Press, 1994).

42   Zygmunt Bauman, *Liquid Modernity* (Cambridge: Polity, 2000) and on liquid modernity and informatics see Antony Bryant, *Thinking Informatically: A New Understanding of Information, Communication and Technology* (Lampeter: Mellen, 2006).

43   N. Katherine Hayles, *How We Became Posthuman: Virtual Bodies in Cybernetics, Literature and Informatics* (Chicago: University of Chicago Press, 1999).

44   Arjun Appadurai, *Modernity at Large: Cultural Dimensions of Globalization* (Minneapolis: University of Minnesota Press, 1996), pp. 33–7. For this reference I am grateful to Chin-Tao Wu, 'Biennials without borders', *New Left Review* 57 (2009), pp. 107–15.

45   Samuel Weber, *Mass Mediauras: Forms, Technics, Media* (Stanford: Stanford University Press, 1996), p. 125.

46   This came to mind when one of the participants at the seminar, Elizabeth Cowie, presented later work on time in documentary cinema, as a lecture at the University of Leeds in November 2009. Quotations from this talk did thus appear in *Private Eye* in December 2009. Cowie's paper for the *Film Theory between Indexicality and Virtuality* seminar at CentreCATH (2–3 March 2005) appears as 'Spectres of the Real: Documentary Time and Art', *Differences* 18/1 (2007), pp. 87–127. See <http://www.leeds.ac.uk/cath/ahrc/events/2005/0304/>.

### Chapter 1. Traumas of Code

1   The immense difficulty of reverse engineering object code was the key factor in the Y2K crisis. Although the feared catastrophic failure did not materialize, attempts to correct the problem vividly demonstrated code's opacity.

2   Robert Bach, vice president of Microsoft's Marketing Desktop Application division, reports that the company employed 750 people, working full-time for two years, to bring Office 97 to market; see 'Office 97 Q and A with Robbie Bach', *Go Inside*, <http://goinside.com/97/1/o97qa.html>. Assuming 40-hour weeks and 50 weeks per year, that amounts to 1.5 million person-hours. To put this number in context, the average person puts in 80,000 person-hours at work during a lifetime. Of course, my argument is concerned with the amount of time necessary to understand the code, whereas the above figures indicate the time required to create and test the Microsoft product. Nevertheless, the comparison gives an idea of why no one person can comprehend a complex large program in its totality.

3   See Adrian Mackenzie, *Cutting Code: Software and Sociality* (New York: Peter Lang, 2006).

4   See Nigel Thrift, 'Remembering the Technological Unconscious by Foregrounding Knowledges of Position', *Environment and Planning D: Society and Space* 22/1 (2004), pp. 175–90.

5   See Edwin Hutchins, *Cognition in the Wild* (Cambridge: MIT Press, 1996).

6   See Andy Clark, *Natural-Born Cyborgs: Minds, Technologies, and the Future of Human Intelligence* (Oxford: Oxford University Press, 2003).

7   See Antonio Damasio, *Descartes' Error: Emotion, Reason, and the Human Brain* (New York: Penguin, 2005).

8   See Thomas Whalen, 'Data Navigation, Architectures of Knowledge', <http://www.banffcentre.ca/bnmi/programs/archives/2000/living_architectures/transcripts/living_architectures_thomas_whalen.pdf>.

9   See Bessel van der Kolk and Onno van der Hart, 'The Intrusive Past: The Flexibility of Memory and the Engraving of Trauma', in Cathy Caruth (ed.), *Trauma: Explorations in Memory* (Baltimore: Johns Hopkins University Press, 1995), pp. 158–82.

10  Dominick LaCapra, *Writing History, Writing Trauma* (Baltimore: Johns Hopkins University Press, 2000), p. 57.

11  See, for example, the study conducted at the Human Interface Technology Laboratory at the University of Washington, Seattle, 'VR Therapy for Spider Phobia', <http://www.hitl.washington.edu/projects/exposure/>. For a comprehensive list of publications on the subject, see the Delft University of Technology and the University of Amsterdam website on collaborative research at a number of universities, especially Charles van der Mast, 'Virtual Reality and Phobias', <http://graphics.tudelft.nl/~vrphobia/>.

12  See William Gibson, *Pattern Recognition* (New York: Putnam, 2003).

13  This definition and insight is offered in W. J. T. Mitchell, 'Ekphrasis and the Other', in *Picture Theory: Essays on Verbal and Visual Representation* (Chicago: University of Chicago Press, 1994), p. 152.

14  See *Avalon*, DVD, dir. Mamoru Oshii (Miramax, 2001).

15  See Jason Nelson, *Dreamaphage*, <http://www.heliozoa.com/dreamaphage/opening.html>.

16  Gibson: *Pattern Recognition*, p. 305.

17  For more information on steganography techniques and countermeasures, see Neil F. Johnson, Zoran Durig, and Sushi Jajodia, *Information Hiding: Steganography and Watermarking: Attacks and Countermeasures* (New York: Kluwer Academic, 2000).

18  See Cathy Caruth, *Unclaimed Experience: Trauma, Narrative, and History* (Baltimore: Johns Hopkins University Press, 1996), in which she comments on the infectious power of trauma. Even more eloquent is Shoshana Felman's account of the devastating effects that reading about trauma and listening to interviews with Holocaust survivors had on the members of her graduate class; see Felman, 'Education and Crisis, or the Vicissitudes of Teaching', in Caruth: *Trauma*, pp. 13–60.

19  Gibson: *Pattern Recognition*, p. 255.

20  The contrast between the precise details that are everywhere in Gibson's novel and the lack of historical and geographical markers in the footage is remarked upon by Fredric Jameson, 'Fear and Loathing in Globalization', *New Left Review*, 23 (2003), pp. 113–14.

21  For more information on Cayce, see Thomas Sugrue, *There Is a River: The Story of*

*Edgar Cayce* (New York: Holt, Rinehart & Winston, 1945), and Sidney Kirkpatrick, *Edgar Cayce: An American Prophet* (New York: Riverhead, 2000); the range of publication dates indicates enduring interest in this phenomenon.

22  Gibson: *Pattern Recognition*, p. 115.

23  Manovich comments that 'the database becomes the center of the creative process in the computer age'. Lev Manovich, *The Language of New Media* (Cambridge: MIT Press, 2001), p. 227.

24  Kathleen Fitzpatrick discusses at length the fears of print writers—especially young white male writers—that the novel is about to become obsolete. She interprets their fear symptomatically, seeing it as a move to claim the cachet of being an at-risk minority while still occupying a hegemonic position; see Kathleen Fitzpatrick, *The Anxiety of Obsolescence: The American Novel in the Age of Television* (Nashville: Vanderbilt University Press, 2006), chapter 1. Nevertheless, the evidence that a number of writers do fear the obsolescence of the print novel is overwhelming.

25  For a discussion of this motto, see Timothy Lenoir, 'All but War Is Simulation: The Military Entertainment Complex', *Configurations* 8 (2000), pp. 289–335.

26  Brian Ruh, whose interpretation of the ending is almost orthogonal to my own, cites Oshii's comments on the significance of the dog: 'For the main character, the dog can be considered as the symbol of "reality" itself. The meaning of the disappearance of the dog is important in the film, but whether or not the dog existed in the first place is an even more important question', quoted in Brian Ruh, *Stray Dog of Anime: The Films of Mamoru Oshii* (New York: Palgrave Macmillan, 2004), p. 181. While Ruh interprets this comment to mean that Ash may be fantasizing the dog's existence, it seems to me to allude to the possibility that her entire world is a simulation.

27  Mamoru Oshii, quoted in *Akadot*, <http://www.akadot.com/article.php?a_109>.

28  Jacques Derrida, *Of Grammatology*, trans. Gayatri Spivak (Baltimore: Johns Hopkins University Press, 1976), p. 158.

29  Nelson: *Dreamaphage*, Book 4, <http://www.heliozoa.com/dreamaphage/book4.html>, pp. 4–10.

30  See N. Katherine Hayles, 'Narrating Bits', *Vectors* 1 (2005), <http://www.vectorsjournal.org/index.php?page=7&projectId=6>.

31  See Neal Stephenson, *Snow Crash* (New York: Bantam, 1992).

32  See Joseph Weizenbaum, *Computer Power and Human Reason: From Judgment to Calculation* (New York: Penguin, 1976).

33  The ELIZA program was designed to prompt its human interlocutor by picking up and repeating key phrases and words as questions or comments. For example, if the human mentioned, 'I saw my father yesterday,' the computer would respond, 'Tell me about your father.' See Weizenbaum, 'ELIZA—A Computer Program for the Study of Natural Language Communication between Man and Machine', *Communications of the Association for Computing Machinery* 9/1 (1966), pp. 36–7.

34  See John R. Koza, Forrest H. Bennett, David Andre and Martin A. Keane, *Genetic Programming III: Darwinian Invention and Problem Solving* (San Francisco: Morgan Kaufmann, 1999).

### Chapter 2. Of Mice and Mien

1  For more details on this workshop, see <http://is2.lse.ac.uk/events/ssit5/>.

2  See <http://www.kevinwarwick.org/>.

3  See, for example Ben Goldacre, 'The return of Captain Cyborg', *Guardian*, 29 April 2004, <http://www.guardian.co.uk/science/2004/apr/29/badscience. science>.

4  See Lester Haines, 'Captain Cyborg terrorises UK conference: Gives speech on, er, speechless communication', *The Register*, 12 May 2004 <http://www. theregister.co.uk/2004/05/12/captain_cyborg_conference/> for an overview of some of Warwick's exploits.

5  Polly Curtis, 'Scientist becomes world's first cyborg', *Guardian*, 22 March 2002, <http://www.guardian.co.uk/education/2002/mar/22/research.higher education1>.

6  Team Register, 'Home truths: Bionic man takes the Metal Mickey', *The Register*, 4 July 2000, <http://www.theregister.co.uk/2000/07/04/home_truths_bionic_ man_takes/>. Further examples of Warwick's accomplishments can be found through *Wikipedia* (<http://en.wikipedia.org/wiki/Kevin_Warwick>) and *The Register*.

7  Warwick has his own understanding of virtuality—linked to a *cyborg* future—but he does not seem to have any inkling about indexicality.

8  Warwick seems to delight in stating the outrageous—as loudly and often as possible; and he seems to embody the liquid modern victory of style over substance. As will be seen later it is not with his more outrageous and self-publicizing statements that I wish to engage. It might, however, be noted with some alarm that despite his Captain Cyborg reputation, Warwick has twice been appointed as a member of one of the panels that determines the basis for, and allocation of, public research funding for UK universities: the RAE panel for Electrical and Electronic engineering (RAE 2001 and 2008).

9  N. Katherine Hayles, *How We Became Posthuman: Virtual Bodies in Cybernetics, Literature and Informatics* (Chicago: University of Chicago Press, 1999), p. 1.

10  David Smith, '2050—and immortality is within our grasp: Britain's leading thinker on the future offers an extraordinary vision of life in the next 45 years', *The Observer*, 22 May 2005, <http://www.guardian.co.uk/science/2005/may/22/ theobserver.technology>.

11  See Waldemar Kaempffert, 'In the Next Fifty Years', *Popular Mechanics*, February 1950 <http://books.google.com/books?id=ANkDAAAAMBAJ&pg=PA112& dq=Popular+Mechanics&lr=&as_brr=0&as_pt=MAGAZINES&source=gbs_t oc_pages_r&cad=0_1#PPA113,M1>. This article was reprinted by *Popular Mechanics* in 2000, but the reprint appears not to have been included in Google's *Popular Mechanics* archive.

12  James Meek, 'Robot with living brain created in US', *Guardian*, 18 April 2001, <http://www.guardian.co.uk/international/story/0,3604,474397,00.html>.

13  Neil Berg, 'Brain-Machine Interfaces: Current and Future Applications', *CHI Labs* (2002), <http://personal.bgsu.edu/~nberg/chilabs/bmi.htm> .

14  Berg: 'Brain-Machine Interfaces', emphasis added.

15  Garry Goettling, 'Harnessing the Power of Thought', *Georgia Tech Alumni Magazine* 76/1 (1999), <http://gtalumni.org/Publications/magazine/sum99/ harnessing.html>.

16  Kristin Cobb, 'Mind Meld', *Science Notes* (2002), <http://scicom.ucsc.edu/ SciNotes/0201/lo/mind/>.

17  Cobb: 'Mind Meld', emphasis added.

18  Zina Moukheiber, 'Mind Over Matter', *Forbes Magazine*, 15 March 2004, <http://www.forbes.com/home/free_forbes/2004/0315/186.html>, emphasis added.

19  Duncan Graham-Rowe, 'Brain implants "read" monkey minds', *New Scientist*, 8 July 2004, <http://www.newscientist.com/article.ns?id=dn6127>.

20  This is reminiscent of Tom Lehrer's story, from the song 'In Old Mexico', about 'the late doctor Samuel Gall, inventor of the gall-bladder', who went on to 'specialize in diseases of the very rich'.

21  This being an American film aimed at the widest possible market, Smith did not have to remove his underwear—state agencies not having stooped so low as to wire his pants, or *shorts* as they say in America. Synopsis available at <http://www.imdb.com/title/tt0120660/>.

22  'The Numskulls', on *TheFreeDictionary*, <http://encyclopedia.thefreedictionary.com/The%20Numskulls>.

23  Baroness Professor Susan Greenfield, 'The Brain of the Future', Butterfield Memorial Lecture 2001, Royal Society for the Encouragement of the Arts, Manufacture and Commerce, London, <http://www.collegeofteachers.ac.uk/older/news/events_bml2001.htm> (accessed 9 January 2007; no longer available).

24  Greenfield does take account of the research that puts microchips in people's brains, concluding that 'in general we're going to have more monitoring of our lives at all levels: at the level of genes, molecular events, more screening and potential for engineering for good and ill'.

25  In her discussion of the Macy Conferences, Hayles notes the critical role of metaphor in the inter-disciplinary dialogues between participants. See Hayles: *How We Became Posthuman*, p. 51.

26  Donald Schön, 'Generative Metaphor: A perspective on problem setting in social policy', in Andrew Ortony (ed.), *Metaphor and Thought*, 2nd edn (Cambridge: Cambridge University Press), p. 152.

27  Schön: 'Generative Metaphor', p. 150, original emphasis.

28  Schön: 'Generative Metaphor', p. 159.

29  Michael Reddy, 'The conduit metaphor: A case of frame conflict in our language about language', in Andrew Ortony (ed.), *Metaphor and Thought*, 2nd edn (Cambridge: Cambridge University Press), p. 166.

30  Reddy: 'The conduit metaphor', p. 166.

31  Reddy: 'The conduit metaphor', p. 170.

32  Reddy: 'The conduit metaphor', p. 171.

33  Jeffrey C. Alexander and Philip Smith, 'The Strong Programme in Cultural Sociology', in J. C. Alexander, *The Meanings of Social Life: A Cultural Sociology* (Oxford: Oxford University Press, 2003), p. 11.

34  See Stuart Hall, 'The Television Discourse—Encoding and Decoding' [1974], in Ann Gray and Jim McGuigan (eds), *Studying Culture: An Introductory Reader* (London: Edward Arnold, 1997), pp. 28–34; Stuart Hall, 'Encoding/Decoding' [1980], in Paul Marris and Sue Thornham (eds), *Media Studies: A Reader* (Edinburgh: Edinburgh University Press, 1996), pp. 41–9.

35  The similarities, complementarities, and differences between the work of Shannon, Reddy, and Hall require far more attention and analysis than can be offered at this juncture.

36 Raymond Williams, *Communications*, 3rd edn (Harmondsworth: Penguin, 1976).

37 Reddy: 'The conduit metaphor', p. 188.

38 See <http://en.wikipedia.org/wiki/Vulcan_(Star_Trek)>.

39 Cobb: 'Mind Meld'.

40 Reddy: 'The conduit metaphor', p. 188.

41 For the original story, see 'Girl, 10, used geography lesson to save lives', *Telegraph*, 1 January 2005, <http://www.telegraph.co.uk/news/1480192/Girl-10-used-geography-lesson-to-save-lives.html>. Such was the subsequent fame of Tilly Smith, however, that a plethora of stories and awards followed. See, for example <http://news.bbc.co.uk/1/hi/uk/4229392.stm> and the ultimate accolade, an entry in *Wikipedia* <http://en.wikipedia.org/wiki/Tilly_Smith>.

42 Nora Boustany, 'As Ukraine Watched the Party Line, She Took the Truth Into Her Hands', *Washington Post*, 29 April 2005, <http://www.washingtonpost.com/wp-dyn/content/article/2005/04/28/AR2005042801696.html>.

## Chapter 3. A Virtual Indication

1 Mark Wallace, 'The Game Is Virtual. The Profit Is Real', *New York Times*, 29 May 2005, <http://www.nytimes.com/2005/05/29/business/yourmoney/29game.html>, emphasis added.

2 Nicholas Barbon, *A Discourse on coining the new money lighter, in answer to Mr. Locke's considerations, etc.* (London: Richard Chiswell, 1696), pp. 2, 3. Quoted in: Karl Marx, *Capital*, vol. 1, trans Ben Fowkes (Harmondsworth: Penguin, 1976), p. 125 n. 2. See also Nicholas Barbon, *Discourse of Trade* (London: Thomas Milbourn, 1690), pp. 14–15: 'Wares, that have their Value from supplying the Wants of the Mind, are all such things that can satisfie Desire; Desire implys Want: It is the Appetite of the Soul, and is as natural to the Soul, as Hunger to the Body.'

3 Marx: *Capital*, vol. 1, p. 125, translation modified.

4 Wallace: 'The Game is Virtual'.

5 See Wallace: 'The Game Is Virtual': 'An active market also exists for the services provided by "power gamers", who in return for a fee will show new players the ropes or even take control of their characters for a few days or weeks to earn them quick advancement.'

6 The Call for Papers for the conference at which this paper was first presented began by noting that 'the current opposition of virtuality to materiality' is 'in need of critical re-evaluation', but also goes on to suggest that 'opposing virtuality to indexicality insists upon the problematic of semiosis and representation'. Call for Papers, *CongressCATH 2005: Ethics and Politics of Virtuality and Indexicality*, <http://www.leeds.ac.uk/cath/ahrc/congress/2005/call.html>.

7 Charles Sanders Peirce, 'Letters to Lady Welby', in: C. S. Peirce, *Selected Writings*, ed. Philip P. Wiener (New York: Dover, 1966), p. 391.

8 Gilles Deleuze, *Difference and Repetition* [1968], trans. Paul Patton (London: Athlone, 1994), p. 208 ff. See also my discussion of this in: Samuel Weber, 'The Virtuality of Media', *Sites* 4/2 (2000), pp. 297–319.

9 Charles Sanders Peirce, *The Philosophical Writings of Peirce*, ed. Justus Buchler (New York: Dover, 1955), p. 108.

10 Deleuze: *Difference and Repetition*, p. 209.

11 Peirce: *Philosophical Writings*, p.114.

12 René Descartes, 'Second Meditation', in: *Meditations on First Philosophy: A Bilingual*

*Edition*, ed. and trans. George Heffernan (Notre Dame: University of Notre Dame Press 1990), pp. 102–5. It should be noted that the present participle and gerund in English often render the present indicative or infinitive in Descartes' Latin.

13  Descartes: *Meditations*, p. 89.

14  I refer here implicitly to the notion of *iterability* as developed by Jacques Derrida beginning with 'Signature, Event, Context' and culminating in *Limited Inc*. See Jacques Derrida, *Limited Inc* (Evanston: Northwestern University Press, 1988).

15  'Datsun Saves!' was the short-lived slogan of an advertising campaign of the predecessor of Nissan Motors in the 1980s. It had to be rapidly abandoned after it evoked the massive protests of religious groups. But for a brief moment it revealed the connection between the automobile as paradigmatic consumer good and 'Capitalism as Religion'—that is, as the religious successor to traditional Christianity.

16  '*Also heimlich ist ein Wort, das seine Bedeutung nach einer Ambivalenz hin entwickelt, bis es endlich mit seinem Gegensatz unheimlich zusammenfällt.*' Sigmund Freud, 'Das Unheimliche', in *Gesammelte Werke*, vol. 12 (Frankfurt am Main: Fischer, 1947), p. 237, translation mine. See also Sigmund Freud, 'The "Uncanny"', trans. Alix Strachey, in *The Standard Edition of the Complete Psychological Works of Sigmund Freud*, vol. 17, ed. James Strachey (London: Hogarth, 1955), p. 226.

17  Martin Heidegger, *Hölderlin's Hymn 'The Ister'*, trans. William McNeill and Julia Davis (Bloomington: Indiana University Press, 1996). See also, M. Heidegger, *Hölderlins Hymne 'Der Ister'*, Gesamtausgabe 53 (Frankfurt am Main: Vittorio Klostermann, 1984).

18  See Martin Heidegger, *Introduction to Metaphysics*, trans. Gregory Fried and Richard Polt (New Haven and London: Yale University Press, 2000), pp. 156–75.

19  Sophocles, *Antigone*, lines 333–4, translation mine.

20  Sophocles: *Antigone*, lines 360–75, translation mine, emphasis added. See also Heidegger: *Hölderlin's Hymn*, pp. 56–61.

21  In German: '*Hochüberragend die Stätte, verlustig der Stätte/ist er, dem immer das Unseiende seiend/der Wagnis zugunsten.*' Heidegger: *Hölderlin's Hymn*, pp. 58, 60.

## Chapter 4. The Future Birth of the Affective Fact

1  Louise-Maude Rioux Soucy, 'Le virus de la prochaine pandémie de grippe n'existe pas encore', *Le Devoir*, 19 October 2005, A1, <http://www.ledevoir.com/2005/10/19/92964.html>.

2  George W. Bush, *Dallas Morning News*, 10 May 2000, cited in Mark Crispin Miller, *The Bush Dyslexicon* (New York: Norton, 2002), p. 251.

3  Eric Schmitt and Richard W. Stevenson, 'Admitting Intelligence Flaws, Bush Stands by Need for War', *New York Times*, 10 July 2004, A9.

4  By 'actual fact' I mean the situation defined (by rule, convention, or consensus) by a normative system for the establishment of publicly recognized fact, under whose jurisdiction the question normally falls when that system's operation is not pre-empted (for example, a judicial system, an administrative review process, a peer-review process, etc.).

5  Gary Dorrien, *Imperial Designs: Neoconservatism and the New Pax Americana* (New York: Routledge, 2004), p. 186.

6  On Bush and gut feeling as decision-making principle, see Bob Woodward, *Bush at War* (New York: Simon & Shuster, 2002), pp. 16, 136–7, 145, 168.

7  The classical doctrine of war allows pre-emptive action in cases where there is a

'clear and present danger' of attack. Pre-emption is only allowed defensively, in the face of actual danger. The contemporary neoconservative doctrine of pre-emption justifies offensive action against threats that are not fully emergent, or more radically that have not even begun to emerge. President Bush spelled this out in the address to the nation in which he formally enunciated the new doctrine for the first time in the lead-up to the war in Iraq: 'If we wait for threats to fully materialize, we will have waited too long. We must take the battle to the enemy, disrupt his plans and confront the worst threats before they emerge.' President George W. Bush, 'Graduation speech at West Point United States Military Academy, June 1 2002', in Carl C. Hodge and Cathal J. Nolan (eds), *U. S. Presidents & Foreign Policy: From 1789 to the Present* (Santa Barbara: ABC-CLIO, 2007), p. 408.

8    The Abu Ghraib images first came to light in April 2004. For a compendium of Bush administration documents justifying the use of torture, see Karen L. Greenberg and Joshua L. Dratel (eds), *The Torture Papers: The Road to Abu Ghraib* (Cambridge: Cambridge University Press, 2005).

9    See for example, Brian Knowlton, 'Bush Insists Al Qaeda in Iraq Threatens U.S.', *New York Times*, 24 July 2007, <http://www.nytimes.com/2007/07/24/washington/24cnd-prexy.html?hg>.

10   President George W. Bush, Radio Address, 18 June 2005, <http://en.wikisource.org/wiki/Presidential_Radio_Address_-_18_June_2005>.

11   See for example, 'ADM (Aéroports de Montréal) soutient que la sécurité des passagers a été améliorée', *La Presse* (Montreal), 10 May 2005, p. A7. See in particular the photo and caption.

12   The affective tainting of objects or bodies implicated in a threat-event can go so far as to functionally substitute the affective fact of the matter for what is accepted as actual fact (as defined above in note 4). The actual fact is neither directly contested nor forgotten, yet is disabled. It slips behind the affective fact, which comes to the fore to take over as the operative reality. To cite an example of this affective-factual eclipse, in August 2007 President Bush retracted earlier statements expressing an intent to close the extraterritorial prison camp at Guantánamo Bay. Guantánamo Bay had become a political liability after the torture scandal at Abu Ghraib, revelations of shady 'black site' prisons into which 'enemy combatants' disappeared without a trace, and criticism of CIA kidnapping of suspects on foreign soil for delivery to third nations known systematically to use torture (known euphemistically as 'rendition'). What placed Guantánamo Bay in the same category as these other extraterritorial practices is that they all aim to pre-empt regulated governmental treatment of suspects according to standard juridical procedures. The strategy is to surge in, in order to rush the production of the *results* of normal juridical procedures before they have had a chance to operate. Imprisonment and punishment come suddenly, before any actual crime is proven. The grabbed bodies are treated, a priori, as guilty. This is done purely on the basis of *signs of threat* that happened to actualize in their vicinity. Some of the inhabitants of Guantánamo who were subsequently released after years of imprisonment were swooped up in Afghanistan during the US invasion, and turned out simply to have been in the wrong place at the wrong time. The treatment of the detainees as a priori guilty attaches this quality to them for life, regardless of their actual actions and the actual danger they posed. They are stained, *as if* they had been guilty all along. The felt quality of guilt has its own affective ambience, which can transmute into a number of specific emotions:

hatred, resentment, disgust, distrust. The detainee becomes an affective pariah. According to the Bush administration, certain prisoners scheduled for release will not be taken in by any country, even their own country of origin. These are detainees whom the US military has not been able to bring to trial, meaning that their cases are not strong enough to transfer into the domestic criminal system— or even bring before the newly established Military Commissions where the bar of the burden of proof is set extravagantly low and the accused's possibilities of defence are sorely limited. Bush explained, without displaying a hint of irony or in any way acknowledging the paradox, that it is because of cases such as these that Guantánamo Bay must be kept open. The prison doors must remain closed in order to detain those who are technically innocent. 'This is not as easy a subject as some may think on the surface,' the explanation went. 'A lot of people don't want killers in their midst, and a lot of these people are killers.' 'These people' should be released because they are innocent, but can't be released because they are 'killers'. Bush's reasoning is not as illogical as it might be supposed as judged by the standards of normative logic. The apparent inconsistency corresponds to a change in factual level occurring between the recognition of innocence and the assertion of guilt. A shift has occurred mid-logic from actual to affective fact. The affective fact is that these innocents are as good as killers. Nothing will change the fact that those pre-emptively treated as guilty are now, as a result of affective tainting, permanently guilty *in effect*. They are *effectively* guilty (presumably, they would have if they could have). Indefinite internment is now the hard, life-wasting affective fact of their situation. Affective facts stand only on their own pre-emptive occurrence. Yet they may come effectively to stand in for actual facts. See 'President Bush Holds a News Conference: Transcript', *Washington Post*, 9 August 2007, <http://www.washingtonpost.com/wp-dyn/content/article/2007/08/09/AR2007080900714.html>.

13  'ADM (Aéroports de Montréal) soutient que la sécurité'.

14  Vikas Bajaj, 'Bloomberg Cites "Specific Threat" to NY Subways', *New York Times*, 6 October 2005.

15  Michael Weissenstein, 'Officials: NYC Terror Plot Uncorroborated', *USA Today*, 9 October 2005.

16  After this incident, there was no questioning in the press about who had been pre-emptively attacked based on the now incredible information, or what their present circumstances might be. Had they been killed? Had they been 'renditioned' to a third country? Disappeared into a 'black site' prison? Sent to Guantánamo for indefinite detention? Would their cases ever be heard? The question, it seemed, occurred to no one. The event was not taking place at that actual-factual level, but rather on the affective level where threat plays itself out through fear. See note 12 above.

17  Rudolph Giuliani, 'Towards a Realistic Peace', *Foreign Affairs*, September/October 2007, <http://www.foreignaffairs.org/articles/62824/rudolph-w-giuliani/toward-a-realistic-peace>.

18  The invocation of 9/11 makes good populist political sense given that, according to a Zogby International Poll, a full six years after the event 81% of Americans listed it as the most important event of their lives. The percentage rises to 90% on the East Coast. 'Attacks were most important historical events in our lives: poll', *Montreal Gazette*, 11 September 2007, A17.

19  'Plus de panique!', *La Presse* (Montreal), 17 May 2005, A22 (report on comments by then Homeland Security 'Czar' Tom Ridge). The French headline captures the ambivalence of pre-emption: taken in isolation it can be read either as 'more panic' or 'no more panic' (the latter interpretation being the one suggested in the body of the article).

20  Kevin Dougherty, 'Province to Rid Schools of Junk Food. Youth Obesity a Pandemic: Couillard', *Montreal Gazette*, 14 September 2007, A8.

21  Michel Foucault characterized American neoliberalism, the economic politics which created the conditions for the neoconservative move toward pre-emption and away from normative governmental logic, as a governmentality becoming '*environmentality*'. Environmentality, he writes, represents a 'massive pull-back with regard to the normative-disciplinary system […] [which had] as its correlate a technology of human behaviour, an individualizing 'governmentality' comprising: disciplinary gridding (*quadrillage*), ongoing regulation, subordination/classification, the norm'. Neoliberalism and neoconservatism remain closely imbricated operative logics, with many positive feedbacks coupling them. They overlap in their mutual embrace of 'environmentality'. They ply the same far-from-equilibrium global threat environment, in different but strongly reciprocally presupposing ways. Michel Foucault, *The Birth of Biopolitics: Lectures at the Collège de France 1978–1979* [2004], trans. Graham Burchell, ed. Michel Senellart (New York: Palgrave Macmillan, 2008), p. 260, translation modified.

22  Gilles Deleuze and Félix Guattari analyse the relations between modes of power in terms of 'a threshold or degree' beyond which what is already active as a tendency 'takes on consistency'. Gilles Deleuze and Félix Guattari, *A Thousand Plateaus*, trans. Brian Massumi (Minneapolis: University of Minnesota Press, 1987).

23  What is being called operative logics here correspond to what Deleuze and Guattari call 'machinic processes' or 'abstract machines'. 'We define social formations by *machinic processes* and not by modes of production (these on the contrary depend on the processes). […] Precisely because these processes are variables of coexistence that are the object of a social topology, the various corresponding formations are coexistent.' 'There is not only an external coexistence of formations but also an intrinsic coexistence of machinic processes. Each process can also function at a "power" other than its own; it can be taken up by a power corresponding to another process.' 'Everything coexists, in perpetual interaction.' Machinic processes operate according to 'reverse causalities that are *without finality* but testify nonetheless to an action of the future on the present' which implies 'an inversion of time. […] These reverse causalities shatter evolution. […] It is necessary to demonstrate that what does not yet exist is already in action, in a different form than that of its existence.' The machinic processes of most concern to Deleuze and Guattari in this chapter form 'apparatuses of capture'. 'As a general rule, there is a primitive accumulation whenever an apparatus of capture is mounted, with that very particular kind of violence that creates or contributes to the creation of that which it is directed against, and thus presupposes itself.' Violence creative of that which it is directed against employs 'anticipation-prevention mechanisms'—in other words, it acts productively by acting pre-emptively. 'Anticipation-prevention mechanisms have a high *power of transference*' or of contagion between processes and their corresponding formations. In Deleuzo-Guattarian terms, the pre-emptive power analysed here is an emergent species of highly vir-

ulent apparatus of capture effecting a 'primitive accumulation' of threat-value, and spreading its operative logic through affective contagion. Deleuze and Guattari: *A Thousand Plateaus*, pp. 430, 431, 435, 437, 439, 447.

One of the modes in which there is effective interaction between operative logics 'in a different form than that of their existence' is termed negative prehension by A. N. Whitehead. 'A negative prehension is the definite exclusion of [an] item from positive contribution to the subject's [the process's] real internal constitution. [...] The negative prehension expresses a bond [...] Each negative prehension has its own subjective form, however trivial and faint [...] it adds to the emotional complex [the affective atmosphere], if not to the objective data [...] [negative prehensions] are required to express *how* any one item is felt [...] the negative prehension of an entity [a process] is a positive fact with its emotional subjective form [it is an affective fact]; there is a mutual sensitivity of the subjective forms of prehensions [there is an ecology of reciprocal presupposition effectively extending to what is negatively prehended]. Alfred North Whitehead, *Process and Reality* (New York: Free, 1979), pp. 41–2.

In Deleuze and Guattari's vocabulary, the 'bond' constituted by a negative prehension is an example of the 'non-localizable liaisons' characteristic of capture (*A Thousand Plateaus*, p. 446). Threat, at the limit where it is 'trivially and faintly' felt only as an atmospheric quality independent of any actual instance of itself, constitutes such a non-localized bond, even when it is not specifically expressed in a sign of alarm. It still contributes in a real but abstract way to the 'how' of the mutual sensitivity of subjective forms, even when it is not positively felt. It still adds to the shared 'emotional complex' that is the affective environment conditioning *how* forms feelingly pursue their individuation. This is particularly the case once the 'primitive accumulation' of threat-value has reached a certain level and extension throughout the environment due to the 'high transference power' of its processual mechanisms. Threat operating in this way, at the limit where it is not actually signed but still negatively prehended, felt vaguely and purely qualitatively, constitutes what in earlier work I described as 'low-level' background fear capable of insinuating itself into the constitution of subjectivities. It is affective fact at its most abstract. See Brian Massumi, 'Everywhere You Want to Be: Introduction to Fear', in B. Massumi (ed.), *The Politics of Everyday Fear* (Minneapolis: University of Minnesota Press, 1993), pp. 3–38.

24    Charles Sanders Peirce, *The Essential Peirce*, vol. 2 (Indianapolis: Indiana University Press, 1998), pp. 4–5.

25    Peirce: *Essential Peirce*, vol. 2, p. 5,

26    Peirce: *Essential Peirce*, vol. 2, p. 16.

27    Peirce: *Essential Peirce*, vol. 2, p. 478.

28    Peirce: *Essential Peirce*, vol. 2, p. 171.

29    Alfred North Whitehead, *Adventures of Ideas* (New York: Free, 1933), p. 212.

30    Whitehead, *Adventures of Ideas*, pp. 211, 217.

31    Whitehead, *Adventures of Ideas*, p. 211.


## Chapter 5. For a Comparative Film Studies

1    For an account of the belated arrival of modernism in cultural theory, see Andreas Huyssen, *After the Great Divide: Modernism, Mass Culture, Postmodernism* (Bloomington: Indiana University Press, 1986), pp. 178–221.

2    Peter Uwe Hohendahl, *Building a National Literature: The Case of Germany 1830–*

*1870*, trans. Renate Baron Franciscono (Ithaca: Cornell University Press, 1989), pp. 334, 351.

3 Franco Moretti, 'Conjectures on World Literature' [2000], reprinted in Christopher Prendergast (ed.), *Debating World Literature* (London: Verso, 2004), pp. 148–62.

4 Arjun Appadurai, *Modernity at Large: Cultural Dimensions of Globalization* (Minneapolis: University of Minnesota Press, 1996).

5 Moretti: 'Conjectures on World Literature', p. 151.

6 Peter Wollen, *Paris Hollywood: Writings on Film* (London: Verso, 2002), pp. 216–32. Wollen argues for the symptomatic value of canons in terms of the aesthetic frameworks they convey. However, he does not take into consideration the socio-economic frames within which those ideological moves take place. This allows him to note that 'postmodern' film theory is derivative and 'seems unclear about its aesthetic commitments' (p. 232), rather than noting, as the situation demands, that the use of 'postmodernism' signals an inversion in the relations between aesthetics and marketing. Whereas previously canonizing labels were devised with an eye on the need to propagate and market a particular aesthetic, the label 'postmodernism' announces the triumph of marketing over aesthetic considerations. Henceforth, the problem is no longer what one sells, but how much profit can be made from selling whatever it is. Consequently, it can be said to 'seem unclear about its aesthetic commitments'.

7 Moretti: 'Conjectures on World Literature', p. 152. See also Franco Moretti, *Atlas of the European Novel 1800–1900* (London: Verso, 1998).

8 See, for instance David A. Cook, *Lost Illusions: American Cinema in the Shadow of Watergate and Vietnam, 1970–1979*, History of the American Cinema, vol. 9 (Berkeley: University of California Press, 2000), pp. 11–14.

9 US Department of Commerce and Office of International Trade, *World Trade in Commodities* 6/3 (1948), p. 8.

10 The issues become even murkier when we take into consideration that the US has been and continues to be dominated by anti-modernist forms of modernization, as shown in T. J. Jackson Lears, *No Place of Grace: Antimodernism and the Transformation of American Culture 1880–1920* (New York: Pantheon, 1981). In cinema, especially, the American people continue to be shielded from the quintessential modern experience of having one's screens occupied by non-domestically produced films.

11 Richard Abel, *The Red Rooster Scare: Making Cinema American, 1900–1910* (Berkeley: University of California Press, 1999).

12 Moretti: 'Conjectures on World Literature', p. 154.

13 It is also debatable whether Hollywood's films are considered as models to be emulated. In fact, Hollywood's 'global' empire only encompasses about 10 countries which yield over 80 per cent of its foreign earnings, and the only Asian country among them is Japan. No doubt Hollywood is currently making strenuous efforts to occupy the screens of China and India as well, but as Charles R. Ackland noted, the globalization thrust attributed to the mid-1990s was in fact the solidification and intensification 'of longstanding routes of cultural commerce'. Charles R. Ackland, *Screen Traffic: Movies, Multiplexes, and Global Culture* (Durham: Duke University Press, 2003), p. 30. In other words, to quote Ronald Reagan, as far as globalization is concerned 'you ain't seen nothing yet'. What seems more likely is that non-American film producers very much want to make the same

piles of dollars that US media conglomerates say they are making, which is not at all the same as wanting to emulate Hollywood films.

14 Examples would be the procedures of state formation, the particular ways in which social relations are transformed and the resistances to that transformation, the particular dynamics involved in the shift from pre-modern modes of surplus appropriation to capitalist production, the transformation of people's physical energy into labour power, the competition for power between different fractions of capital and so on.

15 David Harvey, *The Limits to Capital* (London: Verso, 1999).

16 Since writing this paper, I have come across a challenging essay by Jane Gaines, written a few years ago, calling for a similar reconsideration. Jane Gaines, 'Machines that make the body do things', in Pamela Church Gibson (ed.), *More Dirty Looks: Gender, Pornography and Power* (London: BFI, 2004), pp. 31–44.

17 Christian Metz, *Language and Cinema*, trans. Donna Jean Umiker-Sebeok (The Hague: Mouton, 1974).

18 Roland Barthes, *S/Z*, trans. Richard Miller (London: Jonathan Cape, 1975), p. 184.

19 Roman Jakobson, 'Linguistics and Poetics', in David Lodge (ed.), *Modern Criticism and Theory: A Reader* (London: Longman, 1988), pp. 32–57.

20 Walter Benjamin, *The Arcades Project*, trans. Howard Eiland and Kevin McLaughlin (Cambridge: Harvard University Press, 1999), p. 392.

21 Benjamin: *The Arcades Project*, p. 391.

22 Benjamin: *The Arcades Project*, p. 394.

23 Peter Wollen, *Signs and Meaning in the Cinema*, rev. edn (London: BFI, 1998), pp. 83–4.

24 Wollen: *Paris Hollywood*, pp. 208–9.

### Chapter 6. *Night Passage*

1 Philip Rosen, *Change Mummified: Cinema, Historicity, Theory* (Minneapolis, London: University of Minnesota Press, 2001).

2 Timothy Binkley, 'Refiguring Culture', in Philip Hayward and Tana Wollen (eds), *Future Visions: New Technologies of the Screen* (London: BFI, 1993), quoted in Rosen: *Change Mummified*, p. 319.

3 The formation *pol(e)itics* was the title of *Documenta X* in 1997, and I am thinking of *Night Passage* as a film that functions in the way that Gayatri Spivak understands the relation between the political and the poetic when she writes the following in an interview for the *Documenta X* book: 'the political is a calculus. That is why class must remain. But one must make it play, and when one makes it play then the 'e' comes in. That is when you loosen not just the rights but the responsibility in this very peculiar sense: attending to the other in such a way that you call forth a response. To be able to do this is what I am calling the poetic for the moment, because that brings in another impossible dimension, the necessary dimension of the political.' Cathérine David and Jean François Chevrier, *Documenta X: Pol(e)itics* (Ostfildern-Ruit: Hatje Cantz Verlag and New York: Distributed Art Publishers, 1998), p. 768.

4 Gilles Deleuze, *Francis Bacon: The Logic of Sensation*, trans. Daniel W. Smith (London: Continuum, 2003), p. 42.

5 Trinh T. Minh-ha, 'Still Speed', in *The Digital Film Event* (London and New York: Routledge, 2005), pp. 10–11.

## Chapter 7. Tension, Time and Tenderness

I would like to thank Cathy Johns for her editorial help. Additional thanks to Emma Shercliff and the research students at the Royal College of Art.

1   Rozsika Parker's groundbreaking work in helping to establish this discourse should be mentioned here. See Rozsika Parker, *The Subversive Stitch: Embroidery and the Making of the Feminine* (London: Women's Press, 1984).

2   Claire Pajaczkowska, 'On stuff and nonsense: the complexity of cloth', *Textile: The Journal of Cloth and Culture* 3/3 (2005), pp. 220–49; Claire Pajaczkowska, 'Thread of attachment', *Textile: The Journal of Cloth and Culture* 5/2 (2007), pp. 140–52.

3   Roland Barthes, *Mythologies* [1957], trans. Annette Lavers (London: Vintage, 1993), pp. 97–9.

4   Barthes: *Mythologies*, pp. 109–59.

5   Roland Barthes, *The Fashion System* [1967], trans. Matthew Ward and Richard Howard (London: Jonathan Cape, 1983).

6   See, for example Christian Metz, *The Imaginary Signifier: Psychoanalysis and the Cinema* [1977], trans. Celia Britton, Annwyl Williams, Ben Brewster and Alfred Guzzetti (Bloomington: Indiana University Press, 1982); Stephen Heath, 'Narrative space', in *Questions of Cinema* (Bloomington: Indiana University Press, 1981), pp. 19–75; Peter Wollen, *Signs and Meaning in the Cinema* (London: Secker and Warburg/BFI, 1969); Jean-Louis Comolli and Jean Narboni, 'Cinema/Ideology/Criticism' [1969], trans. Susan Bennett, *Screen* 12/1 (1971), pp. 27–36; 12/2 (1972), pp. 145–55; 13/1 (1972), pp. 120–31; Catherine Dormor, 'skin:textile:film', *Textile: The Journal of Cloth and Culture* 6/3 (2008), pp. 238–53.

7   The cultural significance of the collar and lapels is discussed in Barry Curtis and Claire Pajaczkowska, 'Looking sharp', in Marketa Uhlirova (ed.), *If Looks Could Kill: Cinema's Images of Fashion, Crime and Violence* (London: Koenig, 2008), pp. 62–6.

8   As discussed in Richard Sennett, *The Craftsman* (New Haven: Yale University Press, 2008).

9   Anton Ehrenzweig, 'The four stages of the articulation process', in *The Psychoanalysis of Artistic Vision and Hearing* (London: Routledge and Kegan Paul, 1953), pp. 116–25.

10  Gilles Deleuze, *The Fold: Leibniz and the Baroque* [1988], trans. Tom Conley (London: Continuum, 2006). See also Gen Doy's examination of the cultural significance of drapery in art, *Drapery: Classicism and Barbarism in Visual Culture* (London: I.B.Tauris, 2002).

11  Sigmund Freud, 'The Ego and the Id' [1923], trans. Joan Riviere, in *The Standard Edition of the Complete Psychological Works of Sigmund Freud*, vol. 19, ed. James Strachey (London: Hogarth, 1960), p. 27.

12  Donald W. Winnicott, 'Transitional objects and transitional phenomena' [1953], in *Collected Papers: Through Paediatrics to Psycho-analysis* (London: Tavistock, 1958).

13  Sennett: The Craftsman.

14  See Parker: *The Subversive Stitch* for a discussion of the cultural history of women's sewing activity.

15  Kathryn Sullivan Kruger, Antonia Harrison and James Young (eds), *The Fabric of Myth* (Warwickshire: Compton Verney, 2008). This catalogue accompanied the exhibition *The Fabric of Myth* at Compton Verney, 21 June–7 September 2008.

16 Winnicott: 'Transitional objects'; Wilfred R. Bion, *Elements of Psycho-Analysis* (New York: Basic, 1963).

17 Sándor Ferenczi, 'Confusion of tongues between adults and the child' [1933], in *Final Contributions to the Problems and Methods of Psycho-analysis* [1955], ed. Michael Balint, trans. Eric Mosbacher *et al.* (London: Karnac, 1994), pp. 156–67.

18 Roland Barthes, 'The grain of the voice', in *Image, Music, Text*, trans. Stephen Heath (London: Fontana, 1977), pp. 182–3.

19 Laura U. Marks, The Skin of the Film: Intercultural Cinema, Embodiment, and the Senses (Durham: Duke University Press, 2000).

20 The frontier of research opened up by the new medical textiles is discussed in Chloe Colchester, *Textiles Today: a Global Survey of Trends and Traditions* (London: Thames & Hudson, 2007).

21 Alfred Gell, *Art and Agency: an Anthropological Theory* (Oxford: Oxford University Press, 1998).

**Chapter 8. Look, No Wires!**

1 Edgar Allan Poe, *The Raven* [1845], <http://www.heise.de/ix/raven/Literature/Lore/TheRaven.html>.

2 Donald Morton, 'Birth of the Cyberqueer', *PMLA* 110/3 (1995), pp. 369–81.

3 'Semiotics', in *The Internet Semiotics Encyclopaedia*, <http://filserver.arthist.lu.se/kultsem/encyclo/indexicality.html>.

4 Clearly this is a widely shared preference from thinkers as diverse as Giorgio Agamben to Mieke Bal, and there is a common sense that Benveniste enables the multiple insertion of other language theories into critical practices. Émile Benveniste, *Problèmes de linguistique générale* (Paris: Gallimard, 1966).

5 The work of Henri Meschonnic is much less current in visual and cultural studies that that of Julia Kristeva, whose *Révolution du langage poétique* is canonical. The following quotation from Gabriella Bedetti is useful in condensing the point of my comparison: 'value plays the role of an element of the system of the work, to the extent that the work constitutes itself through certain differences. These differences may relate to phonemes, words, characters, objects, places, scenes, etc. There is no value in the pure state but only in the interior of a system.' Gabriella Bedetti, 'Henri Meschonnic: Rhythm as Pure Historicity', *New Literary History* 23/2 (1992), pp. 431–50.

6 T. S. Eliot, *The Waste Land* [1922] (London: Faber, 1936), p. 72.

7 Giorgio Agamben, *Remnants of Auschwitz: The Witness and the Archive*, trans. Daniel Heller-Roazen (New York: Zone, 1992).

8 Julia Kristeva, *La révolte intime. Pouvoirs et limites de la psychanalyse II* (Paris: Fayard, 1997).

9 Laura Mulvey, 'Delaying Cinema', in *Death 24x a Second: Stillness and the Moving Image* (London: Reaktion, 2006), pp. 144–60.

10 Laura Mulvey, 'The Index and the Uncanny', in Carolyn B. Gill (ed.), *Time and the Image* (Manchester: Manchester University Press, 2000), pp. 139–48.

11 See Margaret Wertheim, *The Pearly Gates of Cyberspace: A History of Space from Dante to the Internet* (London: Virago, 1999).

12 George S. Hendry, 'Nothing', *Theology Today* 39/3 (1982), <http://theologytoday.ptsem.edu/oct1982/v39-3-article4.htm>.

13  See Adrian Rifkin, 'Gay Paris, Trace and Ruin', in Neil Leach (ed.), *The Hiero-glyphics of Space: Reading and Experiencing the Modern Metropolis* (London: Routledge, 2002), pp. 125–35. See also Maurice Halbwachs, *The Collective Memory*, trans. Francis J. Ditter, Jr., and Vida Yazdi Ditter (New York: Harper & Row, 1980).

14  T. S. Eliot, 'Little Gidding', in *Four Quartets* [1943] (London: Faber, 1959), p. 53.

15  See Lev Manovich, *The Language of New Media* (Cambridge: MIT Press, 2001).

16  See, for example, Saint John of the Cross, *Dark Night Of The Soul*, trans. Mirabai Starr (New York: Riverhead, 2002). Also Doriano Fasoli and Rosa Rossi, *Le estasi laiche de Teresa d'Avila: psicoanalisi, misticismo e altre esperienzi culturali a confronto* (Rome: Edizione Associate, 1998).

17  Jacques Lacan, *Le Séminaire Livre V: Les Formations de l'inconscient*, texte établi par Jacques-Alain Miller (Paris: Seuil, 1998), p. 213 ff.

18  Jean-Bertrand Pontalis, *Entre le rêve et la douleur* (Paris: Gallimard, 1977). See especially 'Naissance et reconnaissance du "soi" Pour introduire à l'espace potentiel', p. 159 ff.

19  Philo of Alexandria, *De Providentia*, quoted in Marian Hillar, 'Philo of Alexandria', in *The Internet Encyclopedia of Philosophy*, <http://www.iep.utm.edu/philo/>.

20  See *Megilat Kohelet/Koheles/Ecclesiastes: a new translation with a commentary anthologized from Talmudic, Midrashic and Rabbinic sources*, trans. and ed. Rabbi Meir Zlotowitz (New York: Artscroll Studios, 1976), pp. 123–57.

21  To quote Segal in full: 'I think that one thing that helps me is that these ideas that we discussed together are so much part of my functioning. Of course they change over fifty years—I've brought many modifications to my theories—but they are me, and part of my thinking. So in some way it is very old and very fresh at the same time.' Hanna Segal, 'Motivation: The artist and the psychoanalyst', transcript of ResCen seminar with Hannah Segal, 21 September 2004, Royal Festival Hall, London, <http://www.rescen.net/archive/motivationpsych204.html>.

22  André Green, 'Lear ou les voi(es)x de la nature', in *La Déliaison. Psychanalyse, anthropologie et littérature* (Paris: Hachette, 1992), p. 181 ff.

23  Moïse Maïmonide, *Le Guide des égarés, suivie du Traité des huit chapitres* (Paris: Verdier, 1979). See p. 258 ff. for the discussion on the meanings of the word 'angel'. See also Moïse Maïmonide, *Le Livre des commandements* (Paris: L'Âge d'Homme, 1990), for various discussions of sexuality.

24  Moses Maimonides, 'Helek: Sanhedrin, Chapter Ten', in Isadore Twersky (ed.), *A Maimonides Reader* (New York: Behrman House, 1972), p. 418.

25  Jacques Derrida, *Le toucher: Jean-Luc Nancy* (Paris: Galilée, 2000); Jacques Lebrun, *Le pur amour de Platon à Lacan* (Paris: Seuil, 2002); Jean-Louis Vaysse, *L'inconscient des modernes: essai sur l'origine métaphysique de la psychanalyse* (Paris: Gallimard, 1999).

**Chapter 9. Airport**

1.  Martha Rosler, *In the Place of the Public: Observations of a Frequent Flyer/An der Stelle der Offentlichkeit: Beobachtungen einer Vielfliegerin* (Ostfildern-Ruit: Hatje Cantz, 1998), p. 28.

2.  Benedict Anderson, *Imagined Communities: Reflections on the Origin and Spread of Nationalism*, rev. edn (London: Verso, 1991).

3  *New York Times Magazine*, 8 March 1998.

## Chapter 10. Dossier
*On Fidelity*


1.  Sigmund Freud, 'From the History of an Infantile Neurosis' [1918], trans. Alix and James Strachey, in *The Standard Edition of the Complete Psychological Works of Sigmund Freud*, vol. 17, ed. James Strachey (London: Hogarth, 1955), p. 97.
2.  Jacques Lacan, 'The Subject and the Other: Alienation', in *The Four Fundamental Concepts of Psycho-analysis*, trans. Alan Sheridan (London: Hogarth, 1977), p. 214.
3.  Walter Benjamin, 'On the Theory of Knowledge, Theory of Progress', in *The Arcades Project*, trans. Howard Eiland and Kevin Mclaughlin (Cambridge: Harvard University Press, 1999), p. 463.
4.  For *Circa 1968*, I remade Rey's photograph in compressed lint (formed in the filter screen of a domestic dryer, 10,000 pounds of washing over a six month period), combining 180 units to form an image 256.5 × 266.7 cm over all. In the installation, the work is recessed in the gallery wall and light noise with a slow fade (90-second loop) is projected onto the surface of the lint image. The work was first exhibited in the *Whitney Biennial* in 2004. With reference to Roland Barthes and the two times of the photograph, see Laura Mulvey, 'The Pensive Spectator', in *Whitney Biennial 2004* (New York: Whitney Museum, 2004).
5.  Alain Badiou, 'Search for a Method', in *The Century*, trans. Alberto Toscano (Cambridge: Polity, 2007), p. 9.



*Legacies of Resistance*

1   Jacques Lacan, *The Four Fundamental Concepts of Psycho-analysis*, trans. Alan Sheridan (New York: Norton, 1978), p. 103.
2   Roland Barthes, *Camera Lucida* (New York: Hill and Wang, 1981), p. 96.
3   Sigmund Freud, 'Screen Memories', in *Collected Papers*, vol. 5 (New York: Basic, 1959), p. 69.
4   Bertolt Brecht, 'Popularity and Realism', in Charles Harrison and Paul Wood (eds), *Art in Theory: 1900—1990* (Oxford: Blackwell, 1995), p. 492.


## Chapter 11. Mary Kelly's *Ballad of Kastriot Rexhepi*


1   The work was subsequently exhibited at Cooper's Union Houghton Gallery, New York (21 November–21 December 2002) and at the Museo Universitario de Ciencias y Arte, Mexico City (18 October–12 December 2003).
2   Ernest Larsen, 'About a Boy', *Art in America*, December 2002, p. 99.
3   Roland Barthes, 'The Photographic Message', *Image, Music, Text*, ed. and trans. Stephen Heath (London: Fontana, 1977), pp. 30–31.
4   Mary Kelly and Elsa Longhauser, 'A Conversation with Mary Kelly and Elsa Longhauser', in *Mary Kelly: The Ballad of Kastriot Rexhepi* (Los Angeles: Santa Monica Museum of Art, 2001), p. 6.
5   Larsen: 'About a Boy', p. 101.
6   Maurice Berger, 'Mea Culpa: The Art of Mary Kelly', in *Mary Kelly: The Ballad of Kastriot Rexhepi* (Los Angeles: Santa Monica Museum of Art, 2001), p. 9.
7   This is the crucial point argued for by Jacqueline Rose in her response to a wave of feminist critique of the asocial character of psychoanalysis. See Jacqueline Rose, 'Feminism and the Psychic', and 'Femininity and its Discontents', both in *Sexuality in the Field of Vision* (London: Verso, 1986), pp. 1–24; 83–103.
8   Rose: 'Feminism and the Psychic', p. 7.

9   Scott Glover, 'War Orphan Regains Name—and Family', *Los Angeles Times*, 31 July 1999, <http://articles.latimes.com/1999/jul/31/news/mn-61426>.

10  Mary Kelly, *The Ballad of Kastriot Rexhepi*, canto 3, lines 20–21, reproduced in *Mary Kelly: The Ballad of Kastriot Rexhepi* (Los Angeles: Santa Monica Museum of Art, 2001), p. 18.

11  Kelly and Longhauser: 'A Conversation', p. 7.

12  Kelly and Longhauser: 'A Conversation', p. 7.

13  Susan Sontag, *On Photography* (London: Picador, 1977), p. 19. 'For me it was the photographs of Bergen-Belsen and Dachau which I came across by chance in a bookstore in Santa Monica in July 1945. Nothing I have seen—in photographs or real life—ever cut me as sharply, deeply, as instantaneously. Indeed it seems plausible to divide my life into two parts, before I saw those photographs (I was twelve) and after.' (pp. 19–20). For an excellent historical analysis of the exact impact of the photographs versus the prose press reports see Barbie Zelizer, *Remembering to Forget: Holocaust Memory through the Camera's Eye* (Chicago: University of Chicago Press, 1998).

14  Sontag: *On Photography*, p. 20.

15  Roland Barthes, 'Myth Today', in *Mythologies*, ed. and trans. Annette Lavers (London: Paladin, 1972), pp. 109–58.

16  Juli Carson and Mary Kelly, 'Mea Culpa: A conversation with Mary Kelly', *Art Journal* 58/4 (1999), p. 77.

17  In conversation about this discovered episode—the ready-made of a war experience—Mary Kelly has remarked on the significance of these words of cold blooded enmity emerging fully formed from the mouth of a child, already inducted into the terms of ethnic violence. The child repeats what he has heard as the normal response, his own imaginary already inhabited by the given terms of ethnic conflict.

18  Martha Rosler made a series of major photomontage works on this moment titled *Bringing the War Home* (1967–72; 2004). See Catherine de Zegher (ed.), *Martha Rosler: Positions in the Life World* (Cambridge: MIT Press, 1998).

19  Carson and Kelly: 'Mea Culpa', p. 75, emphasis added.

20  Carson and Kelly: 'Mea Culpa', p. 76.

21  Carson and Kelly: 'Mea Culpa', p. 79.

22  Dori Laub, 'Bearing Witness, or the Vicissitudes of Listening' in Shoshana Felman and Dori Laub, *Testimony: Crises of Witnessing in Literature, Psychoanalysis and History* (London: Routledge, 1992), pp. 72–3.

23  See Griselda Pollock, 'Painting as a Backward Glance That Does not Kill: Fascism and Aesthetics', *Renaissance and Modern Studies* 43 (2001), pp. 116–44; Griselda Pollock, 'Abandoned at the Mouth of Hell or A Second Look that Does not Kill: The Uncanny Coming to Matrixial Memory', in *Looking Back to the Future: Essays on Art, Life and Death* (Amsterdam: G+B Arts International, 2001), pp. 113–77.

24  Dori Laub, 'An Event Without a Witness: Truth, Testimony and Survival', in Shoshana Felman and Dori Laub, *Testimony: Crises of Witnessing in Literature, Psychoanalysis and History* (London: Routledge, 1992), pp. 75–92.

25  Bracha L. Ettinger, 'Traumatic Wit(h)ness-Thing and Matrixial Co/in-habit-(u)ating', *parallax* 5/1 (1999), p. 93.

26  I am thinking here of Julia Kristeva's definition of aesthetic practices as 'signifiance'—that which transforms and renovates the unities of the symbolic

order. See Julia Kristeva, 'The System and the Speaking Subject', in Toril Moi (ed.), *The Kristeva Reader* (Oxford: Blackwell, 1986), pp. 24–33.

## Chapter 12. Nomad-Words

This is a substantially revised version of a paper presented at the 12th BIRTHA (Bristol Institute for Research in the Humanities and Arts) Conference, 'Sublimely Visual: The Art of the Text', 5–7 September 2008.

1   Gilles Deleuze, 'Part I. The Signs' [1964], in *Proust and Signs,* trans. Richard Howard (London: Athlone, 2000), p. 97.

2   Bracha L. Ettinger, *The Matrixial Borderspace* (Minneapolis: University of Minnesota Press, 2006); see also Anna L. Johnson, *Bracha Ettinger's Theory of Matrix and Metramorphosis: Contexts and Commentary* (PhD thesis, University of Leeds, 2006). In part, the present essay follows on from a limit reached in the above research project, where I set out to explicate and contextualize the conceptual architecture upon and through which Ettinger articulated her theoretical propositions. This research was built on a specific methodology, one that finds its echoes here: the assembly of an archive of Ettinger's published texts—a body of work that continues to exist in its very own state of diaspora—and an exclusive focus on that textual archive as an entity distinct from the visual or spoken elements of her work. Testing out Ettinger's proposition of *the matrixial* as a theory in this manner produced a limit in the form of a set of specifically textual questions relating to the role played by language and writing in her work, and the movement(s) it makes between art/practice and theory. At that time, I resisted the idea—raised as a surprising objection to my characterization of the Matrix as a concept—of Ettinger's writing as simply 'poetic', a ludic adjunct of her studio practice, and as such not an appropriate object of critical analysis; such a view, to my mind, undermined the very real possibilities her theoretical propositions open for a feminist project to reconceive the foundations of subjectivity and sexuality. Although to an extent I retain this view, it has since become clear that neither abstraction of Ettinger's work—as non-conceptual play, or as theoretical architectonic—is itself sufficient to account for the complex movements between art and theory that take place within it.

3   Bracha L. Ettinger, 'Trans-Subjective Transferential Borderspace,' in Brian Massumi (ed.), *Canadian Review of Comparative Literature* 24/3 (1997), p. 633.

4   Bracha L. Ettinger, 'Woman-Other-Thing: a Matrixial Touch', in *Bracha Lichtenberg Ettinger: Matrix—Borderlines* (Oxford: Museum of Modern Art, 1993), p. 11.

5   Genesis 17: 9–11.

6   See Exodus 32: 19–23. 'And the LORD said, "I will cause all most goodness to pass in front of you, and I will proclaim my name, the LORD, in your presence. I will have mercy on whom I will have mercy, and I will have compassion on whom I will have compassion. But," he said, "you cannot see my face, for no-one may see me and live."

    Then the LORD said, "There is a place near me where you may stand on a rock. When my glory passes by, I will put you in a cleft in the rock and cover you with my hand until I have passed by. Then I will remove my hand and you will see my back; but my face must not be seen."'

7   See Jacques Derrida, 'Freud and the Scene of Writing' [1966], in *Writing and Difference*, trans. Alan Bass (London: Routledge, 1978), pp. 196–231.

8   See Christine Buci-Glucksmann, 'Images of Absence in the Inner Space of Painting', in M. Catherine de Zegher (ed.), *Inside the Visible: An elliptical traverse of twentieth-century art* (London: MIT, 1996), pp. 89–92; Brian Massumi, 'Painting: The Voice of the Grain', in *Bracha Lichtenberg Ettinger: Artworking 1985-1999* (Brussels: Palais des Beaux-Arts, 2000), pp. 9–32; Griselda Pollock, 'Abandoned at the mouth of hell or a second look that does not kill: the uncanny coming to matrixial memory', in *Looking back to the future: essays on art, life and death* (Amsterdam: G+B Arts International, 2001), pp. 113–74.

9   In interview, Ettinger describes this process of writing: 'When I write, I take what I find, I take pieces of paper to write on and then I may cut and staple them together to make a *Carnet* out of it. When I am painting I at least partly know what I am doing. I sit down to paint, it's completely different. When I write I find the first blank space in the first *Carnet* I find, and I write. There is no continuity, from one moment of writing to another, and I feel that that's not alright, that's not the way you write'. Interview with Caroline Ducker, June 1994, cited in C. Ducker, 'Translating the Matrix: The Process of Metramorphosis in the Notebooks of Bracha Lichtenberg Ettinger', *Versus occasional papers* 1 (1994), p. 11. The suggested association here, between writing and the improper, and writing and discontinuity (or rupture), recalls of course Rousseau's ambivalent dependence on the discontinuities of writing. See Jacques Derrida, *Of Grammatology* [1967], corr. edn, trans. Gayatri Chakravorty Spivak (Baltimore: Johns Hopkins University Press, 1997).

10  Ettinger herself dates the movement from 'private language' to 'theoretical proposition' to some time between 1989 and 1990. Bracha L. Ettinger, 'Matrix and Metramorphosis', *Differences* 4/3 (1992), p. 197.

11  See Bracha L. Ettinger, *Matrix Halal(a)—Lapsus: notes on painting*, trans. Caroline Ducker and Joseph Simas (Oxford: Museum of Modern Art, 1993), p. 28.

12  Deleuze: 'Part I. The Signs', p. 101.

13  See Jean Laplanche, *The Unconscious and the Id: A volume of Laplanche's* Problématiques [1981], trans. Luke Thurston and Lindsay Watson (London: Rebus, 1999), pp. 109–12. Laplanche uses Hjelmslev's division of the semiotic field into the planes of expression and content, and further subdivision into form and substance, to argue against the one-to-one correspondence of signifier and signified that constitutes not only the Saussurean sign, but also Lacan's obliteration of the signified.

14  Bracha L. Ettinger, 'The becoming threshold of matrixial borderlines', in George Robertson *et al.*, *Travellers' Tales* (London: Routledge, 1994), p. 38.

15  There is a suggestive geographical or topographical preoccupation in *Matrix Halal(a)—Lapsus*, that makes an association between European earth/nature as both the scene and cover for the Holocaust, and the (Israeli) desert as a place of meeting and redemption: 'Europe and the desert of Judea. Israeli-European archeology. The earth and all that filth underneath; underneath—Europe must be looked at. During every journey I see the filth underneath. Nature, and all that it has swallowed. The plain desert: blessed drought, or drought wounded' (Ettinger: *Matrix*, p. 29). This is then extended into a reflection on Hebrew and European

languages: 'Tree in Hebrew or in the desert; tree in French or in the forest. It will never mean the same thing to me. It will never leave the same trace in the language, nor in painting, nor in my life. (Hebrew, to sustain me against nature.)' (p. 34). For a brief discussion of the appearance of God to Moses in a no-place 'beyond the desert', and of Moses, in his consignment to the desert—*'the wanderer who will not attain the promised land'*—as a specifically *matrixial* figure, see Ettinger: 'The becoming threshold', pp. 40, 53. Such reflections also evoke Levinas's criticisms of Heidegger's pagan attachment to place, dangerous insofar as it founds tribalism: 'the very splitting of humanity into natives and strangers'. The freedom Levinas perceives in Judaism with regard to both place and nature leads him also to make a specific alliance with technology, taken to its apotheosis in Gagarin's hour 'beyond any horizon'. Such extreme uprootedness from 'the Place', in abstracting the human from the earth, is an opportunity 'to perceive men outside the situation in which they are placed, and let the human face shine in all its nudity' (Emmanuel Levinas, 'Heidegger, Gagarin and Us' [1961], in *Difficult Freedom: Essays on Judaism*, trans. Séan Hand (Baltimore: Johns Hopkins University Press, 1990), pp. 232, 233. See also E. Levinas 'The Poet's Vision' [1956], in *Proper Names*, trans. Michael B. Smith (Stanford: Stanford University Press, 1996), pp. 136–9, and Howard Caygill, *Levinas and the Political* (London: Routledge, 2002), pp. 49–93. With thanks to Bill Allen for suggesting this connection.

16   Ettinger: *Matrix*, p. 11.

17   Ettinger: *Matrix*, p. 39.

18   Ettinger: 'Matrix and metramorphosis', p. 202.

19   Ettinger: *Matrix*, pp. 54, 47, 58, 92.

20   See Johnson: *Bracha Ettinger's Theory of Matrix and Metramorphosis*, pp. 15–76.

21   Ettinger: *Matrix*, p. 72.

22   If controversially: see Julian Morgenstern, 'The Etymological History of the Three Hebrew Synonyms for "to Dance," HGG, HLL and KRR, and their Cultural Significance', *Journal of the American Oriental Society* 36 (1916), pp. 321–2.

23   See Ernest Klein, *A comprehensive etymological dictionary of the Hebrew language for readers of English* (Jerusalem: Carta, 1987), pp. 152, 210, 215, 216, 219.

24   Ettinger: *Matrix*, pp. 12, 23, 65.

25   Ettinger: *Matrix*, pp. 12, 16, 37, 74. See also Klein: *A comprehensive etymological dictionary*, p. 18.

26   Ettinger: *Matrix*, p. 93.

27   A major example of this is in Ettinger's discussion (following Buber and Scholem) of EHIE ASHER EHIE—the form of God's self-presentation to Moses in Exodus. She criticizes its translation as 'I am that I am, or I am that is', insofar as it 'signifies an immanent being, a superposition of present and presence, an a priori subject, a tautological identity, a congruence of signifier and signified, of an identifying I and an identified I, a conjunction of centre, origin and identity, in present time and space' (Ettinger: 'Becoming threshold', p. 39). EHIE however, is not limited to *being*, she argues, also translating as '*I will become.*' From this duality of meaning, Ettinger draws out another translation of EHIE ASHER EHIE as '*I will be/become that I will be/become*': 'a future departure leading to another future departure with no resting point or destination'. Although she duly acknowledges the difficulties inherent in translating EHIE ASHER EHIE into European lan-

guages where being and becoming are counterposed, she argues also that 'the total abolition of becoming and future from this name is a criminal displacement' (p. 40), going on to link this displacement to a foreclosure and exclusion of the feminine which re-emerges in the form of matrix and metramorphosis. See also Ettinger: *Matrix*, p. 89. Interestingly enough, some English translations beside the King James version do recognize this issue. For example, the recent TNIV (Today's New International Version) translation (2004) gives two renderings of EHIE ASHER EHIE (although not in the combined form suggested by Ettinger), as 'I am who I am' and 'I will be what I will be' (Exodus 3: 14–15).

28  Klein: *A comprehensive etymological dictionary*, p. xii.

29  This association has also been noted in passing by Christine Buci-Glucksmann, in her 'Images of Absence', in *Bracha Lichtenberg Ettinger: Matrixial Borderline* (Herblay: Cahiers des Regards, 1993), p. 13

30  This fragment also evokes Freud's account of the translation of latent dream-content into dream-thoughts: 'The dream-thoughts and the dream-content are presented to us like two versions of the same subject-matter in two different languages. Or, more properly, the dream-content seems like a transcript of the dream-thoughts into another mode of expression, whose characters and syntactic laws it is our business to discover by comparing the original and the translation. The dream-thoughts are immediately comprehensible, as soon as we have learnt them. The dream-content, on the other hand, is expressed as it were in a pictographic script, the characters of which have to be transposed individually into the language of the dream-thoughts'. Sigmund Freud, *The Interpretation of Dreams* [1900], trans. and ed. James Strachey, Penguin Freud Library, vol. 4 (London: Penguin, 1976), p. 382. From this passage, Derrida has also drawn out some important implications for the relation between speech and writing that are highly relevant for Ettinger's language-work. See Derrida: 'Freud and the Scene of Writing', p. 218: 'The overall writing of dreams exceeds phonetic writing and puts speech back in its place. As in hieroglyphics or rebuses, voice is circumvented.'

31  The material work on this word-letter-image is also accompanied by a notebook fragment, dated 1989, that plays upon this spelled out sound and its phonic identity with the Hebrew word for nothing or negation: 'In Hebrew, the same sound for *eye* and *nothing* (*Aïn*). The same sound for *eye of* and *there is none* (*Eïn*)' (Ettinger: *Matrix*, p. 53).

32  See Geoffrey Bennington, *Jacques Derrida* (Chicago: University of Chicago Press, 1993), p. 150: 'The I-here-now implied in every enunciation and lost in writing is in principle recuperated in the signature appended to the text.'

33  Ettinger: *Matrixial Borderspace*, p. 113.

34  Luce Irigaray, *This Sex Which Is Not One* [1977], trans. Catherine Porter and Carolyn Burke (Ithaca: Cornell University Press, 1985), p. 134, ellipsis in original.

35  Gilles Deleuze, *Essays Critical and Clinical* [1993], trans. Daniel W. Smith and Michael A. Greco (London: Verso, 1998), p. 5.

36  Roman Jakobson, 'Two aspects of language and two types of aphasic disturbances', in Roman Jakobson and Morris Halle, *Fundamentals of Language* (The Hague: Mouton, 1956), p. 59.

37  As Jean-Gérard Lapacherie points out: 'From a semiological point of view, punctuation marks, underlining, numbers, blanks (and other typographic devices) are very different from letters and stand at the opposite pole of the alphabet. They

do not replace any unit of language. They have no value (in the sense that they do not stand for a unit), but they signal a meaning, a rupture, a hierarchy, an analysis'. J. G. Lapacherie, 'Typographic Characters: Tension Between Text and Drawing', trans. Anna Lehmann, *Yale French Studies* 84 (1994), p. 69.

38 Although in English translation Derrida's neographism is more usually rendered as *différance*, and indeed does not carry the same meaning if 'fully' translated into a parallel English coinage, the retention of the French dilutes the characteristic of the term that is relevant here—'it is read, or it is written, but it cannot be heard'—hence the deliberate Anglicization. See Jacques Derrida, 'Différance' [1968], in *Margins of Philosophy*, trans. Alan Bass (Hemel Hempstead: Harvester Wheatsheaf, 1982), pp. 1–27.

39 Derrida: 'Différance', p. 5.

40 Hans Marchand, *The Categories and Types of Present-Day English Word-Formation: A Synchronic–Diachronic Approach*, 2nd edn (Munich: C. H. Beck'sche, 1969), p. 336.

41 Bracha L. Ettinger, 'Matrixial Gaze and Screen: other than phallic, Merleau-Ponty and the late Lacan', *PS: Journal of the Universities Association for Psychoanalytic Studies* 2/1 (1999), p. 33.

42 Marchand: *The Categories and Types of Present-Day English Word-Formation*, p. 368: 'Denominal verbs are verbalized sentences. The noun is the object of the verb in *calve*, for instance, the object complement in *cash* 'convert into cash', the subject complement in *father* 'be, act as father', the adverbial complement in *corner* 'put in a corner', *butter* 'coat with butter', *alcoholize* combine with alcohol.'

43 Ettinger: *Matrixial Borderspace*, p. 90: 'Beyond the field of aesthetics, the matrix has ethical implications. In the phallus, we confront the impossibility of sharing trauma and phantasy, whereas in the matrix, to a certain extent, there is *an impossibility of not sharing them.*' Thus, although *witnessing* undeniably has ethical dimensions, in the sense that the act of witnessing necessarily involves a relation to an other, it is still constituted by a singular self that bears witness to an event. *Wit(h)nessing* on the other hand, fundamentally modifies the idea of bearing witness as a *trans-subjective* inscription.

44 This also seems to make sense of Derrida's statement that 'The materiality of a word cannot be translated or carried over into another language. Materiality is precisely that which translation relinquishes'. Derrida: 'Freud and the Scene of Writing', p. 210.

45 In a brief comment on Ettinger's coinage of *wit(h)nessing*, Griselda Pollock also notes a visual dimension of Ettinger's language work, but does not allow for the complexity of its etymological status (something I believe to be clearly evident in Ettinger's various plays, far more extensive than those cited here, on the use of witness, withness and wit(h)ness as distinct terms). Pollock writes: 'to define the specific moments or elements of non-psychotic transitivity that may be incited in the aesthetic experience (of making as well as of viewing) [Ettinger] alters the word *witness* visually to create "wit(h)nessing". Introducing the letter "h" from the word *with* breaches the dominant formulations of the conditions of subjectivity in which the subject only emerges when it ceases to be with an other, separates itself, defines its boundaried ego through a scarifying gap through which hole will whistle the subjective engine of desire'. Griselda Pollock, 'Mary Kelly's *Ballad of Kastriot Rexhepi*: Virtual Trauma and Indexical Witness in the Age of Mediatic Spectacle', in this volume, p. 214.

46 Freud: *Interpretation of Dreams*, p. 403.
47 Freud: *Interpretation of Dreams*, p. 400.
48 Bracha L. Ettinger, 'Plaiting a Being-in-Severality and the Primal Scene', *Almanac of Psychoanalysis* 3 (2002), p. 93.
49 This recalls precisely the subordination of speech within the dream-work, registered initially by Freud and then elaborated by Derrida: '[…] Freud, like Artaud later on, meant less the absence than the subordination of speech on the dreamstage. Far from disappearing, speech changes purpose and status. It is situated, surrounded, invested (in all senses of the word), constituted. It figures in dreams much as captions do in comic strips, those picto-hieroglyphic combinations in which the phonetic text is secondary and not central to the telling of the tale […]' (Derrida: 'Freud and the Scene of Writing', p. 218).
50 As a final aside, there is another, inadvertent signification to this hieroglyphic term, covered over by its reference to a French *outside-the-text*: the *English* word *fam*. A shortening of the late Middle English *famble*—meaning both *hand* and *to speak imperfectly, to stammer* or *to stutter*—*fam* is both a hand and to feel; evoking both the tactility of writing, and its disruption of speech, to *fam* in language is to feel one's way, to stammer or stutter.

# BIBLIOGRAPHY

The editors have sought to ensure that all URLs for websites referred to in this book are correct and active at the time of going to press, unless otherwise stated.


Abel, Richard, *The Red Rooster Scare: Making Cinema American, 1900–1910* (Berkeley: University of California Press, 1999).

Ackland, Charles R., *Screen Traffic: Movies, Multiplexes, and Global Culture* (Durham: Duke University Press, 2003).

'ADM (Aéroports de Montréal) soutient que la sécurité des passagers a été amélioriée', *La Presse* (Montreal), 10 May 2005, p. A7.

Agamben, Giorgio, *Remnants of Auschwitz: The Witness and the Archive*, trans. Daniel Heller-Roazen (New York: Zone, 1992).

Alexander, Jeffrey C., and Smith, Philip, 'The Strong Programme in Cultural Sociology', in J. C. Alexander, *The Meanings of Social Life: A Cultural Sociology* (Oxford: Oxford University Press, 2003), pp. 11–26.

Althusser, Louis, 'Freud and Lacan', *New Left Review* 1/55 (1969), pp. 49–65.

Anderson, Benedict, *Imagined Communities: Reflections on the Origin and Spread of Nationalism*, rev. edn (London: Verso, 1991).

Appadurai, Arjun, *Modernity at Large: Cultural Dimensions of Globalization* (Minneapolis: University of Minnesota Press, 1996).

Arendt, Hannah, 'Prologue', in *The Human Condition* [1958] (Chicago: University of Chicago Press, 1998).

'Attacks were most important historical events in our lives: poll', *Montreal Gazette*, 11 September 2007, A17.

Bach, Robert, 'Office 97 Q and A with Robbie Bach', *Go Inside*, <http://goinside.com/97/1/o97qa.html>.

Badiou, Alain, 'Search for a Method', in *The Century*, trans. Alberto Toscano (Cambridge: Polity, 2007), pp. 1–10.

Bajaj, Vikas, 'Bloomberg Cites "Specific Threat" to NY Subways', *New York Times*, 6 October 2005.

Bal, Mieke, *The Point of Theory: Practices of Cultural Analysis* (Amsterdam: University of Amsterdam Press, 1994).

—— *The Practice of Cultural Analysis: Exposing Interdisciplinary Interpretation* (Stanford: Stanford University Press, 1999).

—— *Travelling Concepts in the Humanities: A Rough Guide* (Toronto: University of Toronto Press, 2002).

Barbon, Nicholas, *Discourse of Trade* (London: Thomas Milbourn, 1690).

—— *A Discourse on coining the new money lighter, in answer to Mr. Locke's considerations, etc.* (London: Richard Chiswell, 1696).

Barthes, Roland, *Camera Lucida* (New York: Hill and Wang, 1981).

—— *The Fashion System* [1967], trans. Matthew Ward and Richard Howard (London: Jonathan Cape, 1983).

—— *Image, Music, Text*, trans. Stephen Heath (London: Fontana, 1977).

—— *Mythologies* [1957], trans. Annette Lavers (London: Vintage, 1993).

—— *S/Z* [1970], trans. Richard Miller (London: Jonathan Cape, 1975).

Bauman, Zygmunt, *Liquid Modernity* (Cambridge: Polity, 2000).

Bazin, André, 'The Ontology of the Photographic Image' [1960], trans. Hugh Gray, in *What is Cinema?*, vol. 1 (Berkeley: University of California Press, 1967), pp. 9–16.

Bedetti, Gabriella, 'Henri Meschonnic: Rhythm as Pure Historicity', *New Literary History* 23/2 (1992), pp. 431–50.

Benjamin, Walter, *The Arcades Project*, trans. Howard Eiland and Kevin McLaughlin (Cambridge: Harvard University Press, 1999).

—— 'The Work of Art in the Age of Mechanical Reproduction'[1935], in *Illuminations*, ed. Hannah Arendt, trans. Harry Zohn (London: Fontana, 1973), pp. 217–51.

Bennington, Geoffrey, *Jacques Derrida* (Chicago: University of Chicago Press, 1993).

Benveniste, Émile, *Problèmes de linguistique générale* (Paris: Gallimard, 1966).

Berg, Neil, 'Brain-Machine Interfaces: Current and Future Applications', *CHI Labs* (2002), <http://personal.bgsu.edu/~nberg/chilabs/bmi.htm> .

Binkley, Timothy, 'Refiguring Culture', in Philip Hayward and Tana Wollen (eds), *Future Visions: New Technologies of the Screen* (London: BFI, 1993), pp. 92–122.

Bion, Wilfred R., *Elements of Psycho-Analysis* (New York: Basic, 1963).

Boustany, Nora, 'As Ukraine Watched the Party Line, She Took the Truth Into Her Hands', *Washington Post*, 29 April 2005, <http://www.washingtonpost.com/wp-dyn/content/article/2005/04/28/AR2005042801696.html>.

Brecht, Bertolt, 'Popularity and Realism', in Charles Harrison and Paul Wood (eds), *Art in Theory: 1900—1990* (Oxford: Blackwell, 1995), pp. 489–93.

Bryant, Antony, *Thinking Informatically: A New Understanding of Information, Communication and Technology* (Lampeter: Mellen, 2006).

Buci-Glucksmann, Christine, 'Images of Absence', in *Bracha Lichtenberg Ettinger: Matrixial Borderline* (Herblay: Cahiers des Regards, 1993).

—— 'Images of Absence in the Inner Space of Painting', in M. Catherine de Zegher (ed.), *Inside the Visible: An elliptical traverse of twentieth-century art* (London: MIT, 1996), pp. 89–92.

Bukatman, Scott, *Terminal Identity: The Virtual Subject in Postmodern Science Fiction* (Durham: Duke University Press, 1993).

Bush, George W., 'Graduation speech at West Point United States Military Academy, June 1 2002', in Carl C. Hodge and Cathal J. Nolan (eds), *U. S. Presidents & Foreign Policy: From 1789 to the Present* (Santa Barbara: ABC-CLIO, 2007), p. 408.

—— Radio Address, 18 June 2005, <http://en.wikisource.org/wiki/Presidential _Radio_Address_-_18_June_2005>.

Carson, Juli and Kelly, Mary, 'Mea Culpa: A conversation with Mary Kelly', *Art Journal* 58/4 (1999), pp. 75–80.

Caruth, Cathy, *Unclaimed Experience: Trauma, Narrative, and History* (Baltimore: Johns Hopkins University Press, 1996).

Castells, Manuel, *End of Millennium*, The Information Age: Economy, Society and Culture, vol. 3 (Cambridge and Oxford: Blackwell, 1998).

—— 'Informationalism and the Network Society' in Pekka Himanen, *The Hacker Ethic and the Spirit of the Information Age* (New York: Random House, 2001), pp. 155–78.

—— *The Informational City: Information Technology, Economic Restructuring, and the Urban Regional Process* (Oxford: Blackwell, 1989).

—— *The Power of Identity*, The Information Age: Economy, Society and Culture, vol. 2 (Cambridge and Oxford: Blackwell, 1997).

—— *The Rise of the Network Society*, The Information Age: Economy, Society and Culture, vol. 1 (Cambridge and Oxford: Blackwell, 1996).

Caygill, Howard, *Levinas and the Political* (London: Routledge, 2002).

Clark, Andy, *Natural-Born Cyborgs: Minds, Technologies, and the Future of Human Intelligence* (Oxford: Oxford University Press, 2003).

Cobb, Kristin, 'Mind Meld', *Science Notes* (2002), <http://scicom.ucsc.edu/ SciNotes/0201/lo/mind/>.

Colchester, Chloe, *Textiles Today: a Global Survey of Trends and Traditions* (London: Thames & Hudson, 2007).

Comolli, Jean-Louis and Narboni, Jean, 'Cinema/Ideology/Criticism' [1969], trans. Susan Bennett, *Screen* 12/1 (1971), pp. 27–36; 12/2 (1972), pp. 145–55; 13/1 (1972), pp. 120–31.

Cook, David A., *Lost Illusions: American Cinema in the Shadow of Watergate and Vietnam, 1970–1979*, History of the American Cinema, vol. 9 (Berkeley: University of California Press, 2000).

Cooper, Stephen D., 'A Concise History of the Fauxtography Blogstorm in the 2006 Lebanon War', *American Communication Journal* 9/2 (2007), <http://www. acjournal.org/holdings/vol9/summer/articles/fauxtography.html>.

Cowie, Elizabeth, 'Spectres of the Real: Documentary Time and Art', *Differences* 18/1 (2007), pp. 87–127.

Curtis, Barry and Pajaczkowska, Claire, 'Looking sharp', in Marketa Uhlirova (ed.), *If Looks Could Kill: Cinema's Images of Fashion, Crime and Violence* (London: Koenig, 2008), pp. 62–6.

Curtis, Polly, 'Scientist becomes world's first cyborg', *Guardian*, 22 March 2002, <http://www.guardian.co.uk/education/2002/mar/22/research.higher education1>.

Damasio, Antonio, *Descartes' Error: Emotion, Reason, and the Human Brain* (New York: Penguin, 2005).

David, Cathérine and Chevrier, Jean-François, *Documenta X: Pol(e)itics* (Ostfilderen-Ruit: Hatje Cantz Verlag and New York: Distributed Art Publishers, 1998).

Deleuze, Gilles, *Difference and Repetition* [1968], trans. Paul Patton (London: Athlone, 1994).

—— *Essays Critical and Clinical* [1993], trans. Daniel W. Smith and Michael A. Greco (London: Verso, 1998).

—— *The Fold: Leibniz and the Baroque* [1988], trans. Tom Conley (London: Continuum, 2006).

—— *Francis Bacon: The Logic of Sensation* [1981], trans. Daniel W. Smith (London: Continuum, 2003).

—— 'Part I. The Signs' [1964] in *Proust and Signs*, trans. Richard Howard (London: Athlone, 2000), pp. 1–102.

Deleuze, Gilles and Guattari, Félix, *A Thousand Plateaus* [1980], trans. Brian Massumi (Minneapolis: University of Minnesota Press, 1987).

Derrida, Jacques, 'Différance' [1968], in *Margins of Philosophy*, trans. Alan Bass (Hemel Hempstead: Harvester Wheatsheaf, 1982), pp. 1–27.

—— 'Freud and the Scene of Writing' [1966], in *Writing and Difference*, trans. Alan Bass (London: Routledge, 1978), pp. 196–231.

—— *Limited Inc* (Evanston: Northwestern University Press, 1988).

—— *Of Grammatology* [1967], corr. edn, trans. Gayatri Chakravorty Spivak (Baltimore: Johns Hopkins University Press, 1997).

—— *Le toucher: Jean-Luc Nancy* (Paris: Galilée, 2000).

Descartes, René, 'Second Meditation', in *Meditations on First Philosophy: A Bilingual Edition*, ed. and trans. George Heffernan (Notre Dame: University of Notre Dame Press 1990).

Doane, Mary Ann, *The Emergence of Cinematic Time: Modernity, Contingency and the Archive* (Cambridge: Harvard University Press, 2002).

—— 'Indexicality: Trace and Sign: Introduction', *Differences: A Journal of Feminist Cultural Studies*, 18/1 (2007), pp. 1–6.

Dormor, Catherine, 'skin:textile:film', *Textile: The Journal of Cloth and Culture* 6/3 (2008), pp. 238–53.

Dorrien, Gary, *Imperial Designs: Neoconservatism and the New Pax Americana* (New York: Routledge, 2004).

Dougherty, Kevin, 'Province to Rid Schools of Junk Food. Youth Obesity a Pandemic: Couillard', *Montreal Gazette*, 14 September 2007, A8.

Doy, Gen, *Drapery: Classicism and Barbarism in Visual Culture* (London: I.B.Tauris, 2002).

Ducker, Caroline, 'Translating the Matrix: The Process of Metramorphosis in the Notebooks of Bracha Lichtenberg Ettinger', *Versus occasional papers* 1 (1994).

Edwards, Steve, *The Making of English Photography: Allegories* (University Park: Penn State University Press, 2006).

Ehrenzweig, Anton, 'The four stages of the articulation process', in *The Psychoanalysis of Artistic Vision and Hearing* (London: Routledge and Kegan Paul, 1953), pp. 116–25.

Eliot, T. S., 'Little Gidding', in *Four Quartets* [1943] (London: Faber, 1959).

—— *The Waste Land* [1922] (London: Faber, 1936).

Ellul, Jacques, *The Technological System* [1977], trans. Joachim Neugroschel (New York: Continuum, 1980).

Ettinger, Bracha L., 'The becoming threshold of matrixial borderlines', in George Robertson *et al.*, *Travellers' Tales* (London: Routledge, 1994), pp. 36–82.

—— 'Matrix and Metramorphosis', *Differences* 4/3 (1992), pp. 176–208.

—— *Matrix Halal(a)—Lapsus: notes on painting*, trans. Caroline Ducker and Joseph Simas (Oxford: Museum of Modern Art, 1993).

—— *The Matrixial Borderspace* (Minneapolis: University of Minnesota Press, 2006).

—— 'Matrixial Gaze and Screen: other than phallic, Merleau-Ponty and the late Lacan', *PS: Journal of the Universities Association for Psychoanalytic Studies* 2/1 (1999), pp. 3–39.

—— 'Plaiting a Being-in-Severality and the Primal Scene', *Almanac of Psychoanalysis* 3 (2002), pp. 91–109.

—— 'Trans-Subjective Transferential Borderspace,' in Brian Massumi (ed.), *Canadian Review of Comparative Literature* 24/3 (1997), pp. 625–47.

—— 'Traumatic Wit(h)ness-Thing and Matrixial Co/in-habit-(u)ating', *parallax* 5/1 (1999), pp. 89–98.

—— 'Woman-Other-Thing: a Matrixial Touch', in *Bracha Lichtenberg Ettinger: Matrix—Borderlines* (Oxford: Museum of Modern Art, 1993), pp. 11–18.

Fasoli, Doriano and Rossi, Rosa, *Le estasi laiche de Teresa d'Avila: psicoanalisi, misticismo e altre esperienzi culturali a confronto* (Rome: Edizione Associate, 1998).

Felman, Shoshana, 'Education and Crisis, or the Vicissitudes of Teaching', in Cathy Caruth (ed.), *Trauma: Explorations in Memory* (Baltimore: Johns Hopkins University Press, 1995), pp. 13–60.

Felman, Shoshana and Laub, Dori, *Testimony: Crises of Witnessing in Literature, Psychoanalysis and History* (London: Routledge, 1992).

Ferenczi, Sándor, 'Confusion of tongues between adults and the child' [1933], in *Final Contributions to the Problems and Methods of Psycho-analysis* [1955], ed. Michael Balint, trans. Eric Mosbacher *et al.* (London: Karnac, 1994), pp. 156–67.

Fitzpatrick, Kathleen, *The Anxiety of Obsolescence: The American Novel in the Age of Television* (Nashville: Vanderbilt University Press, 2006).

Foucault, Michel, *The Birth of Biopolitics: Lectures at the Collège de France 1978–1979*, trans. Graham Burchell, ed. Michel Senellart (New York: Palgrave Macmillan, 2008).

'Framing the Story', *Washington Times,* 9 August 2006, <http://www.washington times.com/news/2006/aug/09/20060809-090136-3068r/>.

Freud, Sigmund, 'The Ego and the Id' [1923], trans. Joan Riviere, in *The Standard Edition of the Complete Psychological Works of Sigmund Freud*, vol. 19, ed. James Strachey (London: Hogarth, 1960), pp. 3–66.

—— 'From the History of an Infantile Neurosis' [1918], trans. Alix and James Strachey, in *The Standard Edition of the Complete Psychological Works of Sigmund Freud*, vol. 17, ed. James Strachey (London: Hogarth, 1955), pp. 3–122.

—— *The Interpretation of Dreams* [1900], trans. and ed. James Strachey, Penguin Freud Library, vol. 4 (London: Penguin, 1976).

—— 'Screen Memories' [1899], in *Collected Papers*, vol. 5, ed. James Strachey (New York: Basic, 1959), pp. 47–69.

—— 'The "Uncanny"' [1919], trans. Alix Strachey, in *The Standard Edition of the Complete Psychological Works of Sigmund Freud*, vol. 17, ed. James Strachey (London: Hogarth, 1955), pp. 217–52.

—— 'Das Unheimliche', in *Gesammelte Werke*, vol. 12 (Frankfurt am Main: Fischer, 1947), pp. 227–68.

Friedberg, Anne, *Window Shopping: Cinema and the Postmodern* (Berkeley: University of California Press, 1994).

Gaines, Jane, 'Machines that make the body do things', in Pamela Church Gibson (ed.), *More Dirty Looks: Gender, Pornography and Power* (London: BFI, 2004), pp. 31–44.

Gell, Alfred, *Art and Agency: an Anthropological Theory* (Oxford: Oxford University Press, 1998).

Gibson, William, *Neuromancer* [1984] (London: Harper Collins, 1993).

—— *Pattern Recognition* (New York: Putnam, 2003).

'Girl, 10, used geography lesson to save lives', *Telegraph*, 1 January 2005, <http://www.telegraph.co.uk/news/1480192/Girl-10-used-geography-lesson-to-save-lives.html>.

Giuliani, Rudolph, 'Towards a Realistic Peace', *Foreign Affairs*, September/October 2007, <http://www.foreignaffairs.org/articles/62824/rudolph-w-giuliani/toward-a-realistic-peace>.

Glover, Scott, 'War Orphan Regains Name—and Family', *Los Angeles Times*, 31 July 1999, <http://articles.latimes.com/1999/jul/31/news/mn-61426>.

Goettling, Garry, 'Harnessing the Power of Thought', *Georgia Tech Alumni Magazine* 76/1 (1999), <http://gtalumni.org/Publications/magazine/sum99/harnessing.html>.

Goldacre, Ben, 'The return of Captain Cyborg', *Guardian*, 29 April 2004, <http://www.guardian.co.uk/science/2004/apr/29/badscience.science>.

Graham-Rowe, Duncan, 'Brain implants "read" monkey minds', *New Scientist*, 8 July 2004, <http://www.newscientist.com/article.ns?id=dn6127>.

Green, André, 'Lear ou les voi(es)x de la nature', in *La Déliaison. Psychanalyse, anthropologie et littérature* (Paris: Hachette, 1992).

Greenberg, Karen L. and Dratel, Joshua L. (eds), *The Torture Papers: The Road to Abu Ghraib* (Cambridge: Cambridge University Press, 2005).

Greenfield, Baroness Professor Susan, 'The Brain of the Future', Butterfield Memorial Lecture 2001, Royal Society for the Encouragement of the Arts, Manufacture and Commerce, London, <http://www.collegeofteachers.ac.uk/older/news/events_bml2001.htm> (accessed 9 January 2007; no longer available).

Grosz, Elizabeth, *Architecture from the Outside: Essays on Virtual and Real Space* (Cambridge: MIT Press, 2002).

Habermas, Jürgen, *Knowledge and Human Interests*, trans. Jeremy J. Shapiro (London: Heinemann: 1972).

Haines, Lester, 'Captain Cyborg terrorises UK conference: Gives speech on, er, speechless communication', *The Register*, 12 May 2004 <http://www.theregister.co.uk/2004/05/12/captain_cyborg_conference/>.

Halbwachs, Maurice, *The Collective Memory*, trans. Francis J. Ditter, Jr., and Vida Yazdi Ditter (New York: Harper & Row, 1980).

Hall, Stuart, 'Encoding/Decoding' [1980], in Paul Marris and Sue Thornham (eds), *Media Studies: A Reader* (Edinburgh: Edinburgh University Press, 2000), pp. 41–49.

—— 'The Television Discourse—Encoding and Decoding' [1974], in Ann Gray and Jim McGuigan (eds), *Studying Culture: An Introductory Reader* (London: Edward Arnold, 1997), pp. 28–34.

Haraway, Donna, 'A Cyborg Manifesto: Science, Technology, and Socialist-Feminism in the Late Twentieth Century' [1985], in *Simians, Cyborgs and Women: The Reinvention of Nature* (New York: Routledge, 1991), pp. 149–81.

Harvey, David, *The Limits to Capital* (London: Verso, 1999).

Hayles, N. Katherine, *How We Became Posthuman: Virtual Bodies in Cybernetics, Literature and Informatics* (Chicago: University of Chicago Press, 1999).

—— 'Narrating Bits', *Vectors* 1 (2005), <http://www.vectorsjournal.org/index.php?page=7&projectId=6>.

Heath, Stephen, 'Narrative space', in *Questions of Cinema* (Bloomington: Indiana University Press, 1981), pp. 19–75.

Heidegger, Martin, *Hölderlin's Hymn 'The Ister'*, trans. William McNeill and Julia Davis (Bloomington: Indiana University Press, 1996).

—— *Hölderlins Hymne 'Der Ister'*, Gesamtausgabe 53 (Frankfurt am Main: Vittorio Klostermann, 1984).

—— *Introduction to Metaphysics*, trans. Gregory Fried and Richard Polt (New Haven and London: Yale University Press, 2000).

Hendry, George S., 'Nothing', *Theology Today* 39/3 (1982), <http://theologytoday.ptsem.edu/oct1982/v39-3-article4.htm>.

HITLab Projects, 'VR Therapy for Spider Phobia', <http://www.hitl.washington.edu/projects/exposure/>.

Hirst, Paul, and Woolley, Penny, 'The Social Formation and Maintenance of Human Attributes' in *Social Relations and Human Attributes* (London: Tavistock, 1982), pp. 23–61.

Hohendahl, Peter Uwe, *Building a National Literature: The Case of Germany 1830–*

*1870*, trans. Renate Baron Franciscono (Ithaca: Cornell University Press, 1989).

Hutchins, Edwin, *Cognition in the Wild* (Cambridge: MIT Press, 1996).

Huyssen, Andreas, *After the Great Divide: Modernism, Mass Culture, Postmodernism* (Bloomington: Indiana University Press, 1986).

Irigaray, Luce, *This Sex Which Is Not One* [1977], trans. Catherine Porter and Carolyn Burke (Ithaca: Cornell University Press, 1985).

Jackson Lears, T. J., *No Place of Grace: Antimodernism and the Transformation of American Culture 1880–1920* (New York: Pantheon, 1981).

Jakobson, Roman, 'Linguistics and Poetics', in David Lodge (ed.), *Modern Criticism and Theory: A Reader* (London: Longman, 1988), pp. 32–57.

—— 'Two aspects of language and two types of aphasic disturbances', in Roman Jakobson and Morris Halle, *Fundamentals of Language* (The Hague: Mouton, 1956), pp. 53–82.

Jameson, Fredric, 'Fear and Loathing in Globalization', *New Left Review*, 23 (2003), pp. 105–14.

Johnson, Anna L., *Bracha Ettinger's Theory of Matrix and Metramorphosis: Contexts and Commentary* (PhD thesis, University of Leeds, 2006).

Johnson, Neil F., Zoran Durig, and Sushi Jajodia, *Information Hiding: Steganography and Watermarking: Attacks and Countermeasures* (New York: Kluwer Academic, 2000).

Kaempffert, Waldemar, 'In the Next Fifty Years', *Popular Mechanics*, February 1950 <http://books.google.com/books?id=ANkDAAAAMBAJ&pg=PA112&dq= Popular+Mechanics&lr=&as_brr=0&as_pt=MAGAZINES&source=gbs_toc _pages_r&cad=0_1#PPA113,M1>.

Kelly, Mary, *Mary Kelly: The Ballad of Kastriot Rexhepi* (Los Angeles: Santa Monica Museum of Art, 2001).

Kirkpatrick, Sidney, *Edgar Cayce: An American Prophet* (New York: Riverhead, 2000).

Klein, Ernest, A comprehensive etymological dictionary of the Hebrew language for readers of English (Jerusalem: Carta, 1987).

Knowlton, Brian, 'Bush Insists Al Qaeda in Iraq Threatens U. S.', *New York Times*, 24 July 2007, <http://www.nytimes.com/2007/07/24/washington/24cnd-prexy.html?ex=1187582400&en=2f3c040687c73ebd&ei=5070>.

Koza, John R., Bennett, Forrest H., Andre, David and Keane, Martin A., *Genetic Programming III: Darwinian Invention and Problem Solving* (San Francisco: Morgan Kaufmann, 1999).

Kristeva, Julia, *La révolte intime. Pouvoirs et limites de la psychanalyse II* (Paris: Fayard, 1997).

—— 'The System and the Speaking Subject', in Toril Moi (ed.), *The Kristeva Reader* (Oxford: Blackwell, 1986), pp. 24–33.

Lacan, Jacques, *The Four Fundamental Concepts of Psycho-analysis*, trans. Alan Sheridan (London: Hogarth, 1977).

—— *Le Séminaire Livre V: Les Formations de l'inconscient*, texte établi par Jacques-Alain Miller (Paris: Seuil, 1998).

LaCapra, Dominick, *Writing History, Writing Trauma* (Baltimore: Johns Hopkins University Press, 2000).

Lapacherie, Jean-Gérard, 'Typographic Characters: Tension Between Text and Drawing', trans. Anna Lehmann, *Yale French Studies* 84 (1994), pp. 63–77.

Laplanche, Jean, *The Unconscious and the Id: A volume of Laplanche's* Problématiques [1981], trans. Luke Thurston and Lindsay Watson (London: Rebus, 1999).

Laplanche, Jean, and Pontalis, Jean-Bertrand, *The Language of Psychoanalysis* [1967] (London: Karnac, 1988).

Larsen, Ernest, 'About a Boy', *Art in America*, December 2002, pp. 98–101.

Lebrun, Jacques, *Le pur amour de Platon à Lacan* (Paris: Seuil, 2002).

Lenoir, Timothy, 'All but War Is Simulation: The Military Entertainment Complex', *Configurations* 8 (2000), pp. 289–335.

Levinas, Emmanuel, 'Heidegger, Gagarin and Us' [1961], in *Difficult Freedom: Essays on Judaism*, trans. Séan Hand (Baltimore: Johns Hopkins University Press, 1990), pp. 231–5.

—— 'The Poet's Vision' [1956], in *Proper Names*, trans. Michael B. Smith (Stanford: Stanford University Press, 1996), pp. 127–39.

Mackenzie, Adrian, *Cutting Code: Software and Sociality* (New York: Peter Lang, 2006).

Maimonides, Moses, *Le Guide des égarés, suivie du Traité des huit chapitres* (Paris: Verdier, 1979).

—— 'Helek: Sanhedrin, Chapter Ten', in Isadore Twersky (ed.), *A Maimonides Reader* (New York: Behrman House, 1972), pp. 401–23.

—— *Le Livre des commandements* (Paris: L'Âge d'Homme, 1990).

Manovich, Lev, *The Language of New Media* (Cambridge: MIT Press, 2001).

Marchand, Hans, *The Categories and Types of Present-Day English Word-Formation: A Synchronic–Diachronic Approach*, 2nd edn (Munich: C. H. Beck'sche, 1969).

Marks, Laura U., *The Skin of the Film: Intercultural Cinema, Embodiment, and the Senses* (Durham: Duke University Press, 2000).

Marx, Karl, *Capital*, vol. 1, trans Ben Fowkes (Harmondsworth: Penguin, 1976).

Massumi, Brian, 'Everywhere You Want to Be: Introduction to Fear', in B. Massumi (ed.), *The Politics of Everyday Fear* (Minneapolis: University of Minnesota Press, 1993), pp. 3–38.

—— 'Painting: The Voice of the Grain', in *Bracha Lichtenberg Ettinger: Artworking 1985–1999* (Brussels: Palais des Beaux-Arts, 2000), pp. 9–32.

—— *Parables For the Virtual: Movement, Affect, Sensation* (Durham and London: Duke University Press, 2002).

Meek, James, 'Robot with living brain created in US', *Guardian*, 18 April 2001, <http://www.guardian.co.uk/international/story/0,3604,474397,00.html>.

*Megilat Kohelet/Koheles/Ecclesiastes: a new translation with a commentary anthologized from Talmudic, Midrashic and Rabbinic sources*, trans. and ed. Rabbi Meir Zlotowitz (New York: Artscroll Studios, 1976).

Metz, Christian, *The Imaginary Signifier: Psychoanalysis and the Cinema* [1977], trans. Celia Britton, Annwyl Williams, Ben Brewster and Alfred Guzzetti (Bloomington: Indiana University Press, 1982).

—— *Language and Cinema*, trans. Donna Jean Umiker-Sebeok (The Hague: Mouton, 1974).

Miller, Mark Crispin, *The Bush Dyslexicon* (New York: Norton, 2002).

Mitchell, W. J. T., 'Ekphrasis and the Other', in *Picture Theory: Essays on Verbal and Visual Representation* (Chicago: University of Chicago Press, 1994).

Moretti, Franco, *Atlas of the European Novel 1800–1900* (London: Verso, 1998).

—— 'Conjectures on World Literature' [2000], in Christopher Prendergast (ed.), *Debating World Literature* (London: Verso, 2004), pp. 148–62.

Morgenstern, Julian, 'The Etymological History of the Three Hebrew Synonyms for "to Dance," HGG, HLL and KRR, and their Cultural Significance', *Journal of the American Oriental Society* 36 (1916), pp. 321–32.

Morton, Donald, 'Birth of the Cyberqueer', *PMLA* 110/3 (1995), pp. 369–81.

Moukheiber, Zina, 'Mind Over Matter', *Forbes Magazine*, 15 March 2004, <http://www.forbes.com/home/free_forbes/2004/0315/186.html>.

Mulvey, Laura, 'Delaying Cinema', in *Death 24x a Second: Stillness and the Moving Image* (London: Reaktion, 2006), pp. 144–60.

—— 'The Index and the Uncanny', in Carolyn B. Gill (ed.), *Time and the Image* (Manchester: Manchester University Press, 2000), pp. 139–48.

—— 'The Pensive Spectator', in *Whitney Biennial 2004* (New York: Whitney Museum, 2004).

Nelson, Jason, *Dreamaphage*, <http://www.heliozoa.com/dreamaphage/opening.html>.

O'Sullivan, Simon, *Art Encounters Deleuze and Guattari: Thought Beyond Representation* (Basingstoke: Palgrave Macmillan, 2006).

Pajaczkowska, Claire, 'On stuff and nonsense: the complexity of cloth', *Textile: The Journal of Cloth and Culture* 3/3 (2005), pp. 220–49.

—— 'Thread of attachment', *Textile: The Journal of Cloth and Culture* 5/2 (2007), pp. 140–52.

Parker, Rozsika, *The Subversive Stitch: Embroidery and the Making of the Feminine* (London: Women's Press, 1984).

Peirce, Charles Sanders, *The Essential Peirce*, vol. 2 (Indianapolis: Indiana University Press, 1998).

—— 'Letters to Lady Welby', in: C. S. Peirce, *Selected Writings*, ed. Philip P. Wiener (New York: Dover, 1966), pp. 380–432.

—— *The Philosophical Writings of Peirce*, ed. Justus Buchler (New York: Dover, 1955).

Perlmutter, David D., 'Photojournalism in crisis', *Editor and Publisher Online*, 17 August 2006.

Perlmutter, David D., and Hamilton, John Maxwell (eds), *From Pigeons to News Portals: Foreign Reporting and the Challenge of New Technology* (Baton Rouge: Louisiana State University Press, 2007).

Philo of Alexandria, *De Providentia*, quoted in Marian Hillar, 'Philo of Alexandria', in *The Internet Encyclopedia of Philosophy*, <http://www.iep.utm.edu/philo/>.

'Plus de panique!', *La Presse* (Montreal), 17 May 2005, A22.

Poe, Edgar Allan, *The Raven* [1845], <http://www.heise.de/ix/raven/Literature/Lore/TheRaven.html>.

Pollock, Griselda, 'Abandoned at the Mouth of Hell or A Second Look that Does not Kill: The Uncanny Coming to Matrixial Memory', in *Looking Back to the Future: Essays on Art, Life and Death* (Amsterdam: G+B Arts International, 2001), pp. 113–77.

—— 'Painting as a Backward Glance That Does not Kill: Fascism and Aesthetics', *Renaissance and Modern Studies* 43 (2001), pp. 116–44.

Pontalis, Jean-Bertrand, *Entre le rêve et la douleur* (Paris: Gallimard, 1977).

'President Bush Holds a News Conference: Transcript', *Washington Post*, 9 August 2007, <http://www.washingtonpost.com/wp-dyn/content/article/2007/08/09/AR2007080900714.html>.

Reddy, Michael, 'The conduit metaphor: A case of frame conflict in our language about language', in Andrew Ortony (ed.), *Metaphor and Thought*, 2nd edn (Cambridge: Cambridge University Press), pp. 164–201.

'Reuters Doctoring Photos from Beirut?', *Little Green Footballs*, 5 August 2006 <http://littlegreenfootballs.com/article/21956/>.

'Reuters drops Beirut Photographer', *BBC News*, 8 August 2006, <http://news.bbc.co.uk/1/hi/5254838.stm>.

Rifkin, Adrian, 'Gay Paris, Trace and Ruin', in Neil Leach (ed.), *The Hieroglyphics of Space: Reading and Experiencing the Modern Metropolis* (London: Routledge, 2002), pp. 125–35.

Rioux Soucy, Louise-Maude, 'Le virus de la prochaine pandémie de grippe n'existe pas encore', *Le Devoir*, 19 October 2005, A1, <http://www.ledevoir.com/2005/10/19/92964.html>.

Rose, Jacqueline, *Sexuality in the Field of Vision* (London: Verso, 1986).

Rosen, Philip, *Change Mummified: Cinema, Historicity, Theory* (Minneapolis, London: University of Minnesota Press, 2001).

Rosler, Martha, *In the Place of the Public: Observations of a Frequent Flyer/An der Stelle der Öffentlichkeit: Beobachtungen einer Vielfliegerin* (Ostfildern-Ruit: Hatje Cantz, 1998).

Ruh, Brian, *Stray Dog of Anime: The Films of Mamoru Oshii* (New York: Palgrave Macmillan, 2004).

Sack, Warren, 'Social Networks', lecture at University of California, Santa Cruz, 24 January 2005, <http://dmedia.ucsc.edu/FDM20c/Winter2005/Lectures/24.01.2005/lecture.ppt>.

Saint John of the Cross, *Dark Night Of The Soul*, trans. Mirabai Starr (New York: Riverhead, 2002).

Schmitt, Eric and Stevenson, Richard W., 'Admitting Intelligence Flaws, Bush Stands by Need for War', *New York Times*, 10 July 2004, A9.

Schön, Donald, 'Generative Metaphor: A perspective on problem setting in social policy', in Andrew Ortony (ed.), *Metaphor and Thought*, 2nd edn (Cambridge: Cambridge University Press), pp. 137–63.

Segal, Hanna, 'Motivation: The artist and the psychoanalyst', transcript of ResCen seminar with Hannah Segal, 21 September 2004, Royal Festival Hall, London, <http://www.rescen.net/archive/motivationpsych204.html>.

'Semiotics', in *The Internet Semiotics Encyclopaedia*, <http://filserver.arthist.lu.se/kultsem/encyclo/indexicality.html>.

Sennett, Richard, *The Craftsman* (New Haven: Yale University Press, 2008).

Shiels, Maggie, 'The US Virtual Economy is Set to Make Billions', *BBC News*, 29 December 2009, <http://news.bbc.co.uk/1/hi/technology/8425623.stm>.

Smith, David, '2050—and immortality is within our grasp: Britain's leading thinker on the future offers an extraordinary vision of life in the next 45 years', *The Observer*, 22 May 2005, <http://www.guardian.co.uk/science/2005/may/22/theobserver.technology>.

Sontag, Susan, *On Photography* (London: Picador, 1977).

Stephenson, Neal, *Snow Crash* (New York: Bantam, 1992).

Sugrue, Thomas, *There Is a River: The Story of Edgar Cayce* (New York: Holt, Rinehart & Winston, 1945).

Sullivan Kruger, Kathryn, Harrison, Antonia and Young, James (eds), *The Fabric of Myth* (Warwickshire: Compton Verney, 2008).

Tagg, John, *The Burden of Representation: Essays on Photographies and Histories* (Basingstoke: Macmillan, 1988).

Team Register, 'Home truths: Bionic man takes the Metal Mickey', *The Register*, 4 July 2000, <http://www.theregister.co.uk/2000/07/04/home_truths_bionic_man_takes/>.

Thrift, Nigel, 'Remembering the Technological Unconscious by Foregrounding Knowledges of Position', *Environment and Planning D: Society and Space* 22/1 (2004), pp. 175–90.

Trinh, T. Minh-ha, 'Still Speed', interview with Elizabeth Dungan, in *The Digital Film Event* (New York and London: Routledge, 2005), pp. 3–20.

US Department of Domestic Commerce and Office of International Trade, *World Trade in Commodities* 6/3 (1948).

van der Kolk, Bessel and van der Hart, Onno, 'The Intrusive Past: The Flexibility of Memory and the Engraving of Trauma', in Cathy Caruth (ed.), *Trauma: Explorations in Memory* (Baltimore: Johns Hopkins University Press, 1995), pp. 158–82.

van der Mast, Charles, 'Virtual Reality and Phobias', <http://graphics.tudelft.nl/~vrphobia/>.

Vaysse, Jean-Louis, L'inconscient des modernes: essai sur l'origine métaphysique de la psychanalyse (Paris: Gallimard, 1999).

Wallace, Mark, 'The Game Is Virtual. The Profit Is Real', *New York Times*, 29 May 2005, <http://www.nytimes.com/2005/05/29/business/yourmoney/29game.html>.

Weber, Samuel, *Mass Mediauras: Forms, Technics, Media* (Stanford: Stanford University Press, 1996).

—— 'The Virtuality of Media', *Sites* 4/2 (2000), pp. 297–319.

Weissenstein, Michael, 'Officials: NYC Terror Plot Uncorroborated', *USA Today*, 9 October 2005.

Weizenbaum, Joseph, *Computer Power and Human Reason: From Judgment to Calculation* (New York: Penguin, 1976).

—— 'ELIZA—A Computer Program for the Study of Natural Language Communication between Man and Machine', *Communications of the Association for Computing Machinery* 9 (1966), pp. 36–45.

Wertheim, Margaret, *The Pearly Gates of Cyberspace: A History of Space from Dante to the Internet* (London: Virago, 1999).

Whalen, Thomas, 'Data Navigation, Architectures of Knowledge', <http://www.banffcentre.ca/bnmi/programs/archives/2000/living_architectures/transcripts/living_architectures_thomas_whalen.pdf>.

Whitehead, Alfred North, *Adventures of Ideas* (New York: Free, 1933), p. 212.

—— *Process and Reality* (New York: Free, 1979).

Williams, Raymond, *Communications*, 3rd edn (Harmondsworth: Penguin, 1976).

—— *Television: Technology and Cultural Form* (London: Fontana, 1974).

Winnicott, Donald W., 'Transitional objects and transitional phenomena' [1953], in *Collected Papers: Through Paediatrics to Psycho-analysis* (London: Tavistock, 1958).

Wollen, Peter, *Paris Hollywood: Writings on Film* (London: Verso, 2002).

—— *Signs and Meaning in the Cinema*, rev. edn (London: BFI, 1998).

Womack, Jack, 'Afterword' to the twentieth anniversary edition of William Gibson, *Neuromancer* (New York: Ace, 2004).

Woodward, Bob, *Bush at War* (New York: Simon & Shuster, 2002).

Wu, Chin-Tao, 'Biennials without borders', *New Left Review* 57 (2009), pp. 107–15.

Zegher, Catherine de (ed.), *Martha Rosler: Positions in the Life World* (Cambridge: MIT Press, 1998).

Zelizer, Barbie, *Remembering to Forget: Holocaust Memory through the Camera's Eye* (Chicago: University of Chicago Press, 1998).

# CONTRIBUTORS

**Antony Bryant** is Professor of Informatics at Leeds Metropolitan University, Leeds, UK. His initial studies and his PhD were in the social and political sciences. He later completed a Master's in Computing, followed by a period working as a systems analyst and project leader for a commercial software developer.

He has written extensively on research methods, being Senior Editor of *The SAGE Handbook of Grounded Theory* (SAGE, 2007), co-edited with Kathy Charmaz, with whom he has worked extensively within the areas of grounded theory and research methods in general.

He has developed and taught a wide range of postgraduate courses in South Africa, Malaysia and China. He is currently ASEM Professor at the University of Malaya, and Visiting Professor at the University of Amsterdam.

His current research includes investigation of the ways in which the open source model might be developed as a feature of the reconstructed financial sector in the wake of the recent economic meltdown.

**Juli Carson** is Associate Professor in the Studio Art Department at the University of California at Irvine (UCI), where she teaches critical and curatorial practice in contemporary art and directs the University Art Gallery. She was curator of *Exile of the Imaginary: Politics Aesthetics Love* (Generali Foundation, Vienna, 2007). She also curated the archival exhibition accompanying Mary Kelly's *Post-partum Document* (Generali Foundation, Vienna, 1998). Her essays on conceptualism and psychoanalysis have been published in *Art Journal*, *Documents*, *October*, *Texte Zur Kunst* and *X-Tra*, as well as in numerous critical anthologies. She is currently completing her forthcoming book, *The Conceptual Unconscious: A Poetics of Critique*.

**N. Katherine Hayles,** Professor of Literature at Duke University, teaches and writes on the relations of literature, science, and technology in the twentieth and twenty-first centuries. Her recent books include *How We Became*

*Posthuman: Virtual Bodies in Cybernetics, Literature, and Informatics* (University of Chicago Press, 1999), *My Mother Was a Computer: Digital Subjects and Literary Texts* (University of Chicago Press, 2005), and *Electronic Literature: New Horizons for the Literary* (University of Notre Dame, 2008). She is currently at work on a book entitled *How We Think: The Transforming Power of Digital Technologies*.

**Anna Johnson** is an independent scholar who received her PhD from the University of Leeds, UK. She has been instrumental in the production of several volumes in the New Encounters series (I.B.Tauris 2007–2010). Her research interests include technologies of reading, and the history and future of the book.

**Mary Kelly** has contributed extensively to the discourse of feminism and postmodernism through her large-scale narrative installations and theoretical writings. Her recent exhibitions include Documenta XII (Kassel, 2007), *WACK! Art and the Feminist Revolution* (Museum of Contemporary Art, Los Angeles, 2007), the 2004 Whitney Biennial (Whitney Museum of American Art, New York) and the 2008 Sydney Biennale. She is the author of *Post-Partum Document* (RKP, 1983; reprinted by Generali Foundation, Vienna and University of California Press, 1998) and *Imaging Desire* (MIT Press, 1996). A survey of her work, *Mary Kelly*, was published by Phaidon Press in 1997. She is Professor in the School of Art and Architecture at the University of California, Los Angeles.

**Brian Massumi** specializes in the philosophy of experience, art and media theory, and political philosophy. He is the author of *Parables for the Virtual: Movement, Affect, Sensation* (Duke University Press, 2002), *A User's Guide to Capitalism and Schizophrenia: Deviations from Deleuze and Guattari* (MIT Press, 1992), and, *First and Last Emperors: The Absolute State and the Body of the Despot* (with Kenneth Dean; Autonomedia, 1993). He is editor of *The Politics of Everyday Fear* (University of Minnesota Press, 1993) and *A Shock to Thought: Expression After Deleuze and Guattari* (Routledge, 2002). His translations from the French include Gilles Deleuze and Félix Guattari's *A Thousand Plateaus*. Website: <http://www.brianmassumi.com>.

**Claire Pajaczkowska** learned Art History from Charles Harrison at Watford College of Art and Design in 1974, was a student at Goldsmiths College Fine Art course in the late 1970s and studied Contemporary Cultural Studies at Middlesex University. She learned linguistics and psychoanalysis from Julia Kristeva at Columbia University, translating her essays for English language publication. Her doctoral thesis 'Before Language: the Rage at the Mother' compared historical and psychoanalytic materialisms, proposing that textual analysis needs a theory of pre-Oedipal subjectivity. As Reader in Psycho-analysis and Visual Culture at Middlesex University she researched the relationship between visual and verbal knowledge. As Leverhulme Research Fellow she completed research into the popular sublime. Senior Research Tutor at the Royal College of Art, Pajaczkowska tutors designers in Fashion, Textiles and Applied Arts, with the aim of enabling the collective articulation of the relationship between tacit knowledge, workshop practice and thought, on the basis that design practice can lead the formulation of a theory of knowledge that incorporates, rather than subjugates, the unconscious knowledge of states of mind. Recent publications include *Shame and Sexuality: Psychoanalysis and Visual Culture* (with Ivan Ward; Routledge, 2008), 'On Humming: Marion Milner's Contribution to British Psychoanalysis' in Lesley Caldwell (ed.), *Winnicott and the Psychoanalytic Tradition* (Karnac, 2008), 'Looking Sharp', with Barry Curtis in Marketa Uhlirova (ed.), *If Looks Could Kill* (Koenig, 2008), *Sublime Now* (edited with Luke White; Cambridge Scholars' Press, forthcoming 2010).

**Griselda Pollock** is Professor of Social and Critical Histories of Art and Director of Centre for Cultural Analysis, Theory and History. She works between histories of art and cultural studies with special interests in Modern Jewish Studies, Feminist Studies in the Visual Arts and Psychoanalysis and Aesthetics. A series of strategic interventions, starting from *Old Mistresses: Women, Art and Ideology* (with Rozsika Parker; Routledge & Kegan Paul, 1981), through *Vision and Difference* (Routledge, 1988, recently reissued as a Routledge Classic, 2003) to *Generations and Geographies in the Visual Arts: Feminist Perspectives* (Routledge, 1996) and *Differencing the Canon: Feminist Desire and the Writing of Art's Histories* (Routledge, 1999) have systematically challenged dominant phallocentric and Eurocentric models of art and cultural history. She is currently working on trauma and cultural memory in a trilogy of books including a study of Charlotte Salomon, and post-modern engagements with psychoanalysis and aesthetics. She is directing a research project title 'Concentrationary Memories: The Politics of Representation of the Holocaust' and is editing a major series of books in cultural analysis starting with *Conceptual Odysseys* (I.B.Tauris, 2007). Recent publications include *Psychoanalysis and the Image* (Blackwell, 2006), *Encountering Eva Hesse* (Prestel, 2006), *Museums after Modernism* (Blackwell, 2007) and *Encounters in the Virtual Feminist Museum* (Routledge, 2007) and forthcoming *Theatre of Memory: Charlotte Salomon's Leben? oder Theater?* (Yale University Press). Further information is available at <http://www.leeds.ac.uk/cath/>.

**Adrian Rifkin** is Professor of Art Writing in the Department of Art at Goldsmiths College, University of London. His website is <http://www.gai-savoir.net>.

**Martha Rosler** works in multiple media, including photography, sculpture, video and installation. Her work on the public sphere centres on everyday life and the media as well as architecture and housing, with an eye to women's experience. Investigating landscapes of the everyday, she has produced works on systems of aeroplane, automobile, and metro travel. Rosler has long produced works on war and the 'national security climate'; recent solo exhibitions have centred on the wars in Afghanistan and Iraq. Other works, from bus tours to sculptural recreations of architectural details, are excavations of history. An ongoing project, the Martha Rosler Library, has toured the US and Europe from 2005 through 2009. She has recently opened an archive exhibition of *If You Lived Here…*, a series of exhibitions and forums on housing, homelessness, and the built environment that she organized in New York City in 1989. Rosler's work is in major international collections and has been seen in many solo and group exhibitions, including Documenta XII and skulptur projekte münster (both 2007). Rosler teaches at the Städelschule in Frankfurt and at Rutgers University in New Brunswick, New Jersey. She has published 18 books in several languages.

**Alison Rowley** is Senior Lecturer in Historical, Critical and Theoretical Studies in Visual Art in the School of Art and Design, University of Ulster. Her book *Helen Frankenthaler: Painting History, Writing Painting* was published by I.B.Tauris in 2007. Her writing on contemporary art includes essays on AES+F, Chantal Akerman, Richard Billingham, Willie Doherty, Sarah Lucas and Jenny Saville.

**Trinh T. Minh-ha** is a filmmaker, writer and music composer. Her work includes seven feature-length films that have been honoured in 37 retrospectives around the world, including Documenta XI (Kassel, 2002), and several art installations, including four large multi-media installations: *Old Land New Waters* (Okinawa and Guangdong, 2007–9); *L'Autre marche* (Paris, 2006–9) and *The Desert Is Watching* (Kyoto, 2003) with Jean-Paul Bourdier; *Nothing But Ways* (San Francisco, 1999) with Lynn Marie Kirby. She is also the author of seven books, of which the more recent are: *The Digital Film Event* (Routledge, 2005), *Cinema Interval* (Routledge, 1999), *Framer Framed* (Routledge, 1992) and in collaboration with Jean-Paul Bourdier, *Habiter un monde* (Alternatives, 2005) and *Drawn from African Dwellings* (Indiana University Press, 1996).

**Samuel Weber** is Avalon Foundation Professor of Humanities at Northwestern University and directs that University's Paris Program in Critical Theory. His most recent book publications are *Benjamin's -abilities* (Harvard University Press, 2008), *Targets of Opportunity: On the Militarization of Thinking* (Fordham University Press, 2005) and *Theatricality as Medium* (Fordham University Press, 2004). He is currently working on two projects, tentatively called *Towards a Politics and Poetics of Singularity* and *A Critique of Economic Theology*.

**Paul Willemen** was born near Antwerp in Belgium in 1944. After working at the Belgian Cinémathèque in Brussels, he moved to London in 1968 and worked at the British Film Institute. He was part of the Screen group in the 1970s, edited *Framework* in the 1980s and was Professor of Film Studies and Critical Theory at Napier University (Edinburgh) and Ulster University (Coleraine). He is the author of *Looks and Frictions* (Indiana University Press, 1994), *Questions of Third Cinema* (edited with Jim Pines, 1989), *The Encyclopaedia of Indian Cinema* (with Ashish Rajadhyaksha; BFI/Oxford University Press, 2005), *Theorizing National Cinema* (edited with Valentina Vitali; BFI, 2006) and many other books on cinema. He has lectured widely in Europe, Asia and the United States on a wide variety of topics relating to film cultures.

# INDEX